D1599814

CLASS AND POWER IN SUDAN

Class and Power in Sudan

The Dynamics of Sudanese Politics, 1898–1985

Tim Niblock

State University of New York Press

First published
in U.S.A. by
State University of New York Press
Albany

For information, address State University of New York Press,
State University Plaza, Albany, N.Y. 12246

Printed in Great Britain

Library of Congress Cataloging-in-Publication Data
Niblock, Tim.
    Class and power in Sudan.
    Bibliography: p.
    Includes index.
    1. Sudan—Politics and government. 2. Sudan—
History—1899–1956. 3. Sudan —Economic conditions.
I. Title.
DT156.7.N53 1987   962.4'05   86–23059
ISBN 0–88706–480–9
ISBN 0–88706–481–7 (pbk.)

To Rida

who helped me understand the bountiful and
generous Sudanese people

Contents

x *Contents*

List of Tables and Figures

TABLES

xii   *List of Tables and Figures*

FIGURES

Preface

I owe an immense and abiding debt to the colleagues and students with whom I worked over my eight years at the University of Khartoum (1969–77). My initial inclination was to list the names of as many as I could. Alas, the list would continue for pages, and I would probably cause offence by omitting some. I must, therefore, simply extend a generalised expression of gratitude to the academic community in the University of Khartoum, from which I learned so much. The memory of the high level of intellectual integrity found among colleagues and students in the Faculty of Economic and Social Studies, and in the Institute of African and Asian Studies, remains with me.

Outside of the University of Khartoum also, many individuals gave me assistance with ideas, information and advice. The warmth, hospitality and candour of the Sudanese people provided the most favourable setting within which one could hope to pursue research.

My wife, to whom this book is dedicated, deserves my apologies for the obsessive single-mindedness which has been required to complete this work, as also do my three effervescent daughters, Sally, Kathleen and Rebecca. Their support is much appreciated.

The typing of the manuscript was expertly undertaken by Mrs Susan Ridler, and useful secretarial assistance was provided by Mrs Fay Burgoyne. Their professional expertise and good humour never failed.

Acknowledgement is due to *MERIP Reports* for permission to reproduce the map in Figure 1.1, and to *African Affairs* and *The Arab Researcher* for permission to reprint material by the writer originally published in those two journals, and to Professor Mohamed Omer Beshir for permission to reproduce three tables which appear in his book *Educational Development in the Sudan 1898–1956*.

The spelling of Sudanese place-names and tribe-names follows that given in the *Index Gazetteer of the Anglo–Egyptian Sudan* (1931), which follows customary usage. For other Arabic names and words, however, a separate system of transliteration has been employed.

My greatest hope is that this book may help to spread understanding of a country which, and a people who, truly merit understanding.

Tim Niblock
University of Exeter

Introduction

The politics of Sudan stand once more at a turning point. The collapse of the Nimairi regime throws into question the direction which events will take in this huge country, with its substantial economic potential and its strategic importance.

The pattern of political and economic development in Sudan holds significant implications for the wider context of Africa, the Arab countries and the underdeveloped world. The largest country in Africa, Sudan has some 80 million feddans (1 feddan = 1.036 acres) of cultivable land. Much of this land is composed of highly fertile soil, constituted by silt washed down from the Ethiopian highlands. The Blue and White Niles, converging in Khartoum, provide an ample supply of water for irrigation. With only some 5 per cent of the cultivable land actually under cultivation at the time of independence, Sudan seemed set to complement its strength in cotton production with equal strength in food production.

Such were the hopes at independence. At the time of writing, 30 years later, Sudan is undergoing a desperate economic crisis. Far from producing a surplus for export, the agricultural sector has in recent years retreated even from the goal of self-sufficiency in basic foodstuffs. Some 4 million of the country's 20 million population face starvation. While Sudan may constitute a particularly salient case, many other underdeveloped countries have undergone a similar experience characterised by disappointed hopes and unfulfilled potential. It may be hoped that a careful analysis of how political, social and economic factors have interacted to frustrate Sudan's development aspirations should create a deeper understanding of the processes of development and underdevelopment elsewhere in Africa and the Arab world. The potential remains.

The development perspective, however, does not constitute the only dimension in which Sudan merits attention. Sudanese political life has been exceptionally rich and sophisticated. Despite the attempts of governments to limit the spontaneous vitality of political life, by imposing centrally controlled structures and ideas on the population, political consciousness has remained high. A wide variety of political movements, responding to the problems which Sudan has faced over the last half-century, have held the stage – often articulating well-developed and highly coherent political ideologies.

This political vitality has been based on a substantial body of well-educated people, a strong and active trade union movement (at least up to 1971), and a society which is not only culturally diverse but which has remained open to cultural influences from outside of the country's borders. Sudan has in fact had a very distinctive political tradition over the past 50 years. The parties which dominated the political stage for most of the 1950s and 1960s, and which may well now regain their earlier dominance, adhered strongly to a form of liberal democracy. The Sudanese Communist Party, at times possibly the strongest communist party on the African continent and one of the two strongest in the Arab world, has mostly been content (and even eager) to work within a liberal democratic setting. A continuing interaction has occurred between Islamic conceptions (some stemming from Sudan's indigenous Sufi tradition) and modern forms of political organisation and action. While the Muslim Brother movement has taken the lead in the latter sphere, it has not been alone.

At a time when political life in so many other Arab countries lacks any spontaneous vitality, the re-emergence of articulate and active political movements in Sudan – giving expression to an established political tradition – may have a beneficial effect on the politics of the region as a whole.

This book seeks to explain the dynamics of Sudanese nationalism and of events in Sudan since independence (1956) in terms of the economic and social structures built up under the Condominium (1898–1956). The emphasis given to the pre-1956 economic and social structures, and the detail with which they are described, may seem excessive. Such emphasis and detail, however, are crucial: without them, the political dynamics of post-independence Sudan cannot be understood.

Some will argue, no doubt, that the concept of 'class', formulated with a view to explaining the workings of Western industrialised societies, is ill-suited to the analysis of African or Arab societies. It is clear, however, that economic differentiation does occur in Sudan (as elsewhere in the region) and that this differentiation has political effects. Class structure is defined here as that economic differentiation which places differences in earnings and wealth within the context of the sources of income in the structure of economic production and organisation. The existence of class-consciousness is not necessarily implied: the political actions of individuals may reflect their economic interests whether or not they feel a group-consciousness with those who share these interests. The extent to which class-consciousness exists is revealed in the manner in which social movements, political parties and political institutions function.

The relatively simple class divisions of the developed capitalist world, in any case, are not likely to occur in countries whose economies incorporate a variety of different modes of production. The class structure will inevitably be more complex. With respect to Sudan's rural population alone, for example, great differences exist in the manner in which economic life proceeds and in the way in which it is organised. One important distinction is between those whose livelihood depends on settled agriculture and those whose livelihood depends on nomadism.[1] Along the Nile valley in the northern two-thirds of the country, in the Nuba mountains and in some parts of central Kordofan, in the hilly areas of Darfur, round the ironstone plateau and in the hill masses of the South, and in parts of the central clay plains, the predominant means of livelihood is settled farming. In other areas nomadism is the principal means of livelihood – as among the cattle-owning Nilotic tribes of the southern clay plains and the Baggara tribes stretching over southern Darfur and southern Kordofan, and among the camel-owning tribes such as the Kababish of northern Kordofan, the Rufa'a al-Hoi of the southern Gezira area, the Shukriya of the Butana to the east of the Blue Nile, the Beja tribes inhabiting the Red Sea hills and the Ababda to the east of the Nile close to the Egyptian border.

Overlaying both the settled and the nomadic ways of making a livelihood is the distinction between those communities which produce almost exclusively for their own subsistence, and those which to varying degrees have become involved in the market economy. The market economy has generally been most advanced along the Nile valley in the northern part of the country.

Especially with regard to settled farming, a further significant distinction relates to the techniques used in agricultural production. Government statistics on, and policies towards, the Sudanese economy distinguish between the 'modern' sector and the 'traditional' sector. Under the former heading is included not only the urban economy but also that part of agriculture which makes use of modern aids to production, such as tractors, water-pumps and large-scale gravity irrigation.[2] Even in the traditional sector, however, there can be widespread differences in the extent to which relatively more modern agricultural techniques – such as the use of oxen for drawing agricultural implements – are employed.

Another distinction, or set of distinctions, lies in the organisation of production in settled regions. This may be considered with relation to the ownership of land. In some cases the land is regarded as communally owned[3] and, in areas with plenty of land available and only primitive implements being employed, every individual within the community is deemed to have a right to cultivate – up to the limit of his or his family's physical ability. As every individual has the opportunity to cultivate, no hired labour exists. Where good land is scarce, especially when relatively modernised agricultural techniques are employed, those who have been able to obtain the right to use good land may be in a position to hire the services of those who do not have good land to cultivate.

In other cases private ownership of land exists. Not all such cases are legally recognised, but in so far as the land may be bought, sold and inherited, it enjoys the principal characteristics of private ownership. This land may be in the form of small peasant holdings, of large or small farms run by the landowner, or of schemes where the landowner divides the land into tenancies. The latter tenant schemes are themselves of many different types. On some, the tenants pay a fixed rent. On others, the produce of the land is divided between the tenants and the landowners. On yet others, the relationship between tenants and landowners has been almost feudal in nature. Where the landowner is a prominent religious or tribal leader, tenants may donate all the land's produce to the landowner in return for patronage, protection and such subsistence as the landowner sees fit to provide.

Elsewhere, on land for which the government has assumed responsibility, the government may run farm or tenant schemes itself, or else may let the land to private operators for the same purposes.

Obviously all of these differences which affect the form and nature of production in the rural areas of Sudan mean that the resulting socio-economic structure is bound to be extremely complex. There are many diverse groups, with particular interests and particular outlooks involved in production. The discussion so far, moreover, has been limited to the rural sector. If the industrial, commercial and services sectors are taken into account, within each of which there are widely differing levels of operation, the complexity becomes yet greater.

The central theme in this book is that the socio-political structure left behind by the Condominium state was such that the problems of social and regional inequality which had grown up prior to 1956 continued, and indeed were intensified, after 1956. The independent state initially enjoyed little autonomy of those class groupings which benefited from the inequalities. After 1969 the Sudanese state was rather less dependent on these class groupings, but its greater autonomy was subsequently lost in a different direction. A directly dependent relationship between the state and international capital developed.

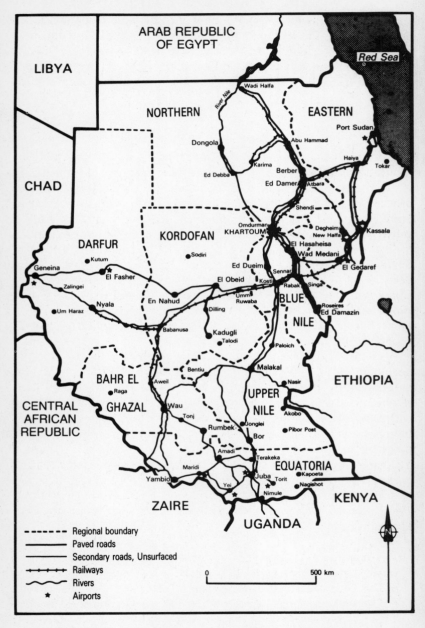

Figure 1.1   General Map of Sudan, Showing pre-1978 Provinces

1 The Development of the Economy up to 1930

I BEFORE 1898

The defeat of the Mahdist forces under the Khalifah 'Abd Allahi at the Battle of Omdurman in 1898, and the consequent establishment of the Anglo–Egyptian Condominium in Sudan, undoubtedly ushered in a new era for Sudan economically as well as politically. Some have described the economic change as a transition from a subsistence economy to a market economy. While there is some truth in this, it is a characterisation which obscures as much as it reveals. Several centuries before 1898 a market economy had been in existence in some parts of Sudan. Moreover, even at the end of the Condominium in 1956 subsistence production still made up a very substantial part of the Sudanese economy. The economic developments before 1898 in fact had a considerable effect, social as well as economic, on the post-1898 period.

A major trading network had been established in Sudan from the beginning of the 16th century.[1] The Funj rulers of the Sennar sultanate, once they had spread their authority over most of the northern riverain Sudan in 1504–5, developed a system of administered trade with the outside world. 'Administered trade' refers here to a pre-bourgeois form of commerce where the trade is organised and dominated by the ruler rather than by a class of profit-seeking merchants.[2] The ruler's objectives in such trade are to obtain exotic articles from abroad – for his own consumption, or for gifts to gain support, or for re-sale so as to obtain funds. The sultans of Sennar in the 16th and 17th centuries, then, organised caravans to import luxury items from abroad. They:

> . . . had the exclusive right to sponsor caravans to the outside world, particularly Egypt . . . Funj consular agents, often relatives of the king, were stationed in Egypt (and perhaps elsewhere) to entice persons with valuable skills or merchandise to Sennar. These latter would join the caravan of royal merchants on its return to the Sudan. When the caravan reached the capital the

sultan's goods were placed on the market first while the demand was greatest and the prices highest.[3]

One indication of the central role played by the sultan in the international trade at this stage is found in the nature of the goods exported. Gold and slaves figured prominently among the exports, and in both of these 'commodities' the sultan controlled much of the supply within the sultanate.[4] All of the larger nuggets of gold mined automatically became the property of the sultan, while smaller nuggets might go to court officials. As for slaves, the sultan had the sole right to sponsor slave-hunts, and these were carried out annually in the Nuba Mountains, White Nile and Southern Funj areas. After a slave-hunt (known as *salatiyah*), one half of all the slaves captured became the property of the sultan while the remainder were divided up among those who had carried out the expedition. The main items exported, then, were items in which the sultan controlled most of the supply.

Other articles exported from the Sennar sultanate were gum arabic, ivory, rhinoceros horn, civet, ostrich feathers and perfumes.[5] Camels and grain were also periodically sold in areas close to the sultanate's borders. Goods imported included spices, soap, perfumes, sugar and cotton manufactures. Trade with the Arabian peninsula, India and the Indies was carried on through the Red Sea port of Suakin, while trade with Egypt was carried on by way of the desert caravan routes.

Besides the administered international trade, it seems probable that the 16th and 17th centuries also saw some development in free domestic trading in subsistence commodities.[6] The main crops grown in the northern riverain Sudan at this time were grain (sorghum and millet) on rain-fed land, and some cotton and dates in addition to grain on land watered by the Nile's flood or by artificial irrigation from the Nile.[7] Away from the riverain area, the nomadic tribes herded their camels (in the northern part) and cattle (in the southern part). In the villages some petty commodity production was undertaken, such as that involved in the weaving of coarse cotton cloth (known as *dammur*) and in making leather articles.[8] It was in these commodities, therefore, that domestic trading developed during the 16th and 17th centuries.

The commercial system within the Sennar sultanate was at this stage based on the gold ounce as a 'currency'. The value of the gold ounce could effectively be controlled by the sultan, in so far as not only gold nuggets but also gold dust, when first mined, became the property of the sultan's court, and therefore:

> . . . by tightening or loosening the flow of gold dust out of the royal treasury according to the fluctuating demands of the market, the sultan could effectively control the value of the gold ounce . . . The value of the gold ounce was high relative to the market price of most articles of trade in Sennar, and the actual circulation of gold must have been restricted to comparatively large exchanges. For the economy at large the most important function of the gold ounce was probably that of a 'fictitious currency' or standard of evaluation for the commonplace goods that actually changed hands.[9]

The Keira sultanate in Darfur practised the same kind of administered trade as was found in Sennar. In the case of the Keira sultanate, however, the trade started rather later – around the mid-17th century.[10] The trade was mainly with Egypt, along the famous *darb al-arba'in* caravan route which connected the Keira capital, El Fasher, with the Egyptian town of Assiut. Principal exports were slaves, ivory, tamarind, rhinoceros horn, ostrich feathers and natron.[11] Imports included spices, soap, fine cloth, weapons, saddlery and jewellery. At its height, towards the end of the 18th century, the trade must have been quite substantial. The British traveller W. G. Browne, who visited Darfur between 1793 and 1796, estimated that the value of the goods carried by the caravan with which he returned to Egypt was about £115,700.[12] Some caravans comprised 5000 camels.

It is notable that the international trade of the Sennar and Keira sultanates depended much on the export of items which were in fact brought from outside their own administered territories. The slaves, the ivory and some of the rhinoceros horn were obtained from the areas to the south of both sultanates – the Nuba Mountains, the Ethiopian foothills and what is today Sudan's southern region. In so far as these items were obtained largely by force, the regions concerned were affected by the commercial system but drew no benefit from it.

In the latter part of the 17th century and the early part of the 18th

century a change of considerable social and economic importance
began to take place in the Sennar sultanate. The system of administered trade began to break down, and the sultan's role in organising
international trade was increasingly taken over by profit-seeking
merchants.[13] This development was to some extent an effect of the
foreign influence which the administered trade had introduced over
the two previous centuries. Foreign merchants and craftsmen who
had come to Sudan with the royal caravans had become established in
Sennar. At the end of the 17th century there were Egyptians, Turks,
Ethiopians, Arabians, Jews, Portuguese, Greeks and Armenians
resident in Sennar. These merchants and craftsmen in fact had to
operate within a framework of regulations which kept them fairly
closely under the sultan's control. Any goods they imported could
only be placed on the market after the sultan's imported goods had
been sold, and they could only buy slaves, gold and some other
specified commodities from the sultan – at prices set by the sultan. By
their very presence, however, they did help to spread the commercial
system and, moreover, they set an example to local people of how
profits could be made through international trading. Some of the
'local people' who were attracted to dealing in international trade
had previously been petty traders in subsistence products; others
were officials in the sultan's court. As these new aspiring merchants
in international trade were part of local society, they could not be so
easily controlled as the foreign merchants had been. Many of the new
merchants, moreover, could improve their economic opportunities
by making use of a relationship with the sultan's court, or with those
who wielded power in the provinces. These, then, were the profit-
seeking merchants who became involved in international trade from
the end of the 17th century.

The development of an increasingly independent merchant group
dealing in international trade was aided by the introduction of new
means of exchange – currencies which had been brought in by the
foreign merchants so as to enable them to escape from the sultan's
total economic control. A number of foreign currencies were in
circulation at the end of the 17th century, and during the 18th century
the Spanish dollar became the standard currency. The circulation of
such currencies was, of course, only among a very small part of the
population, but the effect was to undermine the sultan's control of
the economy and correspondingly to improve the position for profit-
seeking merchants. The sultan was no longer able to regulate prices
by determining how much gold dust should reach the market.

The rise of the new merchants was in part a cause and in part an effect of the disintegration of the sultanate itself. To take the latter aspect first, the Sennar sultanate was at this time becoming subject to separatist and dynastic schisms. As a result of a rebellion in 1659 followed by a more serious one in 1705–6, the Shaigia area around Meroe broke away from the sultan's authority. After this, other northern provinces of the sultanate tended to become effectively independent. Within Sennar itself, dynastic and court disputes further weakend the sultan's authority. The disintegration of existing authority made it possible for the merchants to take over some of the sultan's prerogatives in trade. In doing this, however, the merchants themselves became a factor aiding the further disintegration of that authority.

The sultan's prerogatives in international trade were not always taken over by merchants. In some cases the now independent or semi-independent local rulers established their own administered trade. Sometimes this was done in cooperation and collaboration with a group of merchants within the area.

The fact that there was an increasing number of merchants dealing in international trade is just one part of a broader social and economic phenomenon, for there was also an increasing number of merchants involved in domestic trading of subsistence articles. The phenomenon referred to, therefore, is the development of a merchant class. The relationship between the international and the domestic traders, and the background and character of the new class, are explained by O'Fahey and Spaulding as follows:

> The core of the new merchant community was composed of Sudanese traders in lowly commodities, who were eager to collaborate with the foreigners and expand their commerce to items previously monopolised by the king. Many of these traders were from nomadic groups, and among them the Beja were predominant by virtue of their strategic location between the Nile and the Red Sea and their long tradition of commercial expertise. Beja merchants established residences on the Nile, swelling the population of the new trading centres such as Berber and Shendi, as well as of the older town of Arbaji.

> . . . The life-style of the new middle class was most evident in trading centres such as Shendi and Arbaji. Rectangular courtyard houses replaced *tukuls* (conical huts); dwellings of the more

prosperous had rooftop terraces and occasionally a second storey or private bathing pool.[14]

O'Fahey and Spaulding consider the rise of this class as one of the two crucial factors (the other being the spreading influence of the *sufi* communities) which undermined the authority of the Sennar sultanate and led to its final collapse.[15] This provides some evidence of the strength and position of the class. There were about fifteen settlements within the sultanate where trade and commercial activities were carried on at the beginning of the 18th century, and of these the major ones were Shendi, Arbaji, Berber, Ed-Damer, Suakin, Wad Medani and Sennar itself.[16] In each trading centre the merchants were well organised under the leadership of a *sirr al-tujjar* chosen from among their number.[17] Although the collapse of the Sennar sultanate was followed by anarchy in some areas, the merchant class survived in a strong position.

Accompanying the emergence of a merchant class in the riverain northern Sudan was another important socio-economic development. Private ownership of land – involving purchase, sale, renting and inheritance – was beginning to replace communal ownership.[18] While the sultanate's authority still held, the sultan issued charters allocating land to particular individuals.[19] Such land could be inherited by the heirs of the original grantee, and could be subdivided among tenant farmers, although it could at this stage not be sold. When the sultanate's authority weakened, the sale and purchase of land became possible. In some parts of the Nile valley wealthy and influential individuals (sometimes merchants) established estates where the land was tilled by slaves. Elsewhere, landowners divided their land into tenancies and drew their rent through share-cropping. The rights of land-use which peasants had held on communally-owned land tended to come closer to actual ownership.

In the relationship between the merchants on the one side and the peasants and tenants on the other, a large part was played by the exploitative system known as *shail*. This operated as follows:

It was not uncommon for a peasant family to run short of food during the weeks immediately preceding the major harvest each year. At that time the farmer might borrow a certain amount of grain valued at a set monetary amount from the storehouse of a private merchant. After the harvest the farmer would ordinarily be able to repay his debt, but since the price of grain plummeted at harvest time when the market was flooded, he would have to return to the merchant a considerably larger quantity of grain than he had originally borrowed in order to discharge his debt.[20]

Peasants and tenants who failed to repay their debts would bring down upon themselves a severe retribution from the local rulers, for the latter tended to be on good terms with, or perhaps under the influence of, the merchants. Some local rulers, moreover, engaged in trade themselves.

The emergence of a merchant class in the Sennar sultanate, and the associated socio-economic developments, do not seem to have been mirrored in the Keira sultanate in Darfur. The system of administered trade continued to be predominant there until the middle of the 19th century. Groups of merchants did exist in the principal Darfur trading centres, Kobbei and El Fasher, but they were never able to act independently of the sultan.

The conquest of the disintegrated remains of the Sennar sultanate by the Turko–Egyptian forces under Muhammad 'Ali in 1821 naturally brought about changes in the economic life of the area. Muhammad 'Ali's objectives in Sudan were in part concerned with what could be obtained from the country.[21] Primarily, the Egyptian viceroy was wanting slaves to work in the many agricultural and industrial enterprises which he was establishing in Egypt and to swell the army which he needed to spread his power and confront the Ottoman sultan. He was also hoping to obtain gold – in which he believed Sudan abounded – and to a lesser extent other resources. A conquest motivated in part by such objectives inevitably led to a further opening-up of Sudan to trade with Egypt and the rest of the world.

Communications necessary to the expansion of trade were improved, although this improvement was not carried through very quickly or very extensively.[22] The introduction of a fleet of government steamers on the Nile (numbering fifteen in 1870), together with some sailing craft, opened up new potential for trade within the Sudan and between the Sudan and Egypt. The extension of the Egyptian railway system from lower Egypt to upper Egypt in the 1870s, and the construction of a local railway at about the same time around Wadi Halfa, circumventing the second cataract in the Nile, made it easier for goods from Sudan to reach the Egyptian delta. The improvement of harbour facilities in Suakin and the increasing use made of the port by ocean-going vessels created new trade outlets to the world at large. The spread of telegraph services, such that by 1880 there were over 3000 miles of telegraph line under the control of a self-contained Sudan telegraphs service, improved contacts between those involved in trade and thereby facilitated commerce. Moreover, the military power of the Turko–Egyptian administration was sufficient to re-open and keep open the routes of communication which had been disrupted after the disintegration of the Sennar sultanate.

Trade was also encouraged by economic changes and developments in Sudan. Some new basins[23] were brought into use along the Nile, thereby expanding the amount of cultivable land available and the quantity of agricultural produce on the market.[24] The *shaduf* method of irrigation was increasingly replaced by the more effective waterwheel (*sagiah*), driven by bullocks, which also made it possible to bring more land under cultivation. As a result of experiments with new crops, sugar-cane was successfully and extensively grown on plantations in Berber and Sennar provinces, and some other new crops were introduced on a smaller scale. Cotton, which had previously been grown only in the Nile valley, was introduced in the Gash and Baraka deltas, although not on the large scale for which its initiators had hoped. The establishment of warehouses at the main trans-shipment points along the routes to Egypt assisted the collection and transit of goods bound for Egypt, as the construction of watering places assisted the export of cattle.

Between 1821 and 1838 Sudan's external trade was handled as an exclusive monopoly by the Egyptian state. It was the Egyptian state, therefore, that drew the most substantial profits from Sudan's economy. There were, nevertheless, some private merchants who prospered considerably through selling to and buying from the state trading organisation, as well as by engaging in domestic trading. These merchants were of two different backgrounds. Some had been established merchants before 1821 – i.e. those merchants whose emergence as a class has been discussed above. It was with such merchants that the state trading organisation first arranged commercial exchanges in the newly-conquered territory. In each trading centre the *sirr al-tujjar* would be approached and, through them, business would be conducted with the other established merchants. Other traders arrived in Sudan only after the Turko–Egyptian conquest. Most of these traders, engaging in petty exchange, came from Egypt, but there were some from Turkey, Greece and elsewhere.

After 1838, the state monopoly was gradually loosened and by 1841 almost all aspects of the monopoly had been abolished. This resulted from pressures exerted by European trading powers, which saw in Sudan a rich field of profit for their traders. With the ending of the state monopoly, then, a new kind of merchant entered the field. European traders – British, Austrian, Italian and others – established themselves in Khartoum, the recently-founded centre of the Turko–Egyptian administration. Many of these were agents for commercial houses in their home countries; others were acting independently. Their main trading interest, at the outset, was in obtaining ivory, gum arabic and ostrich feathers. The position of the traders was strengthened through the setting up of consulates in Khartoum by the European trading powers. The foreign consuls not only supported and protected the interests of their country's traders, but frequently engaged directly in trade themselves.

Ivory was perhaps the most important lure which brought the traders to Sudan, and it was this lure that led them into increasingly nefarious activities.[25] As the ivory was to be found in the southern Sudan, where Turko–Egyptian authority was barely established and where the Turko–Egyptian administration showed little concern for the welfare of the inhabitants, the methods used to obtain ivory were under no effective control. When ivory became scarce, the traders' expeditions increasingly took on the form of raiding parties. Hostages were taken from local tribes to force those tribes to supply ivory. If no ivory was forthcoming, it was an easy step for the traders to begin dealing in slaves. Although the Egyptian viceroy banned the slave trade throughout his domains in 1854, such that no further slaves could be sold in Egypt, it was still possible for slaves to be sent illicitly to the Arabian peninsula.

The activities of the European traders in Sudan reached their climax in the 1850s and 1860s. It was at this time that a chamber of commerce was formed in Khartoum, to protect the interests of the big merchants, and an attempt was made to found a bank – the Banque du Soudan.[26] The latter failed in 1873. In the 1870s the anarchic conditions in southern Sudan, for which the European traders were themselves largely responsible, made the activities of these traders difficult and resulted in the withdrawal of some of them.

The trade developed by the European traders led, especially in the 1870s, to the emergence of a number of local merchant 'magnates'. Many of the latter had started off as agents and expedition leaders of the European traders. They then established themselves in their own right, copying the methods used by the European traders. Such magnates as Zubair Rahamah Mansur, whose commerce was based on western Bahr el Ghazal, controlled large private armies and wielded effective power over large parts of southern Sudan.

One effect of the expanding interests of merchants based in Khartoum (whether foreign or local) was that the administered trade of the Keira sultanate in Darfur was undermined. As mentioned before, the Keira sultanate's exports to Egypt consisted to a significant extent of goods which were obtained to the south of the sultanate's territory. When the Khartoum merchants extended their activities into Bahr el Ghazal they cut the Keira sultanate off from an important source of goods for export. This undoubtedly weakened the sultanate, making it easier for the Turko–Egyptian forces to overthrow it in 1874.[27]

The developments in trade were accompanied by important changes in some other aspects of Sudan's economy. The circulation of money (Egyptian currency) became rather more widespread than before. The trend towards private ownership of land superseding communal ownership in the northern Nile valley continued and accelerated. In some parts Egyptian beys purchased land from local tribal leaders and established estates. For the first time, moreover, economic production in Sudan became significant to one part of the global economy. The 19th century saw a big increase in the manufacture of confectionery and paper in Europe, and in both of these gum arabic was an important ingredient. Gum arabic production in Sudan increased quickly during the 19th century and by 1880 Sudan had become the main source of gum arabic for the largest user of this commodity – the United Kingdom.

With the overthrow of the Turko–Egyptian regime in Sudan by Mahdist forces, completed in 1885, the opportunities for international trade naturally diminished.[28] Although the Egyptian government did not deliberately impose a boycott on commercial exchanges with the Sudan, the mutual suspicions and fears rendered any large-scale trade impossible. In so far as the Red Sea port of Suakin remained under Egyptian (effectively British) control, all of the Sudan's trade outlets were prejudiced by the hostile relations with Egypt. A residual and unofficial export trade in gum arabic and ostrich feathers continued through Suakin, and it seems probable that Sudanese nomadic tribes continued to sell camels in Egyptian trading centres. Domestic trade also diminished, due to the disruption caused by the four-year long struggle for control, the invalidity of the currency previously in use, and the serious drought which struck Sudan at this time. Evidence that a market economy still continued, however, is found in a map of Omdurman market drawn around the year 1890 by a prisoner of the Khalifah 'Abdallahi, Rossignoli.[29] The map shows a market with over 30 sections, where the products on sale include shoes, cloth, jewellery and metal goods, in addition to a wide range of foodstuffs.[30] Cloth dealers, druggists, greengrocers, salt and meat vendors, gold and silver smiths, blacksmiths, carpenters, tailors and barbers, coffee shop owners and restaurateurs, firewood vendors, builders and shoemakers were each allocated a fixed place in the market. Rudolf Slatin also describes some aspects of the market economy at the time, specifically relating to petty commodity production, saying that there was a considerable manufacture of spears, stirrup irons, horse and donkey bits, knives, agricultural implements, wooden saddles, amulets, scabbards and hippopotamus hide whips.[31]

It is clear, then, that a market economy and domestic and international trade were in existence long before 1898. Some petty commodity production was practised. These developments naturally involved the existence of a class of merchants and some artisans. By far the greatest part of the economy, however, was restricted to production for subsistence alone.

II DETERMINING THE DIRECTION OF ECONOMIC DEVELOPMENT AFTER 1898

As with other countries under colonial rule, Sudan's economy during the colonial period was moulded by the needs of the colonial power. Although Sudan was nominally an Anglo–Egyptian Condominium between 1898 and 1956, it was the interests of Britain that were predominant – largely because Egypt itself was for most of the time under heavy British influence.

An important element of Britain's economic needs at the turn of the century related to cotton. The Lancashire cotton industry, which up to the end of the 19th century had occupied a paramount position in the world textile industry, was at that time facing increasingly fierce competition from Germany and the United States.[32] Especially in the production of coarse cotton textiles, the Lancashire cotton industry found it difficult to compete with its rivals and the Lancashire mills therefore came to concentrate on fine cloths. Production of the latter required long-staple cotton, which at the time was grown only in Egypt, Peru and the United States. The quantity of cotton grown in Egypt was steadily declining due to the over-taxation of the

Egyptian *fallahin*, and this made the British cotton industry heavily dependent on sources outside of British control. It became essential, then, for the Lancashire cotton industry to find and develop a dependable new source of long-staple cotton.[33] 'Dependable' naturally involved the source being under British control. In 1902 a British Cotton Growing Association was formed, with the express object of securing an increased supply of cotton drawn from within the Empire. When the climate and terrain of Sudan were found to be suitable for the growing of long-staple cotton, the way was open for the quick development of cotton growing there.

The economic position of the Condominium government itself ensured that the needs of the Lancashire cotton industry would be met. Faced with the task of administering a vast and potentially rebellious territory, the government naturally needed a reliable source of revenue with which to maintain and strengthen its administration. As Sudan's economy, in its existing state, was largely of a subsistence nature there was only limited opportunity for raising funds through taxation within the country. The Condominium officials were, moreover, well aware that the imposition of heavy taxes during Turko–Egyptian rule had been one of the factors leading to the downfall of that rule at the hands of the Mahdi.[34] No direct financial help could be expected from the British government, for the latter was upholding the principle that colonies and other dependent territories should be self-sufficient with respect to the costs of basic administration. From the Egyptian government funds could be, and indeed were, obtained. The deficit in the budget (up to 1913) was covered in this way, and the Egyptian government also extended or backed loans to finance the construction of the railways and paid for much of the cost of defence and security.[35] Yet this source of funds was unsatisfactory to the British officials who headed the Condominium administration. The latter were loath, for political reasons, to continuing dependence on Egypt. Besides, the Egyptian government was already strained by its existing commitments in Sudan and could hardly be expected to contribute significantly to any expansion of the administration.

In order to maintain and expand its administration, therefore, the Condominium government needed to create an economic basis within the Sudan from which it could draw revenue. Having insufficient funds to start projects itself, the government could not afford to neglect the opportunities opened up by investors – with powerful support in Britain – who wanted to develop cotton production in the

Sudan. Through such investment an economic basis would be created from which revenue could be obtained, and all without the Condominium government having to bear any significant short-term financial burden. British government-backed loans would enable the infrastructure of one or more major projects in this field to be laid down. The investors themselves would provide the necessary skilled personnel and undertake such financial risks as there might be in the initiation of the projects. There would, moreover, be a virtually guaranteed market for the produce. An enthusiastic acceptance was therefore given to the approaches made by cotton interests, and the enhancement of cotton production became the main feature of Sudan's economic development under the Condominium government.

The genesis of the plans for expanding cotton growing in Sudan greatly affected the form of organisation under which that expansion took place. The object of satisfying the British market, the desire to provide the government with a source of revenue, and the need to create a context within which investment could take place all had definite implications for the form of organisation. Rather than trying to expand production of cotton in the peasant small-holdings along the Nile, the main concentration was on developing centrally-managed schemes or estates where, within a limited area, the agricultural work could be carefully supervised. In this way production could be maximised, investors could ensure a healthy return for themselves in a suitable framework for investment, and the government could be sure of obtaining a reasonable share of the proceeds. Such organisation was efficient and economic but, as has generally been remarked of plantation-type projects in underdeveloped countries,[36] it did little to improve the conditions of the many million small farmers outside of the schemes.

III   THE INCEPTION OF THE COTTON SCHEMES

From the early years of the century, then, investment in cotton began. In 1904, a Sudan Experimental Plantation Syndicate (SEPS) was established, registered in London. The SEPS later changed its name to the Sudan Plantation Syndicate (SPS). In 1906 the syndicate established a cotton scheme at Zeidab on the main Nile near Ed Damer.[37] In spite of some initial setbacks, by 1910 the Zeidab scheme was operating fairly successfully and covered a total of 11 000 feddans.[38] The scheme was based on pump irrigation from the Nile.

In 1911 the Condominium government itself started a small (600 feddans) experimental scheme at Tayiba in the Gezira area, also based on pump irrigation.[39] Once the Tayiba scheme had been shown to be successful, it was handed over to the SPS to operate. The SPS, benefiting from its experience at Zeidab and Tayiba, started new pump irrigation schemes in the Gezira area at Barakat (6000 feddans, started in 1914), Hag Abdalla (19 500 feddans, started in 1921–2) and Wad el Nau (30 000 feddans, started in 1923–4).

The major expansion of cotton growing, however, was based not on pump irrigation but on gravity irrigation. In 1913 the Condominium government began raising a £6 million loan, backed by the British government, on the London market. The loan was to finance the construction of a dam on the Blue Nile at Sennar, commanding a network of canals over a large part of the eastern Gezira. Work on the dam began in 1914 but had to be suspended during the First World War, and it was not finally completed until 1925. Additional loans of £3 million, £1.5 million and £2 million were raised on the London market during the 1920s and early 1930s to cover enlargement and extension. The total funds raised therefore met most of the £13 million basic infrastructural cost of the completed Gezira scheme. In view of the Sudan Plantation Syndicate's success in the earlier schemes, the running of the huge new scheme was handed over to the syndicate on a concession to last until 1950. The earlier pump irrigation schemes in the Gezira were incorporated into the new scheme. A gross area of 240 000 feddans was irrigated in the Gezira in 1925, rising to 300 000 in 1926, 667 000 in 1931, 852 000 in 1938, and almost one million in 1956.

The organisation of the Gezira scheme has often been described as a partnership between the government, which supplied the main part of the infrastructure, the syndicate, which administered the scheme and ran the attendant risks, and the many thousands of tenant farmers who carried out the main part of the agricultural work within plots which were alloted to them. The division of gains took place as follows.[40] The proceeds from every bale of cotton lint and every bag of cotton seed sold were credited to a 'joint cotton account'. Against this account were debited the costs of ginning, sacks and baling materials, transport, insurance and freight, and marketing. The resulting profits were then allocated according to a ratio of 25 : 35: 40 between the syndicate, the government and the tenants respectively. The gains from crops other than cotton were the exclusive property of the tenant farmer, but, as explained below, only a limited part of every plot could be devoted to such crops.

The process by which land was taken over and tenancies distributed was one which preserved some of the social and economic inequalities which had existed in the Gezira area before the scheme's initiation.[41] Large landowners (mostly tribal leaders) were able to obtain a significantly larger share in the scheme than smaller landowners or those without land. At the beginning, the size of each tenancy was set at 30 feddans, but this was soon raised to 40 feddans. An individual who owned 40 feddans or more was entitled to at least one tenancy; if he owned 80 feddans or more he was entitled to two. Such individuals were known as 'right tenants'. If a right tenant owned 120 feddans or more, he was entitled to name an heir – and the heir would be given a tenancy. Even this did not exhaust a landowner's ability to affect the distribution of tenancies, for if he owned 160 feddans he could nominate another individual to be given a tenancy; if he owned 200 feddans he could nominate two; and if he owned 240 he could nominate three. Tenants who obtained tenancies in the latter way were known as 'nominees'. By nominating their close associates, a large landowner could therefore ensure that 240 feddans of irrigated land would be under the control of himself and those close to him. Only after the needs of right tenants had been satisfied could the needs of others be considered. 'Preferential tenants' were those who owned less than 40 feddans. Provided there was sufficient land available in the relevant locality, they could be granted a tenancy or half-tenancy (20 feddans). If there were still tenancies not yet taken up after the preferential tenants had been satisfied, the remaining plots (usually in half-tenancies) could be given to landless cultivators from the area or else to outsiders.

This method of distributing tenancies in fact exaggerated some of the pre-existing inequalities due to the procedures employed in determining land ownership and in assessing compensation. The land on which the scheme was founded was either purchased outright or else rented from the existing owners. Where no single individual was regarded as owning the land, the land was deemed to be government property.[42] In such cases, of course, no price or rent needed to be paid. Much of the land in the Gezira had in fact been communally owned, by tribes or villages. This land was usually under the administrative management of the tribal or village leader. When land was being registered prior to the scheme's inception, tribal and village leaders often sought to register the communally-owned lands as their own private property. Other inhabitants of the area generally failed to contest such claims, for they had nothing to gain by doing so. (If the tribal leader's claim was not upheld the land simply became government property – in the government's eyes – and was therefore not subject to compensation). In this way, then, tribal and village leaders were often able to establish ownership rights over large areas which had not been their property. Some leaders succeeded in having claims to several thousand feddans recognised. On the basis of their newly recognised ownership rights, tribal and village leaders were therefore able to acquire control of more tenancies than was their real entitlement.

Obtaining recognition of ownership rights over large areas was also of some value at the outset in terms of the rent which could be gained. The syndicate rented land at 10 piastres[43] per feddan per annum, which at the time was the going rate for land rental. The income which some of the larger landowners received from this could be quite significant in the early years of the scheme – relative to prices and incomes at that time. In the long term, gains from renting land to the syndicate became relatively less and less significant. As the rent was fixed for 40 years, with provision that rises in the value of the land due to the irrigation would not be taken into account at the end of the 40 years, the rent paid did not keep up with rising prices and incomes. Nevertheless, the sums paid to landowning tenants[44] did help to differentiate them from some of their co-tenants. It will be shown later that many of the richer tenants, benefiting from rent and drawing gains from more than one tenancy, were able to accumulate capital which they then re-invested in commerce and in agricultural machinery.

Allowing existing leaders to maintain some economic pre-eminence in the Gezira was seen by the Condominium government as a political necessity. The government feared that tribal and village leaders could mobilise their people to resist the new scheme. Only by giving these leaders a strong economic incentive to remain complaisant could the scheme's future be ensured.

The organisation of the Gezira scheme was significant in one other respect. The operation of the scheme was very similar to the operation of an industrial undertaking. The role of the tenants was in many ways closer to that of workers in a factory than to that of small-holding peasants. There was considerable central direction, backed up if necessary by compulsion. The syndicate issued administrative directives which the tenants were obliged to accept. In 1927 and 1939 a large number of rules and orders were issued forcing the tenants, on pain of fine or imprisonment, to undertake certain cultivation procedures, directing what crops were to be grown, laying down regulations about the keeping of animals, instructing on the size and nature of ridges, etc.[45] The most important part of this framework was that relating to the crops to be grown: on a 40-feddan tenancy, 10 feddans had to be devoted to cotton, 5 feddans to sorghum or lubia, and the remainder had to stay fallow.

Under this regime it is hardly surprising that the tenants in many ways came to behave more like industrial workers than small-holding peasants. This was particularly true of those tenants who were unable to accumulate capital and develop commercial activities as a sideline. It would be wrong to over-emphasise their proletarianisation, for most of them were themselves employers of labour (i.e. cotton pickers[46]), but in such actions as forming unions to represent their interests, confronting the syndicate with their demands for more favourable treatment and threatening if necessary to go on strike, they tended to copy the ways of industrial workers. Many tenants conceived of themselves more as employees than as self-employed.

The effects of the Gezira scheme's organisation have been explained in some detail here partly because of the central role which the scheme played in the country's socio-economic structure, and partly because the other cotton schemes to be mentioned below were all based on the same system as the Gezira and they all therefore had similar effects. When touching upon the organisation of the other schemes, only the minor differences between them and the Gezira scheme need to be discussed.

While work was proceeding in the Gezira, cotton growing was at the same time being expanded and developed in eastern Sudan. In this case the infrastructural cost was less than in the Gezira, for the schemes in eastern Sudan required no dams – nor did they require any pumping equipment as at Zeidab. They were based on flush irrigation in the deltas of the seasonal Gash and Baraka rivers. The inland delta of the Gash, from which the waters have no escape except by absorption in the soil or evaporation by the sun, had been seen as a suitable area for expanding cotton growing from the 19th century. In the early years after the reconquest, the Condominium government began investing small sums of money in digging canals to channel the seasonal flood waters. The main development of the Gash scheme, however, took place after 1924 when the Kassala

Cotton Company took over the management of the area on a 30-year concession.

The Kassala Cotton Company, (KCC) registered in London and enjoying links with the Sudan Plantation Syndicate, supervised the digging of a series of canals whereby the waters of the Gash could be effectively guided and evenly divided over the land prepared for cultivation.[47] While the first three years of the KCC's concession saw great developments, however, the scheme also encountered serious difficulties. The company, pursuing strictly commercial objectives, failed to take sufficient account of the interests of the local population. Nomadic Hadendowa tribesmen had previously used the Gash delta to graze their camels, especially in dry years, and there had also been some settled Hadendowa cultivators. There was, therefore, a basic conflict over the right to use the land, aggravated by the company's preference for giving tenancies to industrious western Sudanese (and sometimes non-Sudanese Fellata[48]) rather than to the local Hadendowa who were regarded as lazy and unsuited to agricultural work. In 1927 the government was forced to resume responsibility for the scheme, which it delegated to a Gash Board, and the Kassala Cotton Company was given a concession in the Gezira as compensation.[49]

The area covered by the Gash scheme was, naturally, dependent on the size of the flood each year, but as a result of the canalisation there was a quick growth after 1924. The average area covered rose from 9100 feddans between 1920/21 and 1924/25 to 29 400 between 1925/26 and 1929/30. In 1956/57 it reached 68 600 feddans. As with the Gezira scheme, gains were divided on a share-cropping basis between the Gash Board (or the Kassala Cotton Company while it remained responsible), the government and the tenants. The ratio in this case, however, was 30 : 20 : 50.

The scheme on the Baraka river near Tokar required even less infrastructural investment than the Gash scheme, and as such the Condominium government was able to organise and develop the whole scheme from its own resources. Due to the violence of the Baraka river during its flood season, no canal system was feasible in this case, and the scheme simply involved permitting the river to spread its waters over its mainly inland delta and then dividing the flooded land into annual tenancies. Such channels and drainage khors as were dug, and such banks as were constructed, were only of marginal importance and involved little investment. Cotton had, as mentioned above, been grown in the Baraka delta since the 1860s, so the government was simply re-starting and re-organising an existing practice. From 1910 the Tokar scheme usually covered 30–40 thousand feddans annually. This remained roughly constant up to and after Sudan's independence. The gains of the scheme were divided on a 25 : 70 ratio between the government and the tenants.

Outside of the major cotton schemes mentioned above, little else was done to encourage cotton growing. That is to say, peasant small-holders in the rainlands and on the river banks were given no particular encouragement in this direction. The only exception was in the Nuba Mountains where some encouragement was given, from the 1920s, for the growing of short- and medium-staple cotton.

IV   OTHER ECONOMIC DEVELOPMENTS

The main economic preoccupation of the Condominium in the early years was therefore the expansion of cotton growing on large centrally organised schemes. Other economic developments were of less significance. Some non-cotton developments do, however, require a mention.

Beside the Nile in Northern province, seven projects for the growing of food and fodder crops were established by the government. These projects, based on pump irrigation, each covered between 2000 and 4000 feddans.[50] They were initiated during the First World War and their object was partly to provide a guaranteed source of food within the country and partly to meet the demands for fodder made by the British cavalry regiments in Egypt. Their organisation was similar to that of the cotton schemes: each was divided into tenancies, and the tenants were given instructions as to the crops to be grown. In the food and fodder schemes, however, instead of the produce being shared between the government and the tenants, the government took its gain through levying a fixed water rate on all tenants. All the income from the sale of crops went to the tenants, then, but out of their profits the tenants had to pay for the irrigation water with which the government provided them. On average the water rate took up about 50 per cent of the gains a tenant had made through the sale of crops.[51]

Investment in communications services helped to create conditions favourable for the expansion of domestic and international trade. The building of a railway system, initially mainly for military purposes, was the most important element here. By December 1899

Khartoum North was already connected by rail with Wadi Halfa on the northern frontier, and soon afterwards a line was built from Atbara to the Red Sea coast.[52] A bridge was then built over the Blue Nile at Khartoum and the line was extended southwards to Sennar, and thereafter westwards across the Gezira and White Nile to El Obeid, which it reached in 1912. The gum arabic producing area of central Kordofan was thus linked by rail to the Red Sea coast. In the east, a line was built to link Kassala and the Gash cotton growing area with Port Sudan, so as to enable the cotton crop to be exported. That line was later extended through Gedaref to cross the Blue Nile and meet the existing line at Sennar in 1929. Most of the costs involved in the construction of the railway system at this stage were met, in different ways, by Egypt. The first developments, made necessary by security considerations, were undertaken directly by the Egyptian army. The later ones were paid for by grants and loans from the Egyptian government and by loans from the Egyptian National Bank.

The construction of a harbour at Port Sudan, completed in 1909, also facilitated international trade. The ancient port of Suakin had not been suitable for receiving the large ocean-going ships which now passed through the Red Sea.[53] The construction of the new harbour was financed directly by the Condominium government. Meanwhile, the potential for domestic trade and contact was improved by the establishment of an effective steamer service on the navigable stretches of the Nile and its tributaries.[54]

Both directly, by deliberate government policy and indirectly, as a result of the various developments discussed above, encouragement was given to the spread of the cash economy. In order to promote the trend towards a cash economy, the government adopted the practice of paying tribal leaders in cash, and in some cases raising taxes in cash. Agricultural shows were held in the provinces so as to spread knowledge of modernised agricultural techniques, with the idea that farmers would in this way be given an incentive to produce for cash wherewith to purchase new implements.[55] Meanwhile, the existence of growing urban centres encouraged the cash economy through providing a larger market than before for such foodstuffs as fruit, grain, meat, vegetables and dairy produce. The most significant 'urban centre' was, naturally, that constituted by the Three Towns (Khartoum, Khartoum North and Omdurman). The population of the Three Towns rose from an estimated 81 880 in 1904 to 202 381 in 1930, while in the 1956 census it was recorded as 245 736.[56] The expanding population was, of course, based on a growing need for labour – the labour required to implement the various elements of the Condominium's administration and developments. The labour force in the Three Towns probably totalled about 15 000 in 1908, steadily rising thereafter until it reached just less than 90 000 in 1956.[57] This cash-paid labour force naturally created an important market, drawing some of the peasant small-holders and nomads living close to the Three Towns into greater involvement with the cash economy. The same was true, to a more limited extent, with relation to other urban centres such as Port Sudan, Atbara, Wad Medani and El Obeid. The expansion of trade and of the cash economy brought benefit to the merchant class, to whom reference has previously been made.

The pattern which emerges, then, is one of increasing production and trade over the 1898–1930 period. Sudan was emerging as one of the world's major cotton producers, and by 1930 had become the world's major source of gum arabic – simply as a result of the improved communications which enabled the gum of central Kordo-fan to be exported. While raw cotton, cotton seed and gum arabic made up on average about 90 per cent of exports in the later years of this period, exports of hides and skins, cattle and camels, pulses, groundnuts and melon seed were also growing.[58] The effect of the above changes on the population as a whole, however, should not be exaggerated. In 1930 about 75 per cent of gross domestic product was still accounted for by subsistence production. To the majority of the population, then, the economic changes were of little (if any) direct benefit.

2 Economic Developments 1930–56

I THE RE-INVESTMENT OF ACCUMULATED CAPITAL

The emphasis in this chapter is on how capital, which had accumulated as a result of the economic developments between 1898 and 1930, was used and re-invested in the 1930–56 period. It is contended that this process provided the main dynamic of economic development in the later period, particularly with relation to the non-government sector.

The re-investment of accumulated capital cannot, of course, account for all economic developments between 1930 and 1956. In the government sector, some loans and grants continued to be received from the Egyptian and British governments, and these financed a number of important projects. In the private sector, a small influx of foreign private investment was involved in the establishment of two industrial projects: a cement factory in Atbara (1939), owned by the British Portland Cement Company, and a brewery in Khartoum North, owned by British brewing interests. Foreign private investment also supported the establishment and growth of banks and trading companies – branches of British institutions. Some minor capital sums were brought into the country and invested by Syrian, Greek and Egyptian traders.

Moreover, not all the capital accumulated in Sudan was available for use or re-investment within Sudan. Some of the capital left the country as profits for private investors. The largest amount of money leaving the country in this way was, of course, that emerging from the largest privately managed project: the Gezira scheme. The profits made by the Sudan Plantation Syndicate were almost entirely taken out of the country and used for paying dividends to shareholders. Details of the profits can be found in Table A.9 in the Appendix. It will be noted, for example, that between 1947 and 1950, the last four years of the Syndicate's concession, total profits came to rather more than £$9\frac{1}{2}$ million. Expatriated profits of other private investments within the country (such as the cement and beer factories) probably came to only a fraction of those of the syndicate.

In spite of such instances where economic development was not just a case of the re-investment of the capital which had accumulated through projects started between 1898 and 1930, it is still useful to take the process of re-investment as central. This approach does help to show how developments in the second half of the Condominium were in many ways an effect of those in the first half. In the private sector, individuals who had accumulated capital in the earlier period were able to re-invest it and strengthen their economic position in the latter – with significant economic, social and political effects.

It is difficult to make an estimate of the extent of privately accumulated capital in 1930 and thereafter, but in the government sector accumulation of capital is portrayed in the figures for government revenue. Total government revenue rose from £E242 309 in 1901 to £E1 814 098 in 1918. In 1928 it stood at £E4 680 189 and in 1929 at almost £E7 000 000. The 1930s world depression hit Sudan's economy very severely, as the cash economy was dependent on an export crop for which demand fell abruptly. Government revenue in 1938 thus stood at £E5 131 635, still not having regained the peak of 1929. By the 1955/56 fiscal year, revenue had reached £E33 630 000.[1]

That the increase in government revenue did in fact owe much to the Gezira and other cotton schemes is revealed clearly in official statistics. In 1942 revenue came to £E5 894 591, and of this the government had earned directly from the schemes the following sums:[2]

	£E
Gezira scheme	1 369 829
White Nile Alternative Livelihood scheme	155 492
Gash scheme	50 793
Tokar scheme	21 224
Pumping schemes	51 555
Rain-grown schemes	10 000
Total	1 658 893

In addition to what was earned directly (i.e. through the government taking its share of gains in each case), further revenue was obtained by taxing cotton exports. In 1942 such taxes came to about £E1 million.[3] Without taking into account some of the more indirect ways in which government revenue benefited, therefore, almost one half of revenue in 1942 arose from the growing and export of cotton.

The proportion rose during the late 1940s and early 1950s, as a result of the rising world market price of cotton.[4] By 1955/6, however, it had declined to about one third due to the fall in world cotton prices at that time.[5]

II THE GOVERNMENT SECTOR: ADMINISTRATION AND SERVICES

As the government's main objective in the early developments had been to provide itself with funds with which to expand and secure its administration, much of the capital which accumulated in the government's hands was naturally expended on the administration and on associated services. Administration was inevitably expensive, bearing in mind the high emoluments paid to colonial officials. While the statistics make it impossible for one to estimate precisely what percentage of government expenditure was devoted to this, some indication can be drawn from the sums which needed to be spent on pensions. In 1938 (a typical year), for example, the pensions alone for these officials came to 6.9 per cent of total expenditure.[6] Defence was an added expense. Whereas the Egyptian and British governments had initially borne all the costs of this, involving as it did the stationing of units of their armies in Sudan, the Condominium government had to undertake the establishment and development of a Sudan Defence Force following the British–Egyptian confrontation of 1924. In 1938, defence took up 8.9 per cent of total expenditure[7] – a percentage which was little changed in the 1955/6 financial year.[8] The government also needed to repay with interest the loans which had been raised for the Gezira scheme and for the development of the railways. In 1938 such repayments and interest payments came to about 13 per cent of total government expenditure.[9]

From the second half of the 1930s the government began (for the first time in a coherent manner) to spend money on social services. Social welfare, health and educational programmes were moderately expanded. Expenditure in these fields made up about 9 per cent of the total in 1938,[10] rising to about 25 per cent in 1955/6.[11] The overall structure of the educational and health services which had been built up by 1955/6 can be seen from Tables 2.1 and 2.2.

Table 2.1 Government Education Statistics, 1956

No. of students attending schools:	
Technical Schools	1 027
Sub-grade Schools	66 036
Elementary Schools	137 150
Intermediate Schools	10 314
Secondary Schools	3 790
Teacher Training Colleges	712
University of Khartoum	802
Total	219 831
Expenditure of Ministry of Education:	£
Current	4 436 246
Capital	2 002 560
Total	6 438 806

Note: Not all schools benefited from government finance or support. The sub-grade schools were largely independent of government support, as also were some of the elementary schools. About 65 per cent of the students in intermediate schools were in non-government schools (either privately financed or financed by the Egyptian government), while at the secondary level about 50 per cent were in non-government schools.

Source: Republic of Sudan, *Internal Statistics 1960 and 1961* (Department of Statistics, Khartoum, 1961), p. 69.

III THE GOVERNMENT SECTOR: PRODUCTIVE INVESTMENT

Only a relatively small part of government revenue was spent on undertakings which could be expected to be productive in the short term. Expenditure on agriculture and animal resources, communications and transport, power, industry and commerce usually made up no more than 20 per cent of total government expenditure during the 1930s, 1940s and early 1950s.[12] The percentage was still around 20 per cent in the year in which the Sudan became independent.[13]

Agricultural advisory and veterinary services were modestly expanded, bringing some benefit to the traditional agricultural sector. Communications were improved in a minor way through the construction of a railway track from Sennar to Roseires (begun in 1954, completed in 1956), and the establishment of Sudan Airways in 1950.

Table 2.2 Medical Statistics

Year	Number of hospitals	Number of beds	In-patients	Out-patients	Number of dispensaries and dressing stations	Expenditure by medical departments (£S)
1948	40	7 765	140 511	9 820 304	346	895 419
1949	40	7 687	151 011	10 186 668	367	1 015 745
July 1951/June 1952	40	8 254	168 251	12 181 931	383	2 013 773
July 1952/June 1953	40	8 355	164 331	13 966 390	395	2 189 099
July 1953/June 1954	40	8 383	172 675	14 483 366	417	2 581 873
July 1954/June 1955	44	8 760	171 092	15 453 895	438	2 806 290
July 1955/June 1956	47	8 737	154 903	17 694 550	458	2 662 204

Source: Republic of Sudan, *Internal Statistics 1960 and 1961* (Department of Statistics, Khartoum, 1961), p. 70.

Power resources were developed by means of setting up small thermal stations in the main urban centres, together with a hydro-electric station at Sennar – with lines enabling the power to reach the Three Towns.

The main part of the government's attention in economic development, however, was focused (as before) on agricultural schemes either under the direct control of the government or with the government as a partner. The Gezira scheme was expanded by an extra 330 000 feddans, reaching a total of almost one million feddans in 1956/7,[14] and the Gash scheme was developed such that in 1956/7, 68 600 feddans were under cultivation as opposed to the average of 29 400 between 1925/6 and 1929/30.[15] Many smaller new schemes, based on pump irrigation and run directly by the government, were started along the White Nile (between Khartoum and Kosti), the Blue Nile (between Khartoum and Sinja), and the main Nile north of Khartoum.

On the White Nile seven major government schemes were undertaken, mostly in the late 1930s and early 1940s. These schemes covered in all about 25 000 feddans in 1944.[16] The schemes were intended to provide an alternative means of livelihood for farmers whose lands had been submerged following the completion of the Jebel Aulia dam in 1936. The latter dam, situated on the White Nile 24 miles south of Khartoum, was made necessary by the interests of Egypt rather than those of Sudan. It was to regulate the flow of the Nile in such a way that more water than before was available in Egypt during the river's 'low season'. Being required in Egypt's interest it was financed by the Egyptian government, and the Egyptian government paid the Condominium government £E 750 000 compensation for the loss of agricultural land in the permanently flooded area.[17] The compensation money was used to pay for most of the infrastructural costs of the above-mentioned schemes. All of the schemes were placed under the control of a semi-independent White Nile Alternative Livelihood Board,[18] and the main crop grown was cotton.

On the Blue Nile the only major scheme started was at Guneid. This, the largest pump scheme in the country, involved the irrigation of 30 000 feddans. The scheme became fully operational in 1955, and in its first years of operation was devoted entirely to the growing of cotton. On the main Nile north of Khartoum two new pump schemes were started and some existing ones extended, such that the total area under government irrigation schemes in Northern province was doubled. In 1944 these Northern province schemes covered 32 220 feddans, and this total remained roughly constant up to 1955/6.[19] Food and fodder crops were the principal ones grown.

The area covered by government pump schemes, therefore, grew steadily between 1930 and 1956. In 1930 the total stood at about 17 000 feddans, almost entirely in Northern province. By 1944 it had reached 58 000 feddans – 32 220 in Northern province, 25 050 in Blue Nile province,[20] and some 500–600 accounted for by small schemes in Khartoum, Upper Nile and Equatoria provinces.[21] By 1950 it was 80 000 feddans and by 1955 about 120 000.[22]

The organisation of the new irrigation schemes was in most respects similar to that of the ones discussed earlier. On all of them the land was divided into tenancies, with the relationship between the government and the tenants being characterised as 'partnership'. The manner in which the gains from the schemes were divided between the government and the tenants varied according to the area. In the Northern province, the new schemes copied the system practised by the earlier ones there: tenants took all the gains from the produce of their tenancies, but were obliged to pay an annual water rate. On the schemes along the Blue and White Niles a share-cropping system similar to that on the Gezira scheme was adopted: 40 per cent of the gains from cotton were taken by the tenant and 60 per cent went to the government. Gains from such other crops as might be grown went exclusively to the tenant, but only limited areas in each tenancy could be devoted to non-cotton crops. As in the earlier schemes, directives and regulations laid down by the scheme managements played a big part in agricultural production.

The pattern of land ownership and control of tenancies on the new schemes, however, was in some cases rather different from that outlined above for the Gezira. In Northern province only 8 per cent of the land in the new schemes was privately owned,[23] while in the Gezira the major part of the land had been privately owned. This was due to the nature of the land employed: it was the land which lay behind the *salukah* and *sagiah*[24] lands along the river and, in an area where rainfall was not sufficient to produce a crop, it had therefore not been cultivated or otherwise used before. Consequently on most of this land tenancies could be distributed on the basis of one per individual. There were few who could claim prerogatives over the land. Such private land as there was on the Northern province schemes, mostly that closest to the river, remained under the control of the owners. It was not split up into separate tenancies by the scheme management, no rent or compensation was paid to the owners, and the owners had no entitlement to obtaining tenancies elsewhere on the scheme. Although such landowners were referred to as tenants,[25] they could not be removed or otherwise controlled by the scheme management. Some of the larger landowning tenants themselves split their land up into sub-tenancies, dividing the gains from the land (after the water rate had been paid) between themselves and the sub-tenants. At Guneid on the Blue Nile, and on the White Nile schemes, the pattern was more similar to the Gezira. In both cases most of the tenancies were allocated on a compensatory basis to those who had owned land before – either in the area itself or in the White Nile regions flooded by the construction of the Jebel Aulia dam. This allocation took into account the previous inequalities in sizes of holdings, such that large landowners could establish rights over up to four tenancies and could nominate other individuals to be granted tenancies.[26] The size of the tenancies themselves varied according to the scheme. In the Northern province schemes the average tenancy covered 4.5 feddans,[27] on the White Nile schemes all tenancies covered 25 feddans, and at Guneid the size was fixed at 15 feddans.[28]

Besides the various schemes involving irrigated agriculture mentioned above, government agricultural investment also went into one scheme of a very different nature. This was the Zande scheme, a major new project which had industrial as well as agricultural dimensions. The Zande scheme stands apart from most other economic developments during the Condominium era – indeed, from most other economic developments in the whole of Africa during colonial times. It was aimed at developing the south-west corner of the country (inhabited by the Azande peoples) on a basis of self-sufficiency.[29] Within a comprehensive strategy for the area, crops would be grown not for export but for local processing into the consumer goods required by the population. Such goods as would be exported from the area would not be raw materials but manufactured or processed products. The whole population would be involved in, and would benefit from, the scheme. It was initially hoped that cotton cloth, soap, sugar and coffee could be produced, but technical difficulties soon caused the plan to produce coffee to be abandoned.

The major part of the Zande scheme's infrastructure was financed from a £1 million grant from the British government – given to the Sudan as a reward for the positive role it played in the Second World War. The scheme began operation in 1948 under the management of a semi-independent body, the Equatorial Projects Board. The latter board had other activities besides managing the Zande scheme – the most important of these being the establishment and operation of bush shops all over southern Sudan. These shops were intended to offer a broader range of goods than the existing traders offered, and so stimulate the production of cash crops. The Zande scheme, however, soon became the most significant undertaking for which the Equatorial Projects Board was responsible. So that effective services could be provided and so as to enable the land to be redivided into plots of 25–40 feddans (depending on the quality of the soil and the availability of land), the local Azande population had to be resettled in new villages. By 1951 one thousand new villages had been established containing 50 000 families, or nearly 200 000 inhabitants.

No individual was entitled to more than one plot (i.e. 25–40 feddans) as no extensive private ownership of land had hitherto been recognised among the Azande. Rights of use of land had existed, but the land which an individual had the right to use could not normally exceed what lay within his own or his family's power to cultivate. Without private ownership over large areas, no one needed to be compensated through the grant of more plots than others. Most of those who wanted plots were able to obtain them, for there was sufficient land available and ample rainfall to water it.

The organisation and implementation of the Zande scheme undoubtedly had many deficiencies. A fundamental one concerned the resettlement of the population. The somewhat brutal administrative directives through which people were shifted from their traditional villages led some Azande to conceive of their new government-provided villages as concentration camps.[30] Nevertheless, the basic conception was a sound one, and in the early 1950s the scheme's objectives were finding fulfilment. Cloth, cotton-seed oil and cake, soap and some coarse sugar were being produced through the processing of the crops grown by the farmers. In 1954/55 production of these commodities was as follows:[31]

Cotton cloth	1 635 868 plain yards
Cotton-seed cake	510 tons
Cotton-seed oil	122 tons
Soap	118 tons
Sugar	216 tons

The scheme was not making an overall profit, but that had not been one of its primary objectives. The government recognised from the outset that a profit was unlikely during the early years. The ultimate failure of the scheme after 1955 was due not to inherent deficiencies but to the rapid deterioration of the security situation in the area following the 1955 mutiny in the Southern Corps of the Sudan Defence Force.[32]

Investment in the above schemes, then, constituted the main focus of productive investment undertaken by the Condominium government between 1930 and 1956. There was in addition some investment in mechanised rain-fed agricultural projects, but government activities in this field were soon superseded by those of private investors, so mention of it will be left to the section below on private sector investment. The only major industrial investment undertaken by the government in these years, besides that involved in the Zande scheme, was geared not towards producing goods which would satisfy the needs of the population but to further encouraging the export of the main agricultural crop, cotton. Three large ginneries were established, in Port Sudan, Sennar and Atbara, and six very small ginning units were set up in Kordofan.[33]

IV THE PRIVATE SECTOR: INVESTMENT IN PUMP SCHEMES

The pattern of re-investment of capital which had accumulated in private hands was perhaps of more significance in the long term – socially as well as economically – than that which took place in the government sector. Private capital was re-invested in five different fields: pump schemes, mechanised agricultural schemes (rain-fed), real estate, commerce and petty manufacturing. It was in these fields that those with accumulated capital were able to re-invest, obtain a substantial return on their capital, and thereby reinforce their economic position. Through the process of accumulation and re-investment the basis was laid for the emergence of ever-growing economic divergences between different sectors of the population.

The first and major field of investment to which capital was attracted was that of private pump schemes. In the late 1920s a large private pump scheme was established at Aba Island on the White Nile near Kosti, and from the late 1930s similar schemes (though smaller in size) spread over much of the White Nile area between Jebel Aulia and Kosti. During the 1940s such schemes also began to spread along the main Nile in Northern province. The Zeidab scheme, mentioned earlier, was sold by the Sudan Plantation Syndicate to local entrepreneurs in the mid-1940s.[34]

By 1955 there were about 1000 private schemes in operation, covering a total of 620 000 feddans.[35] Approximately two-thirds of this area was in Blue Nile province (including the White Nile area), one-fifth was in Northern province and the remainder was in scattered schemes in Khartoum, Kassala and Upper Nile provinces.[36] The importance of these private schemes can be judged from the fact that they accounted for almost one-third of all irrigated land in Sudan by 1956.

The inception of, and the pattern adopted by, the private pump schemes owed much to the pump schemes in the government sector. The government had shown how profit could be made in this way, had proved the viability of growing various kinds of crops, and had ensured both that the necessary inputs and the required trading outlets would be available. Private individuals now saw the opportunity for their own profit. As with the government schemes, most of the schemes in Blue Nile province concentrated on cotton, while those in Northern and Khartoum provinces restricted themselves largely to food crops. Also on the pattern of the government sector, the private pump schemes (especially the larger ones) were mostly run on a tenancy system, with the gains being shared between the operator[37] and the tenants. There were, however, some schemes that were simply farms – the operator carried out or managed the farming himself, employing such labour to work for him as he deemed necessary.

In Blue Nile province the division of gains between operator and tenants was similar to that on the government schemes there. The operators took 60 per cent of the gains from the cotton produced while the tenants took 40 per cent. In Northern province, however, the water-rate system used on the government schemes in that province was not copied. Operators generally took a share of all crops grown, but the size of the share varied according to who owned the land, how much pressure the tenants were able to exert on the operators, the quality of the land, and what crops were grown. The most common basic division was 50–50 between operators and tenants.[38] Where the operator himself owned the land (or had leased it from the government), however, he could either charge the tenant a fixed land rent or else increase his share of the crops to 55 per cent or 56.25 per cent. On good quality land (known as *qurair*) he could claim 56.25 per cent, while on poorer quality land (known as *kuru* or *jardiqah*) he could only claim 55 per cent. Where the tenant owned the land, the tenant's share could rise to 55 per cent or 56.25 per cent, depending on the quality of the land.

The above-mentioned manner of dividing gains on Northern province schemes was not fixed. On some of the earlier schemes it was more common for the operator to receive 60 per cent as against the tenant's 40 per cent. There were even cases where the tenant's basic share was as low as 25 per cent. Individuals obliged to accept so low a share generally fell into one of two different categories. Some were of ex-slave origin, and their disadvantageous social position put them in a weak bargaining position. Others were sheep or cattle rearers from the nomadic areas away from the river, who wanted land to grow fodder for their flocks and herds. The sheep and cattle rearers were usually eager to preserve good relations with the leaders of the settled community, and were therefore reluctant to make strident demands. At the other extreme, the share of some tenants could reach 66.7 per cent. This was most common on vegetable schemes, where the labour contribution was higher than for other crops. It depended, however, on whether the tenants were able to put sufficient pressure on the operator, and whether the operator felt that by conceding a higher percentage he could provide the tenants with an incentive to raise production.

Although the overall division of gains on private schemes (especially in Blue Nile province) was similar to that on government schemes, the tenants were generally worse off than their counterparts in the government sector, for they did not enjoy some of the fringe benefits which their counterparts enjoyed. There was no provision for social welfare or for reserve funds in case of adversity, and the tenants often had difficulty in obtaining loans and advances.[39] On occasions, moreover, tenants experienced difficulty in securing the share of the gains to which they were entitled.

The private schemes varied considerably in size. The largest such scheme, on Aba Island, covered 30 000 feddans. Some other schemes along the White Nile covered more than 10 000 feddans.[40] In Northern province the size of scheme was generally smaller, with only a few schemes covering more than 1000 feddans. Schemes of 1000 feddans or more accounted for about four-fifths of the area under private irrigation in Blue Nile province, but for less than one-half in Northern province. At the lower end of the scale, there were a few schemes which covered only 20 feddans or less. More than half the total number of private schemes covered less than 75 feddans each, but while such schemes were numerous they accounted for only a small part of the total area under private irrigation – less than 5 per cent.

The land on which the private schemes were based did not all belong to the operator (as has already been acknowledged). About three-quarters of the land used in the schemes, in fact, was government land[41] and was leased from the government at a nominal rent – usually one piastre[42] per feddan per year. Of the remaining one-quarter, the major part belonged to the operators, with a small proportion belonging to tenants. The privately owned land was in most cases the land close to the river, previously irrigated by *sagiah*, while the government lands were the uncultivated parts behind the *sagiah* area. In addition to paying rent on government land the operator also had to pay a small licence fee to the government for permission to use pumps.[43] The length of lease on the land was generally tied to the duration of the licence, and this was usually about ten years.

The nature of the ownership of private pump schemes followed one of four different patterns.[44] Most common was individual ownership: more than two-thirds of all the schemes in 1956 were the property of single individuals. The next most common pattern was partnership, where schemes were owned by a small number of individuals working together. Rather less than a quarter of all the schemes in 1956 belonged to partnerships. A few schemes were owned by companies. The differences between these three forms of ownership were not very significant, for the partnerships were usually among the members of one family or else among the wealthy elements in one closely-knit community, and the companies were usually built up around one individual once his economic activities had reached a certain level.[45]

The fourth pattern of ownership, however, did differ to some extent from the others. About 5 per cent of all schemes in 1956 were owned by cooperative societies, where the people of one area owned a scheme collectively and shared the proceeds. Most of these cooperative irrigation societies were to be found on the Dongola–Meroe reach of the Nile in Northern province. On cooperatively-owned schemes the tenants were usually obliged to give 60 per cent of their produce to the society. The society would use the proceeds from this to pay for the maintenance of the pump and the irrigation channels, would put some money in a reserve fund, and whatever was left would be paid back to the members.

While these cooperative schemes differed considerably from those under other forms of ownership, they cannot be seen as entities where the supplier of labour drew all the benefits of his own work or where there was a fundamental equality among the participants.[46] Not all of the members of the cooperative were themselves farmers. Most of the societies would not have had sufficient funds to lay down the necessary infrastructure of the schemes if they had relied for finance only on the subscriptions of those who would ultimately farm within the scheme.[47] As it was difficult for them to raise finance in any other way,[48] they usually had to draw in local merchants and money-lenders, in addition to some members of the local community who had gone to work in Cairo, Khartoum or elsewhere,[49] as 'associate members' or 'non-resident members'. These associate or non-resident members would then be entitled to a share in the proceeds.

Moreover the members of a cooperative society did not all hold an equal share in the society and therefore they were not all entitled to an equal share of the proceeds (i.e. after the society had covered the costs of pumps, maintenance, etc.). In the early days there was no limit as to how large the share of one individual in a cooperative could be, and sometimes one individual held a larger share than all the other members put together. Such an individual would naturally be entitled to the major part of the proceeds. The 1948 Cooperative Societies Ordinance laid down that no individual could hold more than a 20 per cent share.[50] While this regulation eliminated some of the grosser imbalances, it still permitted a high level of inequality among the members. Those with larger shares were generally the associate or non-resident members. Before the 1948 Ordinance, moreover, there was no restriction on the size of the dividend which could be paid to the members (i.e. from the proceeds). Dividend rates of 40 per cent were not uncommon,[51] and it could therefore be very profitable for a merchant or an emigré element to acquire a share in a cooperative society. Such investment drew a healthy return. After 1948 the dividend rate was limited to 12 per cent, but even this return seems to have been sufficient to entice investors, for non-resident and associate members continued to play a prominent part in the societies. In some societies 50 per cent of the total share ownership was held by such members in the 1950s, although in others the percentage could be only 20 per cent.[52] Whether the dividend was in reality kept down to 12 per cent may be questioned; it seems probable that in many cases ways were found of arranging for a higher dividend. Those with significant sums invested would have had a strong interest in the adoption of procedures ensuring this, and through their crucial role in providing finance they would have had a powerful means of influencing their co-members in this direction.[53]

The private pump schemes, therefore, provided a vital field – the most important field – for the re-investment of accumulated private capital between 1930 and 1956. Even in the case of the cooperatives, it has been contended, individuals with available funds could find a fruitful field for the investment of their capital. Profitability varied according to the nature of the scheme and the period concerned, but in the 1940s and early 1950s most schemes were doing well. Schemes growing high-value vegetable crops were generally highly profitable to the scheme operator, often earning profits within one year which were more than the operator's original investment. The cotton schemes in Blue Nile province were also highly profitable at times when the price of cotton on the world market was high, as was the case in the late 1940s and early 1950s. Some of the schemes growing grain in the Northern province, however, were only marginally profitable to the operator.

V   THE PRIVATE SECTOR: INVESTMENT IN MECHANISED FARMING IN THE RAINLANDS

Investment in mechanised rain-fed farming was not the second most important field of investment for privately accumulated capital between 1930 and 1956. It was surpassed by all of the three main items mentioned under section VI below. Yet it was a field of great significance for the future. After 1956 the economic importance of investment in mechanised agriculture was possibly even greater than that of investment in pump schemes. Private investment did not begin to go into mechanised rain-fed farming until the 1950s yet by 1956 the effect of this investment was already substantial. By 1956, moreover, the pattern according to which future development was to take place had been laid down.

The development of mechanised rain-fed farming in the Sudan began in the public sector.[54] Through a series of transformations the nature of the undertakings changed until investment in this field was largely in the hands of the private sector. During the Second World War the Condominium government became aware that there was an impending grain shortage within the country. As the deficiency could not be made good by imports, due to the wartime dislocation of shipping, some action needed to be taken to boost grain production.

In 1943, accordingly, the government rounded up some of the unemployed from Omdurman and Khartoum, and sent them off to work at the hand production of sorghum near Gedaref. The experiment was only partially successful as the labourers produced only marginally more than they consumed. The project was abandoned in 1944.

Following the relative failure of this first experiment, the government's thinking turned to using mechanised agricultural means to cultivate and grow grain on some of the expanses of under-utilised land which were available in Sudan.[55] The latter plan emerged from some contacts and interchanges with the Middle East Supply Corporation (MESC). The MESC was concerned that there would be a shortage of fats at the end of the war, and in 1943 it approached the Condominium government about the possibility of expanding the Sudan's production of edible fats. The MESC suggested the large-scale mechanisation of sesame production. The Condominium government rejected the idea of growing sesame on such a large scale, stating that the varieties of sesame deemed suitable were all of the type which required considerable speed in harvesting, and it was doubtful whether sufficient labour could be gathered for successful large-scale cultivation. The government suggested instead that the MESC should mechanise sorghum production, so that some of the labour involved in this would also be available for the hand-production of sesame. This plan was finally accepted by the MESC.

In 1945, therefore, the MESC began mechanised production of sorghum. The scheme, known as the Mechanised Crop Production Scheme (MCPS) was situated at Ghadambaliya, to the east of Gedaref. The latter area was chosen due to the availability of land and to the long tradition of sorghum production in the region as a whole. (Of 100 000 tons of sorghum marketed in Sudan at the end of the Second World War, 30 000 tons came from the Gedaref region). The MCPS covered 12 000 feddans in 1945 and 21 000 the following year. In 1947 the MESC withdrew from the scheme, having encountered labour troubles and having found that there was little opportunity for expanding sesame production.

The running of the MCPS was then taken over by the Condominium government. From a desire to avoid the labour problems encountered by the MESC, and wishing to associate the local people more closely with the scheme's management, however, the government adopted a new form of organisation. The latter was based on tenants, or 'participating cultivators', similar to the Gezira scheme.

Each cultivator was allocated either 28 feddans (in the drier parts) or 20 feddans (in the damper parts), and the cultivators and scheme management were given clearly defined roles. The scheme management was to provide the land, machine services for ploughing, sowing and early weeding, seeds and insecticides, water supply, timber for housing, marketing arrangements and small 3–5 feddan garden plots for each cultivator. The cultivators were responsible for resowing any areas which had not been satisfactorily sown by machine, clearing straw off the land, protecting the crop against pests, and weeding, thinning and harvesting the crop. The gains from the sale of the produce would then be divided 50–50 between the scheme management and the cultivators.

Under this arrangement the MCPS functioned between 1947 and 1953. Rather more than 1000 cultivators were involved in it, with the scheme covering about 25 000 feddans. The new form of organisation, however, was itself found to have failings. Unlike the farmers beside the Nile, the cultivators around Gedaref had had no tradition of crop-sharing and the idea found little acceptance.[56] It was, moreover, easy for the cultivators to smuggle some of the sorghum out of the scheme and sell it privately, taking all the benefit themselves. A strike of tractor drivers also created difficulties. The realisation that there were failings did not by itself ensure the abandonment of the participating-cultivator form of organisation. Political pressures from private individuals did the rest. Individuals with accumulated capital saw the chance for investing capital profitably, and in the course of 1952 and early 1953 a number of members of the Legislative Assembly appealed to the government to make provision for private investment in mechanised agriculture. The readiness of private investors to take over mechanised agriculture from the government was highly welcome to the latter, and the decision was taken to abandon the participating-cultivator system and replace it with granting leaseholds for mechanised agricultural schemes to private investors.

That private investors needed to intercede with the government before investing in mechanised agriculture, and that the issue was one of taking over from the government rather than expanding into new areas, was due to laws restricting the use of mechanised agricultural implements. People were not permitted simply to buy a tractor, acquire vacant land and start a scheme. Mechanised implements, such as tractors and harvesters, could only be used on land which the government had specified for that purpose. Laws to this effect had been introduced by the Condominium government and were to continue in force after independence as well. The object of the regulation was to protect the environment: the use of mechanised implements could result in the large-scale removal of the trees and shrubs which had previously kept the topsoil from being blown away. A dustbowl could result. It will be noted later that illegal mechanised farming – the use of tractors and mechanised implements on land outside of the areas designated by the government – was to have damaging effects in the 1960s and 1970s.

In 1954, then, the MCPS area was divided up, mainly into plots of 1000 feddans each, and private individuals were given the opportunity of taking a lease on the plots for the purpose of mechanised agriculture. A small number of such plots had in fact been available before 1954, for since 1950 the MCPS management had been experimenting with the idea. It was perhaps the experience of the early plot-holders that had led other private investors to demand the opening up of further opportunities. The allotment of the plots (after 1954) was the responsibility of a Gedaref District Allotment Board. The original intention seems to have been that no individual should be given leases to more than one plot, but this was not rigorously upheld.

Under the new arrangement mechanised agriculture went ahead very quickly. Although it was only in 1954 that the new system had been introduced, by 1956, 388 000 feddans were covered by the private schemes (all in the Ghadambaliya area near Gedaref). Over 300 separate undertakings were involved. The entrepreneurs were at this stage generally given eight-year leases, although in some cases one-year leases could also be granted – usually when the land was to be used for testing out agricultural machinery.[57]

The role of the government was limited to providing advice, exercising general control over land use and management, and (up to 1960) providing a machine repair service. The 'general control over land use and management' involved promulgating regulations as to how the land was to be treated, such that the fertility of the soil would be retained in the long term. A four-year rotation was laid down, with four years of sorghum (or sesame) being succeeded by four years of fallow. It is questionable whether the regulations were strictly adhered to by the private investors. They had no long-term stake in the land, and their interest was in making a quick and massive profit – whatever the effect on the fertility of the soil might be. Government inspectors, some of whom may have been subject to bribery and to social pressures, were probably not in a position to curb activities which infringed the regulations.

Most of the schemes were under individual ownership, but there were also some owned by companies and partnerships. Up to 1956 no schemes had been established under cooperative ownership. Priority in the allotment of plots was supposed to have been given to the inhabitants of the area and to people currently engaged in agriculture, but in fact most of those who obtained plots came from outside of the area and had little if any previous experience of agriculture. The new scheme operators were basically entrepreneurs with a keen eye for profitable investment, not farmers. Few of them resided on or close to their schemes, and the running of the schemes was usually put in the hands of a hired manager while the agricultural work was done by labourers.

The failure of the local farmers to obtain plots, in spite of the priority which they were supposedly given, is not difficult to understand.The schemes required capital and therefore could only be taken on by those who had accumulated capital. Although mechanised agricultural schemes needed less capital than pump schemes, the necessary sum was still well beyond the resources of most Gedaref farmers. In the early years, £S2000 to £S2500 was considered necessary to initiate a scheme – including the purchase of a tractor and other basic equipment, but not inclusive of the running costs (for which loans could easily be obtained).[58] Unless such capital was available, the allotment board would not consider an application. The priority which was supposed to be shown to the local farmers, therefore, meant little in practice.

VI   THE PRIVATE SECTOR: INVESTMENT IN REAL ESTATE, COMMERCE AND PETTY MANUFACTURING

Investment in real estate, commerce and petty manufacturing was of considerable importance between 1930 and 1956. In all years the quantity of investment in real estate, and in some years that in commerce, was higher than that in either pump schemes or mechanised agriculture. Yet the long-term economic significance of investment in pump schemes or mechanised agriculture was undoubtedly greater.

Although the ownership of buildings (real estate) may only have contributed a small percentage to gross domestic product – 3 per cent in 1955/56 – the share of private capital formation taken up by this form of investment was often very substantial.[59] In 1955/56 the share was as high as 83 per cent. The latter figure was in fact a freak caused by a number of factors: the recent promotion of many Sudanese civil servants to take over from the departing British officials (i.e. the 1953–4 Sudanisation process) meant that many new people had access to government housing loans; the approach of independence created fears of instability and this encouraged investors to opt for a secure form of investment; and the high cotton prices brought about by the Korean War put money into the hands of many tenant-farmers and merchants whose most immediate concern was to improve their housing conditions. Nevertheless, although the share of private capital formation taken by ownership of buildings in 1955/56 was higher than in any previous or subsequent year, declining to 38 per cent in 1958, the share was always substantial.

From the information available, it is impossible to tell how many of those who constructed buildings were doing so primarily for their own personal use[60] or primarily to make a profit (through renting the building to others). No doubt the majority of buildings were primarily for the use of the owner. That there was substantial renting of buildings, however, is indicated by later housing surveys. The 1964/65 Population and Housing Survey of Omdurman, for example, showed that 34 per cent of the population of Omdurman was living in rented accommodation.[61] It seems probable that a similar percentage held for the mid-1950s.

In the case of high-quality houses, especially, renting out property could often be very profitable. This was particularly true around the time of independence when the influx of embassies put pressure on available facilities. Generally, investment was attracted to real estate by the low level of capital which was needed to begin investment, by the conviction that this was a secure field where loss was unlikely, and by the incentives which individuals had to improve their own housing conditions. Civil servants and some private sector executives, moreover, were able to obtain loans at concessionary rates to finance house construction.[62] The latter factor helps to explain a prominent characteristic of this sphere of investment: the large part played by civil servants. Investment financed by such loans was, of course, not based on previously accumulated private capital but on private capital in the process of accumulation.

In commerce also there was substantial investment. We will

include privately-owned transport services within this field, as transport and trade were closely intertwined. In 1955/56 transport and distribution made up 13 per cent of gross domestic product, of which about one-half was probably contributed by the private sector.[63] Capital formation in transport and distribution (private sector) stood at only 3 per cent of total private capital formation in 1955/56, but in most of the years around then it came to between 6 per cent and 10 per cent.[64] The size and importance of the field can be seen from the numbers who gained their livelihood within it. The 1956 population census recorded that 55 000 people drew the main part of their income from commerce.[65] Due to the limited activities of the government in commerce, very few of the 55 000 would have been public sector employees. The long tradition of commerce in Sudan, as described earlier, and the existence of families which had been immersed in trade for many generations, help to account for the prominence of the private commercial sector.

The official figures make it impossible to distinguish between large-scale commercial undertakings and small-scale (petty shop-keeper) activities. Most of the contribution to gross domestic product must have been made by the many thousands of petty traders scattered throughout the towns and villages of the Sudan. Nevertheless, it is clear that a number of large trading organisations were in existence by 1956. Private entrepreneurs had purchased means of transport and established widespread trading networks. With fleets of lorries they were able to collect crops from the farmers, and either sell these crops in the urban markets or else prepare them for export. Some idea of the development of these trading organisations can be obtained from information on the registration of means of transport, for it was lorries and trucks that constituted the principal infrastructure of the organisations. In 1939 there were 2099 registered trucks and lorries in the country, in 1945, 2718, and in 1956, 10 798.[66] In each of these years approximately two-thirds of the total consisted of privately-owned vehicles. The total for 1956 was composed in the manner indicated in Table 2.3.

As the greater part of the 7880 lorries and trucks in the private sector would have been owned by merchants and trading organisations,[67] it is evident that large-scale commerce was well established by 1956. Some merchants and trading organisations also owned buses and sometimes taxis.[68] In 1956 there were 353 privately-owned buses in the country and 1784 privately-owned taxis.

The most profitable commercial activity was probably import–

Table 2.3   Numbers of Lorries and Trucks Registered, 1956

	Private	Government	Total
Lorries	6 247	2 131	8 378
Trucks	1 633	787	2 420
Total	7 880	2 918	10 798

Source: Republic of Sudan, *National Income of Sudan 1960/61* (Department of Statistics, Khartoum, 1963), p. 35.

export. At the time of independence there were about 30 local companies which were engaged in this.[69] The major part of the import–export trade, however, was still in the hands of foreign companies, and a large number of the local companies were in fact owned by Sudanese of foreign origin (mainly Greek, Lebanese and Egyptian).

Finally, petty manufacturing. Although there were a few large-scale manufacturing undertakings, the great majority of undertakings in this field were on a very small scale.[70] Moreover, the two main large-scale units that did exist, the brewery and the cement factory, were owned by British interests and were not the result of private capital accumulation within the Sudan. Such privately accumulated capital as went into manufacturing, then, was in small-scale enterprises.

The principal fields of petty manufacturing which attracted investment were oil presses, mineral water factories, flour mills, engineering workshops, soap factories, ice factories, sweet factories, printing presses, carpentry workshops and tin factories. Figures for the 1955/56 output of manufacturing industry in these various fields (together with cement and brewing) can be found in Table 2.4.

Production from all of these manufacturing activities, however, made up less than 1 per cent of the gross domestic product in 1955/56,[71] and private capital formation in manufacturing came to only 5 per cent of total capital formation (private sector).[72] The total sum invested in manufacturing in 1955/56 was little more than £S$\frac{1}{2}$ million.[73]

The main characteristics of the manufacturing sector, its small absolute size and the smallness of the individual units of production, are reflected in the pattern of employment within the sector. In 1955/56 employment in manufacturing stood at no more than 9500 people, and of this number 90 per cent were working in units where

Table 2.4   *Output of Manufacturing Industry in Sudan, 1955/6*

Type of Industry	Net Output 1955/6 (thousand £S)
Oil pressing	1 000
Mineral water factories	347
Flour mills	340
Cement factory	228
Engineering workshops	152
Brewing	137
Soap factories	131
Ice factories	106
Sweet factories	84
Printing presses	77
Carpentry workshops	67
Tin factories	38
Total	2 736

Source: C. H. Harvie and J. G. Kleve, *The National Income of Sudan 1955/56* (Department of Statistics, Khartoum, 1959), p. 31.

less than ten people were employed.[74] A further prominent characteristic of the manufacturing sector at this stage was related to the origin of the investors. By far the largest group to invest in this sector consisted of merchants. A survey in the late 1950s showed that almost 50 per cent of all local investors came from that background, and it seems probable that in the early 1950s the percentage was even higher.[75]

In addition to the fields of real estate, commerce and petty manufacturing, investment in two lines of activity which do not quite fit into any of the three categories requires a mention. First, the saltworks in Port Sudan. The latter were established in 1934, and by 1955/56 the value of output had reached £S113 000.[76] Although this output only made up a very small part of gross domestic product, the saltworks were a substantial undertaking for local private enterprise. Second, construction companies. The increasing level of investment going into ownership of buildings naturally led to the growth of companies and contractors specialising in construction. In 1955/56, private sector construction accounted for 5 per cent of gross domestic product,[77] and capital formation in this field accounted for 1 per cent of total capital formation (private sector).[78] Unfortunately there are no adequate statistics on the number and size of the contracting businesses involved, but the pattern seems to have been of a small number of medium-sized companies and a large number of very small under-takings.[79]

VII THE ECONOMIC POSITION IN 1956

It remains now to bring out and emphasise some of the economic trends inherent in the pattern of development just described.

First, Sudan had benefited from very little industrialisation by 1956. As stated above, manufacturing in 1956 made up less than 1 per cent of the gross domestic product, and involved only about 0.03 per cent of the working population. The contribution of manu-facturing to GDP was in fact less than one-third of that made by traditional craft industry (i.e. mat making, rope making, carpentry, spinning and weaving, tailoring, cap making, pot making, *marisah* making,[80] leather tanning, shoe making and shoe repairing, snuff mak-ing, ivory-work and gold-work).[81]

The failure of private investors or the government to invest sub-stantially in industry is explained by a number of factors. The govern-ment was convinced that agricultural development held the exclusive key to the future, and that investment in industry would be wasteful and perhaps socially harmful. The possibility of substantial govern-ment investment in industry seems never to have been seriously entertained. For private investors, the funds needed for investment in this field were greater than most local investors had at their disposal. This inherent obstacle confronting private investment in industry was in no way alleviated or circumvented by government policy. Indeed, the policies of the Condominium government added to the difficulties. The trading policy under the Condominium in-volved facilitating exchange between Sudan's agricultural produce and the manufactured goods of the United Kingdom (and to a lesser extent those of Egypt). As with most territories under colonial control, therefore, the level of tariffs was held deliberately low. Tariffs were raised marginally after the Second World War, but even in 1950 the general rate of import duty stood at only 15 per cent, with rather higher rates for alcoholic drinks, tobacco, silks and artificial textiles.[82] Goods from Egypt imported through Wadi Halfa were mostly exempt from duty. Local industry, then, had little protection. The heavy competition which new industries faced – competition in which the products of large-scale foreign industry inevitably held an advantage over those of small-scale local industry – made industrial investment simply not worthwhile. Local investors recognised the realities of the situation.

A second prominent feature of the pattern of development was the large sector of the economy where the processes of production remained much the same as they had been before the Condominium era. In spite of all the developments mentioned above, in other words, much of the economy was fundamentally unchanged. Official statistics in the Sudan distinguish between the modern sector and the traditional sector. The 'modern' sector is that part of the economy using modern machines and modern methods of production, or where production takes place in an urban setting. The 'traditional' sector is that part where simple tools and implements are used and where the economy is geared largely to subsistence production.[83] In terms of this distinction, the modern sector accounted for 43.6 per cent of gross domestic product in 1955/56 while the traditional sector accounted for 56.4 per cent[84] As productivity in the modern sector was obviously much greater than that in the traditional sector, it is clear that the proportion of the population involved in the traditional sector must have been considerably more than 56.4 per cent. In fact it seems likely that 90 per cent of the population were still enclosed within the traditional sector – some as nomads and others as simple peasant farmers.

While there had been advance in irrigated agriculture,[85] in mechanised agriculture, in transport and distribution, in construction and in some other modern fields, therefore, and while government services had expanded and the growing urban centres had seen an increasing number of artisans catering for the needs of the urban population, the major part of the population were still engaged in that sector of agriculture which employed traditional methods of cultivation and animal husbandry. The existence of a modern sector, it should be noted, does not mean that standards of living within that sector were particularly high. On the contrary, wages for unskilled or semi-skilled workers in government service, manufacturing or commerce, and average returns for tenants, were mostly so low that the individuals concerned were living barely above the subsistence level.[86]

Although the processes of production were unchanged within the 56.4 per cent of the economy made up by the traditional sector, the use of cash and the practice of market exchange within that sector seem to have grown considerably. The development of communications and the establishment of the private sector trading companies must have been largely responsible for this. Lorries owned by the trading companies now covered the country in the search for crops to purchase, thereby drawing many more farmers than before into a national market. The precise share of gross domestic product accounted for by cash exchanges, however, is not revealed in official statistics.

A third feature was the extent of the economy's dependence on foreign trade.[87] In 1955/56 the total of imports and exports was equivalent to 40 per cent of gross domestic product,[88] and about 80 per cent consisted of one crop: cotton. This naturally made the economy very vulnerable to fluctuations. A downward turn in the price of cotton (such as occurred in the second half of the 1950s) would suddenly deprive the country of the expected level of foreign exchange earnings. As the manufacturing sector was so little developed and the need for manufactured goods had to be satisfied from imports, a drop in foreign exchange earnings from exports would naturally restrict the quantity of manufactured goods which could be imported. In so far as development projects were dependent on imports of capital equipment, the pace of development would naturally be affected.[89] Coherent planning was made very difficult.

Moreover, the foundation on which Sudan's trade was built, the exchange between agricultural produce (largely cotton) and manufactured goods, was one which proved increasingly disadvantageous after 1956. From the mid-1950s through to the late 1960s, Sudan's terms of trade were consistently deteriorating. Taking 1968 as the base year, for example, the terms of trade index steadily declined from 125 in 1956 to 95 in 1967, before rising to 100 in 1968.[90]

Sudan's foreign trade in 1956 was, of course, predominantly with the developed Western countries. About 75 per cent of exports went to Western Europe and North America, and rather more than 50 per cent of imports came from those areas.[91] The remaining shares, both of imports and of exports, were mainly taken up by Egypt, India and Japan. The economy, therefore, was in effect closely bound up with that of the capitalist world as a whole.

A final feature, perhaps with some more positive implications than the previous ones, was the substantial flow of income which the government was assured of from its economic undertakings. This was, of course, an effect of the deliberate designs of the Condominium government in the early years, as explained above. The Gezira scheme was responsible for the largest part of revenue earned in this way. In 1950, when the Sudan Plantation Syndicate's concession came to an end, the Gezira scheme was taken over by the government. The government's share of the gains now rose from 35 per cent to 40 per cent while the share which had been taken by the SPS – reduced from 25 per cent to 20 per cent – was given to the administrative body, the Gezira Board, and the tenant's share of 40 per cent remained constant. In the early 1950s the government's share of the gains generally exceeded £S5 million annually.[92] The other cotton schemes, the government pump schemes, Sudan Railways, Sudan Airways and the ginneries all made some contribution.

The Sudan government, therefore, had less need to rely on taxation for revenue than the governments of most African states.[93] Whereas many African governments raised 90 per cent of their revenue from taxation, the Sudan government in 1955/56 drew only 64 per cent of its total revenue from that source.[94] Profits of government enterprises in 1955/56 made up about 20 per cent of the total, and profits on fiscal monopolies most of the remainder. In the years which followed, moreover, the percentage contributed by government enterprises tended to rise. This does not mean that rates of taxation in Sudan were particularly low. The total raised in taxation generally came to about 12 per cent of gross domestic product – an average figure for African countries. The conclusion, rather, is that relative to the size of the country's economy, the Sudan government had more revenue at its disposal than most African governments.

The policies of the Condominium government, then, left the Sudan government in 1956 with a valuable flow of income. The funds made available in this way obviously constituted a useful base from which post-independence governments would be able to launch development programmes. Whether the funds were in fact used for this purpose, or were wasted on inflated salaries for an over-large bureaucracy, will be the concern of later chapters.

3 Social Forces under the Condominium

I INTRODUCTION

We now turn to the manner in which the processes of accumulation and re-investment under the Condominium (as described in Chapters 1 and 2) created and shaped social forces within Sudan. This will lay the basis for describing the political dynamics of the nationalist movement as it developed in Sudan, and the political dynamics of post-independence Sudan. While the pattern of Sudanese politics may, in an immediate sense, have been determined by the struggle between sectarian and ethnic groupings and between adherents and opponents of unity with Egypt, our concern here lies at a more fundamental level. The focus is on the factors which created the whole framework within which Sudanese politics moved. How, for example, did sectarian and ethnic groupings come to be in a position to play a political role?

Two aspects of inequality, or imbalance, inherent in the economic structure of Sudan under the Condominium provide the key to understanding the country's emerging social and political dynamics. The first is the division between those individuals who were in a position to benefit from the Condominium economy and re-invest in productive fields of investment which further strengthened their economic position, and the remainder of the population. The second is the division between those parts of the country which saw economic development under the Condominium and those which did not. The Condominium's developmental efforts were concentrated in an area resembling an inverted 'T' imposed on Sudan: composed of the valley of the Nile to the north of Khartoum, the Blue and White Nile areas immediately south of Khartoum, central Kordofan, and the southern part of Kassala province. The social and political effects of these two inequalities or imbalances were crucial: together, they have given Sudanese politics its particular dynamics.

II REINVESTMENT AND THE ECONOMIC ELITE[1]

This section seeks to identify the social elements which were in a position to benefit from the Condominium economy and re-invest their funds. While companies, organisations and individuals based outside Sudan were substantial beneficiaries, the focus here is exclusively on domestic elements. As the latter elements were to play a crucial role in the politics of Sudan after independence, it is clearly important to identify what background they came from and how they related to the rest of the Sudanese population. The political role played by those who composed the economic elite was not based solely on their economic position. Personal wealth, rather, buttressed an existing position of social influence or social control. The economic elite was constituted of individuals who came from four distinct social/occupational categories: religious leaders, tribal leaders, merchants and higher civil servants/politicians. Not all members of these categories were able to draw substantial benefit and re-invest; other factors have to be brought in to explain why some could benefit and some could not.

(a) Religious leaders

The leading families of the Sufi religious orders (*turuq*, sing. *tariqah*) and of the Mahdist movement were frequently in a position to accumulate funds.[2] Such funds came mainly from the dues and contributions paid by the order's or movement's followers and through the services which these followers rendered. The religious dues generally came to one-tenth of the follower's income, while the rendering of 'services' usually involved the follower cultivating land owned by a religious leader – a service which was given free if done on a part-time basis, or in return for the bare means of subsistence if done on a full-time basis. Followers on occasions donated their landholdings to their religious leader, sometimes continuing to work the land in return for payment of a subsistence allowance (or the means of subsistence).

The extent to which religious leaders were in a position to accumulate and re-invest funds depended on a variety of factors: whether the *tariqah* or movement was strongly centralised (such that all contributions and dues flowed to a single leader or family at the centre – as was the case with the Mahdist Ansar) or decentralised (such that contributions and dues flowed to localised leaderships – as with the

Sammaniyyah order); the size of the *tariqah* or movement; whether the leadership was oriented towards involvement in the economy, or saw its role simply in terms of providing the upkeep of mosques and provision of charitable services; and whether the *tariqah* or movement's membership resided in an area where incomes were rising (and hence where the population could afford to make significant contributions).

The ability of particular religious leaders (or leading families) to emerge in positions of economic strength, however, was not influenced only by factors internal to the order or movement. The Condominium authorities took an active part in enabling some such leaders to establish themselves economically – partly so as to reward them for their loyalty to the Condominium regime, and partly (especially in the case of Sayyid 'Abd al-Rahman al-Mahdi[3]) in the hope that by enabling such leaders to emerge as prominent businessmen they could defuse the political threat posed by tightly organised movements capable of fanaticism. On the basis of government support, the economic role played by Sayyid 'Abd al-Rahman expanded rapidly. In 1908 he obtained permission from the government to cultivate some land on Aba Island; the land was to become his after five years.[4] Further grants followed. Government support, combined with the financial acumen of the recipient, had impressive results:

In 1915 Sayed Abdel Rahman was given additional land on Aba Island. In 1925 he obtained, together with Sayed Abdullahi Al Fadil and Mohamed Al Khalifa Sherif, a lease of about 600 feddans of land at Gondal for the growing of cotton. A loan of £4500, later converted into a gift, was made to him in 1926. By 1933 he had some 13 000 feddans under cultivation in Aba Island, the Funj, the White Nile and Kassala Provinces. His annual income was estimated at between £15 000 and £40 000. On Aba Island alone he had a labour force of about 4500. He was in 1936, by any standards, economically prosperous and politically important.[5]

Sayyid 'Abd al-Rahman also seems to have benefited from a supportive governmental attitude towards his contracting activities. The interruption in fuel supplies to Sudan caused by the First World War led to him obtaining contracts for the supply of wood to government river steamers (the wood coming from Aba Island's forests). Contracts for the supply of materials needed in the construction of Sennar Dam in the early 1920s also went to Sayyid 'Abd al-Rahman.[6] In all these economic activities Sayyid 'Abd al-Rahman's religious role was complementary to his economic role. Much of the labour used on his projects was constituted by Mahdists who had migrated to the Aba Island area from Darfur and Kordofan, so as to benefit from Sayyid 'Abd al-Rahman's *barakah*.[7] These *ansar* earned no income; they were simply given food and clothing for subsistence. The religious role strengthened Sayyid 'Abd al-Rahman's economic effectiveness. So also was his economic well-being used to build up both the religious and political strength of the Mahdist movement.

Similar support, although not nearly as substantial, was given to Sayyid 'Ali al-Mirghani[8] of the Khatmiyyah order, and Sharif Yusif al-Hindi[9] of the Hindiyyah order. Both of these religious leaders were given substantial allowances from the outset of the Condominium era. Sayyid 'Ali was granted land in the Red Sea province and the Northern province to develop agriculture,[10] and Sharif Yusif was granted land in the Gezira on the grounds that both he and Sayyid 'Abd al-Rahman 'claim to be regarded as natives of the Blue Nile province to whom (as influential natives of the province) the Governor might owe special consideration in the allotment of land.'[11] Neither Sayyid 'Ali nor Sharif Yusif proved as adept in business as did Sayyid 'Abd al-Rahman.

Other families which were able to make use of positions of religious leadership to expand their economic role (albeit without direct British assistance), included the al-Majdhub family of the Majdhubiyyah *tariqah* (who invested in agricultural schemes around Ed Damer), the Nur al-Da'im family of the Sammaniyyah (who owned pump schemes on the White Nile), the Siwar al-Dahab family of the Qadiriyyah (with pump schemes around Dongola), and the al-Makki family of the Isma'iliyyah (who operated a profitable trading concern covering Kordofan and Darfur).

(b) Tribal leaders

The traditional tribal leaders of Northern Sudan had been in a position before the Condominium to extract part of the economic surplus from agricultural production (settled and nomadic) in the areas which fell under their sway – through their control of grazing rights, or water resources (wells, *hafirs*, etc.), and of the allocation of gum gardens.[12] At that time, however, the economic surplus was generally limited and tribal leaders were seldom in a position to re-invest funds accumulated in this way outside the traditional agricultural sector.

Under the Condominium the political and economic roles of tribal leaders grew stronger. This was in part the effect of deliberate government policy: the Condominium authorities had neither sufficient economic resources nor sufficient personnel to maintain an administrative presence in all areas of the country, so from the outset of Condominium rule tribal leaders were given the support and assistance necessary for them to administer their tribal territories effectively.[13] Following the nationalist uprising of 1924, moreover, the government further strengthened this role: the educated Sudanese were now deemed an unreliable stratum on which to build an administrative framework and, with the reduced role now given to Egyptians in the administrative system, it became government policy to entrust as much local administration to tribal leaders as they could realistically handle. Many tribal leaders were now enabled to extend their authority to semi-urban areas adjacent to the tribal areas which they had previously administered – areas which had perhaps been part of the tribal domain in a previous age, but which had long since established an effective independence of the traditional tribal leadership. The tribal make-up of these semi-urban areas was usually different from that of the surrounding rural areas – the population being made up of traders who had moved into the area from outside (most commonly, this involved Shaigi, Ja'ali and Danagla traders from the riverain areas of Northern province who had migrated to the small towns and villages of the rest of Sudan).

Under the Condominium, then, the tribal leaders (some more than others) encountered new opportunities for accumulating funds and investing in profitable enterprises. The formal support from a strong centralised government improved their ability to collect the dues (for use of gum gardens, etc.) which had been their traditional right;[14] the expansion of their authority to cover some semi-urban areas gave them some control over trade licences and some other aspects of commercial life (which could on occasions be manipulated profitably). Moreover, as has already been mentioned in the case of the Gezira,[15] the process of land registration, carried out by the Condominium government in its early years, made it possible for tribal leaders to establish ownership rights over land which had in fact been communal property – belonging to the tribe as a whole, not to the tribal leader. Where the land which tribal leaders acquired was fertile and could be irrigated, the way was open for them to invest in pump schemes, dividing the land into share-cropping tenancies.

The administrative role of tribal leaders, moreover, meant that they were often responsible for – or deeply involved in – taking supposedly governmental decisions affecting their own interests. It was, therefore, relatively easy for them to tailor decisions to suit their own entrepreneurial interests. The registration of land under the *Title of Lands Ordinance 1899*, for example, was carried out by provincial and district commissions appointed by the Governor-General. These commissions consisted of three commissioned officers of the Egyptian army and two Sudanese notables – usually the shaikhs of the most powerful tribes in the area.[16] Tribal leaders, moreover, held responsibility for leasing out government land which fell within their tribal domains. They were also members of the pump scheme boards which allocated licences for pump schemes. It was thus possible for some tribal leaders to arrange the registration of communal land in their own names; to grant themselves the lease of government land which could be developed through the introduction of pump irrigation; and to arrange for themselves to be given a pump licence so as to develop the land. The good standing of tribal leaders in governmental eyes ensured access to commercial bank loans for agricultural schemes.

The Habbani family, traditional leaders of the Hassaniya tribe along the White Nile in the Ed Dueim area, was one of the families which grew in economic strength through the procedures described above. Over the Condominium period they established a total of fifteen pump schemes along the White Nile, covering a total of 15 000 feddans.[17] Similarly the family of Malik al-Zubair (tribal leaders of the Danagla) established a number of schemes around Dongola; the family of Surur Ramli (tribal leaders of the Ja'aliyin) established schemes around Shendi; and the family of Muhammad Ahmad Abu Sinn (tribal leaders of the Shukriya) established schemes along the Blue Nile. Most such schemes were devoted to cotton growing and earned substantial profits for their owners in the late 1940s and early 1950s when the price of cotton was high.

(c) Merchants (traders)

The continued existence of a merchant grouping in Sudan, from the Funj empire through the Turko–Egyptian regime and the Mahdiyyah into the Condominium era, has been described in Chapter 1. New merchants entered the Sudan in the 19th and early 20th centuries from outside and gradually became integrated within the local merchant community.[18] In the Turko–Egyptian era most of the immigrants who established themselves as merchants came from Egypt (apart from the European traders mentioned previously, who did not become integrated into the local merchant community), while under the Condominium they came from a wider range of Eastern Mediterranean countries – mainly from Greece, Syria and Lebanon (as well as Egypt). The migrants who emerged as important merchants (and petty manufacturers) under the Condominium were mostly based in Port Sudan – where they played a prominent part in shipping and exporting, gaining at the same time a prominent holding in the town's real estate (e.g. the Barbari family) – and in Khartoum, where they were prominent in trade and, subsequently, petty manufacturing.

The sphere of commerce in which most money was made was that of import–export. The commanding heights of this sector were occupied by foreign companies, but Sudanese merchants could nevertheless create for themselves a profitable role. The import side was almost entirely in the hands of British-owned or Greek-owned companies (principally Sudan Mercantile and Mitchell Cotts in the former category, and Contomichaelos and Tchivaglou in the latter), which between them held the vast majority of agencies for foreign suppliers.[19] The export side, however, was more open. Even when the actual exporting procedure was carried out by foreign companies, Sudanese merchants often played the crucial role of buying in the products which the foreign companies would subsequently export.

The main exports of Sudan in the Condominium era were gum, livestock, oilseeds (sesame, groundnuts and cotton-seed) and cotton. An examination of the scale and structuring of each of these fields of exporting activity gives an idea of the kind of gains which could accrue to Sudanese merchants. Even before the Condominium, the Sudan had emerged as the leading producer of gum in the world. Prices for gum were rising in the early part of the century, and the extension of the railway in 1913 to El Obeid – in the centre of the gum-growing area – gave a considerable boost to gum exports. The first gum market in Sudan was established in Tisra (1900), with new markets coming into existence in Kosti, Ed Dueim and Goz Abu Goma in 1903 and 1904.[20] When the railway reached El Obeid in 1913, a gum market was established there – and this soon became (as it remains) the biggest gum market in the world. Table 3.1 shows the growth which occurred in Sudan's exports of gum arabic over the latter half of the Condominium era, and the proportion of world gum

Table 3.1   World Exports of Gum Arabic (in tonnes with percentages in brackets; four-year averages)

Year	Sudan	French West Africa	Nigeria	Tanzania	Total
1926–29	20 890 (79.2)	4 850 (18.4)	75 (0.3)	575 (2.2)	26 390
1930–33	19 175 (76.8)	4 705 (18.9)	375 (1.5)	700 (2.8)	24 955
1934–37	21 485 (76.4)	5 330 (19.0)	525 (1.9)	775 (2.8)	28 115
1938–41	22 005 (72.0)	6 765 (22.1)	575 (1.9)	1 200 (3.9)	30 545
1942–45	14 980 (72.1)	3 035 (14.6)	1 450 (7.0)	1 300 (6.3)	20 765
1946–49	31 365 (78.2)	6 100 (15.2)	1 450 (3.6)	1 200 (3.0)	40 115
1950–53	37 950 (84.0)	3 990 (8.8)	1 760 (3.9)	1 485 (3.3)	45 185
1954–57	43 220 (85.0)	5 050 (9.9)	1 090 (2.1)	1 470 (2.9)	50 830

Source: A. A. Bishai, *Export Performance and Economic Development in Sudan* (Ithaca Press, London, 1976), p. 103.

exports which this constituted. The purchase of gum from the collectors and its sale in the gum markets was organised by Sudanese merchants, operating at different levels.

The organisation of the gum trade was left to the merchants, who created a chain of small traders and brokers to link them with the producers. These merchants eventually delivered the product to the export companies, which were mainly British.[21]

Livestock exports grew steadily through the Condominium period. Unlike the other three export items covered here, this trade was exclusively in the hands of Sudanese merchants, with sheep and cattle being exported to Egypt through Wadi Halfa and sheep being exported to Saudi Arabia through Port Sudan or Suakin. Only a small proportion of total livestock exports went to Saudi Arabia. Table 3.2 gives an idea of growth in the livestock export trade. The high figures for 1942 stem from the role which Sudanese livestock exports played during the Second World War – constituting an important source of meat for the British and allied forces in North Africa.[22]

As with the gum trade, the organisation of the livestock trade involved a chain of agents, brokers, petty traders and merchants, linking the farmers and nomads with the export market. The major role in establishing and maintaining the trade, however, was played by a small group of big merchants.[23] Before the Second World War, in fact, a single individual held a pre-eminent position: Muhammad Ahmad al-Birair. In the early 1940s al-Birair came together with three other livestock exporters (Sa'ad Abu al-'Ila, 'Abd al-Hamid

Table 3.2   Livestock Exports in Selected Years

	Sheep	Cattle	Camels*
1904	7 846	1 661	n.a.
1910	67 387	n.a.	n.a.
1921–6 (average)	25 000	16 000	n.a.
1942	151 782	50 890	n.a.
1956	107 000	53 000	38 000

Total value of livestock exports in 1956: £1 496 000

* No figures on camel exports are available until the end of the Condominium period. As most of the camels were exported on the hoof over the desert, the Condominium authorities experienced difficulty in collating the relevant information. The camel trade was, in any case, organised more by nomadic tribal leaders than by merchants.

Sources: The figures for 1904, 1910, 1921–6 and 1942 are taken from F. Mahmoud, 'Origin and Development of the Sudanese Private Capitalist Class', PhD thesis, University of Hull, 1978, pp. 88–9; the figures for 1956 (numbers of animals exported, and their value) are taken from C. A. Harvie and J. G. Kleve, *The National Income of Sudan 1955/56*, (Department of Statistics, Khartoum, 1959), p. 19.

al-Mahdi, and Ahmad Kardaman) to form a new company, *al-Sharikah al-Rubaiyah* ('the company of four'). This company dominated livestock exporting for most of the two decades which followed. It was at this level that the most substantial profits accrued.

Oilseed exports also grew steadily under the Condominium. Table 3.3 shows the pattern of growth in the three principal types of oilseed. These figures in fact understate the growth which occurred in the closing years of the Condominium period – in all three types of seed, exports underwent a rapid expansion in the mid-1950s.[24]

The organisation of the oilseed trade again involved a chain of traders and merchants, with a few prominent merchants coming to dominate the substantial trade of the 1940s and 1950s – partially as suppliers to foreign-owned import–export companies, partially as exporters in their own right. A characteristic of this sector was the close link between trade and manufacturing. Even before the Condominium, oilseed merchants had set up camel-driven oil presses in Kordofan and Darfur. Funds accumulated through the oilseed trade under the Condominium were often invested in mechanised oil presses and mills and, in 1956, oil-pressing accounted for some 36 per cent of total manufacturing output.[25] Merchants in the oilseed trade,

Table 3.3   Oilseed Exports, Selected Years (thousand tons)

	1914	1924	1934	1944	1952
Cotton-seed	3.0	18.0	56.4	136.1	92.3
Sesame	n.a.	9.0	13.0	n.a.	14.0
		(1922)	(1932–4)		(1952–4)
Groundnuts	n.a.	2.7	3.9	n.a.	28.8

Source: A. A. Bishai, *Export Performance, and Economic Development in Sudan* (Ithaca Press, London, 1976), pp. 147, 177, 211 and 217.

thus, were prominent among those who emerged as manufacturers in the closing years of the Condominium.

The role of Sudanese merchants in the cotton trade was less significant than the role played by Sudanese merchants in the three spheres of commercial activity mentioned so far. As large-scale cotton production in Sudan was brought into being by British investors specifically to supply the Lancashire cotton industry, it is hardly surprising that British companies retained control of the export of the commodity. There was, nevertheless, a small number of Sudanese merchants who and companies which – in one way or another – became involved in cotton trading. In most cases these merchants and companies were the owners of large pump schemes producing cotton, and were thus cotton producers as well as cotton traders. Among such elements were Sa'ad Abu al-'Ila, 'Abd al-Mona'im Mohamed, Uthman Salih and the Dairat al-Mahdi (the holding-group of the Mahdi family's economic undertakings). Here also, as with oilseeds, there was a link between trading and manufacturing (or, at least, processing). The merchants and companies of the kind mentioned above invested in ginning factories to prepare cotton for export. In this way they gained extra profit not only from the cotton grown on their own schemes but also from that grown by the smaller pump-scheme owners. The smaller pump-schemes were, in fact, often under the influence of the larger pump-scheme owners. Not only did the latter provide the ginning facility for the former, they also extended loans to the smaller pump-scheme owners. The smaller pump-scheme owners, therefore, became highly dependent on the larger ones.

In a variety of different areas of commercial activity, therefore, Sudanese merchants accumulated funds and re-invested under the Condominium. The re-investment involved expanding their commercial networks, processing goods which they had previously traded as primary products and, in some cases, entering new fields of petty manufacturing: flour milling, printing, and the production of soaps, soft drinks, sweets, etc. Many merchants made their money in the provinces (Darfur, Kordofan, Red Sea and Blue Nile) and then transferred their operations to Khartoum in the 1950s.[26]

(d) Higher civil servants and professionals

Higher civil servants and professionals (doctors, lawyers, engineers, etc.) were to be prominent after independence among those accumulating funds and re-investing in agriculture, real estate, contracting, commerce and petty manufacturing. Up to 1956, however, only a small number had done so. The principal reason for this, of course, was that few Sudanese held high administrative positions until the eve of independence. In 1946 the Condominium government appointed a Sudanisation committee to consider the replacement of non-Sudanese officials by Sudanese, and in 1948 the committee produced a plan to Sudanise 62.2 per cent of the posts held by non-Sudanese over the next fourteen years.[27] The percentages of civil service and professional jobs held by Sudanese in 1948 was as follows:

Administrative officers	14.3
Agriculturalists	8.5
Civil engineers	25.5
Doctors	39.0
Educationalists	17.4
Judges and law officers	44.4
Scientific officers	4.6[28]

It was, however, not until the establishment of the Sudanisation Commission in 1953, following the Anglo–Egyptian agreement, that a major change occurred: 647 of the 1111 posts held by British personnel were marked for immediate Sudanisation, and 87 of the 108 posts held by Egyptians.[29] This was carried out in the course of 1954. A further 200 British officials resigned voluntarily.

Although the majority of top administrative posts only fell into Sudanese hands in the last two years of the Condominium era, a small number of Sudanese had occupied such posts before 1954. In 1952, for example, there were 119 Sudanese in the Political Service (the body of administrators under the Condominium holding key central and local government administrative responsibility).[30] While there are no figures showing how many Sudanese pursued professional occupations in that year, the number was probably slightly larger than that of the administrators.

Not all of the officials and professionals just mentioned were in a position to accumulate funds and re-invest – most would still have been too junior and too new in their positions to do so. In the early 1950s, nevertheless, officials and professionals were beginning to acquire urban real estate, and a small number were investing in mechanised dry farming, pump schemes and contracting businesses. Real estate provided the main field of investment for government officials: they enjoyed access to low-interest or interest-free loans intended to enable them to build their own houses, while living in low-rent government housing. Although these officials were supposed to vacate government housing once their own houses were built, many remained in government houses and rented out their newly built properties. The benefits which could be drawn from this course of action were particularly prominent at the time of independence when foreign embassies and their employees were seeking accommodation in Khartoum.

(e) Composition of policy-making bodies: representation of the economic elite in the Legislative Assembly and the first Parliament

The role which the economic elite was to play in the Sudanese nationalist movement and in the politics of independent Sudan inevitably had many facets. This will become evident in the analysis given in subsequent chapters of the dynamics of Sudanese politics. One particular facet concerns us in this subsection: the prominence of individuals from the economic elite in the central advisory and legislative institutions established in the closing years of the Condominium. An examination of the social backgrounds of the members of these institutions reveals that all but a small minority came from one or other of the four groupings discussed above. Tables 3.4–3.6 provide the information to support this contention. Virtually all of the members of the Advisory Council came from one or other of the four groupings; so also did virtually all of the northern members of the Legislative Council and over half of the southern members. In the first parliament, as is indicated in Table 3.7, some 70–75 per cent of the members of the House of Representatives came from one of these four groupings, and between 75 per cent and 85 per cent of the members of the Senate. These latter percentages, moreover, understate the real strength in parliament of members from one or other of the four groupings. As effective power lay in the hands of political parties based in northern Sudan, it is significant that most of the members from less privileged backgrounds were southern Sudanese. In both houses of parliament combined there were only some fifteen northern Sudanese from less privileged backgrounds.

As Sudan was proceeding through self-government into independence, therefore, the preponderance of the legislators were from those parts of the population capable of accumulating funds and re-investing. This is not to say that all those capable of accumulation and re-investment in fact pursued such activity: some did, others did not. The favoured economic position enjoyed by such elements, however, inevitably put its stamp upon the economic and social policies which Sudanese legislative bodies were inclined to support.

Table 3.4   Social Backgrounds of the Members of the Advisory Council for Northern Sudan, 1944–7

1. Babu 'Uthman Nimr	— paramount *nazir* of the Messeriya
2. Yahiah Ahmad 'Umar	— deputy *nazir* of the Jawama'a
3. 'Abdallah Bakr	— *nazir* of Dar Bakr
4. Muhammad Muhammad Al-Amin al-Tirik	— paramount *nazir* of the Hadendowa
5. Muhammad Ahmed Abu Sin	— *nazir* of the Shukriya
6. Ibrahim Musa Madibbo	— *nazir* of the Rizeigat
7. Muhammad Bahr al-Din	— *sultan* of Dar Masalit
8. Ayubi 'Abd al-Majid	— head of the local administration in Berber
9. Al-Zubair Hamad al-Malik	— head of the local administration in Dongola
10. Hasan Adlan	— *makk* of the Funj district
11. Fahal Ibrahim	— *shaikh* of the Haj Abdallah area
12. Ahmad Yusif Alqam	— *nazir* of the south-central Gezira
13. Idris 'Abd al-Qadir Salih	— *nazir* of the Hassaniya
14. Surur Muhammad Ramli	— *shaikh* of an area in Northern province
15. Khalil 'Akashah	— prominent merchant in El Obeid
16. 'Uthman 'Abd al-Qadir	— prominent merchant in Wadi Halfa
17. Hasan Shiklawi	— senior government official
18. Hamid al-Sayyid	— chief clerk in Darfur province administration

Table 3.4 continued

19. Makki Abbas	— inspector of adult education
20. Mirghani Hamzah	— engineer in the Public Works Department
21. Muhammad 'Ali Shawqi	— deputy-registrar of lands

Note: For the translation of Arabic terms used in this table see the glossary on p. 356; also see the section on tribal leaders, pp. 52 to 54.

Source: M. H. 'Awad, *Al-Istighlal wa Fasad al-Hukm fi al-Sudan*, (Exploitation and the Corruption of Government in Sudan), (no publisher or date given), pp. 117–18.

Table 3.5 *Social Backgrounds of the Members of the Legislative Assembly, 1948–53*

A *Direct elections*

1. 'Umar Aqabain	— prominent merchant (Atbara)
2. Ahmad Yusif Hashim	— editor and proprietor of *al-Sudan al-Jadid* newspaper. Member of the Hashimab family which was closely associated with orthodox religious leadership in northern Sudan (Khartoum East)
3. Zain al-'Abdin 'Abd al-Tam	— doctor (Khartoum West)
4. 'Abdallahi al-Fadil al-Mahdi	— nephew of Sayyid 'Abd al-Rahman al-Mahdi, with an involvement in some of the latter's agricultural schemes (Omdurman North)
5 Muhammed al-Haj al-Amin	— government official and member of Omdurman town bench (Omdurman West)
6. Muhammad Adam Adham	— doctor (Omdurman South)
7. Muhammad 'Abd al-Rahman Nuqdallah	— merchant, owning some agricultural and commercial enterprises; some of the latter developed through Nuqdallah's links with Sayyid 'Abd al-Rahman al-Mahdi (Wad Medani)

Table 3.5 continued

8. Salih 'Abd al-Qadir al-Mubarak	— government official (Khartoum North)
9. 'Umar Kisha	— prominent merchant (Port Sudan)
10. Al-Zain 'Ubaid Ahmad	— prominent merchant (El Obeid)

B Indirect Elections

11. Muhammad Salih Dirgham	— government official (Wadi Halfa)
12. Al-Zubair Hamad al-Malik	— head of the local administration in Dongola (Dongola)
13. Muhammad Taha Sorij	— *shaikh* of a branch of the Shaigia and president of the Shaigia court (Merowe)
14. 'Abdallah Ayubi	— member of the Berber town bench, and son of the head of the local administration in Berber (Berber)
15. Muhammad Ibrahim Farah	— *nazir* of the Shendi area (Shendi)
16. Surur Muhammad Ramli	— *shaikh* of a branch of the Ja'aliyin (Khartoum Rural, North)
17. Muhammad Nasir	— *shaikh* of a branch of the Ja'aliyin (Khartoum Rural, South)
18. Ahmad al-Jid al-Shaikh al-Abbas	— religious notable (Kamlin)
19. Muhammad Ahmad Abu Sin	— *nazir* of the Shukriya, and president of the Shukriya court (Rufaa)
20. Muhammad Musa'id	— *nazir* of the Messellemia area (El Hasaheisa)
21. Iman Bata'alah Muhammad Iman	— religious notable (Halawin)
22. Ahmad Yusif Alqam	— *nazir* of the south-central Gezira; held a number of tenancies on the Gezira scheme (Wad Medani, North)
23. Qasm al-Sid 'Abdallah al-Nur	— *shaikh* of a branch of the Kawahla, and president of the Kawahla court (Wad Medani, South)

Table 3.5 continued

24. Ahmad ʻAbd al-Bagi Muhammad	— vice-president of the Managil court (Managil)
25. ʻUthman ʻAli	— *shaikh* of Sennar district (Sennar)
26. Yusif al-Ajab	— *shaikh* of the Rufaʻa al-Sharq (Funj nazirate)
27. Hasan Adlan	— *makk* of the Funj district (Sinja)
28. Muhammad al-Khalifah Sharif	— religious notable from a branch of the al-Khalifa family (Kosti North)
29. Makki Ahmad Asakir	— *nazir* of the Baggara confederation (Kosti South)
30. Muhammad ʻAbd al-Qadir Habbani	— member of the leading family of the Hassaniya (Ed Dueim East)
31. Yusif Idris Adam Habbani	— deputy-*nazir* of the Hassaniya (Ed Dueim West)
32. Mustafa Ahmad Unur	— deputy-*nazir* of the Hadendowa (Tokar)
33. Jaʻafar ʻAli Shiklawi	— *nazir* of the Halenga (Kassala)
34 Muhammad Muhammad al-Amin Tirik	— *nazir* of the Hadendowa (Hadendowa)
35. Muhammad Karrar Kujur	— school headmaster, and vice-president of the Red Sea Bisharin court (Amarar Bisharin)
36. Ahmad Hamad Abu Sin	— deputy-*nazir* of the Shukriya (Gedaref North)
37. ʻAbdallah Bakr	— *nazir* of Dar Bakr (Gedaref South)
38. Muhammad Timsah Simawi	— *nazir* of Dar Hamid (Dar Hamid)
39. Fadlallah al-Tom	— acting *nazir* of the Kababish (Kababish and Hawawir)
40. Munʻim Mansour	— *nazir* of the Hamar (Dar Hamar)
41. Babu ʻUthman Nimr	— *nazir* of the Messeriya (Dar Messeriya)
42. Al-Amin ʻAli ʻIsa	— *makk* of the Nuba (Jebels A)
43. Nawwal Muhammad Rahal	— religious notable (Jebels B)
44. Al-Tayib Adam Gaili	— religious notable (Tegale)
45. Saʻid Ali Matur	— acting *nazir* of the Jawamaʻa (Eastern Kordofan)
46. Mirghani Husain Zaki al-Din	— deputy *nazir* of the Bederiya (Dar Bederiya)
47. Abu al-Qasim ʻAli Dinar	— member of the traditional ruling

Table 3.5 continued

	family of the Fur (Northern Darfur)
48. Ibrahim Daw al-Bait	— *shartai* in Eastern Darfur (Eastern Darfur)
49. Al-Malik Rahmatallah Mahmud	— head of the native administration in El Fashir, and president of El Fashir court (Central Darfur)
50. Ibrahim Musa Madibbo	— *nazir* of the Rizaigat (Southern Darfur)
51. 'Abd al-Hamid Abu Bakr Ibrahim	— *'Umda* in Western Darfur (Western Darfur)
52. Abu 'Abd al-Rahman Muhammad Bahr al-Din	— deputy-*sultan* of Dar Masalit (Dar Masalit)

C Elected by Province Councils of the Southern Provinces

Equatoria Province

53. Andarea Gore	— a chief of the Bari
54. Benjamin Lwoki	— school headmaster
55. Korokongwa Hassan	— a chief of the Moru
56. Siricio Iro	— government official; began work as an accountant and ended as a sub-*ma'mur*
57. Yona Kaka	— junior government official

Upper Nile Province

58. Buth Diu	— government official; began work as a clerk, subsequently promoted to station officer and administrative assistant
59. Edward Odok Dedigo	— government official; began work as a clerk, subsequently promoted to station officer and administrative assistant
60. Muhammad 'Abdallah	— prominent merchant
61. Lual Deng Kaak	— a chief of the Dinka

Bahr al-Ghazal Province

62. 'Abdallah Adam	— army officer
63. Cyer Rihan	— a chief of the Dinka
64. Khamis Mursal	— junior government official
65. Stanislaus Paysama	— government official; began work as a clerk, subsequently promoted to station officer and administrative assistant

Table 3.5 continued

D	Nominated Members	
66.	'Abd al-Karim Muhammad	— senior official in the Education Department
67.	'Abdallah Khalil	— army officer, being the first Sudanese to reach the rank of *miralai*
68.	Ahmad al-Hashim Dafa'allah	— *shaikh* of the Ma'ahad, and president of Hoi branch court
69.	Fadl Bashir	— editor of *al-Amil* newspaper
70.	James Tembora	— government official
71.	Ibrahim Qasim Makhayir	— pharmacist
72.	Ibrahim Yusif al-Hindi	— religious notable; son of the founder of the Hindiyyah order
73.	Muhammad Ahmad al-Birair	— prominent merchant
74.	Muhammad Ahmad Mahjub	— served as a district judge, then became an advocate; from the leading family associated with the Shadhiliyyah order
75.	Muhammad Salih Shinqiti	—judge of the High Court

Note: For the translation of Arabic terms used in this table see the glossary on p. 356; also see the section on tribal leaders, pp. 52 to 54.

Source: Civil Secretary's Office, *Sudan Almanac 1950*, (Sudan Government, Khartoum, 1950), pp. 49–51; supplemented by information gathered in the writer's own research.

Table 3.6   Social Backgrounds of the Members of the First Parliament, 1954–8

House of Representatives (92 territorial constituencies; 5 seats for the graduates' constituency)	
1. 'Abdallah Bakr Mustafa	— originally an army officer, he retired from the army in 1928 and became *nazir* of the central Gedarif area; subsequently *nazir* of Dar Bakr (Umma, Gedarif South)
2. 'Abdallah Khalil	— (see no. 67 on Table 3.5) (Umma, Eastern Darfur)

Table 3.6 continued

3. 'Abdallah Muhammad al-Tom	— a *shaikh* of the Arakiyin; a substantial tenant farmer on the Gezira scheme (NUP, Madina)
4. 'Abd al-Hamid Musa Madibbo	— brother of the *nazir* of the Rizaigat; accountant for the Rizaigat administration (SRP, Nyala Baggara East)
5. 'Abd al-Nabi 'Abd al-Qadir	— government official (NUP, Renk and Malakal)
6. 'Abd al-Rahman Muhammad Ibrahim Dibaikir	— veterinarian; brother of the *nazir* of the Bani Hilba (Umma, Nyala Baggara West)
7. 'Abd al-Rahman 'Umar Abdallah	— an employee of the Dairat al-Mahdi (Umma, Dar Hamar North and East)
8. Abu Bakr Badawi Abbakar	— school headmaster (Independent, Dar Masalit North)
9. Abu Fatmah Bakash	— started work as a government agricultural officer, subsequently became president of Wagar court and *shaikh* of the Gash area (NUP, Hadendowa)
10. Ahmad al-Amir Mahmud	— army officer up to 1945, subsequently owner of a pump scheme; son of a prominent Mahdist leader (Umma, Sennar and Kawahla)
11. Ahmad Idris Abu al-Hasan	— started as an army officer, being later transferred as *ma'mur* to the civil administration; served as executive officer of the Shaigiya Council (NUP, Merowe)
12. Akec Khamis Rizgalla	— junior government official (NUP, Aweil West)
13. Alfred Burjuk Vludo	— government official (Independent, Western Bahr al-Ghazal)
14. 'Ali 'Abd al-Rahman	— a *shari'a* judge (NUP, Khartoum North)
15. Amin al-Sayyid	— doctor, and subsequently senior

Table 3.6 continued

	government official: assistant director of the Sudan Medical Service (NUP, Dongola)
16. Arbab Ahmad Shittah Ishaq	— *shartai* of Dar Tarbilla, and president of Kargulla court; son of the *maqdum* of the Fur (NUP, Zalingi South East)
17. Bannaga Muhammad al-Tom	— a substantial tenant on the Gezira scheme; *'umda* of al-Barsi (Umma, Wad al-Haddad)
18. Benjamino Long Jur	— chief of the Twij section of the Dinka; also a teacher and court president (Independent, Jur River North)
19. Benjamin Lwoki	— school headmaster (Southern Party, Yei)
20. Bullen Alier de Bior	— government official: *sub-ma'mur* (NUP, Bor)
21. Buth Diu	— (see no. 58 on Table 3.5) (Southern Political Association, Zeraf Valley)
22. Dak Dei	— began work as a clerk in government service, subsequently becoming administrative assistant and then executive officer; a member of the chief family of the Lau Nuer (Independent, Central Nuer East)
23. Edward Odhok Dedigo	— began work as a clerk in government service, subsequently becoming station officer and then administrative assistant (Southern Political Association, Shilluk)
24. Eriya Kuze	— school headmaster (Southern Party, Zande East)
25. Al-Fadil al-Bushra	— doctor; grandson of Muhammad Ahmad al-Mahdi (Umma, Dar Hamar South West)
26. Al-Fadil Mahmud 'Abd al-Karim	— owner of substantial agricultural schemes; grandson of

Table 3.6 continued

	Muhammad Ahmad al-Mahdi (Umma, Messiriya Humr)
27. Fadlallah 'Ali al-Tom	— tribal leader; son of Sir 'Ali al-Tom, *nazir* of the Kababish (NUP, Kababish)
28. Ferdinando Adyang	— schoolteacher (Liberal, Eastern Equatoria)
29. Qasm al-Sid 'Abdallah al-Nur	— (see no. 23 on Table 3.5) (Umma, Hosh)
30. Hammad Abu Sadur Shallukah Gharr	— school headmaster; brother of the *makk* of Jebel For (NUP, Northern Jebels East)
31. Hammad Muhammad Dafa'allah	— school headmaster; also *'umda* of the Taggat, and son of the *nazir* of the Zurug section of the Messiriya (Umma, Messiriya Zurug)
32. Hammad Tawfiq	— senior government official: inspector of accounts in the Department of Agriculture; had formerly managed his father's pump scheme in al-Hasaheissa (NUP, Messellemiya)
33. Hashim Muhammad Sa'ad	— prominent merchant (NUP, Port Sudan)
34. Hasan 'Abd al-Qadir al-Haj Ahmad	— merchant and journalist; manager of El Obeid Printing Press (NUP, El Obeid)
35. Hasan 'Awadallah Mustafa	— junior government official: book-keeper (NUP, Omdurman West)
36. Hasan Jibril Suliman	— magistrate, and *'umda* of Geneina town (Independent, Dar Masalit South)
37. Hasan Muhammad Zaki	— government official: began work as a clerk, subsequently became an accountant then an auditor (NUP, Southern Funj)
38. Hasan al-Tahir Zarruq	— schoolteacher, dismissed for political activities (Anti-Imperialist Front, Graduates' Constituency)

Table 3.6 continued

39. Ibrahim al-Mahalawi	— head accountant for Sudan Railways, dismissed for political activities; his family was prominent in the administration of Eastern Sudan under Turko–Egyptian rule (NUP, Atbara)
40. Ibrahim al-Hasan Abu al-Ma'ali	— government official: administrator in posts and telegraphs (NUP, Khartoum Rural South)
41. Ibrahim Idris Habbani	— assistant to the *nazir* of the Hassaniya; member of the leading family of the Hassaniya; owner of agricultural schemes and commercial enterprises (Umma, Dueim North-East)
42. Ibrahim al-Mufti	— advocate (NUP, Graduates' Constituency)
43. Ibrahim al-Tayyib Badr	— substantial tenant on the Gezira scheme (NUP, Kamlin)
44. Idris al-Zaibaq Jaili	— '*umda* of Abbasiya; nephew of the *makk* of Tegali (NUP, Tegali North)
45. Imam Dufa'allah	— son of the *nazir* of the Halawin; substantial tenant on the Gezira scheme (Umma, Halawin)
46. Isma'il al-Azhari	— government official in the Department of Education up to 1946, when he resigned to devote himself full-time to political activities; grandson of a prominent religious notable who became *mufti* of Sudan (NUP, Omdurman North)
47. John Majok Mayol	— originally a schoolmaster, subsequently became a farmer and small-scale merchant (Independent, Rumbek)
48. Joshua Malwal	— junior government official: court clerk and interpreter (Independent, Western Nuer Jebel)

Table 3.6 continued

49. Kamal al-Din 'Abdallahi al-Fadil	— son of 'Abdallahi al-Fadil al-Mahdi (see no. 4 on Table 3.5); owner of pump schemes and commercial enterprises (Umma, Dueim South East)
50. Kampouchto Koma	— *makk* of Haiban (Independent, Central Nuer)
51. Khidir Hamad	— senior government official in the Finance Department; resigned from government service in 1946 to join the Arab League, in which he became an assistant director in the Finance Section; resigned from Arab League in 1951 to engage in commerce in Sudan (NUP, Graduates' Constituency)
52. Kosmos Rababu Babunguma	— schoolteacher (Southern Party, Zande West)
53. Liwo Tombe Lako	— junior government official: clerk (Southern Party)
54. Majdhub Abu 'Ali Musa	— landowner, with agricultural schemes in Tokar (NUP, Tokar)
55. Majdhub Ibrahim Farah	— brother of the paramount *nazir* of the Ja'aliyin; prominent merchant, also owning agricultural schemes and a contracting business; *'umda* of Metemma and president of the Metemma court (NUP, Shendi)
56. Mahmud al-Tayyib Salih	— vice-president of Dar Galla administration; brother of the *shartai* of Dar Galla (Umma, Kutum East)
57. Al-Malik Rahmatallah Mahmud	— (see no. 49 on Table 3.5) (Umma, Central Darfur)
58. Al-Mardi Muhammad Rahmah	— merchant and petty industrialist, owning a date-processing factory and managing some agricultural schemes (NUP, Berber)
59. Mashawir Juma'a Sahal	— government official, with strong commercial interests; son of

Table 3.6 continued

	the *nazir* of the Western Maganin tribe (NUP, Dar Hamid West)
60. Michael Canti de Bilkwie	— government official: court clerk; brother of the chief of the Kwil Dinka (Southern Party, Western Nuer Ghazal)
61. Mirghani Hamzah	— senior government official and professional: retired in 1951 as assistant director in the Public Works Department and established a private architectural contracting company; from the prominent Khanadga grouping of the Danagla (NUP, Omdurman South)
62. Mirghani Husain Zaki al-Din	— deputy-*nazir* of the Bedeiriya (Umma, Dar Bedeiriya)
63. Muhammad 'Abd al-Bagi al-Mikashfi	— prominent merchant; son of a religious leader (Umma, Managil)
64. Muhammad Ahmad Abu Sin	— (see no. 19 on Table 3.5) (SRP, Rufa'a)
65. Muhammad Ahmad Mahjub	— (see no. 74 on Table 3.5) (Independent, Graduates' Constituency)
66. Muhammad Jubarah al-'Awad	— school headmaster; resigned from this in 1947 in order to start an agricultural enterprise (NUP, Kassala Town)
67. Muhammad Hamad Abu Sin	— *nazir* of the Kassala Shukriya; president of Kassala Province Shukriya court (NUP, Gedaref North)
68. Muhammad Harun Taimah	— school headmaster (NUP, Jawama'a West)
69. Muhammad Karrar Kujur	— (see no. 35 on Table 3.5) (NUP, Amarar and Bisharin)
70. Muhammad Mahmud Muhammad	— began work as an official of the Sudan Plantations Syndicate; later became a merchant, with significant agricultural interests (NUP, Kassala Rural)

Table 3.6 continued

71. Muhammad Nujumi Ahmad	— a leading merchant in the Jur River area, with a transport and trading business (Independent, Jur River South)
72. Muhammad Nur al-Din	— bank manager; resigned from this in 1947 to devote himself full-time to politics (NUP, Halfa)
73. Muhammad al-Siddiq Muhammad Talhah	— tribal leader (NUP, Khartoum Rural East)
74. Muhi al-Din at-Haj Muhammad	— substantial farmer; member of a family associated with religious leadership in the Tegale area (NUP, Tegale South)
75. Mubarak Zarruq	— advocate; virtually a full-time politician from 1950 (NUP, Graduates' Constituency)
76. Muddathir 'Ali al-Bushi	— originally a *shari'a qadi*, he became *imam* of a mosque in Wad Medani; from a family associated with religious leadership (NUP, Wad Medani)
77. Mustafa Hasan Muhammad	— merchant, with trading interests covering the Western Sudan; *imam* of a mosque in Nyala (Umma, Nyala Maqdumate)
78. Nasrallah Sarmin Silyah	— originally a non-commissioned officer in the Sudan Defence Force, he subsequently became a junior government official (NUP, Northern Jebel West)
79. 'Umar Hamzah Muhammad Ahmad	— government official: Civil Secretary's office (NUP, Khartoum Rural North)
80. 'Uthman Ishaq Adam	— merchant, with a trading concern in Kutum (Umma, Kutum Centre)
81. Phileman Majok	— originally a schoolmaster, he subsequently became a police officer; resigned from police in 1951 and began a large-scale

Table 3.6 continued

	scheme for groundnut cultivation in Yirol (Southern Party, Yirol)
82. Rahmatallah Mahmud	— head of the native administration in El Fasher; president of the Fasher main native court (Umma, Central Darfur)
83. Santino Deng Teng	— government official: agricultural officer (Independent, Aweil East)
84. Al-Shadhli al-Shaikh Birair	— a *shaikh* of the Sammaniyyah order, with some agricultural interests (NUP, Jawama'a East)
85. Al-Sharif al-Sayyid al-Faki	— deputy-*nazir* in the Kosti area; vice-president of the Selim and Ahamda panel (Umma, Kosti South)
86. Siddiq 'Abd al-Rahman al-Mahdi	— general manager of the Dairat al-Mahdi; son of 'Abd al-Rahman al-Mahdi (Umma, Kosti North)
87. Simon Makwac Mayen	— schoolteacher (NUP, Pibor and Eastern Nuer)
88. Simplicio Ataxa	— junior government official: Posts and Telegraphs Department (Southern Party, Torit)
89. Taifur Muhammad Sharif	— '*umda* of Aliab and subsequently *shaikh* of the Aliab branch; member of the Nile Pumps Control Board (NUP, Ed Damer)
90. Al-Tigani Ibrahim Ayif	— merchant, with agricultural interests; brother of the '*umda* of the Awlad Agoi in Dar Hamid (NUP, Dar Hamid)
91. Timon Biro Mbaringwa	— originally a non-commissioned officer in the Sudan Defence Force, he subsequently became a small-scale merchant and a minor tribal chief of the Moru Miza (Southern Party, Moru)
92. Al-Wasilah al-Shaikh al-Samani	— a substantial farmer; grandson

Table 3.6 continued

	of *shaikh* Birair, a noted religious leader in the Dueim area (NUP, Dueim West)
93. Ya'qub Hamid Babikir	— prominent merchant, with shops in Suki and Khartoum; also owner of a contracting business (Umma, Northern Funj)
94. Ya'qub Rahal Ando Kadugli	— junior government official (NUP, Kadugli)
95. Yahia al-Fadli	— government official; resigned from government service in 1940 to devote himself full-time to political activities (NUP, Khartoum South)
96. Yusif 'Abd al-Hamid Ibrahim	— originally a non-commissioned officer in the Sudan Defence Force, he subsequently became a junior government official; son of 'Abd al-Hamid Ibrahim Qarad, tribal leader of the 'Abbasia section of the Kura (NUP, Zalingi North-West)
97. Yusif al-Ajab	— (see no. 26 on Table 3.5) (SRP, Funj Nazirates)

Senate (50 seats: 30 filled by election, 20 nominated; election by provincial electoral colleges, with voting restricted to those with certain requisite educational qualifications)

1. 'Abbas al-'Ubaid al-Shahinabi	— originally a schoolteacher, he resigned from this in 1946 and became a substantial farmer; from a family associated with religious leadership (NUP, Khartoum)
2. 'Abdallah Mirghani	— originally a senior government official: head accountant to the Sudan Government; retired from government service in 1950 and became a prominent businessman, owning the Watania Printing Press (Independent, nominated)

Table 3.6 continued

3. 'Abd al-Majid Ahmad Hitailah	— originally a government official: tax collector; resigned from government service in 1935 and became a prominent merchant, owning some flour mills and a trading concern covering southern Kordofan (NUP, Kordofan)
4. 'Abd al-Rahman 'Abdun	— senior government official: under-secretary of the Irrigation Department (Umma, nominated)
5. 'Abd al-Salaam al-Khalifah	— senior government official: had been a district commissioner in Kordofan, subsequently became under-secretary of the Department of the Interior; son of the Khalifa 'Abdallahi (Umma, nominated)
6. Ahmad Abu al-Qasim	— substantial merchant in northern Darfur (Umma, Darfur)
7. Ahmad Jaili	— senior government official: commandant of police in Darfur province; son of the *'umda* of Rufa'a (NUP, nominated)
8. Ahmad Muhammad Salih	— senior government official: deputy-director of the Education Department; a well-known poet (Independent, nominated)
9. Ahmad Said Haj Ahmad	— prominent merchant, with substantial agricultural interests in the Dueim area (NUP, Blue Nile)
10. Ahmad Yusif Alqam	— (see no. 22 on Table 3.5) (NUP, Blue Nile)
11. 'Ali Mahmud 'Ubaid	— merchant in the Shendi area; secretary of the local merchants committee (NUP, Northern)
12. 'Awad al-Shaikh 'Abd al-Karim	— prominent merchant, with a trading network covering most of Sudan and extending into

Table 3.6 continued

	Egypt; also a petty industrialist: owner of a lemonade factory (NUP, Northern)
13. Babu 'Uthman Nimr	— (see no. 1 in Table 3.4) (Umma, Kordofan)
14. Bashir 'Abd al-Rahim Hamid	— senior government official: divisional engineer for the Irrigation Department (NUP, Blue Nile)
15. Fadl Babikir	— doctor, with private practices in Khartoum and Omdurman (NUP, nominated)
16. Gordon Ayom	— government official: managing editor of the Department of Education's publications bureau (Southern Party, Upper Nile)
17. Hasan 'Abd al-Jalil Dafa'allah	— merchant; chairman of Hasaheisa rural council (NUP, Blue Nile)
18. Hasan Mahjub Muhammad	— merchant (NUP, Northern)
19. Hasan Taj al-Din	— from a family associated with tribal leadership; assistant *qadi* of the Geneina native court; son of a *sultan*, Taj al-Din Isma'il (Independent, Darfur)
20. Ibrahim Yusif Badri	— senior government official: served as a district commissioner among the Dinka, then became director of the Gezira Board (Socialist Republican Party, nominated)
21. Ibrahim Faki Ibrahim	— prominent merchant, with a cotton broking business; member of the Tokar native court (NUP, Kassala)
22. James Gatluak Kuny	— schoolteacher (NUP, Upper Nile)
23. Khalafallah Khalid	— senior government official: originally an army officer, he became an administrator in local government; member of a family associated with tribal

Table 3.6 continued

	leadership; his father, Al-Haj Khalid al-'Umarabi, was *amir* of the 'Umarab during the Mahdia (NUP, nominated)
24. Khalifah Muhammad Adam	— an *'umda* of the Jawama'a up to 1953, he resigned from this position in that year and became president of the Jawama'a native court (NUP, nominated)
25. Mathayo Shambe Leena	— schoolteacher (Independent, Bahr al-Ghazal)
26. Makki Shaibun	— merchant, with trading operations in Kadugli and Dilling (NUP, Kordofan)
27. Mica Bol Ciengan	— junior government official: medical assistant (NUP, Bahr al-Ghazal)
28. Muhammad 'Abdallah al-'Umarabi	— schoolteacher (NUP, Khartoum
29. Muhammad 'Abd al-Rahman Nuqdallah	— (see no. 7 on Table 3.5) (Umma, Blue)
30. Muhammad Ahmad 'Awad	— originally a captain in the Sudan Defence Force, he resigned from the army in 1931 and started some substantial agricultural schemes in the Tokar area (NUP, Kassala)
31. Muhammad 'Ali Abu Sinn	— prominent merchant and transport agent in El Fashir (NUP, Darfur)
32. Muhammad Bakhit 'Ali Habbah	— a leading transport contractor in El Obeid (NUP, Kordofan)
33. Muhammad al-Haj al-Khidir Ali Kamair	— prominent merchant in Khartoum (NUP, nominated)
34. Muhammad Ibrahim Farah	— (see no. 15 on Table 3.5) (NUP nominated)
35. Muhammad Salih Siwar al-Dahab	— from a family associated with religious leadership in the Dongola area; a *shari'ah qadi*, he was appointed judge of the *shari'ah* high court in 1952 (NUP, nominated)
36. Muhammad al-Zaki Ahmad	— government official: chief clerk of the El Fashir main court (NUP, Darfur)

Table 3.6 continued

37. Nyodo Okeich	— originally a junior government official, in 1937 he resigned from this and became a small-scale farmer (NUP, Upper Nile)
38. 'Umar Abu Amnah	— prominent contractor in Kassala province; son of the *'umda* of Gebeit (NUP, Kassala) '
39. 'Uthman Abu al-Ila	— prominent merchant: a partner in the Aboulela Trading Company, one of the main import–export companies in Sudan (NUP, nominated)
40. Paulo Logali Wani	— junior government official: book-keeper (Southern Party, Equatoria)
41. Peter Muarwel Agolder	— a chief of a section of the Dinka, his father held the Amonhom chiefship among the Dinka; served for a time as manager of the Yirol Cooperative Society (Independent, nominated)
42. Redento Ondzi Koma	— junior government official: storekeeper to the Public Works Department in Juba (NUP, Equatoria)
43. Al-Shadhli al-Shaikh al-Rayah	— prominent merchant in Bara (NUP, Kordofan)
44. Siricio Iro Wani	— (see no. 56 on Table 3.5) (Independent, nominated)
45. Stanislaus Abdullahi Peysama	— (see no. 65 on Table 3.5) (Southern Party, Bahr al-Ghazal)
46. Tadros 'Abd al-Masih	— prominent merchant in Omdurman; head of the Coptic community in Omdurman (NUP, nominated)
47. William Garang	— government official: agricultural officer (Independent, nominated)
48. Yoseppa Swokiri Yokwe	— a chief of the Bari; member of Juba district court (Southern Party, nominated)

Table 3.6 continued

| 49. Yusif Idris Habbani | — (see no. 31 on Table 3.5) (Umma, nominated) |
| 50. Ziadah 'Uthman Arbab | — advocate, with a legal practice in Wad Medani (Umma, nominated) |

Note 1: For the translation of Arabic terms used in this table see the glossary on p. 356; also see the section on tribal leaders, pp. 52 to 54.

Note 2: The occupations of Members of Parliament, given in this table, are those which MPs had before entering parliament; government officials winning election had to resign their government posts before taking up their seats. No such rule existed in the case of the Legislative Assembly. The occupations given are those of the individual's primary employment. No mention is made of 'sideline occupations', e.g. when a government official had accumulated funds and, while still retaining his government position, had invested in an agricultural or business scheme.

Note 3: The parties to which individual members are listed as being affiliated are those which they supported at the time of election. A number of MPs changed their party affiliations after the election. The latter mainly came from southern Sudan, abandoning the 'Independent' label and joining either the Southern Party or the National Unionist Party.

Source: Some of the information in this table is taken from Government of Sudan, *Directory of the Republic of Sudan, 1957–8* (Diplomatic Press and Publishing, London, 1958), pp. 145–62; this information, however, has been supplemented by material gathered personally by the writer.

Table 3.7   Numbers of Members of the First Parliament Associated with Tribal or Religious Leadership, or Who Worked as Merchants or Senior Government Officials

House of Representatives	Northern constituencies	Southern constituencies
Members from the backgrounds mentioned in the title	65	9
Members from other backgrounds	11	12

Table 3.7 continued

Senate		
Members from the backgrounds mentioned in the title	35	5
Members from other backgrounds	4	6

Note 1: The five members elected in the graduates' constituency are included under 'Northern constituencies'; all those elected in this constituency came from the northern Sudan. Nominated senators are included under 'Northern constituencies' or 'Southern constituencies' according to whether they were northern Sudanese or southern Sudanese.

Note 2: This table should only be regarded as giving a rough impression of the overall pattern, not a precise one. The dividing lines between senior government officials and junior government officials, between substantive merchants and petty shopkeepers, and between those who figure prominently in tribal or religious leadership as opposed to those with only a loose family connection with such leadership, are inevitably indistinct. To obtain a full and accurate picture of the social composition of the first parliament, it is necessary to look in detail at the backgrounds of individual members, as presented in Table 3.6.

III SOCIAL STRUCTURE: THE SIZE AND CHARACTER OF SOCIO-ECONOMIC GROUPINGS

As the Condominium drew to a close and the independence era began, Sudan's social structure was constituted by a complex network of interlinked social and economic divisions. Here we will examine the economically-based divisions in that social structure, classifying different elements of the Sudanese population according to the role they played in the country's overall economy, and indicating some of the characteristics of these various roles (relationship to other economic strata, potential for members to improve their economic positions, direction and processes of surplus extraction etc.).[31] The arena of political action and conflict was inevitably shaped by the nature of these socio-economic formations.

(a) Peasants

This social category comprises all those agricultural producers who could use land without the payment of rent (whether or not they

formally owned the land they were using[32]) and who were employin
traditional, rather than mechanised, methods of production. Peasan
agriculture occurred on the *salukah* land, flood-watered land an
some of the *sagiah* land, beside the main Nile, Blue Nile and Whit
Nile in northern Sudan, on the ironstone plateau and the hill masse
of southern Sudan, on the hilly formations of Darfur and Kordofan
and in some of the southern parts of Kordofan, Kassala and Blue Nil
provinces where rainfall was sufficient for settled agriculture.

The 1955/56 population census estimated that 2 371 700 peopl
were 'gainfully employed' as farmers.[33] Deducting those who wer
involved in forms of agricultural production other than that covere
in this subsection (e.g. tenant farmers), the number of gainfull
employed peasants comes to about 2 255 700. This constituted abou
59.4 per cent of the gainfully employed population. It may be assume
that peasants and their families constituted a similar percentage of th
total population, which the census estimated at 10 263 000.

Significant differences in economic position existed among th
Sudanese peasantry. The most crucial aspect of these difference
concerned the relationship between a peasant's labour and his farm
ing activity. Peasants may be divided into 'richer', 'middle' an
'poorer' according to the following labour-based criteria:

  (i)   richer peasants: those who employed non-family labour on thei
        farms. (Most such peasants farmed along the main, Blue o
        White Niles in northern Sudan);
 (ii)   middle peasants: those who used only their own and thei
        family's labour on their farms, and who did not work outside o
        their farms;
(iii)   poorer peasants: those unable to subsist on their own farms, an
        needing to work for others[34] (whether richer peasants in th
        neighbourhood or agricultural or industrial schemes elsewhere
        to supplement their income. Such peasants constituted a larg
        proportion of the peasant population in Darfur, southern Kor
        dofan, and parts of the South.[35]

No precise estimate can be made of how many of Sudan'
2 255 700 peasants fell within each of these groupings. The likelihoo
is that the majority were 'poorer peasants'. The existence of
substantial body of poorer peasants – impelled to seek temporar
labour on the agricultural schemes at harvest-time, but able t

support themselves elsewhere for the rest of the year – was a necessity for the Sudanese economy under the Condominium. The poorer peasantry constituted a reserve of cheap labour for the harvesting of cotton, the main export crop around which the economy was built. The labour was 'cheap' both because poorer peasants would not, and did not, demand high wages, and because such labour did not impose a heavy social cost upon the areas where cotton was produced. Temporary labourers, especially those coming from a poor peasant background, would not require sophisticated housing, educational facilities for children, or elaborate medical services.

At the time of the 1956 cotton harvest there were some 200 000 temporary labourers on the Gezira scheme, together with an approximately equal number on agricultural schemes in other parts of the country. Most of these labourers (perhaps 75 per cent) were Sudanese peasants and nomads – a majority of them coming from western Sudan. The remaining approx. 25 per cent were migrants from Chad or Nigeria (some of them making a short stop on their pilgrimage to Mecca).[36] This gives some indication both of the size of the poorer peasant grouping in Sudan's political economy and of the contribution which this grouping was making to maintaining a 'competitive price' for the supply of Sudanese cotton to Lancashire's cotton mills.

The division between 'richer' and 'poorer' peasants should not be taken as a division between rich and poor. The incomes of richer peasants were mostly insufficient for them to accumulate funds and invest in tractors or other mechanised agricultural implements. Those who did accumulate funds tended to enter the commercial field – in part because they could begin trading without requiring substantial resources, and in part because a good return could be earned in the short term as well as the long term. Funds accumulated in trade, with the individual now operating in effect as a merchant, might then find their way back to agriculture. Merchants would buy tractors, pumps and other mechanised implements both for use on such land as they owned themselves and for loan to peasants.

The discussion in Chapter 3 of the means whereby certain social elements could accumulate funds – in effect drawing off a significant part of the small surplus which peasant agriculture produced – is, of course, relevant to the overall economic position of the peasantry. The dues paid to religious and tribal leaders, the high returns which merchants gained from peasants for *shail* arrangements, and the rates levied for water supplied by *sagiahs* or pumps to the peasants' fields,

all reduced the surplus available to peasants. The returns on *shail*
were sometimes equivalent to a 200 per cent rate of interest, and
payments for water supplies often took up three-tenths of a peasant'
gains through the sale of his produce. While some *sagiahs* and pump:
were owned collectively by a group of peasants, it was more common
for merchants and local notables (tribal or religious) to own this vita
resource. It is clear, moreover, that the relationship between mer
chants and peasants was far from equal and, therefore, that mer
chants had little difficulty in ensuring a favourable rate of exchange
(to themselves) between the goods they supplied to, and the good:
they purchased from, the peasants.

(b) Nomads

The 1955/56 census estimated that 1 405 951 people were living in
'rural nomadic areas', constituting 13.70 per cent of the total popu
lation.[37] This probably understates the actual nomadic population: the
census enumeration was carried out at a time of year when many
nomads were temporarily settled, engaged in cultivation outside o
the customary nomadic areas.[38] Evidence of the size and significance
of the nomadic portion of the population is found elsewhere in the
census. The numbers of nomadic animal owners and of 'shepherds'[39]
are given as 95 774 and 710 815 respectively.[40] While not all of the
'shepherds' would have been nomadic, it seems likely that a large
proportion were.[41] Nomadic animal owners and 'shepherds' com
bined comprised 21.23 per cent of the gainfully employed popu
lation.[42] There were, moreover, others who pursued nomadic activi
ties as a 'subsidiary occupation', subsidiary, that is to say, to the
occupation from which they drew their main means of livelihood
22 907 people were enumerated as having a subsidiary occupation
as nomadic animal owners, and 244 599 as subsidiary-occupation
shepherds.[43]

The economic significance of the nomadic portion of the popula
tion is evident from statistics on livestock production. Livestock
production in 1955/56 was valued at £S32 280 000, constituting 11.4
per cent of gross national product.[44] The livestock sector in 1956 was
estimated to comprise some 6.9 million cattle, 6.9 million sheep, 5.7
million goats and 2 million camels.[45] The major part of livestock
production emerged from the nomadic part of the population.

The areas in which nomadic life predominated covered a substan
tial part of the country's land surface: the desert and semi-desert

regions of the Butana and Red Sea hills, the Nubian desert to the east of the Nile in Northern province, the Gezira region south of the irrigated schemes, central and northern Kordofan, the Bayuda desert, the plains of Darfur, and the south-eastern corner and central plains (subject to flooding from the White Nile and its tributaries) of southern Sudan.

Differences in economic well-being among the nomads were reflected, as with the peasants, in the varying ways in which labour was used. Some nomads needed to employ labour ('shepherds') to look after their large herds; others used only their own labour and that of their families; others again had to sell their labour so as to acquire the means for survival. Those who sold their labour would do so either by performing services for other nomads (possibly as a full-time 'shepherd') or by obtaining temporary employment on one of the agricultural schemes. Government taxation (herd tax),[46] together with the increasing availability of goods which the nomads wished to purchase, ensured that a considerable number of nomads every year sought temporary employment at harvest-time on the Gezira, Gash and Tokar schemes.

The accumulation of wealth among nomads was closely linked to political power: wealth accrued mainly to tribal leaders, with such resources often coming from activities outside of the nomadic sphere (rents from settled farmers for the use of gum gardens, involvement in irrigated agricultural schemes established in the tribal domain, etc.).The extent to which a nomad could increase his wealth as a nomad was limited: large herds ultimately became unwieldy, posing a threat of exhaustion to the grazing lands.[47] The more successful nomads would tend to buy a house in a village or town and (sooner or later) become settled.

(c) Tenant farmers

The role of tenant farmers in the Sudanese economy at the time of independence was closely linked to the role of irrigated agriculture: more than 95 per cent of all irrigated land in the country was organised in tenant schemes; similarly, more than 95 per cent of all tenant farmers were working irrigated land. In 1955 some 2 039 472 feddans were being used for irrigated agriculture. Table 3.8 provides information on the proportions of this irrigated land situated in each province, the number of tenants farming the land, and the division between gravity and pump irrigation.

Table 3.8 Numbers of Tenant Farmers on Irrigated Land, 1955

Province	Name (and/or type of scheme)	Number of schemes (pump irrigated schemes only)	Area covered (feddans)	Number of tenants*
Blue Nile	Gezira (gravity)	1	c. 1 000 000**	c. 35 000**
	Pump schemes	581	530 341	c. 23 000
Northern	Pump schemes	430	148 015	c. 33 000
Kassala	Gash (gravity)	1	68 600	c. 13 700
	Tokar (gravity)	1	40 000	c. 8 000
	Pump schemes	4	750	c. 40
Upper Nile	Pump schemes	34	39 587	c. 1 000
Khartoum	Pump schemes	117	22 179	c. 1 700
Total		1 169	2 039 472	c. 115 440

* The numbers given here must only be regarded as approximate. The 1955/56 *First Population Census* provides no information on the numbers of tenant farmers – they are subsumed under the broad category 'Farmers, Hunters and Fishermen'. The numbers given here have been worked out by the writer on the basis of information presented in the 1963 *Report on the Census of Pump Schemes*. The census lists 'cotton cultivators' as numbering 150 143, but makes no distinction between peasants and tenants.

** In 1955/56 the area covered by the Gezira scheme was rapidly expanding, with tenants settling on the new Managil extension. The figures given here for the area covered and the number of tenants, therefore, are necessarily generalised approximations.

Source: Information on pump schemes has been compiled on the basis of Tables 3.2 and 4.6 in Republic of Sudan, *A Report on the Census of Pump Schemes, June–August 1963* (Department of Statistics, Khartoum, 1967), pp. 17(a) and 39. Information on gravity schemes is taken from K. M. Barbour, *The Republic of the Sudan* (University of London Press, 1961), pp. 202 and 222.

The table reveals that there were about 115 440 tenant farmers in Sudan in 1955 (c. 3 per cent of the total labour force); that rather more than half of these tenant farmers (farming more than three-quarters of the country's irrigated land) were in Blue Nile province; that the Gezira scheme accounted for almost half of all the irrigated land in the country (but significantly less than half of all tenant farmers); and that tenant farmers were divided almost equally between those on gravity irrigation schemes and those on pump schemes. The significance of Blue Nile province in irrigated agriculture and tenant farming is perhaps yet greater than the figures suggest: agricultural production in the Gezira scheme was more coherently and effectively organised than elsewhere, with the effect that this area enjoyed greater agricultural productivity. Moreover, the pump schemes in Upper Nile province were all situated in the

Renk area, which is flanked on the east by Blue Nile province; effectively they constituted an extension of the Blue Nile province irrigated area. There are obvious geographic and climatic reasons why irrigated agriculture was restricted to the riverain areas of north-central Sudan.

The role of irrigated agriculture – and hence tenant farming – in the Sudanese economy was crucial. The figures on agricultural production given in government statistics do not differentiate between the produce of irrigated agriculture and that of rain-fed agriculture. Figures on cotton production and exports, however, reveal the significance to the Sudanese economy of irrigated agriculture, as cotton was the principal crop grown on irrigated land and little cotton was grown elsewhere.[48] In 1955 the direct proceeds of cotton production accounted for about 12 per cent of gross domestic product,[49] while cotton exports constituted 63 per cent of total Sudanese exports.[50]

As with peasants and nomads, economic differences among tenant farmers can best be described in terms of the use of labour. Three broad categories existed:

(i) Tenants who undertook little or no agricultural work themselves, and whose families did not participate in agricultural work. All, or almost all, the agricultural work on the tenancy would be done by hired labour, leaving the tenant purely as a manager of agricultural labour.[51]

Such tenants would usually farm over 30 feddans of land and might well have more than one tenancy.[52] They would usually pursue some sideline economic activities outside the sphere of agricultural production: possibly involving themselves in local commerce, hiring out agricultural machinery to other tenants, offering *shail* loans,[53] or owning transport vehicles for taking local produce (or people) to the nearest market towns. A tenant accumulating funds would, in any case, be most likely to invest these funds outside of his tenancy (where there was more opportunity for substantial gain) and would eventually emerge as a merchant.

It has been estimated that in the mid-1960s about 1.7 per cent of tenants on the Gezira Scheme fell into this category.[54] The figure for the mid-1950s would probably have been roughly equivalent. No information is available on the number of tenants elsewhere in this category, but there are unlikely to have been many. Although tenancies on the Blue Nile province and

Upper Nile province pump schemes tended to be reasonably substantial (8.7 and 7.9 feddans respectively on average,[55] as against 26 feddans for the Gezira scheme tenancies), those in the Northern province, Kassala province and Khartoum province pump schemes were much smaller (2.2, 4.4, and 5.0 feddans respectively on average[56]).

(ii) Tenants who spent most of their working hours in farming their tenancies, using also the labour of members of their families. They might in addition employ some hired labour, especially at harvest-time. The area of land farmed would usually be between 11 feddans and 30 feddans. Some of the tenants in this category would, to a limited extent, have been able to engage in some sideline economic activities.

It has been estimated that in the mid-1960s 41 per cent of all Gezira tenants fell into this category.[57] The percentage would probably have been the same in the mid-1950s.

(iii) Tenants who relied almost entirely on their own and their family's labour to farm their tenancies. One or two labourers might occasionally be hired when the burdens of harvesting were too great for the family. Tenants in this category would usually be farming 10 feddans or less. The poorer ones (such as those in the Northern province, where many tenancies covered only one or two feddans) might sell their own labour (either to richer tenants or peasants in the area, or through temporary employment in the towns) for part of the year.

In the mid-1960s (and probably also the mid-1950s) some 57.3 per cent of all Gezira tenants fell into this category. While there is no information on the relevant percentage for schemes elsewhere, it would almost certainly have been higher – especially in Northern province.

Tenant farmers occupied a somewhat paradoxical position in Sudan's socio-economic structure. While enjoying (especially those with tenancies on the Gezira scheme) a higher standard of living than most peasants, they lacked the peasants' apparent freedom of productive activity.[58] Whereas peasants had the opportunity to make their own choices regarding what and how much to produce, tenant farmers had to operate within a tight framework of rules and regulations on production. They were told what to grow, when to plant and when to harvest, and were supervised continually so as to ensure that they were performing their work satisfactorily. If they failed to fulfil their obligations to the scheme management they could be deprived of their land. A tenant farmer in some ways, therefore, played a role similar to that of a worker in industry: supplying his labour for work whose nature and extent were determined by others.[59]

Given the aspects of the tenant farmers' economic role mentioned above, it is scarcely surprising that Sudanese tenant farmers organised themselves socially and politically in a very different manner than did Sudanese peasants. They developed union organisations and threatened strike action when scheme managements proved resistant to their demands. The realities of the tenant farmers' position was that the share of the proceeds of production which they received was affected by the amount of pressure which they could or would exert on the scheme managements – as was reflected in the gradual adaptations made over the years in the Gezira scheme's procedures of division.[60] Tenant farmers generally felt squeezed between the share taken by scheme managements (and/or the government) and the wages they had to pay for hired labour. An estimate of the gains made from a 20-feddan Gezira scheme tenancy in 1951 (the year in which cotton prices reached their highest level ever) suggest that the total gains came to £E2065 and that this sum benefited the government, the tenant and hired labour according to the following division:

	£E
government[61]	1211
tenants	751
labourers	103[62]

In an average year (in the 1940s to 1950s) the overall gains from a 20-feddan Gezira scheme tenancy would only have come to about one-quarter of the gains made in 1951.

(d) Rural labourers

The majority of rural labourers were employed seasonally only. At the time of independence there were some 300 000 seasonal rural labourers; rather more than one-half of these were employed on the Gezira scheme, mainly at harvest-time.[63] Some 20–30 per cent of the 300 000, however, came from outside Sudan (mainly from Chad and Nigeria) and did not form a permanent part of the Sudanese population. Most of the Sudanese seasonal rural labourers were peasants or nomads for the remainder of the year. Besides the seasonal labour employed in irrigated agriculture, some was employed in mechanised dry farming.

The gains which could be made from seasonal rural labour were not substantial. The explanation for the large numbers who took on this employment, therefore, is to be found in the acute needs of the individuals concerned – especially with regard to paying taxes to the government in cash, while their traditional peasant or pastoral life had largely been of a subsistence nature – not in any expectation that they could accumulate funds through such employment. A seasonal labourer on the Gezira scheme could expect to earn about 30 piastres a day, of which two-thirds would be paid in cash and the remaining third paid in subsistence goods and facilities (sorghum, dried fish and accommodation in a grass hut). In a ten-week picking season, therefore, a labourer would earn about £E18. Out of his earnings he would have to cover part of his living expenses while on the Gezira, together with the costs of his return journey to his home village (the outward journey would usually be paid for by those who recruited him). He would be unlikely to return to his home village with more than £E8 or £E9. The gains made on pump and gravity schemes elsewhere in the country would probably have been less than this.

Seasonal labourers contributed the major part of the work needed to grow and harvest cotton, but gained the smallest part of the rewards. In a study of agricultural work on thirteen Gezira villages conducted in 1954, Yusif Abd al-Majid showed that of the 3796 working hours required annually to grow and harvest cotton on a 10-feddan holding, the labourers worked on average 3083 hours and the tenant 713 hours.[64] As indicated on p. 89 above, the tenant nevertheless received a much greater reward.

The numbers of permanent (i.e. not seasonal) rural labourers enumerated in the 1955/56 population census came to 49 282.[65] These too were employed mainly in irrigated agriculture or mechanised dry farming.

(e) Urban workers

This category covers all manual workers in the towns, whether working in manufacturing or in services. Self-employed artisans are included. The total urban population in 1955/56, as given in the population census of that year, was 853 873 (out of a total population of 10 263 000).[66] Table 3.9 presents information given in the census regarding the numbers of urban workers in Sudan.

Table 3.9   Urban Workers in Sudan, 1955/56

Job classification	Numbers
Craftsmen and mechanics	
Metal industries craftsmen	13 568
Metal industries mechanics	1 048
Wood-working craftsmen	13 172
Building craftsmen	13 319
Textile craftsmen	24 098
Light industries craftsmen	37 560
Other craftsmen	6 821
Total	109 586
Personal services	
Shop assistants	26 262
Domestic servants	39 168
Janitors, ghaffirs, messengers, etc.	32 896
Sanitary workers	4 273
Servants (other than domestic)	5 352
Others	231
Total	108 182
Machinery operatives	
Operatives in transport	27 378
Operatives in stationary machinery	4 198
Other machinery operatives	2 072
Total	33 648
Protective services	
Soldiers	6 270
Police and prison	7 509
Total	13 779
General labourers	
Building and construction workers	5 385
Road and railroad workers	4 192
Others	71 481
Total	81 058
Overall total urban workers	346 253

Note: The total number of urban workers given here (346 253) seems large relative to the total urban population (853 873). A number of factors explain this. One is that many men working in the towns left their families at home in the rural areas. Another is that the enumeration of urban workers given here is based not on the place of residence of the worker (i.e. whether in a town or a rural area) but on the nature of his employment (i.e. whether his job is one which is usually performed in an urban setting). Some 'urban workers', therefore, may be enumerated in the census as living in the rural areas. The census definition of 'urban areas' seems to have been broad, including substantial villages as well as the towns.

Source: Compiled from information given in Republic of Sudan, *First Population Census of Sudan 1955/1956* (Department of Statistics, Khartoum, 1962), vol. 2, pp. 123–4.

In 1955/56 there were only some 9500 workers employed in manufacturing industry,[67] constituting 3.2 per cent of the urban worker grouping. The urban workers, therefore, were mainly employed in services and small-scale craft manufacture. It is significant that there were over four times as many domestic servants as workers in manufacturing industry. The composition of the urban worker grouping had particular implications for the possibilities of mobilising urban workers in political or union organisations reflecting their interests as workers: the scattered nature of their employment, with few large concentrations of workers employed in a single organisation, made it difficult to draw workers into such organisations.

While there were differences in the economic well-being of different urban workers (with those who could organise themselves in unions – such as the railway workers – generally doing best), wages were seldom more than that necessary for fairly simple subsistence. In 1955/56 a worker would have been unlikely to earn more than £S15 per month.

(f) Salariat

The salariat comprises all those earning a monthly-paid salary rather than a weekly wage. There were some common elements to the social and economic position of those falling within this bracket: they all had some measure of education and/or training; they were all based in the urban areas (even though they may have been working in the rural areas as local government officers, etc.); and both in social status and income they enjoyed a more favourable position than manual workers. Significant differences in economic well-being, however, existed between different parts of the salariat. Table 3.10 seeks to classify the salariat into three main divisions according to the standard of living enjoyed, and the effective role in the Sudanese economy and society played by salaried personnel.

The 'senior personnel and professionals' would, in 1955/56, mostly have been earning substantial salaries (relative to the cost of living): in excess of £S1000 per annum. Even where salaries were not deemed sufficient, senior personnel could feel assurance in the prospect of a rising standard of living, either through ascending further the rungs of the administrative ladder or through using their specialised knowledge (or possibly their influential positions) to acquire gains additional to their salaries. Their role in administering Sudan's society and economy (especially with the arrival of self-government in 1953)

Table 3.10   Numbers of Salaried Personnel, Classified by Type of
Employment 1955/56

	Numbers
Senior personnel and professionals	
Accountants, statisticians, etc.	197
University and secondary school teachers	793
Ministers, senior civil servants and local govt officers	1 044
Senior religious occupations	162
Doctors, dentists, etc.	276
Engineers, surveyors, architects	563
Members of House of Representatives and Senate	147
Newspaper and magazine editors	27
Judges, barristers, solicitors, etc.	272
Army officers (above the rank of captain)	52
Senior police and prison officers	29
Managers of large commercial and industrial undertakings	329
Others	290
Total	4 145
Middle-level personnel and semi-professionals	
Book-keepers, cashiers, etc.	3 803
Intermediate and primary teachers	6 397
Junior administrators in civil service and local govt service	716
Medical assistants (dispensers, nursing sisters, pharmacists, etc.)	4 375
Draughtsmen, non-degree engineers and surveyors	909
Senior clerks in civil and local govt services	2 755
Senior clerks in commerce, industry, etc.	1 000
Army officers (up to the rank of captain)	360
Police and prison officers	185
Others	939
Total	21 439
Junior personnel and employees	
Junior religious occupations	1 039
Junior medical helpers (dressers)	3 555
Sub-grade school teachers	5 034
Junior clerks in civil and local govt service	10 426
Junior clerks in commerce, industry, etc.	4 712
Foremen	201
Army non-commissioned officers	684
Police and prison non-commissioned officers	1 619
Total	27 270
Overall total of salaried	52 854

Table 3.10 continued

Note 1: The population census figures do not make it possible to distinguish between professionals working for the government and those working in a private capacity. Although doctors, dentists, engineers, architects, solicitors, etc. may have been working in a private capacity (and were thus not salaried) they have nevertheless been included here within the salariat.

Note 2: One category of individuals who did receive a salary from the Sudan government has been excluded from this table. A total of 27 103 '*umdas, shaikhs* and headmen received such a salary in 1955/56. As these salaries were not intended to cover their living expenses but only to defray some of their expenses, they cannot usefully be deemed salaried personnel.

Sources: Most of the information in this table is taken from Republic of Sudan, *First Population Census of Sudan 1955/56* (Department of Statistics, Khartoum, 1962), vol. 2, pp. 122–4 and 397–410. Where information was lacking on a particular item, however, use has been made of material gathered independently by the writer.

was crucial. Such personnel, furthermore, tended to have access to subsidised government housing and to interest-free loans for building houses.[68]

The 'middle-level personnel and semi-professionals' enjoyed higher incomes and a clearly superior social status to those of urban workers. Their salaries generally ranged between £S400 and £S1000 per annum. Some personnel in this category (specifically the junior administrators and local government officers) could hope to work their way up the administrative ladder to become senior personnel, but the greater part had little prospect of bettering their positions substantially.

'Junior personnel and employees' enjoyed incomes only marginally higher than those of urban workers, between £S300 and £S400 per annum. They did, however, hold a rather higher social status. Such personnel had usually obtained only a rudimentary education or training and had no prospect of improving their positions substantially.

(g) Merchants

The term 'merchants', as used here, covers a wider range of economic entrepreneurs than those described as 'merchants (traders)' in

Chapter 2. It covers not only the owners of commercial enterprises (whether large-scale trading concerns or small-scale shops) but also owners of manufacturing concerns or agricultural schemes (i.e. pump or mechanised crop production schemes). Investment in commercial, industrial and agricultural enterprises cannot usefully be kept separate, because investors tended to straddle the different spheres of economic activity. Rather than there being a rural landowning gentry which invested in agriculture and an urban bourgeoisie which invested in industry, there were entrepreneurs who shifted and developed their economic activities between industry, commerce and agriculture according to where they saw chances of profit at the time.[69] At the stage of economic development which Sudan had reached in 1955/56, moreover, the dividing lines between agricultural, commercial and manufacturing activities were far from clear: manufacturing was sometimes sufficiently small scale for the manufacturer to be also a retail trader in the goods he was producing, while merchants owning agricultural schemes would conduct their trade on the basis of their schemes' produce.

Table 3.11 enumerates merchants according to the nature and scale of the economic activities they pursued. The figures given in this table separating 'major merchants' from 'petty merchants' are only approximate. As the population census classification depended on every merchant's perception of himself (i.e. whether he called himself a trader or the owner of a commercial undertaking, etc.) the picture which emerges is inevitably impressionistic. The overall pattern portrayed by the figures, however, is realistic: of the 66 831 merchants in Sudan, a small number ran substantial businesses while a large number pursued very limited and small-scale trading operations.

Levels of economic well-being varied greatly both between and within the 'major merchant' and 'petty merchant' groupings. As indicated earlier, rich merchants constituted one of the principal social groupings accumulating funds under the Condominium. The incomes of petty merchants, on the other hand, would frequently have been little more than those of urban workers. Yet the economic lot of even the poorest merchants was in one respect more favourable than that of urban workers: unlike the latter, merchants could envisage some betterment of their own conditions, through expanding their trading activities.

Table 3.11　*Classification of Types of Merchants, 1955/56*

	Numbers
Major merchants	
Owners of large commercial undertakings:	
large shops	51
taxi fleets	76
service-selling concerns (cinemas, buses, etc.)	251
Total	378
Owners of pump schemes and mechanised crop production schemes	137
Owners of industrial undertakings	785
Lorry-owners	459
Total	1 759
Petty merchants	
Owners of small shops	6 047
Traders	54 580
Owners of coffee-houses and restaurants	3 286
Owners of workshops	1 159
Total	65 072
Overall total	66 831

Note 1:　The term 'industrial undertakings', as used in the population census (from which this information is taken), appears to be used loosely – or perhaps incorrectly. The large-scale import–export concerns, for example, seem to have been brought under this heading. In some cases this was justified as the concerns did undertake some processing of the products which they exported (cotton ginning, oil pressing, etc.), but it was not justified in all cases. Most of those listed under 'owners of industrial undertakings', in fact, could more properly be described as 'owners of large trading undertakings'.

Note 2:　There were considerably more privately owned agricultural schemes than would appear from the number of 'owners of pump schemes and mechanised crop production schemes' (137) given in this table. It is evident, therefore, that most of those who owned private agricultural schemes held other occupations and were classified in the census under the latter categories. For more information on the total number of private agricultural schemes see Chapter 2.

Source:　Republic of Sudan, *First Population Census of Sudan 1955/56* (Department of Statistics, Khartoum, 1962), vol. II, pp. 122–3 and 399–402.

(h) Class structure

The attempt must now be made to show how the various economic groupings and fractions discussed above may be aggregated into class groupings. Such aggregation does not, of course, constitute evidence of the existence of class consciousness (or of the existence of classes 'for themselves' rather than classes 'in themselves', to use Marx's terminology). Evidence of class consciousness can only be found by examining the course of social and political developments and conflicts – as is done in Chapters 5, 6 and 7. Even without class consciousness, however, the existence of classes 'in themselves' may still be significant, providing an explanation for the character of political and social action.

One should not expect in Sudan under the Condominium a fully-developed class structure similar to that of an industrialised capitalist state. Sudan at that time (and after) was part of a capitalist system of production, but it did not itself constitute a fully capitalist system of production. Pre-capitalist forms of production remained significant. The accumulation of funds by tribal and religious leaders, the limited extent to which labour on the agricultural schemes was free wage-labour,[70] the prominence of subsistence peasants and pastoral production in many parts of the country, and the effective control which tribal leaders held over the allocation of the land used in peasant and pastoral production, all constituted aspects of pre-capitalist forms of production. The configurations of class groupings, therefore, were confused by the overlapping of capitalist and pre-capitalist forms of production. The emergence of classes related to capitalist forms of production can be detected, but the nature of their formation and composition makes it necessary to describe them as incipient or transitional.

Sudanese society, as the Condominium came to an end, consisted of three broad class groupings:

(i) The incipient bourgeoisie. The 'major merchants' constituted the core of the class, owning some of the country's most economically rewarding assets and activities. Although the Condominium state (working together with foreign commercial organisations) occupied the central position in such economic development as occurred, the merchants' involvement in pump schemes and mechanised crop production schemes, their domination of domestic trade and some export–import trade, and their growing investment in manufacturing, created for them a powerful economic role.

Allied to the core element was the highest echelon of the salariat: senior personnel and professionals. The overlapping of interests between major merchants and the higher salariat was evident both in the effective cooperation between them in the organisation of Sudan's economy (the higher salariat, especially after self-government, creating and maintaining the social and economic framework which benefited the merchants), and in the tendency of senior salaried personnel and professionals to move into commercial fields of activity (either concurrently with holding salaried positions or subsequent to abandoning such positions).

Given the weakness of Sudan's industrial infrastructure (and the fact that a significant part of such industry as existed belonged to foreign companies[71]), the merchants and higher salariat cannot be characterised as 'owners of the industrial means of production'. They were, rather, poised to emerge in this role as the economy developed. Hence the necessity for describing them as an 'incipient' bourgeoisie.

(ii) The intermediate strata. The nature of these strata is evident from the name given: their position is characterised by not belonging to either of the more clearly defined class groupings. Members of the intermediate strata held economic roles which – whether by virtue of their having a training needed by the government and private sector, or whether by virtue of having access (by ownership, control or family position) to a sphere of economic activity capable of providing more than a subsistence standard of living – could enable them to escape from the cycle of inevitable poverty in which the urban and rural poor were trapped. For them there was some prospect of economic improvement, yet the bounds within which such improvement could occur were generally limited – unless they succeeded in transferring such gains as they made to other fields of economic activity.[72]

The intermediate strata comprised middle-level and junior personnel and employees in the salariat, the petty merchant grouping, tenant and peasant farmers whose holdings were such that they could rely wholly or mainly on employed labour to undertake the agricultural work, and pastoralists whose holdings of animals similarly allowed them to rely on employed labour.

These strata obviously have much in common with the petites bourgeoisies of industrialised capitalist states. The petty merchant grouping comprises the 'traditional' petite bourgeoisie, the salaried personnel and employees constitute the 'new' petite bourgeoisie, while the richer tenants, peasants and pastoralists can only progress economically by investing their gains in commerce (and thus becoming part of the 'traditional' petite bourgeoisie). To refer to such strata in Sudan as constituting a petite bourgeoisie, however, may impose a spurious unity on a grouping characterised by diversity.

(iii) The urban and rural poor.   Such elements, comprising the great majority of the Sudanese population, were effectively trapped in a cycle of poverty. Whether rural peasants or urban workers, their labour could only earn for them the means for a bare subsistence. Without the ability to generate any surplus income, the majority of peasants could not afford the modern agricultural implements which would have made their labour more productive and earned more substantial rewards. Urban workers, similarly, seldom had any means of breaking out of their existing situation: they lacked the modern-sector training (and the ability to gain one) which could have enabled them to command a higher income, and they lacked the surplus funds necessary to developing a different economic activity. The abundant availability of urban labourers[73] ensured that wages for manual labour remained low.

The groupings included under this heading are the urban workers, the 'middle' and 'poorer' categories of peasants and nomads, the rural labourers, and those tenants who 'relied entirely or almost entirely on their own or their families' labour to farm their tenancies'.[74]

While it is important to have a perspective on the major economic cleavages in Sudanese society, the divisions within each of the three main class groupings remain highly significant. For an understanding of the dynamics of Sudanese politics both of these dimensions must be borne in mind.

APPENDIX: THE SUFI RELIGIOUS ORDERS (*TURUQ*)

The role played by religious leaders in Sudanese politics makes it valuable to provide some background on the Sufi religious orders which, together with the Mahdist movement, have dominated the religious life of northern Sudan.

Sufism can be seen as a reaction to the relatively austere intellectual nature of orthodox *sunni* Islam. The Orthodox Islam of the *'ulama* tended to be dominated by legalistic conceptions, preoccupied more with the organisation of the Muslim community than with the spiritual development of individual Muslims. The *'ulama*, more-over, placed greater emphasis on the transcendence and omni-potence of God than on God's immanence. The remote and legalistic religion of the *'ulama* could not easily constitute a living creed for the mass of the population – especially for the rural people, distant as they were from the big mosques of the great cities. Sufism, named after the simple woollen clothing (*suf*) of travelling holy men, came therefore to fill an important human need: putting forward 'paths' (the literal translation of *'turuq'*) whereby individuals could attain experience of God. Although this mystical approach was regarded with some disapproval by the *'ulama*, it should not be regarded as un-Islamic for the prophet himself clearly believed he had attained a direct personal experience of God.

Individual Sufi mystics attracted groups of followers, committed to pursuing the same path (*tariqah*) in attaining experience of God. These groups, each committed to a particular method of contempla-tive mysticism, eventually became institutionalised into self-per-petuating orders or brotherhoods, sometimes taking the character of monastic establishments. The death of the founding mystic, there-fore, did not bring the community to an end: a *tariqah* had been established which would continue under different leadership (usually under a succession of descendants of the founding mystic, whose *barakah* was deemed to have passed to his descendants). The *silsilah* (continuous chain) linking the founding mystic with the contempor-ary leadership ensured that the *barakah* – God's blessing, conceived as a supernatural power possessed by the individual who enjoys it – remained effective.

The Sufi orders which developed were not sects. On doctrinal issues they were at one with the orthodox *sunni* establishment. Where they differed from the *'ulama* was in their stress on attaining direct experience of God and in the rituals which they practised so as to gain this experience. Common practices and procedures in the exercise of religious devotions, common patterns of prayer (instituted by the founding mystic and developed by others), and the collective act of remembrance of God (*dhikr*) among groups of followers, gave each Sufi order its coherence. Initially, a *tariqah*'s following consisted entirely of dervishes (*darawish*, sing. *darwish*), who committed their whole lives to the service of the order. In time, however, lay mem-bers came to be accepted into the *tariqah*. The lay members would carry on with their usual employment, but deemed themselves under the guidance of the *tariqah*'s leadership and took part in the collective repetition of remembrances of God (*dhikr*). The lay members came in due course to constitute the major part of every *tariqah*'s following.

Sufi orders first emerged in a recognisable form (i.e. as self-perpetuating orders rather than as groups of followers of a living mystic) in the 12th–13th centuries. Among the first orders to be established were the Qadiriyyah, following the path of 'Abd al-Qadir al-Jilani (1077–1166), and the Shadhiliyyah, following the path of Abu al-Hasan al-Shadhili (died 1258). The organisation of each *tariqah* assumed a similar pattern. At the top of the hierarchy was the *shaikh*, bearer of the founding mystic's *barakah*. Below him, responsibility for guiding the mass of followers lay with a number of *khalifah*s – each responsible for a particular region. A regional *khalifah* often developed a following of his own, establishing an individual reputation for *barakah*. On occasions such followings would develop into a new *tariqah*. Although appointments to *khalifah*ships nominally lay with the *shaikh* of the *tariqah*, in pratice particular families dominated these positions. Under the regional *khalifah*s were the sectional leaders – bearing in North Africa the title *muqaddam*, in Egypt '*am*, and in Sudan simply *shaikh*. The sectional leaders carried out the practical work of managing the *tariqah*'s local following, initiating new members, proselytizing, etc.

In Sudan, as in many other Islamic countries, Sufi orders came to constitute the focal point of religious life to the great majority of the Muslim population. The orders began to enter the country shortly before the fall of the kingdom of Alwa; under the Funj Empire they emerged as the dominant force in religious life. Proselytizing members of orders established outside Sudan came to the country from the Hijaz and founded branches of their orders.[75] Thus the Shadhiliyyah order is said to have been brought to Sudan by Sharif Hamad Abu Dunanah, who settled in the Berber district in 1445 (before the fall of the kingdom of Alwa).[76] The descendants of Abu Dunanah have continued to exercise the *khalifah*ship of the order's branch around Berber to this day. Although the Shadhiliyyah enjoyed a position of some significance under the Funj Empire, it did not maintain a substantial following thereafter. Besides the branch around Berber, a small following has continued to exist in Sennar and among peoples of Hijazi or Hadramauti origin on the Red Sea coast.

The Qadiriyyah order was probably introduced into the Sudan by Taj al-Din al-Bahari, who lived in the Gezira for some seven years around 1550. Al-Bahari had travelled to Sudan from Baghdad (where the Qadiriyyah *shaikh* resided) and before he left the country he appointed *khalifah*s to take charge of the order in the central Sudan. Among these were Muhammad al-Amin ibn 'Abd al-Sadiq, who established the Sadiqab branch in al-Suqi; Ban al-Naqa al-Darir, who founded the Ya'qubab branch; and 'Abdallah Dafa'allah al-'Araki, founder of the 'Arakiyyin branch which later transferred its loyalties to the Sammaniyyah order. Each of these branches – whether it remained formally within the Qadiriyyah or not – operated with effective independence. Descendants of the three original *khalifah*s of these branches retain the *khalifah*ships to this day. A substantial proportion of the inhabitants of the Gezira (at least before the Gezira scheme had brought in settlers from western Sudan and beyond) adhered to one or other of these three branches.

A distinctive characteristic of the Qadiriyyah order in Sudan is the looseness of its organisation and the diversity of elements within it. Not all parts of the *tariqah* in Sudan trace the origins of their branches back to al-Bahari. There were other Qadiri holy men visiting Sudan in the early days of the Funj Empire and many of them established their own branches, leaving behind a separate set of *khalifah*s. One such holy man was Idris ibn Arbab, a Mahasi who established a large following at 'Ailafun. The diffuseness of the Qadiriyyah's organisation has meant that despite having a substantial number of adherents – some claim that it has more adherents than any other *tariqah* in Sudan – the *tariqah* has not carried the political weight which some smaller but more centralised *turuq* have carried.

The Sammaniyyah order, although not as long established as the Shadhiliyyah or the Qadiriyyah, has maintained a substantial following in Sudan since the early 19th century (possibly as large as that of the Qadiriyyah). The order is formally a branch of the Khalwatiyyah but in practice it operates independently – especially in Sudan where the parent order has virtually no presence. The Sammaniyyah order was brought to Sudan from the Hijaz around 1800 by Ahmad al-Tayyib ibn al-Bashir, who was appointed *khalifah* for Sudan either by the founder of the Sammaniyyah (Al-Sayyid Muhammad al-Hasan al-Sammani) or by his successor. Al-Bashir was granted lands in the Gezira by the Funj *wazir*, Muhammad Abu Likailak. The order spread quickly, partly as a result of some Qadiriyyah groupings (such as the Ya'qubab) transferring allegiance to the new order. In due course al-Bashir appointed *khalifah*s for the different areas into which the order spread – mainly along the banks of the White Nile, among the Hamar of Kordofan and among the Fadniyyah East, a sub-tribe of the Ja'aliyin.

At the time of the Condominium three families occupied positions of particular influence within the Sammaniyyah order in Sudan. First, the direct descendants of al-Bashir, the Nur al-Da'im family, based at Lake Tabat. A member of this family retained the *khalifah*ship which was often deemed the most senior in the order's Sudanese establishment. For most of the Condominium period the latter position was held by Jaili 'Abd al-Muhammad Nur-Da'im. Second, the Qurashi family. A member of this family, Qurashi al-Zain, had counted Muhammad Ahmad (al-Mahdi) among his adherents – after the latter had quarrelled with the current Nur al-Da'im *khalifah* and before he pronounced himself the Mahdi. The branch of the Sammaniyyah order led by the Qurashi *khalifah* combined belief in the sanctity of Muhammad Ahmad al-Mahdi with continued adhesion to Sammaniyyah beliefs. The family was based at Tayyibah. Third, the al-Hindi family, which was led for most of the Condominium period by one of the most influential Sudanese religious leaders of the era, Sharif Yusif al-Hindi. The branch of the Sammaniyyah led by Sharif Yusif al-Hindi was steadily taking on an independent character, becoming known as the Hindiyyah. It enjoyed strong support among the Kawahla tribe.

The three orders mentioned so far all entered Sudan from outside and continued to operate (theoretically at least) as branches of the wider order. There were, however, some orders which were founded inside Sudan, or else which ceased to have any links or activities outside Sudan. One such was the Majdhubiyyah. This order was started by a Ja'ali mystic, Hamad ibn Muhammad al-Majdhub (1693–1776), in the first half of the 18th century. A distinctive characteristic of the Majdhubiyyah was that despite being very localised (with a following restricted largely to the town and environs of Ed Damer) it enjoyed widespread influence and respect in northern Sudan. The Majdhubiyyah laid stress on religious learning and education, such that under the Funj, Ed Damer became the main centre of education for the riverain tribes of northern Sudan: the Ja'aliyin, Shaigia, Hasaniya, etc.

From its inception, the Majdhubiyyah functioned as a strongly centralised order. Hamad ibn Muhammad al-Majdhub concentrated both spiritual and temporal authority in the Ed Damer district in his own hands. This pattern of authority – at least on the spiritual side – continued through the succession of *wali*s who followed him. The identification of the Majdhub family (or tribe, as it tended to become) with the Majdhubiyyah *tariqah* was strong: followers called themselves collectively the Majadhib (plural of Majdhub) and those who joined the order from outside the family/tribe were effectively absorbed into it.

The centralised character of the *tariqah* enabled it to act as a coherent political force. The Majadhib actively resisted the Egyptian occupation of Sudan in 1821 and strongly supported the Mahdist movement in the 1880s. Although to this day still based at Ed Damer, some dispersion of the following took place under Turko–Egyptian rule and subsequently under the Condominium. By the middle of the 20th century adherents of the Majdhubiyyah could be found on the Red Sea coast, among the Bisharin tribe, and in small communities in most major Sudanese towns. The *wali* (equivalent to the central *shaikh* in other *turuq*) during the later part of the Condominium era was Bashir Ahmad Jalal al-Din.

The Mirghaniyyah or Khatmiyyah order was founded by Muhammad 'Uthman al-Mirghani (1793–1853). Al-Mirghani, a native of Turkestan, travelled to Sudan in 1817 as a proselytizing agent for Ahmad ibn Idris, founder of the Idrisiyyah order in the Hijaz. Although this visit appears not to have been outstandingly successful, the foundations were laid for future development. While in Sudan al-Mirghani married a Dongolawi woman who bore him a son, al-Hasan. Al-Hasan was later seen by al-Mirghani as the 'seal' (*khitm*[77]) binding his African adherents to his order. In 1819 al-Mirghani returned to the Hijaz and served Ahmad ibn Idris through to the latter's death in 1837.

Contention for the leadership of the Idrisiyyah order followed Ahmad ibn Idris's death. The main contenders were the order's two most prominent adherents: Muhammad ibn 'Ali al-Sanusi (founder of the Sanusi order, which ultimately became predominant in spiritual and temporal life in eastern Libya) and Muhammad 'Uthman al-Mirghani. Most of the order's bedouin support followed al-Sanusi while the *'ulama* and the Sharifs of Mecca gave their support to al-Mirghani. Four different orders emerged from the contention: the Sanusiyyah, the Mirghaniyyah, the Idrisiyyah (continuing under the descendants of Ahmad ibn Idris and ultimately gaining both spiritual and temporal predominance in the al-Asir region of south-west Arabia), and the Rashidiyyah (built up around Ibrahim al-Rashid, another of Ahmad ibn Idris's pupils). While all of these orders maintained a presence in Sudan, only the Mirghaniyyah was of any real significance there.

In developing the Mirghaniyyah order, al-Mirghani modified substantially the traditions of Ahmad ibn Idris and gave emphasis to the hereditary sanctity of his own family. His sons were sent out to proselytize for the new order. Al-Hasan, being himself half-Sudanese, proceeded to Sudan where he achieved considerable success in attracting a following among the tribes of northern Kordofan and among the Danagla and Shaigia in what later became Northern province.

The death of al-Mirghani in 1853 led to a further spate of contention, this time within the Mirghaniyyah order itself. Under al-Hasan's leadership the Sudanese branch of the Mirghaniyyah became effectively independent, taking on the name Khatmiyyah. Al-Hasan settled at Kassala, where he established the township of Khatmiyyah – which became and remains the order's centre. Al-Hasan is today a more revered figure to Khatmi adherents than is Muhammad 'Uthman al-Mirghani. On al-Hasan's death in 1869 the succession passed to his son, Muhammad 'Uthman Taj al-Sirr. The latter played a prominent role in mobilising Khatmi followers to support the Turko–Egyptian regime and to oppose the claims of Muhammad Ahmad al-Mahdi in the early 1880s. Shukriyah and Bani 'Amir Khatmi adherents were prominent in the local forces used against the Mahdist forces. Khatmiyyah activity, therefore, came to an end in Sudan during the Mahdiyyah (except in Suakin, which remained under Egyptian control) and the Khatmi leadership spent the years of the Mahdist era in Egypt.

The organisation of the Khatmiyyah under the Condominium contained a paradoxical element: although the leadership was in theory diffuse, in practice the order retained a fairly centralised structure, with a coherent centre. The succession to Muhammad 'Uthman Taj al-Sirr (who died in 1886) was shared between different family members. The division of authority between these family members was arranged, once the order had been able to re-establish itself in Sudan after 1898, on the basis of regional responsibilities. One of Muhammad 'Uthman's sons, Ali (generally known as Sayyid Ali al-Mirghani), took responsibility for Khartoum, Kordofan, Berber, Dongola and Halfa; another son, Ahmad (succeeded by his son Muhammad in 1928), held responsibility for the Kassala, Gedaref and Qallabat areas and for the Shukriya and Hadendowa tribes; a daughter of Muhammad 'Uthman, Maryam al-Mirghani, was responsible for the Red Sea hills area; and a niece ('Alawiyyah al-Bakri) and nephew (Ja'far al-Bakri) were responsible in Eritrea. It is interesting to note the role played by the two women – an unusual aspect in a Sufi order.

While the division of responsibilities might seem to reflect disunity, the arrangement was given coherence by the political pre-eminence of one of the five regional leaders: Sayyid 'Ali al-Mirghani. Condominium government support for the Khatmiyyah, given in the hope that the order's strong following in northern Sudan could be used to counter the re-emergence of an anti-British Mahdist movement, was channelled through Sayyid 'Ali.[78] This both strengthened the Khatmiyyah as an organisation and strengthened the position of Sayyid 'Ali within the leadership.

The Isma'iliyyah *tariqah* is another order which is effectively restricted to Sudan – enjoying, in fact, little support outside of Kordofan province. The founder, Isma'il al-Wali ibn 'Abdallah al-Kordofani (1793–1863), acted initially as a proselytizing agent for Muhammad 'Uthman al-Mirghani when the latter visited Kordofan in 1817. The branch of the Mirghaniyyah formed by Isma'il al-Wali in Kordofan ultimately developed into an independent order, based in El Obeid and benefiting from the strong support of the Bedeiriya tribe. A schism occurred in the order at the time of the Mahdiyyha: Isma'il al Wali's eldest son, Muhammad al-Makki (died 1906), gave support to the Mahdist movement, while the second son, Ahmad al-Azhari, and his family strongly opposed the Mahdi. The al-Makki family continued to hold the central leadership of the *tariqah* throughout the Condominium era, while members of the al-Azhari family rose to prominence in religious and political spheres outside the order. Isma'il al-Azhari, Ahmad's son, became *mufti* of Sudan (1924–32), and the *mufti*'s namesake and grandson ultimately became the first prime minister of independent Sudan.

Of the other *turuq* present in Sudan, none have been as significant as those already mentioned. The Tijaniyyah, introduced into Sudan by Muhammad al-Mukhtar Abd al-Rahman al-Shanqiti (died 1882), has had adherents among migrants from West Africa as well as among educated elements attracted by the order's philosophical mysticism and liberalism. The Sanusiyyah had a following in Darfur, which stemmed from the caravan routes linking Darfur and Cyrenaica, but this following steadily diminished over the Condominium period.

4 Social Movements, Regional Movements and Administrative Organisation, 1898–1956

This chapter examines some of the social and regional movements which came into being under the Condominium, and the system of administrative organisation. The movements and the system of administration were both of importance to the political dynamics which developed in the Sudanese nationalist movement.

I SOCIAL MOVEMENTS AND ORGANISATIONS

Our concern here is with movements and organisations based on employment, occupation or role in life, not with groupings based specifically on political or religious belief, or on ethnic or regional identity. The inclusion of the army as a 'social organisation' may cause surprise. Ranking it under this heading helps to bring out one aspect of the military – the cohesion which enabled the army to act politically as a coherent and unified force. The social differences within the military, however, should not be neglected – for the social backgrounds of different elements in the army obviously affected the form and nature of the army's political involvement.

(a) The labour movement

The 'labour' referred to here is urban labour. The composition and characteristics of the urban labour force has been made clear in the previous chapter. Rural labour was never organised into, or formed part of, a trade union – although between 1953 and 1956 Shaikh al-Amin Muhammad al-Amin, the radical tenants' leader, advocated opening membership of the Gezira Tenants' Union to 'non-tenants', which effectively meant rural labourers.[1] The Sudan government, however, never accepted the change to the constitution of the Tenants' Union which Shaikh al-Amin was seeking and there was, in addition, considerable opposition to the proposal among Gezira tenants (this, indeed, was one of the factors which led to Shaikh al-Amin losing his position as President of the Tenants' Union following the 1956 Union elections).

While a coherently organised labour movement did not come into existence in Sudan until after the Second World War, the beginnings of labour organisation were evident well before that. Sporadic strikes occurred from the early years of the century among workers employed by Sudan Railways, Port Sudan harbour, government departments and the ginning factories.[2] The militant opposition and resistance movement which flourished briefly between 1922 and 1924, moreover, sought both to organise workers and to utilise them in the political struggle: a 'workers' society', apparently operating in conjunction with the White Flag League,[3] recruited a wide range of artisans and labourers (carpenters, tailors, cooks, mechanics and others[4]) and seems to have played a significant part in organising the strikes and demonstrations which occured in different parts of Sudan between June and November 1924.[5] The Governor of Khartoum at this time reported that 'there is in Khartoum a workers' league organised by the White Flag League which was intended in due course to place at the disposal of the White Flag League all local artisans'.[6] The creator and leader of this workers' society was 'Ali Ahmad Salih (an employee at the Government Printing Press), while other active members were 'Uthman Ahmad Sa'id (an employee in the Public Works Department), Ramadan Muhammad (an employee of the Steamers Department) and 'Abdallah Rihan (a tailor in Khartoum).[7] This nascent labour movement, however, proved short lived. It fell victim not only to the Sudan government's overall success in crushing the opposition, but more specifically to 'Ali Ahmad Salih turning king's evidence and revealing his organisation's secrets to the authorities after his arrest.[8] For the remainder of the 1920s, and for most of the 1930s, the urban labour force remained quiescent – mirroring the state of the nationalist movement as a whole. One development of some significance, however, was the establishment of workers' clubs in Atbara (1934), Khartoum (1935) and some other major towns.[9] These clubs, intended to bring workers together for social and cultural activities 'gave impetus to the emergence of industrial labour as a self-conscious class and provided much-needed centres for workers' activities of a recreational and cultural character. They also provided a meeting place and a platform for the more articulate artisans to express their hopes for workers' organisations which would not be limited to social and cultural activities.'[10]

The limited size of the urban workforce, together with its dispersal in a wide variety of different sites of employment, help to account for the failure of any labour organisation to survive the events of 1924. This, however, does not constitute the whole explanation. Following the events of 1924 the Condominium government enacted legislation which imposed severe penalties on membership of 'unlawful associations'. The Unlawful Associations Act of 1924 imposed prison sentences 'which may extend to three years' for simple membership of an unlawful association, while 'whoever manages or assists in the management of an unlawful association, or promotes or assists in promoting a meeting of any such association . . . shall be punished for a term which may extend to seven years . . .'[11] Such legislation inevitably acted as a disincentive for those inclined to experiment with union organisation.

Developments during and immediately after the Second World War created a new situation for trade unionism in Sudan. There were four aspects to this new situation. First, the high inflation rate of the war years had led to a severe deterioration in the standard of living of the urban workforce.[12] Wage rates for railway workers in 1946, for example, had not been changed since 1935 and ranged from £E1.05 to £E2.00 per month.[13] A government enquiry in 1948 reported that the absolute minimum which was needed to maintain a small family was £E4 per month.[14] The cost of living indices in 1946 stood at almost double the 1935 level. Saad ed Din Fawzi comments:

> The decline in real earnings . . . affected all sections of labour, their wages not having been altered since 1935, and the rise in prices having been met to a small extent only by a war allowance, and a cost-of-living allowance granted since the end of the war.[15]

Table 4.1 gives details of the rise in the cost of living between 1943 and 1947, using 1938 as the base year. Expenditure on food comprised over half the spending of poor families; the indices related to food are therefore of particular significance.

These conditions had led to a rash of strikes during the war, in a variety of different spheres of employment.[16] Such strikes, however, seem not to have stimulated the Condominium government to raise wage levels. Or, at least, the Condominium government was slow to act on the issue, despite being aware of the considerable problems

Table 4.1 *Cost of Living Indices for Sudanese with Monthly Incomes of Less Than £12* (base year 1938)

	Year	Food	Clothing	Light, water and fuel	Rent and rates	All items
War	1943	135.3	559.5	121.7	100.0	176.6
	1944	144.4	357.2	121.7	100.0	160.4
Post-war	1945	170.9	285.7	121.2	100.0	170.2
	1946	190.2	285.7	121.2	102.0	183.4
	1947	243.0	357.1	144.6	102.8	229.3

Source: S. E. Fawzi, *The Labour Movement in the Sudan, 1946–55* (Oxford University Press, 1957), p. 22.

faced by the urban workforce. Sir James Robertson, who served as Civil Secretary of the Sudan government from 1944 to 1953, writes:

> Dissatisfaction increased and Government was slow to act, disliking a piecemeal attempt to rectify the situation and wishing to await a comprehensive review of all official salary scales which was to be carried out by a special commission.[17]

Second, the urban workforce had grown in size considerably during the war. This was in part due to the contribution (in support facilities as well as direct military involvement) which Sudan made to the allied war effort in the Middle East, and in part due to the expansion of petty manufacturing which occurred during the war. The latter phenomenon was caused by the need to produce military equipment for the allied armies and consumer goods which, in war conditions, could no longer be imported. Henderson, writing at the end of the Second World War, gives an impressive picture of the Sudan's role in the manufacture of military equipment:

> The Sudan had no factories and no reserve of trained craftsmen, and yet it contrived to produce in the workshops of the Stores and Ordnance Department, the Sudan Railways and the Public Works Department, with the assistance of the big commercial firms, the equivalent of a small military arsenal. These organisations doubled and trebled their staffs and their hours, working overtime far into the night. They supplied equipment to units of the British, Indian, French and Ethiopian forces in addition to their own, for most of these arrived in the country far in advance of their auxiliary services. They serviced their arms and transport, put new and

captured weapons and trucks into action, and trained armourers and mechanics in their use.

The variety of articles manufactured was remarkable, and included camp kit, uniforms, tentage, furniture, stationery, saddlery, and panniers (specially built to carry articles such as W/T equipment) for horses, mules and camels. Innumerable forms, pamphlets and handbooks in various tongues were printed. Local dyes were invented and applied for camouflaging. (Attempts were even made to find a fast dye for white camels.) Armoured cars were built, and an armoured train. Railway trucks were strengthened to carry heavy tanks. Mechanical transport chassis were commandeered or bought from America and converted. (Chassis ordered in Detroit in September were in action before Agordat in January.) Ambulances, gun mountings, stretchers, bomb clips, water tanks, ventilators, fittings for buildings, and aircraft repair stands were constructed. Passenger coaches were converted into ambulance trains, tugs into minesweepers, trucks into flats for carrying mechanical transport. The Surveys Department, in the intervals of turning out thousands of maps for the Army, contrived lithographic processes for printing the Emperor's Amharic messages and broadsheets and reproducing his seal. The Stores covered his State umbrella; the Railways made him a set of copper drums. Meteorological balloons were supplied to Fort Lamy. Requests were received for staffing lighthouses in the Red Sea. Bows and incendiary arrows were manufactured to set fire to huts in the Baro Salient.[18]

The expansion of the Sudan Defence Force during the war, and the need to demobilise many of the soldiers once the war had ended, had particular implications for the development of new attitudes among the urban population. The strength of the force had risen from 4500 men in 1939 to about 30 000 in 1944. Sir James Robertson writes:

The troops had been well paid by Sudan standards. Many had served in the Middle East in Cyrenaica, Eritrea and Tripolitania and while under British army control had enjoyed rations and amenities far higher than those they had known at home. They had seen Egypt and learned ways of life unknown in the country districts of Sudan. Two or three thousand had learned technical trades, as motor drivers, fitters, telegraphists etc., and we wondered how they would settle again into their old ways of life.[19]

It is significant that some of those most active in the trade union movement in the late 1940s were demobilised soldiers (and specifically those who had obtained a technical training while in the army).

Third, the re-emergence of political activism among educated Sudanese during and after the Second World War both embodied and created new opportunities for social and political organisation. On the one hand, the Condominium government had to act more circumspectly than before in its treatment of such social or political entities as emerged from within the Sudanese population. On the other hand, some elements in the new political activism were strongly supportive of the development of trade unions and played a crucial role in advocating and encouraging their formation. Sudanese communists, who in 1944 formed the Sudanese Movement for National Liberation, were particularly prominent in this sphere. An official publication of the Sudan Workers' Trade Union Federation in 1965 described the role of communists in the formation of the Sudanese union movement as follows:

> Due to the efforts of the communists and their explanation of new facts about the means of struggle and the causes of the misery (of workers), the form which could unite the workers began to be clarified . . . that was the trade union organisation.[20]

The communists, however, were not the only political activists involved in and with the labour movement. The Ashiqqah grouping also sought support among the urban work force and ultimately gave assistance in the establishment of trade unions.[21]

Fourth, British government policy following the Second World War became more favourable to the establishment of trade unions in territories under British control. The election of a Labour government in April 1946, and the appointment of a leading trade unionist – Ernest Bevin – as Foreign Secretary, provides the main explanation for this change in policy. Upon assuming office Bevin arranged for the appointment of a labour counsellor at the British Embassy in Cairo.[22] The latter individual (a Mr Audsley, seconded from the British Ministry of Labour) was available to assist the Sudan government in developing labour legislation. Too much significance, however, should not be attached to this factor. The officials of the Condominium government appear to have been unenthusiastic about the new policy and reluctant to take an initiative which would have brought trade unions into existence.[23] It did nevertheless become increasingly difficult for these officials to take a strong stand against the establishment of trade unions.

The initiation of a systematically organised trade union movement took place in Atbara in 1946. The location was not accidental. Contrary to the general pattern of urban worker employment, where labour tended to be divided up into small and diverse units of employment (with different employers, different places of employment and usually different conditions of service), labour in Atbara was fairly homogeneous. Some nine-tenths of the inhabitants consisted of railway workers and their dependants.[24] These railway workers comprised about 40 per cent of all the employees of Sudan Railways. As the Railway School (founded in 1924), the Engine School and the railway workshops were all situated in Atbara, moreover, skilled workers constituted a major part of the Atbara workforce.[25] It was skilled workers who ultimately took the lead in establishing a union organisation among railwaymen – in part because they felt particularly aggrieved. Despite the training which skilled workers had to undergo, their wages were not significantly higher than those of unskilled workers. Sir James Robertson comments:

> There was something to be said for labour's dissatisfaction with their conditions; skilled craftsmen, after many years experience of using machine tools and doing work requiring considerable technical ability, received less pay than their more academically educated young relatives who had obtained employment in the Railways clerical cadres.[26]

In 1944, 6680 of Sudan Railways' 20 000 employees were skilled workers, in the 'mechanical branch'.[27]

As the Second World War ended, the Sudan government became aware of the need for some kind of labour legislation. The only existing legislation in this field was a Workmen's Compensation Ordinance.[28] Problems over demobilised soldiers seem to have been at the forefront of government officials' minds as they considered the need for new legislation – indeed, the first formal proposal for such legislation came from the demobilisation committee which the government established in 1944. The committee recommended 'the establishment of machinery to deal with the labour problems which are now presenting themselves for the first time'.[29] Responsibility for creating the appropriate machinery was given to the Government Labour Board – a body which had been established in 1921 but had been dormant for some years before its resurrection in May 1945.[30] At a meeting of the board held on 18 May 1946, members reached agreement on the form of labour representation which should be instituted. Encouragement was to be given to the formation of works committees in all major places of employment. The secretary of the board was instructed:

> to communicate with all large-scale employers of labour in the Sudan, both government and private enterprise, setting forth fully details of the nature of works committees and stating that the Labour Board strongly favoured the setting up of such bodies whenever practicable, in the interests both of the workers and industry generally.[31]

The new scheme was duly communicated to employers at the beginning of July 1946.

It was hoped that the works committees, consisting of elected representatives of the workers and nominated representatives of the management in each place of work, would provide a forum where workers' demands could be discussed – and hopefully defused – before they led to industrial unrest. The framework of works committees which was now being promoted was based on the 'Whitley-Hartney councils' which had been established in Britain during the Second World War.[32] There was, however, one fundamental difference: whereas the Whitley-Hartney councils operated in conjunction with trade unions, the works committees proposed by the Sudan government were to be introduced in the absence of trade unions.

The railway workers of Atbara, meanwhile, had been developing some very different ideas. Following a series of meetings held in Atbara between 29 June and 16 July 1946, the basis of a new trade union organisation was laid down: the Workers' Affairs Association (WAA).[33] It seems that those who took this initiative were unaware of the proposals put forward on the government side for works committees. Their objectives, in any case, went well beyond those which the Government Labour Board had conceived appropriate to the works committees. The functions which the WAA proposed to fulfil have been summarised as follows:

1. Trade union functions: to link its members in an organised association; to improve their standards materially and culturally; to look after their interests and rights by legitimate action within the boundaries of the law; to act as a link between

workers and employers; to defend the rights of its members against the employers by resorting to legal and other action.

2. Mutual help: to render its members moral and financial assist-'ance . . . ; to establish saving schemes, cooperative societies and the like . . .

3. Cultural functions: to organise literary and scientific lectures in order to improve the educational standards of its members . . .[34]

All of the members of the first fifteen-man executive committee of the WAA were either skilled or semi-skilled workers. The meetings which led to the union's establishment, in fact, had been held in the technical schools' old boys' club in Atbara. Those who were elected to offices were a chargeman in the mechanical transport shop (president); a pattern maker (vice-president); a fitter (secretary); an electrician (assistant secretary); a carpenter (treasurer); a turner (assistant treasurer) and a boiler-shop mechanic (publicity officer).[35]

In the months which followed the WAA's foundation a prolonged confrontation with the Sudan Railways administration developed. The latter sought to persuade the WAA to restrict its activities to the channel of representation opened up by the newly created works committees, while the WAA sought formal recognition and negotiating rights from the Sudan Railways administration.[36] Having failed to obtain recognition from the Sudan Railways administration, the WAA on 16 March 1947 addressed a petition to the Governor-General – with an appeal for his support on the issue of formal recognition.[37] No satisfactory answer was received. What happened next is recounted by Mohamed Omer Beshir:

Faced with the opposition of the management and the disregard of the government the Sudan railway workers resorted to militant action as the only way to obtain recognition. On July 12, 1947, they marched on the railway headquarters in a peaceful demonstration to register their protest and to show that the Workers' Affairs Association was backed by the majority of the railway workers in Atbara. As they approached the railway headquarters the demonstrators were met by armed police who prevented them from proceeding and declared that only the president of the Association would be allowed to take the petition to the management. The workers, however, insisted on continuing their march and presenting their petition as a group. The police advanced to disperse the march and a violent clash took place. The next day the leaders of the Workers' Affairs Association were arrested and the railway workers in Atbara went on a strike which spread to all parts of the country and brought all the trains to a complete standstill. It was only when the Workers' Affairs Association was recognised by the management, following the intervention of representatives of the political parties and the press, that the strike was ended on July 23, 1947.[38]

By mid-1947, therefore, the WAA had succeeded in establishing the legitimacy of trade union organisation in Sudan, and had forced the Sudan government to abandon its own plans for works committees.

The success of the WAA forced the Sudan government to draft a body of labour legislation which would take account of the new situation. The key element in this legislation was the Trade Union Ordinance of 1948, based on the British Trade Union Act of 1871. Also enacted in 1948 were the Regulation of Trade Disputes Ordinance, the Workmen's Compensation Ordinance, the Trade Disputes (Arbitration and Inquiry) Ordinance, the Employer and Employed Persons Ordinance, and the Workshops and Factories Ordinance.[39] The drafting of the legislation was carried out under the supervision of an official seconded to the Sudan government for this purpose by the British Ministry of Labour.[40] The WAA initially opposed the Trade Union Ordinance, mainly on the grounds that (unlike its British equivalent) it required the compulsory registration of trade unions. Following discussions between six representatives of the WAA, six government representatives and three members of the Legislative Assembly (including 'Abdallah Khalil and Muhammad Ahmad Mahjub), however, the government agreed to some minor amendments to the Ordinance and the WAA agreed to work within its framework.[41] Trade union activities, therefore, could now proceed – in effect protected by a strong legislative framework.

Even before the Trade Union Ordinance was passed, workers' groups in different spheres of employment had begun drafting union rules and constitutions, in readiness for registration. The process of registration was duly initiated in 1949, with five unions gaining recognition in that year. In 1951 the number of trade unions registered rose to 86, in 1952 to 99, in 1954 to 123, and in 1956 to 135 – with 87 355 members.[42] Unions were not slow in launching themselves into negotiations with management and, where demands were not met, organising strikes. The WAA called two major strikes on

Table 4.2   *Man-days Lost Through Strikes, 1947–53*
(government sector only)

Man-days lost through strikes in individual government departments

	Sudan Railways	Other departments	Total
1947–8	840 000	—	840 000
1948–9	20 000	13 000	33 000
1949–50	60 000	57 181	117 181
1950–1	141 584	56 721	198 305
1951–2	181 460	78 645	260 105
1952–3	213 938	47 987	261 925

Man-days lost through general strikes

	Number lost	Percentage of loss through all strikes
1947–8	—	—
1948–9	—	—
1949–50	113 251	97
1950–1	130 124	65
1951–2	246 976	95
1952–3	—	—

Days lost per man through strikes

	Sudan Railways	Other departments	Total
1947–8	42	—	42
1948–9	1	0.5	1.5
1949–50	3	2.3	5.3
1950–1	7.1	2.3	9.4
1951–2	8.9	3.2	12.1
1952–3	10.7	2.0	12.7

Source: S. E. Fawzi, *The Labour Movement in the Sudan, 1946–55* (Oxford University Press, 1957), p. 122.

Sudan Railways in January and April 1948, ultimately forcing the government to set up a committee of enquiry into wages. The latter committee recommended the raising of wages – approximately to the level demanded by the WAA.[43] The militancy of trade union activity was such that, over the 1947–53 period, some 1 750 000 man-days were lost through strikes (see Table 4.2). Wage levels were steadily pushed upwards, more than doubling between 1949 and 1955. Although wages in 1955 were still insufficient to afford urban workers more than a subsistence living, the level of wages was increasing rather faster than the rate of inflation.[44]

The strength and coherence of the trade union movement were reinforced by coordination and collaboration among the various unions. In August 1949 a Workers' Congress was formed, grouping together the first fifteen unions to be established. Due to the prominent role played by the WAA in initiating the trade union movement as a whole and the Congress in particular, the Workers' Congress was based in Atbara.

The increasing number of unions gaining registration and the consequently increased significance of collective pressure exerted on the government, however, led to the Workers' Congress being reconstituted in November 1950 as the Sudan Workers' Trade Union Federation (SWTUF) based in Khartoum. The first general secretary of the SWTUF was the general secretary of the WAA, Shafi' Ahmad al-Shaikh. The WAA, itself now reconstituted as the Sudan Railways Workers' Association, had in 1950 a membership of some 25 000 – about one-quarter of all trade union members. The ability of unions to exert pressure on employers was greatly strengthened by collective action through the SWTUF. In August 1951 the federation coordinated action among those unions representing workers in the public sector and organised a strike calling for an overall 75 per cent rise of wages in this sector. The government was forced to undertake a major review of wages, leading to substantial wage rises.[45]

From the outset, the trade unions were deeply involved in politics. Some have seen this as an aberration from their true role, caused by the involvement of extraneous political activists.[46] Although many of the leaders of the trade union movement (including Shafi' Ahmad al-Shaikh) were members of the Sudanese Movement for National Liberation, the political role of trade unions developed naturally from the struggle to improve workers' economic and social conditions. Some specific factors promoted the politicisation of the movement. First, the rising tide of nationalist consciousness affected workers as well as other sectors of the population, giving them political perspectives and political demands. Second, the legitimacy of trade union organisation had been established through confrontation with the Condominium government; there was a strong conviction that unless the unions were politically aware and articulate trade union rights would be withdrawn or restricted.[47] Third, the high proportion of the labour force employed in the government sector made it difficult for unions to differentiate between confronting the employer and confronting the government.

An early indication that Sudanese trade unions would broaden their campaign from the issue of wages and conditions to the wider political and economic structures of the Condominium came in a letter from the WAA to the civil secretary's office in November 1947:

> We fail to understand how either the railway management or the government could make business gains at the expense of lowering the living standards of human beings to such depths, when it was realised that the greater part of those profits went to the central government to be expended largely on the unduly large salaries earned by British officials who led luxurious lives, and out of which were built magnificent mansions, the construction and mainten-ance of which required hundreds of thousands of pounds.[48]

The formation of the Sudan Workers' Trade Union Federation created a new context within which political objectives could be pursued. The SWTUF's constitution, adopted in November 1950, defined the federation's role almost exclusively in terms of labour interests. Soon after its formation, however, the SWTUF entered the political arena: one of its first actions was to protest against the dismissal of 119 Khor Taqqat secondary school students for political activity. The federation threatened to organise a three-day strike if the students were not re-instated.[49] On this occasion, however, the government called the federation's bluff: the students were not re-instated and no strike ensued. More significant was the confron-tation which developed between the SWTUF and the Condominium government in late 1950 and early 1951 over two issues which the SWTUF saw as crucial to its role and existence. First was the issue of registration for the SWTUF under the Trade Union Ordinance of 1948, which would have given the federation some measure of legal protection. The government refused registration on the grounds that the Ordinance only allowed for the registration of individual unions.[50] Second was the federation's opposition to the amendments which the government was seeking to introduce in the Defence of Sudan Ordi-nance. The amendments gave the Governor-General additional powers in the case of strikes. In December 1950 the SWTUF sought unsuccess-fully to organise a strike against the amendments; the amendments were duly adopted by the Legislative Assembly.[51]

The vulnerability of the federation's position, for as long as it was not accorded recognition under the Trade Union Ordinance was made clear in June 1951. A large part of the police force in Khartoum province went on strike for higher pay at the beginning of that month, also demanding the right to form a trade union. The strike inevitably had strongly political overtones. According to M. N. El-Amin, the Sudanese Movement for National Liberation

> . . . jumped at this opportunity and tried to turn the whole affair into a major confrontation with the authorities. The workers were invited to come to the assistance of the police (viz. strikers), and huge demonstrations were held in which the striking members of the police took part and in which communist slogans were loudly and repeatedly shouted.[52]

Not unnaturally – and probably with some justification – the SWTUF leadership was suspected of having instigated the strike. The authorities reacted strongly to the growing disorder: a state of emergency was declared on 10 June. The SWTUF president, Muhammad al-Sayyid Sallam, and the general secretary, Shafi' Ahmad al-Shaikh, were arrested and sentenced to one and two years' imprisonment respectively, charged with abetting the policemen in the desertion of their duty.[53]

As a direct reaction to the tough stance taken by the Condominium government over the registration of the SWTUF and the amendments to the Defence of Sudan Ordinance, the first annual congress of the SWTUF in December 1951 amended the federation's constitution to include some specifically political objectives. These included working for 'the immediate defeat of colonialism in the Sudan in all forms, economic, political, administrative and military' and seeking 'to win for the Sudan the right of self-determination in an atmosphere free from foreign influences'.[54] Such objectives would be pursued through 'absolute non-cooperation with the colonial regime' and 'uniting the Sudanese people in a united front comprising political and other groups whose political aims approach the federation's'.[55]

Even before the SWTUF constitution had been amended, the federation had in fact joined a specifically political alliance. In October 1951 the SWTUF came together with the SMNL, the students' congress, the Liberal Unionists and some smaller political groupings to form the United Movement for the Liberation of Sudan. The Front, whose inception was prompted by the Egyptian government's renunciation of the 1936 Anglo–Egyptian treaty, called for the immediate withdrawal of foreign forces from the Sudan and for the granting of self-determination to the Sudanese people. It denounced both the Umma Party for its collaboration with the British and the Ashiqqah grouping for its contacts with feudal classes in Egypt.

The political dimension of the SWTUF's activities developed in interaction with government policy: the federation needed to gain political allies so as to protect its position, but the closer its alliance with radical forces the more insistent was the government in introducing legislation of a kind which the SWTUF perceived as a threat. In April 1952 the government put before the Legislative Assembly a draft law on 'subversive activities'. A campaign against the draft law was undertaken by the SWTUF and its allies in the United Movement for the Liberation of Sudan. Although the campaign failed to prevent the passage of the Subversive Activities Act, it bore fruit in the longer term. One of the first actions taken by Isma'il al-Azhari's government after self-government was to repeal the Act.[56]

The political role envisaged by the December 1951 amendments to the federation's constitution gained further emphasis in the annual report, presented by the SWTUF committee to the second annual congress in December 1952. This stated:

> The struggles of our labour movement have demonstrated that the demand for better economic and social conditions and the hope for a prosperous and peaceful life always came against a major block which is the imperialist regime in power. Therefore in the final analysis our objectives cannot be achieved until the imperialists are thrown out of the country.[57]

In 1953, however, the SWTUF's political role suffered a setback. Following the Anglo–Egyptian agreement on self-determination for the Sudan (February 1953) the executive committee of the SWTUF denounced the agreement and called for a general strike. The provisions of the agreement, according to the SWTUF executive, would not guarantee true self-determination: the powers given to the Governor-General during the transitional period were excessive; the envisaged pace of Sudanisation (especially in the army and police) was too slow; and Condominium officials were left with too much power in southern Sudan.[58] The SWTUF executive, however, had misjudged the mood of the workers. The preponderant feeling among Sudanese workers appears to have been that the agreement – whatever its deficiencies – did provide the Sudanese population with the prospect of self-determination. Support for a strike was lacking.

Despite the setback, the SWTUF continued to pursue political objectives. The focus of concern in the later part of 1953 was with the programmes put forward by the 'bourgeois' political parties. During the election campaign for the first parliament in 1953, Isma'il al-Azhari, leader of the National Unionist Party, had stated:

> . . . the transitional period is essentially one of liberation, of liquidating the condominium rule, and of preparing for self-determination, not of reconstruction and broad social policies . . . at such a time labour should not press its demands too far, and should certainly not go on strike.[59]

At the SWTUF's third annual congress, held in December 1953, Isma'il al-Azhari and other political leaders were attacked for concentrating only on liberation – not on the social and economic policies which would be pursued once liberation was achieved. The congress resolutions described the strategy of these leaders as being against the trade union movement and stressed that liberation could have no meaning unless it was linked with reconstruction. Failure to link liberation with reconstruction, the resolutions stated, could only serve the interests of colonialism and the ruling classes.[60] This line was pursued consistently through to independence.

(b) The tenants' movement

As indicated in Chapter 3, the rural tenants shared certain characteristics with industrial workers: they were organised (in substantial groups) under a common 'employer', who determined the rate of return for their work; the work they had to perform was set for them by the management; failure to perform the assigned work would lead to sanctions. There was, therefore, a tendency for tenants to use similar techniques to those used by industrial workers in seeking to improve their economic position: to form unions which enabled collective pressure to be exerted on the scheme authorities. While tenants' associations sprang up on a number of different agricultural schemes, the only one substantial enough to play a political role – rather than simply to defend tenants' interests in negotiations with scheme managements – was the Gezira Tenants' Union.

The origins of the Gezira Tenants' Union can be traced back to a strike (itself evidence of the industrial worker parallel) which occured in April 1946. Tenants had become suspicious over the Gezira Board's financial management, believing that tenants were not being paid all the sums to which they were entitled.[61] The paternalistic attitude of the board, which saw no need to enlighten tenants as to the overall financial position, and the absence of any representative body through which information on such matters could be conveyed, created a framework within which mistrust was inherent. Matters came to a head over the 'reserve fund' – a fund which was intended to relieve financial hardship in bad years (when the price of cotton was low) through money deposited in good years. Following the revelation that the sum of £E1 300 000 was in the reserve fund, the tenants went on strike. They refused to begin planting seed for the new season until all of the money in the reserve fund had been paid to them. While there were some individuals (mostly connected with the Ashiqqah grouping in the Graduates' Congress) who coordinated the strike action, the success of the strike was mainly attributable to the spontaneous response of tenants to the assumed unfairness of the board's financial dealing.

The strike was settled through the mediation of a committee of the recently established Advisory Council for Northern Sudan. The sum the £E400 000 was withdrawn from the reserve fund and paid to the tenants. Aware that some of the mistrust and suspicion which had led to the strike could be dispelled by more communication with the tenants, the Gezira Board now accepted the need for a representative body. A Tenants' Representative Body (TRB) was instituted: tenants in each *samadiah* (the village agricultural unit) elected a delegate to their local 'block electoral college' and the latter chose a representative for the 40-member TRB. The first elections were held in April 1947.[62]

Between 1947 and 1951 the TRB played, with some effectiveness, the role which had been allotted to it: defending the tenants' immediate interests and constituting a channel of communications between the board and the tenants. In keeping with the board's conception of the TRB's role, the TRB remained non-political. An early attempt by members of the Ashiqqah grouping to turn it towards national political concerns failed.[63] Although some poorer tenants gained seats on the TRU, the richer tenants (some of whom owned sideline commercial undertakings) tended to be predominant.[64]

A substantial number of tenants, however, remained dissatisfied with the form of organisation which had now been opened up to them. The 1946 strike had created widespread awareness of what could be achieved through collective pressure on the scheme management. The TRB, many tenants believed, was not a suitable instrument for the exertion of collective pressure.[65] Functioning (in part) as a channel for communications between tenants and management, it was in no position to mobilise tenants to confront the management. Moreover, it was widely believed that the indirect form of election, which was supervised by the board's field inspectors, created a more pliable leadership than would have emerged by direct election. The activities of newly formed national political movements, especially the Ashiqqah and the SMNL, also impinged upon the Gezira tenants. A deepening political consciousness led increasing numbers to see the problems of tenants within the context of problems facing Sudanese nationalism. Tenants' organisation, in this perspective, should therefore not be restricted to the non-political concerns of the TRB, but should become politicised.

Pressures from tenants for the establishment of a new representative body, more distinctly independent of the Gezira Board, led to the Tenants' Representative Body adopting a new constitution in 1952.[66] The name was changed to Gezira Tenants' Association (GTA) and provision was made for direct elections to the council of the association. As most of the old TRB leadership simply slipped across into the council of the GTA, however, the split between the established tenants' leadership and the radical tenants who demanded a more militant anti-board line continued. Matters came to a head in the summer of 1953. Intending to confront the Gezira Board with some new demands, the radical tenants – informally led by Shaikh al-Amin Muhammad al-Amin[67] – called on tenants to boycott cotton picking. The GTA leadership repudiated the call. The conflict was resolved by the 1953 elections for the GTA council: Shaikh al-Amin and his supporters won a resounding victory.

Following the 1953 tenants' elections the GTA was reconstituted under a revised constitution as the Gezira Tenants' Union (GTU), with Shaikh al-Amin as president. An active role was pursued by the union between 1953 and 1956, both in inducing the Gezira Board to offer tenants more favourable terms and conditions,[68] and in mobilising tenants for wider political campaigns.[69] Close links were established with the Sudan Workers' Trade Union Federation, with which some joint political demonstrations were organised. The 'unity of struggle of peasants and workers' was proclaimed. Contacts were opened up with some of the smaller tenants' associations in the

Table 4.3   Numbers of Students at Gordon Memorial College, 1920–44

Year	Number	Year	Number
1920	162	1933	410
1921	185	1934	384
1922	191	1935	344
1923	207	1936	291
1924	211	1937	325
1925	235	1938	357
1926	303	1939	411
1927	370	1940	508
1928	442	1941	515
1929	510	1942	524
1930	555	1943	523
1931	563	1944	514
1932	436		

Source: Education Department, *Annual Reports* (Government Printer, Khartoum); and Republic of Sudan, *Sudan Almanacs* (Government Printer, Khartoum).

Northern province and with the association which represented Nuba Mountains cotton cultivators.[70]

(c) The student movement

At a number of critical stages in the development of the Sudanese nationalist movement and in subsequent Sudanese politics, students played a significant role in influencing the course of events. Before examining the development of student political organisation, reference must first be made to the size and structuring of the student community. The focus here must be on the development of secondary and higher education, for it was exclusively students at those two levels who played a political role.

Up to 1944 there was only one government secondary school in Sudan: the Gordon Memorial College. The latter was established in 1903 and was intended, according to the guidelines laid down by the first director of education (Sir James Currie), to make available a small number of Sudanese for work in the civil service.[71] Initially the college also undertook some vocational training, but this division was separated from the college in 1932 and was moved to a technical training school in Omdurman. Table 4.3 shows the numbers of students at Gordon Memorial College between 1920 and 1944. In the non-government sector there were two other secondary schools: the Coptic school, which began admitting a very small number of Sudanese students after 1931, and Comboni College, run by the Verona Fathers and catering almost exclusively for non-Sudanese children.[72]

One further government-sector educational institution which took students from the intermediate schools and gave them further training deserves mention. The Elementary Teachers' Training College at Bakht er Ruda, established in 1934, accepted some 60 students a year for a one-year course. The college began a course for intermediate teachers in 1939, eventually leading to a separate Intermediate Teachers' Training College in Bakht er Ruda in 1949. In the later part of the 1940s new elementary teachers' colleges were established in Dilling, Shendi and Maridi. The location of the Bakht er Ruda college – in a rural setting close to Ed Dueim on the White Nile – and the small number of students meant that little opportunity arose for the involvement of the student body in national politics.

Up to 1938 higher (i.e. post-secondary) education barely existed. Only the Kitchener School of Medicine, established in 1924, was active at this level – training small numbers of Gordon College graduates over a five-year period as general practitioners. Up to 1948 the intake never exceeded 10 per annum. Table 4.4 gives details of recruitment and graduation over the 1924–43 period.[73]

The signing of the Anglo–Egyptian Treaty in 1936, combined with the onset of better times following the depression, were the key factors leading to the expansion of higher and secondary education in Sudan which occurred in the late 1930s and the 1940s. The 1936 treaty effectively ended the exclusion of Egyptian officials from Sudan (maintained since 1924), stipulating that the Governor-General 'will select suitable candidates of British or Egyptian nationality' to fill those positions for which qualified Sudanese were not available.[74] For the Condominium government, the training of more Sudanese for government service was a means of avoiding the presumed political dangers of employing Egyptians.

Following investigations by a number of government-appointed bodies (most crucially the De La Warr Commission, which reported in 1937[75]) the decision was taken in 1938 to expand secondary education and to introduce post-secondary courses in specific fields – leading towards the establishment of a university. Arrangements for the expansion of secondary education were duly undertaken, but the outbreak of the Second World War delayed the implementation of new projects in this field until the mid-1940s. In 1944 the secondary

Table 4.4   Student Intake and Graduation at the Kitchener School of Medicine, 1924–43

Year	Student intake	Numbers graduated	Year	Student intake	Numbers graduated
1924	10	0	1934	10	6
1925	8	0	1935	2	9
1926	0	0	1936	10	5
1927	9	0	1937	0	6
1928	8	7	1938	7	1
1929	9	7	1939	5	7
1930	9	0	1940	9	7
1931	10	5	1941	0	1
1932	10	6	1942	8	0
1933	10	9	1943	0	6

Source: H. Squires, *The Sudan Medical Service: An Experiment in Social Medicine* (Heinemann, London, 1958).

school element at Gordon Memorial College was transferred to a new school at Wadi Seidna (making room for Gordon Memorial College to develop in the field of higher education). New secondary schools were established in Hantoub (1946), Rumbek (1949) and Khor Taqqat (1950). By 1956 there were seven secondary schools in the government sector and five in the non-governmental sector – including an Egyptian secondary school, founded in 1944, which itself reflected the new conditions brought about by the 1936 treaty.[76]

In the field of higher education – where the government did not allow itself to be distracted by the outbreak of war – a number of 'higher schools', intended to initiate post-secondary education in specific fields, were established over the 1938–41 period. Thus, the Veterinary Science School and the Agriculture School accepted their first students in 1938; the Science School and the Engineering School in 1939; the Arts School in 1940; and the Law School in 1941.[77] These schools, initially only comprising a handful of students, awarded diplomas to their graduates – the diplomas being deemed equivalent to a pass degree at a British university.[78] Each school was placed under the control of a specific government department: the Veterinary School coming under the Veterinary Department, the Agriculture School coming under the Department of Agriculture, and the remainder under the Department of Education.

In 1944 the five higher schools were brought together in one

Class and Power in Sudan

Table 4.5   *Educational Development in Northern Sudan
(Government Education): Number of Pupils Attending Schools in
1936, 1944, 1948 and 1956*

	1936	1944	1948	1956
Higher education	18*	163	306	722
Secondary education: boys	291	514	801	1 700
Junior secondary education: boys	—	221	191	280
Intermediate education: boys	1 072	1 847	2 255	4 675
Elementary education: boys	12 402	19 381	26 074	76 996
Teachers' training for elementary schools	62	149	217	438
Sub-grade education	—	12 738	25 640	53 500
Subsidised khalwas	22 400	10 133	7 328	5 000
Technical education: boys	175	221	295	609
Teachers' training: girls	29	90	130	265
Elementary education: girls	2 927	6 681	n.a.	26 581
Intermediate education: girls	—	114	313	1 288
Secondary education: girls	—	—	37	265

* The 18 mentioned here were the students at the Kitchener School of Medicine.

Source: Figures adapted from M. O. Beshir, *Educational Development in the Sudan, 1898–1956* (Oxford University Press, 1969), p. 208.

institution: the new-style Gordon Memorial College, from which the secondary element had now been removed.[79] The college was formally inaugurated in February 1945, with its functions defined as 'teaching and research'. Responsibility for higher education thus passed from government departments to the College Council. In 1946 an agreement was made with the University of London, which enabled Gordon College students to sit for University of London degrees, with syllabuses and degree structures designed for Sudanese needs. In 1951 the college, brought together with the Kitchener School of Medicine, was elevated to the status of a University College. It finally emerged as the University of Khartoum in 1956.

Under the Condominium, therefore, the main development of secondary education and virtually all the development of higher education occurred in the later part of the era. Table 4.5 shows the pattern of overall educational development in Sudan between 1936 and 1956 – indicating how secondary and higher education fitted into the wider structure – while Table 4.6 gives details of the numbers of

Table 4.6   *Higher Education: Number of Students, 1942–56*

	1942	1943	1944	1948	1951	1952	1953	1954	1955	1956
School of Arts	57	73	58	100	112	152	144	183	175	187
School of Agriculture	12	11	11	7	6	37	35	40	40	33
School of Law	n.a.	n.a.	n.a.	36	27	39	84	67	82	99
School of Engineering	17	19	19	14	12	29	39	44	35	46
School of Medicine	21	22	29	32	47	50	70	82	71	128
School of Science	38	31	44	92	100	170	149	185	167	213
School of Veterinary Science	3	5	2	9	13	15	10	10	10	16
Total	148	161	163	290	317	492	531	601	580	722

Source: M. O. Beshir, *Educational Development in the Sudan, 1898–1956* (Oxford University Press, 1969), p. 202.

students in the different fields of higher education. Although second-ary and higher education remained underdeveloped through to the end of the Condominium period, the educational system by the later part of the 1940s contained sufficient numbers of students to form the basis of a politically significant students' movement. Complementing the higher education structure within Sudan, there were also large numbers of Sudanese students at institutes and universities in Egypt – a total of 789 in 1949.[80] While the latter students did not form an integral part of the students' movement which developed within Sudan, their activities in Egypt at times strengthened the movement in Sudan.

In view of the manner in which secondary and higher education developed, it is hardly surprising that formal student organisation was not initiated until the very end of the 1930s and did not gather momentum until the second half of the 1940s. Although the students in Gordon College organised strikes in 1928 and 1931, these were transitory events unconnected with any continuing student organisa-tion. The 1928 strike stemmed from student dissatisfaction with authoritarian procedures in the College,[81] while the 1931 strike was stimulated by currents in the wider Sudanese nationalist movement.[82]

The formation of the Culture and Reform Society in 1938, among students of the old (i.e. secondary school) Gordon College, provided a context within which student political organisation could emerge. The society's constitution laid down its objectives as follows:

(i) To bring together members through personal contact and collective readings of books and magazines.
(ii) To enlighten members through reading books, conducting debates and undertaking scientific expeditions.
(iii) To raise the standard of the people culturally through magazines and also to encourage other cultural activities such as the theatre and writing books.
(iv) To criticise backward habits in newspapers and to expose their disadvantages through plays and any other effective means.[83]

Many of the students in the new 'higher schools' which were opened in 1938 and 1939 joined the society, and it was among higher school members of the society that the idea of forming a union for higher school students was first mooted.[84] Under the auspices of the society, a meeting to discuss the establishment of such a union was convened in June 1940. The meeting recommended that the society's president write to the director of education, seeking approval for setting up a higher schools students' union. In February 1941 the director duly gave his approval, on condition that the union limited itself to organising debates and supervising sports activities, and that the meetings of the union be held only in the students' hostels. The conditions were accepted and elections for the new union's leadership were held forthwith. The first president of the higher schools students' union (subsequently Gordon College Students' Union and ultimately University of Khartoum Students' Union) was Ahmad Khair. Mubarak Zarruq was elected vice-president and Abd al-Majid Imam (who had been the first secretary of the Culture and Reform Society) was elected secretary.

For the first few years, especially while the Second World War continued, the new union concentrated on matters internal to the higher schools and the post-1944 Gordon College. However, with the rising tide of nationalist feeling in the mid-1940s (stimulated by the activities of the Graduates' Congress), the union began to move in a more overtly political direction. Demonstrations of a political character were organised by the union leadership in 1946.[85] Following a warning from the Gordon College principal that he would close the college if the union undertook further political activities, the union executive responded with a memorandum outlining its position as follows:

. . . our position in the Sudan differs from other free countries (*sic*). Alien rule in the Sudan should be removed and it is the duty of the educated Sudanese to do that. The students could not separate themselves from their people who pay the taxes in order to make it possible for them to study.[86]

The college was duly closed and the union dissolved.

In 1947 the college authorities re-opened the college but sought to maintain the ban on the union.[87] A confrontation with the student body ensued. The ultimate retraction of the ban saw the union re-emerge, strengthened in its political role by the confrontation which had occurred. The union executive which was elected in 1947, under the presidency of Muhammad Sa‘id Ma‘ruf, now adopted a new strategy. An effective role for the students in the liberation of Sudan, the executive believed, could only be developed if secondary school students joined the political mobilisation. Through 1947 and the first half of 1948, therefore, the executive was active in promoting the establishment of unions at secondary schools. By the middle of 1948 such unions existed at Hantoub and Wadi Seidna schools in the government sector, and in the Ahlia and Ahfad schools in the private sector. The links between Gordon College union and the school unions were given formal expression by the establishment of a students' congress, intended to coordinate the national students' movement, in 1949.

The political complexion of the students' movement leadership in Gordon College/University College over the 1945–56 period went through three stages. In 1945 and 1946 supporters of the Ashiqqah grouping[88] constituted the predominant element in the union executive. The executive organised its political campaign around the slogan 'The Unity of the Nile Valley'. In 1947, however, the Ashiqqah elements lost their predominance to supporters of the Sudanese Movement for National Liberation (SMNL), later to become the Sudanese Communist Party, which established its first branch in the college in 1946. A new slogan, 'the common struggle of the Sudanese and Egyptian peoples against the British', was adopted. SMNL supporters remained the majority element on the union executive through to 1950. It was while the SMNL controlled the executive, therefore, that the union emerged as part of a national students' movement. SMNL elements were prominent in all of the school unions and formed the leadership of the students' congress. In 1950 a grouping of 'neutrals' won the union elections and for most of the 1950–6 period this grouping retained control of the union executive. The neutrals, who took their name from the 'positive neutralism' associated with Nehru and other rising leaders in the Third World,

combined a broadly radical political perspective (and commitment to
involvement in national politics) with an insistence that the student
body should not be subordinated to national political parties or
movements. In practice the students' union under the neutrals continued to involve itself in national political issues but greater emphasis was given to intra-college concerns.

The emergence of the neutrals in the University College union was
in part a reaction against SMNL involvement with the student body.
A similar reaction against SMNL involvement led in a different
direction. In March 1949, a group of students, under the leadership
of Babikir Karrar, formed the Islamic Movement for Liberation
(ILM) – emphasising their rejection of communism and their adhesion to Islamic values.[89] Muslim Brother groups had been active in
Sudan since 1944 (mostly influenced by, and sometimes directly
controlled by, the Egyptian Muslim Brother movement), but the new
college-based movement was independent of these – both in organisation and in ideology. Unlike the mainstream of the Muslim Brother
movement, the ILM propounded the ideas of 'Islamic socialism'.

The ILM gained rapidly in strength in the early 1950s, coming to
constitute an opposite pole to the SMNL in both college and school
unions. The rising support, however, brought divergences. Some of
the new members drew their inspiration from the Egyptian Muslim
Brother movement and began to seek the re-creation of the ILM in
that mould. A divergence also arose as to the primacy of political
objectives, with some members contending that the initial emphasis
should be on the spiritual regeneration of the Sudanese population.
Political objectives, they maintained, could only be effectively pursued
once a measure of spiritual regeneration had been achieved. These
divergences led to the creation, in 1954, of two separate organisations:
the Islamic Group, which adhered to Babikir Karrar's Islamic socialist
line, and the Muslim Brothers, led initially by Rashid al-Tahir.

The development of strongly differing political tendencies in the
student body inevitably affected the impact which students could
have on political life. The students' congress had at its inception been
intended – at least by the SMNL elements who created it – to unite
secondary and university students behind a radical leadership, committed to promoting the liberation of Sudan.[90] The hope, on the part
of the students' congress leadership, was that future developments
would follow the pattern of 1948 – when students (led by the SMNL-
dominated Gordon College union) had mobilised popular opinion
against the Legislative Assembly. The congress itself, however, ulti-

mately became only one faction among others on the student scene. Remaining under the control of SMNL elements after the latter had lost their predominance in the Gordon College union, the congress re-formed itself as the Democratic Front in 1954.

The significance of the students' movement for the dynamics of the nationalist movement which developed in Sudan will be covered in Chapter 5.

(d) The women's movement

In practice only educated women had the social freedom and political awareness to create and maintain a women's movement in Sudan. The Sudanese women's movement, therefore, could only emerge at the very end of the Condominium era; before that there were simply not enough educated women to constitute a movement.

The origins of public-sector girls' education in Sudan go back to the Condominium's first decade, but this education remained restricted to the elementary level through to 1940. In 1907 two classes for girls were opened at the Khartoum elementary school.[91] Following opposition from the Church Missionary Society, however, which argued that its own school in Khartoum was being made redundant, the girls' classes were transferred to Rufaa where a girls' elementary school was opened in 1911.[92] The success of the latter undertaking led to four other girls' elementary schools being opened between 1911 and 1920, in Kamlin, Merowe, Dongola and El Obeid. The schools taught reading, writing, arithmetic, the Qur'an and embroidery. The significance of this excursion into girls' education, however, was limited: in 1919 the total number of girls attending all five schools combined was only 146.

In 1920 the Education Department began to give more emphasis to girls' education. A Girls' Training College, whose role was to take girl graduates of elementary schools and train them as elementary school teachers, was opened in 1921.[93] An expanded network of elementary schools was envisaged. By 1927 there were ten girls' elementary schools, with an enrolment of 694 girls. Table 4.7 gives details of the expansion of girls' elementary education up to 1956.

Higher-level girls' schools in the government sector were slow to develop. The first intermediate school for girls, the Omdurman Girls' Intermediate School, opened in 1940. New intermediate schools were established in El Obeid and Wad Medani in 1946 and, by 1955, ten such schools were in existence. Enrolment of girls rose from 114 in

Table 4.7   Expansion of Girls' Elementary Education (Government
Sector), 1919–56

Year	Number of schools	Number of pupils
1919	5	146
1927	10	694
1931	23	2 095
1936	n.a.	2 927
1944	n.a.	6 681
1956	173	26 581

Source: Compiled from figures given in M. O. Beshir, *Educational Development in the Sudan, 1898–1956* (Oxford University Press, 1969).

1944, through 313 in 1948, to 1288 in 1956.[94] At the secondary level, a small number of government-financed girls were sent to a private institution – the Unity High School for Girls – from the early 1940s. This practice, however, was discontinued in 1949 when Omdurman Secondary School for Girls was established. In 1956 the latter school, comprising some 265 students, remained the only girls' secondary school in the government sector.[95]

The number of girl students at the university level was even more restricted. The first girl joined Gordon College in 1945, and a further four joined in 1946. There were, still, fewer than 40 girl students at University College in 1956.[96]

The overall pattern of girls' education in the government sector, then, was one of severe underdevelopment. In 1956 less than 4 per cent of Sudanese girls/women were in any sense literate.[97] Such development as occurred at the higher school level took place exclusively in the later part of the Condominium era. Although there were non-government girls' schools (most notably the Unity High School for Girls, established in 1928) these – run by missionary organisations – catered primarily for the Christian communities in the larger towns. Only in southern Sudan did missionary schools contribute significantly to the education of local women.[98]

There was, therefore, no basis for the emergence of a women's movement – dependent as such a movement was on a core of well-educated women – until the late 1940s. Once the educational system had begun to produce girl graduates of higher-level schools, however, wider developments in society impinged to foster the political and social consciousness necessary for women's organisation. The activities of political parties, trade unions and students' unions, together with the general increase in nationalist consciousness, all created conditions in which women's organisation came to appear a natural development.

The first women's organisation to be established in Sudan was the Women's Association (or League), founded in 1947 following a meeting at the Girls' Training College in Omdurman.[99] The first president was Fatmah Talib Isma'il,[100] and the first general secretary Khaldah Zahir.[101] The association, whose objective was to mobilise educated women with a view to enlightening the uneducated, began by organising classes in literacy, health and hygiene for uneducated women in Omdurman. When it came to wider concerns, however, political differences soon emerged. The year 1948 saw widespread demonstrations, organised by the trade unions, the students' unions, the SMNL and the unionist parties, against the Legislative Assembly elections.[102] The more radical Women's Association members wanted the association to align itself with the opposition to the Legislative Assembly and participation in the elections. Others, however, rejected this proposition – whether because they wanted the association to remain strictly non-political or because they were committed (through personal conviction or family allegiance) to one of the political groupings which were participating in the elections. Finding themselves out-numbered in the association leadership, the latter elements withdrew from the association in 1948 and formed the Association for the Advancement of Sudanese Women. The division weakened the movement as a whole: both associations became inactive in the course of 1949.

Although it was not until 1952 that the attempt to establish a national women's movement could be re-launched, significant developments did occur meanwhile at a different level. In 1948 a women teachers' association was established.[103] Envisaged from the outset by its leadership as a trade union, but initially refused recognition as such by the Education Department, the association was eventually registered as the Schoolmistresses Union in December 1951.[104] The association's and union's main focus was on issues specific to women teachers, calling for equal pay with male teachers (as opposed to the ⅘ rate which was the practice), equal chances with male teachers in being sent abroad for further training, and the Sudanisation of the inspectorate grade (for girls' schools) in the Education Department. Some educational concerns of a wider nature were also raised. When the Marshall Committee[105] proposed to place elementary education under the control of local councils, the union opposed the idea, on the grounds that traditional leaders on the councils would restrict the expansion of girls' education. Pressure was consistently exerted on the Education Department to expand girls' education. Women were also active in one other union: the Nurses' Union, established in 1949.

The re-emergence of activity aimed at creating a national women's movement was prompted by a conflict which occurred at the Omdurman Secondary School for Girls in 1951.[106] A group of final year students (who constituted, significantly, the first batch of girls to reach the final year in a government secondary school) wrote a memorandum critical of the government's educational policy generally and of the headmistress's autocratic policy in particular. A bitter confrontation ensued between the students and the school authorities. The confrontation resulted in some links being established between the old Women's Association leadership and the schoolgirl activists. The Sudanese Women's Union (SWU), founded in 1952, grew from these links. The union's first executive committee was constituted from both elements: Fatmah Talib Isma'il and Khaldah Zahir were given leading positions on the committee, as also was Fatmah Ahmad Ibrahim, leader of the schoolgirl activists.

The primary objective of the SWU was to enlighten Sudanese women politically and culturally through educational, cultural and social activities.[107] An educational office was opened in 1953, responsible for promoting girls' education and women's literacy. Afternoon classes for women were run in the buildings of elementary schools (after the children had gone home); pre-school nurseries were initiated, relying on the voluntary work of SWU members; and a small number of girls' schools were established and maintained, including an intermediate school (founded in 1955) in Khartoum South. By 1956 SWU branches were operating in most of the main northern Sudanese towns. Although the educational activities were inevitably most effective in the Khartoum and Omdurman area, where there were sufficient numbers of educated women to run the classes, every branch undertook some activity in the educational field.

Also of importance was the initiation of a monthly women's magazine, *Woman's Voice*, in 1955. The magazine, edited by Fatmah Ahmad Ibrahim, had a circulation of some 3000 copies in the mid-1950s.[108] Emphasis was given to persuading women to abandon such customs as might hinder women from playing a fuller role in society. Among the customs which were discouraged were Pharoaonic circumcision, the *mushat*[109] hair-dressing, the wearing of *hidd*,[110] and expensive marriage practices.

Politically, the SWU tended to align itself with the more radical political groupings and organisations. A number of the most prominent members of the SWU executive committee were active in the Sudanese Movement for National Liberation: Khaldah Zahir had been a founder-member of the SMNL, and Fatmah Ahmad Ibrahim joined the movement in 1954.[111] SWU members participated in demonstrations organised by the SWTUF in 1953 (over the 'subversive activities' legislation), and subsequently in other street demonstrations organised by radical groups or movements. The political militancy led some of the less radical SWU members to split away and form rival, but never very significant, organisations.

(e) The military

The form which Sudanese nationalism took, especially in the events of 1924,[112] cannot be understood without reference to the Sudanese military. In 1924 the Sudanese military – some 9500 soldiers and officers – constituted a substantial organised grouping. At a time when the absence of higher education and the severe restriction of secondary education[113] meant that the foundation for a strong civilian-based nationalist movement (utilising modern forms of organisation and ideology) was lacking, military elements could play a significant role in promoting nationalist organisation. The training which they had undergone, their experience and their close mutual contacts created conditions in which at least some soldiers and officers had the inclination to act collectively in the political sphere.

The nature of the army in which Sudanese soldiers and officers served (up to 1924), moreover, itself increased the likelihood of politicisation. The army was the Egyptian army, within which Sudanese soldiers and officers formed the Sudanese battalions. There was, therefore, an institutional avenue through which vibrations from the nationalist upheavals in Egypt naturally penetrated the Sudanese battalions and politicised those within them. Contact with Egypt was strong: a substantial number of Egyptians served as officers in the Sudanese battalions; Sudanese units and individual officers would on occasions go to Egypt for training – or even serve the Egyptian government in outside conflicts, as occurred during the First World War;[114] and the oath of loyalty given within the Sudanese battalions was to the Khedive/King of Egypt, not to the Sudan government.

The involvement of the Sudanese in modern forms of military organisation was not new under the Condominium. Sudanese were in fact being drawn into modern forms of military organisation from the early part of the 19th century. By the time of the Condominium, therefore, there was already a tradition of military service for some sections of the Sudanese population.[115] The initiation of Sudanese involvement with modern military organisation can be traced back to the Emperor Napoleon's attempt to create a new army in Egypt under French occupation. In 1798 Napoleon wrote to the Fur Sultan, 'Abd al-Rahman al-Rashid, requesting 2000 young men from Darfur for military service.[116] French rule in Egypt collapsed before the planned new army could be created, but the idea of recruiting Sudanese for service in a modernised Egyptian army was taken up by Muhammad 'Ali when he became Viceroy of Egypt in 1805. Large numbers of Sudanese, mainly from Kordofan and Darfur, were recruited into Muhammad 'Ali's army and played a significant role in the campaigns which Muhammad 'Ali pursued in the Hijaz and in Syria, as well as in Sudan itself. There remained substantial numbers of Sudanese in the army which Muhammad 'Ali had created through to the dismantlement of that army following the British occupation of Egypt in 1882. When Napoleon III asked the Egyptian *wali* in 1863 to supply him with troops which were accustomed to tropical conditions, for service in the French campaigns in Mexico, a regiment of Sudanese troops was despatched to Mexico.[117] The latter regiment, which comprised three officers, 23 NCOs and 398 soldiers, served in Mexico for some four years.

When the Egyptian army was re-formed under British control after 1882, the policy of recruiting Sudanese was continued. The first Sudanese battalion in the re-formed Egyptian army was set up in 1884, largely from Sudanese 'blacks'[118] who had served in the pre-1882 Egyptian army. The successes achieved by the Mahdist forces in Sudan during the mid-1880s led increasing numbers of Sudanese to take refuge in Egypt. Many of the latter were ex-soldiers of the pre-1882 Egyptian army. Such elements constituted the basis of five more Sudanese battalions which were set up between 1884 and 1896. As with the first battalion, the Sudanese soldiers and officers of the five later battalions were predominantly black.

The Anglo–Egyptian forces which advanced into Sudan in 1898 comprised some 25 600 men, of which the six Sudanese battalions made up approximately one-third. Once the Khalifah's forces had been defeated and the security of the new regime assured, moreover,

Table 4.8   *Composition of the Egyptian Army Units in Sudan by National Grouping, November 1924*

| Total | | Officers | | Soldiers and NCOs | |
	British	Sudanese	Egyptian	Sudanese	Egyptian
12 943	107	233	407	9 203	2 943

Source: A. A. al-Faki, *Tarikh Quwwah Difaʿ al-Sudan* (Al-Dar al-Sudan-iyyah, Khartoum, 1971), p. 37.

some of the purely-Egyptian regiments of the Egyptian army withdrew from Sudan, leaving a preponderance of Sudanese in those Egyptian army units which remained. As time went by, and Sudanese gradually replaced Egyptians in the officer and NCO ranks, the proportion of Sudanese steadily rose. Immediately before the 1924 military insurrection, Sudanese constituted 84 per cent of all the soldiers in the Egyptian army units based in Sudan, and 31 per cent of all the officers (see Table 4.8).

It is significant that Sudanese served in the Egyptian army not only as soldiers but also as officers. Besides the 9203 Sudanese soldiers serving in the Egyptian army in 1924, there were 233 Sudanese officers – as Table 4.8 indicates. Some of these officers had graduated, in the closing years of the 19th century or the first few years of the 20th century, from the Egyptian Military Academy. The majority, however, were graduates of the Khartoum Military School, established in 1905 with a view to training Sudanese officers in an environment divorced from the ideological contamination of Egypt.[119] The Khartoum Military School drew its cadets mainly from among pupils who had completed their elementary education at Gordon College, with a small number drawn from the NCO ranks of the army. The period of instruction was three years for those who entered direct from Gordon College and two years for any who had come up from the ranks.[120] An account of the training given to cadets, written in 1921, makes it clear that the training was thorough and many-sided:

The indoor subjects include military law (in all its branches, particular attention being devoted to the framing of charges); army regulations (army customs, etiquette, etc.); interior economy, musketry, signalling, financial, clothing, equipment, supplies, pay, accounts relating to army pay, and the making out of monthly accounts, and all army forms; tactics and fortification (theory of field training and infantry field exercises, Infantry Drill vol. ii simple schemes on paper based on military sketches); topography and map-reading (scales, compass, etc., preliminary preparation for practical outdoor instruction, plotting from field-notebook conventional signs, military map-reading, and road and river reports); first aid (St John's Ambulance under an officer detailed by the Staff Medical Officer); official letter-writing; geography (Egypt and the Sudan, principal towns, districts etc., tribes, roads and routes, rivers and produce); arithmetic (proportion, fractions, decimals etc.).[121]

Over the 1905–24 period there were usually some 40–50 cadets training at the Military School, with some 15–25 graduating every year.

Most of the cadets who passed through the school came from that segment of the population which Condominium officials referred to as 'blacks' (see note 118). In 1908, for example, of the fifteen cadets who graduated in the school's first batch, twelve were blacks and only three were listed as 'Arab Sudanese'.[122] The army authorities appear to have deliberately fostered this pattern of officer recruitment. They believed that the soldiers, who were themselves mainly blacks, would hold most respect for officers who shared their ethnic background. It would also seem, however, that Arab Sudanese – associating the army with those of 'slave origin' – were themselves reluctant to join. The Sudanese battalions were organised into three corps: the Equatorial Corps, the Eastern Arab Corps, and the Western Arab Corps.

The changing relationship between Britain and Egypt after the First World War made some change in the security arrangements for Sudan inevitable. The nationalist uprising in Egypt in 1919 created increased concern among British officials of the Condominium government that the Egyptian army could constitute a conduit for the introduction of nationalist ideas to the Sudanese population. Britain's unilateral declaration in February 1922 terminating its protectorate over Egypt, moreover, meant that the Egyptian army was no longer under direct British control. Initially this made little difference: between February 1922 and February 1924 Egyptian governments made no attempt to assert greater Egyptian authority over the army's units in Sudan. The Wafdist success in the 1924 elections in Egypt, however, and the subsequent emergence in February 1924 of a Wafdist government, changed the position. The new Egyptian minister of war announced that he would involve himself closely in the running of the Egyptian army, including its units in Sudan.[123] Conflicts soon arose over the appointment of British officers to the latter units.[124]

Matters came to a head following the assassination of Sir Lee Stack, Governor-General of Sudan and *sirdar* of the Egyptian army, in Cairo on 19 November 1924. On 22 November Lord Allenby, the British High Commissioner in Egypt, issued an ultimatum which demanded that the Egyptian government 'order within twenty-four hours the withdrawal from the Sudan of all Egyptian officers and the purely Egyptian units of the Egyptian army, with such resulting changes as shall be hereafter specified'.[125] A communiqué which followed the ultimatum stated:

> The Egyptian officers and purely Egyptian units of the Egyptian Army having been withdrawn, Sudanese units of the Egyptian Army shall be converted into a Sudan Defence Force owing allegiance to the Sudan Government alone and under the supreme command of the Governor-General, in whose name all commissions will be given.[126]

The arrangements for re-structuring security arrangements in Sudan, phasing out the Egyptian involvement, had in fact been made prior to Stack's assassination.[127]

The Sudan Defence Force (SDF) was formally instituted on 17 January 1925. Financial constraints led to the new military force being both smaller and, initially, less well-armed than the units of the Egyptian army based in Sudan had been. The Egyptian government had borne the full cost of its army units based in Sudan – an estimated £E1 294 300 for the year 1923.[128] Financial responsibility for the new force was assumed by the Sudan government. Although Egypt made a contribution (£E750 000 annually, between 1925 and 1937)[129] towards the expenses of the Sudan Defence Force, the Sudan government was still left with added expenditure for which it had not been fully prepared. A plan put forward in 1924 for reducing the size of the army (covering the transition from Egyptian army units based in Sudan to the Sudan Defence Force) envisaged reductions in the numbers of soldiers, NCOs and officers according to the schedule given in Table 4.9. In fact the reductions went further than proposed in this schedule. In 1927 the actual number of men in the SDF stood at 4500.

Table 4.9   1924 Schedule for Reducing Size of Armed Forces, 1924–7

Date	British officers	Sudanese officers	Sudanese NCOs and soldiers
August 1924 (Egyptian army in Sudan, exclusive of Egyptian personnel)	106	233	9 253
30 June 1925 (SDF)	97	200	8 191
30 June 1926 (SDF)	84	132	6 871
30 June 1927 (SDF)	90	128	5 620

Source: Memorandum of Sir Lee Stack, Governor-General of Sudan, to the British prime minister, 19 August 1924 [E/7134/735/16].

As there was little need for new officers in the Sudan Defence Force, the Khartoum Military School was closed in 1925.[130] Political, as well as practical, reasons lay behind the closure: the 1924 troubles had convinced the British authorities that the officer material produced by the school was politically suspect. Following the Anglo–Egyptian treaty of 1936, the school was re-opened – with a view to increasing the number of Sudanese officers and obviating the need to bring in Egyptians. It was closed again in 1939, apparently because sufficient officers were now deemed to be available, and was not re-opened until 1948 (under a new name: the Khartoum Military College). Such Sudanese as were given commissions in the intervening years were promoted from the ranks.

The Sudan Defence Force was organised on a regional basis, with four regional commands. The Central Command was based in El Obeid, the Western Command in El Fasher, the Northern Command in Shendi, and the Equatoria Command in Torit. Army headquarters were in Khartoum.

Although the Sudan Defence Force's responsibilities were supposedly limited to internal security, leaving external aggression to be countered by the armies of the two co-domini, the Force had to be used to counter the attack on eastern Sudan by Italian forces during the Second World War. The Italian army of occupation in Ethiopia from which the aggression was launched, numbered some 300 000 men at the outbreak of the war. Some 100 000 of the latter could be ısed in the campaign against Sudan, supported by about 200 aircraft. Against these well-armed Italian forces, there were initially only hree British infantry battalions and the 4500 lightly armed men of he SDF. With 600 miles of border to guard, the task was immense.

The events which occurred during the conflict with the Italians in 1940–1 do not concern us here. Ample accounts of the successful actics employed by the SDF – usually aimed at deceiving the Italian orces into believing that a larger and better armed force was facing hem – can be found elsewhere.[131] The impact which these events had on the size of the SDF, however, is significant. The force was rapidly expanded over the war period, reaching some 30 000 men in 1944. Once the threat from the Italians in Ethiopia had been checked, SDF units joined the allied armies fighting the Germans and Italians in North Africa. The ending of the Second World War saw rapid demobilisation. By mid-1946 the SDF had shrunk back to the same number of men as it had had in 1939: 4500.

From mid-1946 to the introduction of self-determination in January 1954, the numbers of men serving in the SDF remained roughly constant, between 4500 and 5000. To cater for the prospec-ive needs of independence, however, the first government of the self-determination period began rapidly to expand the armed forces. A plan adopted early in 1954 envisaged the SDF reaching 15 000 men within three years. The intake into the Khartoum Military College was raised from 10 per annum to 100 per annum.[132]

I   REGIONAL MOVEMENTS AND ORGANISATIONS

(a) The basis of inequality

The economic structure built up in Sudan under the Condominium was such that the pace and nature of economic change varied con-siderably from one part of the country to another. The Condo-minium's development efforts were concentrated on the valley of the Nile to the north of Khartoum, the Blue and White Nile areas immediately south of Khartoum, central Kordofan and the southern part of Kassala province. These areas contained the major agricul-tural schemes (private and public) and benefited most from the spread of education and health services. With the exception of Port Sudan, they were the only parts of the country where significant urban development occurred. Such manufacturing as there was in pre-independence Sudan was carried out, almost exclusively, within these areas.

Although the imbalance in development was often as marked within an individual province as it was between provinces, some indication of the extent of the regional imbalance can be found in inter-province comparisons on the flow of investment. Table 4.10 outlining the regional distribution of gross domestic investment for the financial year 1955/56, shows that Khartoum, Northern and Kassala provinces were collectively obtaining approximately eight times as much private, governmental and public corporation invest ment as the three southern provinces, and about three times as much as Kordofan and Darfur. The combined population of Khartoum, Northern and Kassala provinces stood at 2 319 000, while that of the three southern provinces came to 2 783 000, and that of Kordofan and Darfur to 3 091 000. The investment imbalance in per capita terms was, therefore, more extreme than the investment totals suggest. Although the figures for other years are not available, it seems probable that the regional distribution of investment in earlier years was similar to that in 1955/56.

Stemming from the imbalance in the regional distribution of investment, standards of living also varied considerably between the different provinces. This is clearly reflected in the figures on per capita product, given in Table 4.11. Per capita product in Blue Nile province was three times the level of per capita product in the southern provinces.

Inter-province migration also stemmed from the uneven distribution of investment, with people drifting from the less developed to the more developed provinces in search of work. The 1955/56 population census reveals that at the time of the census some 10 per cent of those classified as 'Western and Eastern Southerners' were living outside of the southern provinces, and that some 15 per cent of those classified as 'Westerners' were living outside of the two western provinces.[133]

The regional imbalance in development created conditions and attitudes among the population in the less developed areas which were to be of political significance. As education in the less developed areas had been relatively limited (especially at the higher levels), few of the inhabitants were in a position to gain government jobs. Those Sudanese who were appointed to administrative posi tions in the less developed 'fringe' generally came from the more

Table 4.10   Regional Distribution of Gross Domestic Investment, 1955/56 (thousand £S)

Provinces	Total investment	Percent of total	Gov. investment	Percent of total	Public corps.	Percent of total	Private enterprise	Percent of total
Khartoum, Northern and Kassala	11 906	56	4 770	64	1 276	32	5 860	60
Blue Nile	4 178	20	1 147	15	721	18	2 310	23
Kordofan and Darfur	3 533	17	1 035	14	1 325	34	1 173	12
Equatoria, Upper Nile and Bahr el-Ghazal	1 616	7	514	7	610	16	492	5
All Sudan	21 233	100	7 466	100	3 932	100	9 835	100

Source: C. H. Harvie and J. G. Kleve, *The National Income of Sudan, 1955/6* (Department of Statistics, Khartoum, 1959), p. 88.

Table 4.11　Regional Distribution of Gross Domestic Product, 1955/56

Provinces	GDP (thousand £S)	Population (thousands)	Per capita Product (£S)
Khartoum, Northern and Kassala	75 788	2 319	33
Blue Nile	86 038	2 070	42
Kordofan and Darfur	83 777	3 091	27
Equatoria, Upper Nile and Bahr el-Ghazal	38 610	2 783	14

Source: C. H. Harvie and J. G. Kleve, *The National Income of Sudan 1955/6*, Department of Statistics, Khartoum, 1959), p. 80.

developed central riverain Sudan. Whereas education had wrough substantial changes in attitudes and customs in the more develope areas (in part by constituting a channel through which nationalis ideas spread), popular attitudes and customs were not subjected t the same transformative influences in the less developed areas. Trad in the latter areas was dominated mainly by merchants from th central riverain Sudan, or else by non-Sudanese companies an individuals. The riverain *jallabah* had, of course, established wide ranging trade networks covering much of western, eastern and south ern Sudan prior to the Condominium, but their ability to maintai and expand these networks depended on increased prosperity in th areas from which they originated – and with which they maintaine contact.

To much of the population in the less developed fringe of Sudan then, the Sudanese state as it emerged at independence seemed distant and alien entity, just as it did in the colonial era. The people of southern Sudan, and most of those in western and eastern Sudan had little access to the benefits which the state bestowed (education health services, remunerative government jobs, etc.). Their mai contact with the state was through those organs which sought to tax administer and control them. The state personnel who faced them i these latter capacities appeared to share little of their cultural o ethnic background.

The political effects which followed from the uneven impact o development varied from one part of the country to another. Th form which such effects took depended on the way in which th economic deprivation interacted with social, historical and politica factors. Where local peoples could identify themselves clearly a belonging to a different ethnic/racial grouping from that of the Arabised population of northern riverain Sudan, regionalist movements – calling for autonomy or independence for a particular ethnic/racial grouping – tended to emerge. Such a tendency was strengthened if there was an historical experience of conflict between local peoples and the northern riverain Sudanese, and if Condominium government policy had given separate treatment to the local peoples concerned.

Where these social, historical and political factors were not present, or were not so marked (as, for example, in the nomadic areas of northern Sudan), the political effects of economic deprivation were different. In such cases, the absence of economic development facilitated the persistence of traditional political structures. Tribal leaderships, not threatened by the emergence of new social forces, could maintain their authority. The tribal following, becoming conscious of a changing world around them in which their own status was falling, looked for reassurance to their traditional leaders.

(b) Regional movements in northern Sudan

Although it was southern Sudan which saw the emergence of the strongest regionalist movements in post-independence Sudan, regionalist movements in the northern Sudan were also to be of some significance. Such movements developed among the Fur of Darfur, the Nuba of southern Kordofan, and the Beja of Kassala province. Even though the social and economic basis for all of these movements was laid down under Condominium rule, however, it was only among the Beja that a concerted movement emerged prior to independence. Regionalist movements among the Fur and Nuba were to come into existence after 1964.

The nature of the Beja's historical experience – the long and peaceful interaction with the peoples of riverain central Sudan, and the absence of any separate treatment under the Condominium – meant that Beja regionalism was unlikely to take a secessionist direction. In the 9th century the Beja had begun to interact with the Arab tribes who entered the Sudan from Egypt and settled and Arabised the riverain areas. The Beja adopted Islam in the course of the 14th and 15th centuries.[134] While the Beja language remained strong in the mid-1950s, spoken as a first language by some 473 000 of the 675 000 Beja enumerated in the 1955/56 census,[135] most of the Beja-speakers could also speak Arabic. The Beja, moreover, shared some of the historical experience of central riverain Sudanese: despite a close association with the Khatmiyyah *tariqah*, the Beja had played a prominent role in the Mahdiyyah.

In addition to the general characteristic of economic deprivation relative to the more developed areas, Beja regionalism was stimulated by some issues specific to the Beja. The development of the Gash scheme enabled some Beja to obtain agricultural tenancies, but it also deprived the nomadic Beja (the majority of the population) of their richest grazing lands. This constituted a significant contributory factor in the severe famines which struck the nomadic Beja in 1925–7, 1930, 1941–2, 1948–9, and 1955–8.[136] The social position of those Beja who sought work in Port Sudan also made the Beja more conscious of their own economic deprivation relative to others. Local administrators in Port Sudan seem to have attempted, largely successfully, to restrict the Beja to the Daim al-Arab on the outskirts of town – an area where the poor living conditions contrasted sharply with the facilities available in the centre of town.[137]

The beginnings of Beja political organisation, in a regional movement, can be traced from 1953. In that year a Beja intellectual, M. D. Isma'il, published a pamphlet entitled *Kifah al-Bija* (The Struggle of the Beja).[138] The pamphlet surveyed the social and economic conditions under which the Beja were living, and pointed to the harmful effects which the development of the Gash scheme and the Gebeit gold mines were having on Beja interests. The comparison which Isma'il drew between the position of southerners and that of the Beja was significant:

> In Eastern Sudan there are tribes which are no less primitive than those of the South. The Beja have not asked, and will not ask, for separation, but they may well ask for something which looks like separation.[139]

The objective now, the pamphlet stated, should be to develop the countryside and its people socially, economically and politically. The pamphlet, and the programme which it put forward, came to constitute a focal point around which the Beja regional movement emerged. Discussion groups were formed among educated Beja, sometimes drawing in Beja workers in Port Sudan, to consider how Beja interests could best be forwarded. As these discussion groups on occasions made representations to local authorities in defence of Beja rights, they gradually evolved towards constituting interest groups.

The elections for the constituent assembly in 1953, and the parliamentary elections of 1958, brought to the constituent assembly and the subsequent parliament a group of members representing predominantly Beja areas. While all of the latter members belonged to national political parties (mainly the PDP), attempts were made to weld them into a regional caucus – for the promotion of Beja interests. A strong move towards putting this caucus on a sound basis, linking it to the regionalist movement outside parliament, was taken when a committee of Beja educated and notables convened a Beja congress in Port Sudan in October 1958. The congress, presided over by Dr 'Ali Muhammad Ballia, sought to draw the attention of Sudan's political leaders to the problems facing the Beja areas. Papers presented to the congress analysed the social and economic problems confronting the Beja. The congress's final resolutions pointed to the distinctive nature of these problems and called for the areas inhabited by the Beja to be granted autonomous status.[140]

The Beja movement seemed set, in October 1958, to make an impact on Sudanese politics. The leaders of both the Umma and People's Democratic parties, seeking to strengthen their positions in parliament, appeared willing to make concessions to the Beja caucus of MPs. In November, however, the parliamentary regime was overthrown by General 'Abbud. Those who had organised the Beja congress were arrested and imprisoned. After 1964, the Beja movement was to re-emerge in a different form – as a political party.

c) The regional movement in southern Sudan

The 'basis of inequality', as outlined earlier, provided the framework within which a regionalist movement developed in southern Sudan. The form and nature of the movement which emerged, however, owed much to other factors. Of critical importance here was the manner in which some of the political structures which had been built up under the Condominium impinged on the southern Sudan.

Some writers, seeking to explain the origins of the civil conflict which was to emerge in Sudan after independence, lay emphasis on the pre-Condominium historical background.[141] In this perspective, the disruption to southern societies caused by slave-raids emanating from northern Sudan – continuing over many centuries, but reaching its climax in the mid-19th century – created a lasting racial antagonism on the part of the negroid southerners towards the Arabs of northern Sudan. A picture is purveyed of 'a fragmented and primitive, but static, people, devastated by the predatory northerner and carrying their fear and anger into the independence period and subsequently into a war of secession against their historical enemy'.[142]

No doubt this element in the historical experience of southern tribes did help to mould the perceptions which southerners had of northern Sudanese at the time of independence. The history of pre-Condominium southern Sudan, however, is complex. To lay primary emphasis on the destructive northern impact may not be justified. The unsettled state of southern Sudan in the 19th century stemmed in part from inter-tribal rivalry, with the larger and more powerful tribes seeking to dominate the smaller tribes.

> The Zande from the south-west were expanding their authority by an organised military force which the smaller tribes could not withstand and from the plains the Dinka (in a characteristically less organised way) were encroaching upon the lands of peoples to the west and south and driving them away. Moreover, within the southern Sudan slavery was already an established, but nonetheless destabilising feature of intra-southern Sudanese relations.[143]

The slave-raiding which emanated from northern Sudan, moreover, was not necessarily organised by northern Sudanese. Especially over the period between 1820 and 1863, a prominent and possibly even predominant part was played by non-Sudanese traders: Europeans, Turks and Egyptians.[144] Some Sudanese writers, furthermore, have stressed that slavery in 19th century Sudan 'had . . . little in common with that which had been operating in the British colonies and the Americas until 1835'.[145] Most slaves in Sudan were brought into domestic service and in that capacity, were integrated closely into the household. They would usually convert to Islam and their children would be assimilated (as freemen) into the Arab community around them.

The historical experience of slavery, then, was not such that inter-racial conflict became inevitable. Southerners, in fact, rather than showing a natural antogonism to the ways and religion of northern Sudanese, often seemed to British Condominium official over-prone to ape Arab ways and to convert to Islam. A Christian missionary, writing in 1908, complained that:

> it is almost fatal, as far as his religion is concerned, for a black man from any of the tribes south of Khartoum to make a sojourn in the capital city of the Sudan, be it ever so short, because it is almost

certain that on his return to his tribe he will announce himself as a Mohamedan.[146]

The determination which was required of Condominium officials in their attempt to eradicate Arab cultural influence in southern Sudan is itself evidence of southerners maintaining a receptive attitude towards influences from the north.

Between 1898 and 1930 Condominium government policy towards the southern Sudan was concerned primarily with the simple maintenance of control. The potential of envisaging or pursuing more far-going objectives was limited. Only a very light administrative presence could be maintained in the southern Sudan and, indeed, 'many years and in some areas decades were to pass before the people actually understood that they were being ruled by Englishmen'.[147] The area was not fully 'pacified' until 1928 when an uprising among the Nuer was suppressed. There was, then, 'little incentive to invest financial or personnel resources in a region of no economic value to the colonial power (either as a market or as a supplier), of no potential for colonial settlement, and of no interest to any competing power'.[148]

Nevertheless, even in this early period the Condominium did pursue policies in the southern Sudan which were distinctively different from those pursued in northern Sudan, and which tended towards creating and maintaining a very different cultural milieu in the South than that which existed in the North. Of crucial importance here was policy towards missionary activity and education. The first two years of Condominium rule in Sudan saw a conflict develop between the missionary societies and the Condominium government. The missionary societies demanded the right to proselytize in any part of Sudan, while the government took a highly cautious attitude towards permitting such activity – fearing for the impact which it would have on opinion within the Islamic world as a whole.[149] A compromise was eventually reached, whereby the societies were allowed freedom of action in the South but not in the North.[150]

Following the compromise agreement between the missionary societies and the Condominium government, each of the major missionary societies with an interest in Sudan was allocated a specific sphere of activity in the South. The American Presbyterian mission was to operate in the Shilluk areas towards the Ethiopian border; the Catholics were to operate in Bahr el-Ghazal and the Zande areas; and the Church Missionary Society was allocated parts of Upper Nile province and the greater part of Equatoria. The government made clear its wish that the societies should lay emphasis on social and educational work,[151] rather than proselytization, but the distinction had little meaning. Mission work and education were to be closely intertwined in southern Sudan: schools formed an integral part of mission activity.

Up to 1922, Christian missions were left wholly responsible for the development of education in the southern Sudan. In 1922 the government began giving some financial assistance to the mission schools. This assistance was substantially increased after 1926, with a view to enabling the mission schools to produce educated personnel suitable for government service (as clerks, teachers, minor administrative officials etc.).[152] With a larger stratum of educated southerners, the government hoped to dispense with the employment of northerners in the administration of the southern provinces. Government assistance to the mission schools was given on condition that the schools accepted government advice with regard to syllabuses and educational practice. Although government-appointed inspectors henceforward monitored education in the South, however, actual control of all the educational institutions there remained with the missionary societies. The first government school in the South, the Atar intermediate school, was not opened until the late 1940s.

From early in the Condominium era, then, education in southern Sudan developed within a framework which was quite separate from that which was being established in northern Sudan. Two characteristics of this mission-based educational structure are worthy of emphasis. First, the cultural milieu of mission education was such that contact with Islam (not unnaturally) and with Arabic was deliberately discouraged. The Rejaf language conference of 1928 made formal a language policy for southern schools which was in practice already being applied (albeit partially): the medium of instruction at the elementary level was to be 'local languages' (Dinka, Bari, Nuer, Latuka, Shilluk and Zande) and at all higher levels, English. Arabic was excluded on the grounds that 'it would open the door for the spread of Islam, Arabise the South, and introduce the northern Sudanese outlook'.[153]

Second, education in southern Sudan remained more limited than in the North. Of particular significance was the lack of emphasis on higher-level education. In 1926, together with numerous 'bush schools', there were 31 elementary schools, two intermediate schools, and one trade school. In 1948 there were 45 boys' and 26 girls' elementary schools (serving about 6600 pupils), and three intermediate schools (serving some 549 pupils).[154] The first secondary school stream in a southern school was that which opened, with the admission of 20 students, at Rumbek in 1950.

General administrative policy also tended, from the outset of the Condominium era, towards creating procedures and structures of authority in the South which were separate and distinct from those emerging in the North. Arrangements were initiated at an early stage to phase out the stationing of northern troops in southern Sudan. It was perceived that northern Sudanese soldiers, through intermarriage with southern women and through the emulation of Muslim customs which their presence engendered, constituted an effective proselytizing agent. An Equatorial Corps, composed of southern soldiers, was formed, and in December 1917 the last garrison composed of northern Sudanese soldiers left the South.[155] In 1918, Sunday, rather than Friday as in the northern Sudan, was made the official day of rest in the South.

The extent to which at least some British Condominium officials were envisaging a future for the South separate from the North is evident from memoranda, presented to the Milner Commission in 1920. A number of these memoranda, presented by senior government officials, make reference to the possibility that the southern provinces could be separated from the North at some future date and linked up with the British-controlled territories in East Africa.[156] The report of the Milner Commission, however, simply suggested some 'measures of decentralisation'. Following publication of the report, the Governor-General instructed the governors of the three southern provinces to hold annual meetings to coordinate policy in the South, and relieved them of the necessity of attending the annual meetings of province governors in Khartoum. The governors of the southern provinces were instructed to keep in touch with their opposite numbers in Kenya and Uganda.[157]

The promulgation of the Passports and Permits Ordinance in 1922 introduced an important new element into government policy in the southern Sudan. The ordinance empowered the Governor-General to declare any part of Sudan a 'closed district'. Ingress into a closed district, whether by Sudanese or non-Sudanese, was made subject to permit. Under the ordinance, the Governor-General could close any part of Sudan to external trade, declare any part of Sudan closed for trading other than by inhabitants of the area, and prohibit the movement of labour from one part of Sudan to another.[158] A Closed Districts Order, promulgated at the same time as the ordinance, declared the whole of the provinces of Equatoria, Upper Nile, Bahr el-Ghazal and Darfur, together with parts of Kordofan, Gezira and Kassala provinces, as closed districts.[159] In 1925 a further measure, the Permits to Trade Order, specified that no non-southerner was permitted to trade in the southern provinces without a permit.[160] While the Closed Districts Order applied to some areas outside the South, the order's principal significance and impact was in the South.

It was, however, only after 1930 that 'Southern Policy' – a strategy aimed at encouraging and safeguarding a distinct and separate cultural identity in southern Sudan – was pursued with any real determination, consistency or coherence. With the South now fully pacified, Condominium government policy could become more explicit. Lugardian principles (i.e. retaining and strengthening native institutions as channels through which colonial authority was exercised), the desire to 'protect' simple and uneducated southerners, the hope that rising nationalism in Sudan could be defused through 'divide and rule' tactics, and simple anti-northern prejudice all played their part in the government's new determination. A confidential memorandum, entitled 'Memorandum on Southern Policy', was drafted by the civil secretary and circulated to senior government officials in January 1930.

Sudan government policy in southern Sudan, the civil secretary's memorandum said, was to 'build up a series of self-contained racial or tribal units with structure and organisation based, to whatever extent the requirements of equity and good government permit, upon indigenous customs, traditional usage and beliefs'.[161] The measures which provincial authorities should be pursuing to this end were the following:

(i) The provision of non-Arabic staff (administrative, clerical and technical).

(ii) The control of immigrant traders from the northern Sudan ('It is the aim of the Government to encourage, as far as possible, Greek and Syrian traders rather than the Gellaba-type. Permits to the latter should be decreased unobtrusively . . .').

(iii) Ensuring that British staff familiarised themselves with the beliefs and customs and the languages of the tribes they administered.

(iv) The use of English where communication in the local vernacular was impossible (' . . . whereas at present Arabic is considered by many natives of the South as the official and, as it were, the fashionable language, the object of all should be to counteract this idea by every practical means').

Between 1930 and 1946 these measures were stringently applied in the three southern provinces. Some government officials in the South deemed the measures unrealistic and harmful, but complied nonetheless.[162] Northern merchants and officials were 'repatriated' to the North, southerners were made to give up Arab names they had adopted, intermarriage between southerners and northerners was discouraged, Arab clothing was banned and (when found) burnt, and a no-man's-land was created between Bahr el-Ghazal and Darfur provinces so as to discourage cultural contact.[163]

Southern policy could only have constituted a coherent strategy in the long term if the ultimate objective was to separate southern from northern Sudan. In such a scenario the South would have been linked, presumably, to British-controlled East Africa. Although some Condominium officials may initially have envisaged this possibility – the South's long-term future was customarily described as 'yet to be determined' – no consensus to this effect emerged in Condominium government circles. The practical difficulties which would ensue from re-structuring the colonial borders, moreover, became increasingly apparent. The British authorities in East Africa expressed themselves 'extremely cool toward any prospect of union with this vast and unproductive land'.[164]

With the rise of nationalist organisation in northern Sudan, some stark choices faced the Condominium government. A primary objective of British policy in Sudan had been to prevent Egypt regaining sovereignty over the country. 'Southern policy' threatened to thwart the achievement of this objective. The resentment which British policy in the southern Sudan engendered among northern Sudanese constituted a prominent factor fostering nationalism, and the more militant nationalists looked increasingly towards Egypt for support. Some of the principal demands raised in the 1942 Graduates' Congress memorandum to the Sudan government related to the southern Sudan: the abolition of the Closed Districts Ordinance, the lifting of restrictions on trade and on the movement of Sudanese within the Sudan, the cancellation of subventions to missionaries, and the unification of syllabuses in northern and southern Sudan.[165] The political dynamics set in train by southern policy, within the context of rising northern Sudanese nationalism, thus seemed capable of delivering at least northern Sudan into the hands of Egypt.

Pressures for a major reconsideration of southern policy grew within the Condominium administration in the early 1940s. A memorandum drafted by the civil secretary in December 1946 marked the formal abandonment of the previous policy. Henceforward, the memorandum stated,

> The policy of the Sudan Government regarding the Southern Sudan is to act upon the facts that the peoples of the Southern Sudan are distinctively African and Negroid but that geography and economics combine (so far as can be seen at the present time) to render them inextricably bound for future development to the Middle Eastern and Arabicised Northern Sudan.[166]

From 1946, therefore, the Condominium government was committed to integrating the South into a unitary Sudan. Although the South could not now be deprived of that distinct cultural identity which had been safeguarded and fostered by earlier policies, the emphasis was placed on conditioning southerners to increased contacts with northerners, drawing the South into national political institutions, and making southern education compatible with the educational system established in the North. With less than seven years before southerners had to cope with the politics of national self-determination, however, it was too late. The possibility of gradual acculturation which could have drawn southerners into the national community, while enabling them to retain local customs and identities, had long since passed.

Southern policy, and the overall basis of regional inequality, fashioned the form in which political organisation emerged in southern Sudan. With higher education very limited, and little economic development of a kind which could stimulate the creation of 'modern' occupational, social or political groupings, political consciousness was slow to arise in southern Sudan. As Howell has written:

> There were not only no councils or representative institutions, but also no clubs or newspapers or professional gatherings. Where interest in politics was acquired it was an informal and random process, often depending upon the tutelary temperament of the local administrator or missionary.[167]

When a southern political elite did eventually emerge in the 1940s, therefore, it was narrowly-based and politically inexperienced. Political organisations based on such an elite were inevitably weak – susceptible to being out-manoeuvred by the more sophisticated political movements of northern Sudan. The elite which emerged, moreover, was culturally distinct from its counterpart in the North. Its members were predominantly Christian by religion and more proficient in English than in Arabic. In human terms, the southern elite had developed in isolation: both practically and intellectually educated southerners had remained far from the nationalist events which had moulded the consciousness and political allegiances of the northern elite from the 1920s onwards.

The nature of the southern elite was to be significant in one further respect to the development of a regionalist movement in southern Sudan. The limited availability of higher education meant that those educated southerners who were in government service (as most members of both the southern and northern elites were) held relatively junior positions. The southern elite, in fact, was composed mainly of junior officials, clerks and teachers. When the government posts held by British and Egyptian officials were Sudanised in 1954–5, therefore, southerners were poorly placed to gain from the process. Of the 734 posts which were Sudanised, in fact, only six went to southerners: four at the Assistant District Commissioner level and two at the *ma'mur* level.[168] Even within the southern Sudan itself, therefore, southerners did not take over the positions of the departing British and Egyptian officials. The latter were replaced, mainly, by northern Sudanese. One externally-supported administration seemed simply to have been replaced by another. The struggle for jobs, linking in with the struggle to give southerners a stronger role in the country's government, coloured the regionalist movement which emerged.

Political organisation in the southern Sudan, then, evolved not as part of the Sudanese nationalist movement, but in reaction to it. It was only when moves towards Sudanese self-determination, impelled by the growth of nationalism in northern Sudan, began to impinge on educated southerners that political organisation in the South began. The first significant political links among educated southerners, in fact, were forged during the Juba Conference of June 1947. The conference had been convened by the civil secretary to discuss the manner in which the South would relate to the new institutional structures being created for Sudan – structures whose proclaimed objective was 'to seek ways and means of associating the Sudanese more closely with the government of their country'.[169] At issue, specifically, was whether the South should be represented in the proposed new Legislative Assembly (as recommended in the report of the Sudan Administrative Conference, March 1947), or whether a separate Advisory Council should be created in the South. There were 17 southerners and five northerners, all hand-picked by the government, who participated in the conference.

Most of the southern participants at the Juba Conference, fearing that the South's underdevelopment left it ill-prepared to articulate and safeguard its own interests, initially opposed southern representation in the Legislative Assembly. They called, instead, for the creation of an Advisory Council for Southern Sudan. By the end of the second day of the conference's proceedings, however, the persuasive arguments of the northern Sudanese participants had convinced them that the South could gain much by representation at the national level.[170] The predominant view was that province councils should be instituted in each of the three southern provinces, and that representatives from these councils should proceed to the Legislative Assembly. On this basis southern representation in the Legislative Assembly, which opened in December 1948, was arranged. The South had thirteen seats in the Assembly.

Although the Juba Conference, and the political fora constituted by the province councils and the Legislative Assembly, created a southern political elite – which sought to articulate southern interests – political organisation still scarcely existed. A Southern Officials' Welfare Committee, formed in 1947, enabled some of the professional grievances of southerners to find expression.[171] No specifically political movement was formed, however, until 1953. It was, ultimately, the Anglo–Egyptian agreement on self-determination for Sudan (1953) which prompted the creation of a southern Sudanese political movement. The British and Egyptian governments had reached agreement on terms which were broadly acceptable to, and following intensive consultations with, the northern Sudanese political elite. The South was not consulted. The sequence of events clearly illustrates the nature of political organisation as it developed in southern Sudan: a reaction to Sudanese nationalism rather than an integral part of it.

III THE ADMINISTRATIVE SYSTEM

The administrative aspects of Condominium rule have been covered in commendable detail in other books.[172] Here we will simply summarise the salient developments. The Anglo–Egyptian agreement of 1898 vested the supreme military and civil command of the Sudan in a single officer, 'the Governor-General of Sudan'. Muddathir Abd al-Rahim sums up the Governor-General's position thus:

> He was to be an Egyptian official, appointed and dismissed by Khedivial Decree. He could not, however, be appointed except on the recommendation of the British government, nor could he be removed without their consent. This, obviously, meant that although the Governor-General was nominally and formally an Egyptian official, he was in fact a British agent.[173]

The first move towards drawing Sudanese into a formal consultative was the creation of an Advisory Council for Northern Sudan in 1943. It consisted of the Governor-General as president, the civil, financial and legal secretaries, and 28 Sudanese members. Of the latter, 18 were elected or nominated from the province councils which had been established in the northern provinces; eight were appointed by the Governor-General; and two were elected by the chamber of commerce. This was superseded in 1948 by a Legislative Assembly, covering the whole Sudan, which remained in existence through to self-government. The assembly contained thirteen members elected by the southern provincial councils, and 52 members directly or indirectly elected to represent the North. An executive council was responsible to the assembly. The development of local government, as opposed to native administration, began on a small scale in 1937, with the passage of three local government ordinances.

5 Sudanese Nationalism and the Attainment of Independence

I   INTRODUCTION

The concern of most earlier writing on the emergence and development of the Sudanese nationalist movement[1] has been to explain how and why Sudanese nationalism came to be divided into 'Sudan for the Sudanese' and 'Unity of the Nile Valley' factions. While this issue is important, and will be given some attention here, the focus of this chapter lies elsewhere.

It will be contended later (in Chapter 6) that the governments which ruled Sudan between 1956 and 1969 sought no fundamental change in the social and economic structures which had been built up under Condominium rule. This is hardly surprising: governments were dominated by those social groupings which had benefited most under the Condominium. These social groupings had a natural interest in maintaining the economic and social framework from which they had benefited. Economic and social policy between 1956 and 1969, therefore, can only be understood with reference to the social characteristics of the movement which brought about the country's independence and which set the pattern for post-independence politics.

The concern of this chapter, then, is to examine the social character of the Sudanese nationalist movement. The focus is on how the values and objectives of the 'incipient bourgeoisie' came to predominate within the movement, such that the leaders who rose to positions of influence gave attention almost exclusively to political liberation – rather than seeking the dismantlement of the pattern of society and economy created or maintained by colonial rule.

While it may in retrospect seem inevitable that Sudanese nationalism took the form which it did, this is not the case. At some critical periods in the movement's development (especially in 1924 and in the early 1950s) a radical nationalism began to emerge, where the radical nationalists were inimical not only to the colonial rulers but also to those Sudanese who were deemed to be benefiting unduly from Condominium rule. Pressure for economic and social liberation, as well as for political liberation, emanated from radical nationalists. Given the deprivation of the rural and urban poor and the economic frustrations of the 'intermediate strata' (as described in Chapter 3), and the trend towards establishing social movements and organisations which sought to protect the interests of some of the less privileged sections of the population (as described in Chapter 4), a strong basis for radical nationalism seemed to exist.

The role played by 'graduates' in the Sudanese nationalist movement is regarded as critical in most writings on this subject. The account given here also gives prominence to the role of graduates, while stressing that this role can only be understood with reference to other groupings with which graduates allied themselves. Graduate nationalism, in short, could move in different directions depending on the links which graduates developed with other elements in society. The term 'graduates', as used in this context, refers to individuals who had emerged from 'institutions of a standard higher than the elementary'.[2] With an educational system which was geared primarily towards training personnel for government service, the majority of graduates were members of the 'middle-level and senior salariat' discussed in Chapter 3.

The social position of graduates gave the graduate grouping a certain natural unity and coherence. The narrowness of the educational system, culminating usually at Gordon College, created close personal links among the limited number who emerged; graduates had a common perception of themselves as an educated and enlightened elite, leading the Sudanese population away from traditionalism into a more modern world; and their employment in the Condominium administration gave them a good knowledge of how the state worked, a belief that they could govern the state as effectively as the British, and a desire to improve their position collectively against the foreigner.

Other factors, however, tended to divide the graduates. As graduates moved up in the government service, reaching positions of responsibility and enjoying the benefits which accrued, they naturally became less inclined towards radical nationalism. While they retained nationalist objectives, therefore, the tactics they adopted were often different from those used by younger graduates. They tended, moreover, to seek different kinds of allies within Sudanese society.

What was in reality a division based on different social positions (younger graduates as 'intermediate strata', older as 'incipient bourgeoisie') found expression as a division between old and young.

II PRIMARY RESISTANCE

The primary resistance to Condominium rule in Sudan, involving armed resistance on the part of tribal or religious-based groups who had never been fully 'pacified' by the Condominium, is sometimes portrayed as an integral part of Sudanese nationalism. Such resistance, however, had little in common with, and virtually no effect on, the Sudanese nationalist movement which developed from 1920 onwards. The graduates and army officers who laid the basis for Sudanese nationalism were inspired by the nationalist activity in Egypt, not by those southern tribes which were still staging sporadic uprisings. Primary resistance may be important as an indication that Sudanese people did not take easily to colonialism, but not as a direct contribution to Sudanese nationalism.

Primary resistance took three forms. First, *nabi 'Isa* movements emerged in the northern Sudan, among parts of the population which had been strongly influenced by Mahdism. Such movements were based on the belief, emanating from Islamic eschatology, that the anti-Christ (*al-dajjal*) who had destroyed the rule of the Mahdi and his successor would in due course be defeated by Jesus (*nabi 'Isa*) descending from heaven and leading the Muslims to victory. A number of self-professed *nabi 'Isa*s arose in the years following 1898. Even the more successful of these, however, only managed to secure a very localised support. The principal *nabi 'Isa* uprisings were those staged by Muhammad al-Amin in Tegale (1903); Adam Wad Muhammad in Sennar (1904); 'Abd al-Qadir Wad Habbuba in the Gezira (1908);[3] Faki Najm al-Din in Kordofan (1912); and Ahmad 'Umar in Darfur (1915).[4]

Second, sporadic tribal uprisings took place in the southern Sudan and in the Nuba mountains over the first 30 years of Condominium rule. Of particular importance was the Nuer resistance, led by Dengkur and Diu (1899–1908); the Zande resistance under Sultan Yambio (1900–1905); the scattered but continuing incidents in the Nuba mountains (going up to 1918); the risings among the Agar Dinka (1901) and the Atwot Dinka (1903–10); and the widely-based rising among the Nuer in 1927.[5] The Condominium authorities suppressed these uprisings mainly by despatching punitive expeditions, with occasional aerial bombardments in the period which followed the First World War.

Third, Sultan 'Ali Dinar of Darfur, who had been recognised by the Condominium government in 1900 as 'independent but tributary', heeded the Turkish call in 1915 for the expulsion of the infidel British from Muslim territory. In April 1915 he renounced his obligations to the Condominium government and prepared himself for a military conflict. Units of the Egyptian army in Sudan were sent against him and in the ensuing battle 'Ali Dinar was killed. On 1 January 1917 Darfur eventually became a province of the Anglo–Egyptian Sudan.

III THE 1924 UPRISING

Nationalist organisation in Sudan was initiated by graduates who were deeply influenced by the 1919 disturbances in Egypt – and, indeed, by the historical experience of Egyptian nationalism as a whole. In 1920 a group of young graduates, predominantly junior officials in government service, formed a Sudanese Union Society. The society's aim was to strengthen the nationalist consciousness of Sudanese, partly through literary activities and partly through directly disseminating views critical of the Condominium government. The need for secrecy caused the founders to organise their society within a structure of five-man cells. Each member of the initial five-man cell recruited four others to form a new cell, and this process was then repeated at lower levels. While any member might have some knowledge about two or three other cells besides his own, therefore, it was intended that none but the founding members would know of the whole structure.[6]

The members of the founding cell had much in common. All five of them were proficient poets or literary critics, playing an active role in the Graduates' Club in Omdurman.[7] Four of the five ('Ubaid Haj al-Amin, Tawfiq Salih Jibril, Mohi al-Din Jamal Abu Saif, and Ibrahim Badri) were junior government officials,[8] while one (Sulaiman Kishah) was an educated merchant.[9] The four who were junior government officials had all passed through Gordon College. All five were 'of good family': 'Ubaid Haj al-Amin was the nephew of two of Sudan's leading *'ulama*; Tawfiq Salih Jibril was the son of a leading Omdurman merchant; Mohi al-Din Jamal Abu Saif was the son of an

Egyptian-born chief clerk; and Ibrahim Badri and Sulaiman Kishah both came from families well known in commerce. As might be expected, the founding five recruited members of a similar social and educational background to themselves. Bakhiet lists some of these:

> . . . Khalafallah Khalid, a well-born sub-*ma'mur*; the school-teacher and literary critic al-Amin 'Ali Madani; Makkawi Ya'qub, a clerk and poet; the army officer 'Abdallah Khalil, who became prime minister in 1956; Muhammad Salih Shinqiti, another sub-*ma'mur*; Babikir Qabbani, another postal clerk; Khalil Farah, perhaps the most celebrated singer and musician of his time; and Muhammad al-'Umarabi, who was unusual in being educated, not at Gordon College, but in Islamic studies at Omdurman mosque.[10]

The society's literary activities consisted mainly of poetry readings, literary festivals and drama. On occasions these activities were pursued in the provinces, but the major part were put on at the Graduates' Club in Omdurman. The 'direct dissemination of views critical of the Condominium government' involved circulating leaflets within Sudan and sending anti-British poems and articles to Egyptian newspapers for publication. As Egyptian newspapers reached Khartoum twice every week, the poems and articles would in due course find their way back to Sudan. The society also sought (not always successfully) to facilitate the travel of Sudanese students to Egypt for further education.

The Sudanese Union Society's leaflets and articles placed considerable emphasis on the common struggle of Egyptians and Sudanese, seen as joint victims of British colonial oppression. The articles written for the Egyptian press, especially those composed by 'Ubaid Haj al-Amin, often went beyond this and stressed the continuing need for political unity between the two countries. In an open letter to Prince 'Umar Tusun,[11] published in *Al-Ahram* on 21 November 1922, 'Ubaid declared that the Sudanese national movement 'supports the Egyptian nation . . . and opposes the partition of Egypt and the Sudan under any circumstances.'[12]

There were, from the outset, two tendencies within the leadership of the society: some gave primacy to the literary activities, while others were more intent on political action (producing leaflets, writing articles for the Egyptian press, etc.). Of the five founding members, 'Ubaid Haj al-Amin (generally regarded as the leader of the society) was most committed to political action, while the remaining four were predominantly 'literary activists'.[13] Most of the society's political activities between 1920 and 1923, in fact, had been organised by 'Ubaid.

In 1923, the differences between the two tendencies caused an open split in the society. Three years of literary activity and covert political action had, 'Ubaid and the political activists believed, adequately prepared the ground for a direct confrontation with the Condominium government. They envisaged a campaign involving strikes and demonstrations. The literary activists baulked at involvement in such an undertaking. In mid-1923, therefore, 'Ubaid and the political activists withdrew from the society and created a new organisation committed to directly confronting the Condominium government: the White Flag League (WFL).

The campaign envisaged by the White Flag League required mobilising a wider part of the population than the mainly graduate elite which had been gathered in the Sudanese Union Society. Seeking a means to broaden support for the new organisation, 'Ubaid turned to 'Ali 'Abd al-Latif, a dismissed army lieutenant, well known to the urban Sudanese population for his ardent nationalism. In 1922 'Ali 'Abd al-Latif had written an allegedly seditious article, intending it for publication in *al-Hadarah* newspaper. Although the editor of *al-Hadarah* declined to publish the article, 'Ali 'Abd al-Latif was arrested, tried and imprisoned for one year. The article, entitled 'Claim of the Sudanese Nation', demanded self-determination for the Sudanese, more education, the ending of the sugar monopoly, and higher posts for Sudanese in the administration. The Egyptian press had given considerable publicity to 'Ali 'Abd al-Latif's trial, such that he emerged from prison clothed in an aura of popular heroism.

'Ali 'Abd al-Latif's social and occupational background gave him direct access, through personal contacts, to parts of society whose support was needed for the political struggle which lay ahead. On the one hand, as a graduate of the Military School and a former army officer, he could move easily in army circles, spreading the spirit of opposition to British rule among soldiers and officers. On the other hand, born of a Dinka mother and a Nuba father (both ex-slaves), his social roots lay in the 'black'[14] community of the Three Towns area – that de-tribalised and fairly numerous section of the urban populace, of southern or Nuba origin, whose vulnerability to politicisation was clearly recognised by the British.[15] The report of the Ewart Commission, established to enquire into the events of 1924, described 'Ali 'Abd al-Latif disparagingly but accurately as:

> a young savage who had begun life by holding horses for halfpence . . . who found himself a military cadet in his teens, and at the age of 22 became a commissioned officer and so was translated at a bound from the dregs to the cream of local society.[16]

'Ali 'Abd al-Latif was given the presidency of the WFL, with 'Ubaid as his deputy. The remaining three members of the initial five-man cell, all postal clerks, were Hasan al-Sharif, Hasan Salih al-Matba'ji and Salih Abd al-Qadir.[17] The league's constitution stated its aim as to 'serve the national ideal in the Sudan and to refuse to be separated from Egypt'.[18] The commitment to Egypt was demonstrated further by the league's insignia: a map of the Nile valley, with an Egyptian flag in one corner.[19] The struggle to remove the British presence from Sudan evidently required a stronger link between Sudanese nationalists and Egypt.[20]

By the beginning of June 1924, the White Flag League had created an organisation and a basis of support suitable for launching its projected campaign of demonstrations. Its 'hard core' membership at this time may have comprised no more than 150 individuals,[21] but this hard core stood at the centre of a more extensive network of contacts. The network drew in a diverse collection of individuals and groupings. In short, the wider social support which 'Ubaid and his mainly graduate following had set out to create was now in existence. The league:

> was represented in many provincial towns and some district headquarters, and had established connections with groups of Sudanese army officers, officials, students, merchants and artisans, and with those in the Gordon College, the Military School in Khartoum and the Omdurman Mosque Institute.[22]

Government intelligence sources indicated that the league's main strength lay in public employees at the 7th and 8th grades (the lower clerical category), and that league activists were mostly aged between 17 and 25.[23] Urban artisan elements, however, were also prominent:

> Through 'Ali Ahmad Salih, a would-be trade union organiser, the League . . . recruited Sudanese artisans, tailors, carpenters, shoemakers, and these together with teachers and disgruntled or dis-

missed government employees played leading parts in the subsequent demonstrations.[24]

The campaign of demonstrations and 'direct action' against the Condominium government covered the five months which followed June 1924. Some 150 incidents took place over this period, with most of the major northern Sudanese towns experiencing at least one significant confrontation between demonstrators and the forces of order deployed by the Condominium government.[25] Over the first two months, the demonstrations involved only civilians and followed a common pattern:

> [All of the demonstrations] were led by a white flag with a map of the Nile in the middle and the Egyptian flag in a corner; all of them shouted 'Long Live Egypt' and for loyalty to its King; all of them were led by five League members composed typically of a Sudanese junior official together with four artisans or small retailers; and typically the leaders were arrested and given six months, the rest being dispersed by the police with batons or flats of swords.[26]

Early in July, 'Ali 'Abd al-Latif was arrested and imprisoned. By the end of that month 'Ubaid was also under arrest. A steady campaign of civilian demonstrations, organised by other members of the league, nevertheless continued through July and into early August. These demonstrations drew their strength and vitality from the ease with which the urban populace (artisans, workers, clerks, unemployed youths, etc.) could be drawn in to participate.

In the course of August, however, the character of the disturbances changed. The severity of government countermeasures, involving the almost inevitable arrest and imprisonment of those who organised demonstrations, had begun to cripple the league's ability to organise civilian demonstrations. But the spirit of opposition had now taken hold within the Sudanese battalions of the Egyptian army. On 9 August cadets in the Military School mutinied and marched in a protest demonstration to Kober prison, where 'Ali 'Abd al-Latif was imprisoned. Although the cadets were eventually persuaded to surrender their arms, and their leaders were arrested, the mutiny initiated a new, army-based, phase in the resistance movement. Over the period between August and October a number of minor mutinies in the Sudanese battalions occurred, organised by White Flag League supporters among soldiers and officers.

A major mutiny eventually erupted in November 1924, sparked off by the assassination in Cairo of the Governor-General of Sudan, Sir Lee Stack, and by the British government's subsequent demand that all Egyptian troops in Sudan be withdrawn forthwith. The Sudanese mutineers had, apparently, counted on support from Egyptian army units based in Khartoum North. Such support, however, was not forthcoming and the mutiny was put down by British troops, with considerable loss of life. By the end of 1924, the White Flag League had in effect been destroyed, bringing this phase in the development of Sudanese nationalism to a rather abrupt end.

The Sudanese nationalist movement between 1920 and 1924, then, developed out of a predominantly literary society among the graduate elite. Radical graduates, splitting away from the Sudanese Union Society, mobilised parts of the wider urban populace in a confrontation with the Condominium government. The confrontation which emerged, however, was not simply between Sudanese nationalists and an alien government. As the radical nationalist movement grew, drawing artisans, workers, clerks, soldiers and officers into demonstrations, it engendered an increasingly concerted and hostile response from the Sudanese 'establishment' – the tribal and religious leaders, the major merchants and some of the senior graduates.[27] No doubt differences over the relative benefits of cooperation with Britain or with Egypt constituted one aspect of the conflict. An aspect of social confrontation, however, was also clearly present: the establishment defending its relatively privileged position against the upstarts who had little to lose. Articles in *al-Hadarah* newspaper, owned by Sudan's three most prominent religious leaders, gave a consistently disparaging view of the social composition of the White Flag League. One such article read:

> The league should know . . . that the country is insulted when its smallest and humblest men, without status in society, pretend to come forward and express the country's opinion.[28]

The article from which the above quotation is taken went on to complain that the dust which the petty riff-raff was stirring up was 'disturbing the commercial class and the financial side', and appealed to all true patriots to 'quell the pro-Egyptian street boys'. Another article baldly stated: 'Low is the nation if it can be led by 'Ali 'Abd al-Latif'.[29]

The suppression of the White Flag League in 1924 led to a protracted quiescence in the Sudanese nationalist movement. An organised movement did not re-emerge until the late 1930s. Many factors explain the lengthy period of retreat: government policy after 1924 was deliberately geared towards strengthening the position of tribal leaders and diminishing the prominence of the graduate class, deemed unreliable; the radical nationalist leadership of the White Flag League had been dispersed (some chose to exile themselves to Egypt; some were imprisoned for lengthy terms, and some died or were executed in or after the disturbances);[30] the failure of Egyptian forces to support the Sudanese mutineers of 1924 had disillusioned some formerly pro-Egyptian nationalists, encouraging them to seek more gradualist means towards Sudanese self-determination;[31] and the withdrawal of Egyptian troops from Sudan, together with the enforced return to Egypt of many Egyptian officials, removed a potent channel for the transmission of anti-colonial political consciousness. Some of the graduates who had been active in the 1924 disturbances, moreover, made their peace with the government and rose within government service, becoming inevitably less susceptible to militancy.

When nationalist organisation re-emerged in Sudan in the late 1930s, it was shaped by new forces, and by a new generation of graduates. Two developments which had occurred during the quiescent years were to constitute important influences on the character of the re-born movement: the creation of quasi-political groupings around some leading figures of the Sudanese establishment, and the formation of literary study groups among the younger generation of graduates.

IV THE CREATION OF QUASI-POLITICAL GROUPINGS AROUND ESTABLISHMENT FIGURES, 1920s AND 1930s

In the late 1920s and early 1930s, each of Sudan's two main religious leaders, Sayyid 'Abd al-Rahman al-Mahdi and Sayyid 'Ali al-Mirghani, began to draw around himself a coterie of educated Sudanese – mainly graduates in government service, but also comprising some educated merchants and private contractors. The members of these coteries played a number of diverse roles: in some respects confidants, in other respects supporters or admirers, and sometimes business advisers, partners, managers or simply contacts. The coterie as a whole constituted a web of relationships, where coterie-members tended to develop similar viewpoints and possibly (in the longer term) to coordinate their activities outside of the coterie.

These coteries were the instruments through which the attitudes and objectives of educated Sudanese (especially those of the senior graduates) were shaped and influenced by the religious/commercial establishment. So also, of course, were the objectives pursued by the religious leaders affected, and their interests enhanced, by gaining a substantial following among the educated elite.

The two religious leaders, it should be recalled, not only wielded religious authority. Considerable economic power also lay in their hands: they were active economic entrepreneurs (Sayyid 'Abd al-Rahman rather more than Sayyid 'Ali), with widespread contacts among the pump-scheme owners and merchants. Family and religious links drew major merchants towards the religious leaders, buttressing the latter's involvement with the commercial sector. The interests of the commercial sector, therefore, inevitably found expression in the coteries around Sayyid 'Abd al-Rahman and Sayyid 'Ali.

The aspect of the coteries which has attracted most attention in the past is their role in promoting division within the Sudanese political elite: Mahdist against Mirghanist. Of equal importance, however, is the role they played in welding together an alliance of senior graduates, religious leaders and merchants, on both sides of the Mahdist/Mirghanist divide. The strength of this coalition of interests, benefiting from the popular following of the religious leaders, the economic power of the commercial establishment, and the positions of administrative influence of the senior graduates, was considerable. The quasi-political groupings into which the coteries developed were well placed to influence the nationalist movement when it re-emerged in the 1930s.

Before describing further the development of the coteries around Sayyid 'Abd al-Rahman and Sayyid 'Ali, however, we need to examine how and why these two leaders had been able to achieve their prominence – enjoying, by the 1920s, positions which combined political influence, economic power and religious authority. The educated Sudanese who joined their coteries, after all, were attracted mainly by the leaders' prominence, and by the benefits which could ensue from associating with them, not by religious allegiance.[32] The roots of the two leaders' prominence must be sought in Condominium policy – specifically, in the means whereby the government, early in the Condominium era, sought to tighten its control over the recently acquired territory.

Condominium government control over Sudan's vast territory and scattered population could not depend exclusively, or even mainly, on British officials. There were too few for this task, even when complemented by Egyptian or Sudanese officials in junior positions. The government, therefore, sought to create a Sudanese 'establishment' with which it could cooperate (or collaborate, depending on one's perspective). This was done by reinforcing the authority of those it chose to regard as the 'natural leaders of Sudanese society'. A statement of Lord Cromer, shortly before the re-conquest, is indicative of the approach adopted:

> In every country, and more especially in a country where the reformer is alien . . ., you cannot afford to alienate . . . the upper classes.[33]

Kitchener, in a circular to governors one year after the re-conquest, made the approach rather more precise:

> The task before us all . . . is to acquire the confidence of the people . . . by being thoroughly in touch with the better class of native, through whom we may hope gradually to influence the whole population.[34]

The development of the Sudanese establishment, prior to the Second World War, passed through three stages: 1898–1915, 1915–24, and 1924–38.

Between 1898 and 1915 Condominium government policy identified the *'ulama*, the orthodox religious leaders, as crucial agents in obtaining popular acceptance of Condominium rule. Believing that the *turuq* were inherently prone to fanaticism (with revelations, visions and notions of *barakah* acting as instruments through which leaders could stir up the populace), the government turned to the rival school within the Sudanese Islamic tradition: the *'ulama*. Rooted in Sunni orthodoxy, the *'ulama*:

> had no central organisation, laid no claim to *barakah*, owed their personal influence locally to scholarship and piety, . . . were quietist in politics and busied themselves chiefly with administering the Holy Law.[35]

By drawing the *'ulama* into a collaborative relationship with the government, therefore, Condominium rule could be 'clothed in the moral authority of orthodox Islam'.

In 1902 the government established a Board of *'Ulama*, centred at Omdurman mosque, to advise on religious affairs. The board's purpose was clearly, albeit confidentially, outlined by a senior Condominium official:

> The Board has been appointed with the object of enabling Government to deal with these religious questions as, ostensibly, the approved agents of orthodox Mohammedanism, rather than as a Government acting on its own initiative. The attitude of Government towards the religion of the country is visibly strengthened in being supported in its measures by the highest orthodox religious opinions in the land.[36]

'Religious affairs' inevitably strayed into the political sphere. The board gave the stamp of Islamic legitimacy to some key government policies, labelled as heresy the *nabi 'Isa*[37] risings against Condominium rule, and, by running the *shari'ah* courts, enabled the government to portray its legal structures as genuinely Islamic. Among the most prominent members of the *'ulama* establishment prior to the First World War were Muhammad Mustafa al-Mirghani (the grand *qadi*), al-Tayyib Hashim (the grand *mufti*) and 'Abd al-'Aal Qasim Hashim (president of the Board of *'Ulama*).

The *'ulama*, however, were not the only 'natural leaders' favoured with government support between 1898 and 1915. While the *turuq* were generally viewed with suspicion, some *tariqah* leaders were nevertheless deemed reliable. Sayyid 'Ali al-Mirghani, of the Khatmiyyah, and Sharif Yusuf al-Hindi, of the Hindiyyah, both benefited from government support – in part through the bestowal of honorary distinctions, in part through direct material assistance.[38] Major merchants (carrying influence, as 'urban notables', on townspeople) and tribal leaders in the countryside were also drawn into a collaborative relationship with government. Such, then, was the Sudanese establishment which the Condominium government patronised and strengthened in the early period.[39]

Mahdism, it should be noted, remained suspect. While the government did pay Sayyid 'Abd al-Rahman (and other Mahdist notables) a small pension, and also provided him after 1910 with a limited quantity of land, the *sayyid* was not drawn into the collaborative establishment. With his movements watched and restricted, he was tolerated more than supported.

Between 1915 and 1924 a new emphasis in government policy emerged. While not abandoning support for any of the strata with which it had previously cooperated, the government began to pay considerably more attention to the *turuq* and to draw Sayyid 'Abd al-Rahman (together with some other prominent Mahdists) into the collaborative establishment. There were two main reasons for this. First, the Condominium authorities had come to understand more fully the real nature of Sudanese religious allegiances. They were now aware that the *turuq* and the *ansar* movement, rather than the *'ulama*, constituted the principal *foci* of these allegiances. Second, the Turkish government's attempt to mobilise Islamic opinion against the British presence in the Middle East, initiated in 1915, impelled the Condominium authorities to widen and deepen their support in religious circles. The *turuq*, imbued with Sudanese particularism rather than orthodox Islamic universalism, were likely to prove more resistant to appeals from Istanbul than were the *'ulama*. The Mahdists, whose campaign against Turko–Egyptian rule in the 19th century had been legitimised by propagating a view of the Turks as renegades from the Islamic faith, were perhaps the least vulnerable element to Turkish propaganda.

The main beneficiary of the new government policy was, with little doubt, Sayyid 'Abd al-Rahman al-Mahdi. The government's initially restrictive policy towards the *sayyid* had already been relaxed prior to the First World War. In 1908 he had been permitted to take up residence in Omdurman and had been given land to cultivate (for the upkeep of himself and his family) on Aba Island. In 1910 he showed his appreciation of the government's more relaxed attitude by making a public speech supportive of the Condominium administration.[40] It was, however, the exigencies of the First World War which brought about the major change in the relationship between the Condominium and Sayyid 'Abd al-Rahman. Aware of the government's desire to counter the propaganda emanating from Istanbul, the *sayyid* offered to mobilise support for the British military effort in the Middle East by touring parts of the country where the population retained a strong Mahdist commitment. The Condominium authorities readily agreed and the *sayyid* proceeded, through 1915, on a series of visits and tours, concentrating on the Baggara in the White Nile area. The fallacies inherent in the Ottoman sultan's call for a *jihad* against the British infidels were duly exposed.[41]

Sayyid 'Abd al-Rahman's move was astute. It enabled him not only to prove his worth to the Condominium government as a valuable collaborator, but also to emerge as the natural and accepted leader of the *ansar*. He took the opportunity to establish his own authority within the Mahdist movement, usually appointing *manadib* (representatives) in the areas he visited – charged with responsibility for organising the Mahdist community and for collecting *zakat*. Benefiting from further land grants during and after the First World War, and enjoying both government support and a position of acknowledged leadership in Mahdist circles, then, Sayyid 'Abd al-Rahman entered the post First World War period as a prominent figure in the Sudanese establishment.

The three best-known leaders of Sudanese popular Islam – Sayyid 'Ali al-Mirghani, Sharif Yusuf al-Hindi and Sayyid 'Abd al-Rahman al-Mahdi – thus stood at the centre of the collaborative establishment between 1915 and 1924. Around this establishment core were gathered the other *tariqah* leaders, the *'ulama*, the merchants, the tribal leaders and some senior graduates. These strata, whose members had been active in rallying Sudanese opinion to support Britain during the First World War, played an equally significant role after the war in countering the anti-British campaigns mounted by Egyptian and nationalist Sudanese groupings and organisations.

In 1919 a petition to the Governor-General, organised by the *tariqah* leaders, the *'ulama*, prominent merchants and some tribal leaders, deplored the disturbances in Egypt and the attacks which were being made on British troops and installations there.[42] The object, evidently, was to dissuade those Sudanese who were intent on following a similar path from doing so. In 1920 the three *sayyids* established a newspaper, *al-Hadarah*, through which they hoped both to lead and to shape Sudanese opinion. As has already been noted, the paper pursued a rather combative course to this end during 1924. A further petition, entitled the 'Petition of the Sound Elements' was organised in June 1924 – bolstering the government's position at a time when the activities of the White Flag League were posing a threat to public order. The list of signatories of the petition (Table 5.1) gives a clear picture of the Sudanese establishment at that time, with a few notable omissions.[43]

Between 1924 and 1938 the government's collaborative links with prominent Sudanese remained within the same framework as had existed prior to 1924. A different emphasis, however, did develop. The 1924 disturbances led the government to seek to strengthen

Table 5.1   List of Signatories to the Petition of Sound Elements, June 1924

Names	Occupations
1. 'Abd al-Rahman al-Mahdi	Religious leader
2. Al-Tayyib Hashim	*Mufti* of Sudan
3. Isma'il al-Azhari (senior)	Inspector of *mahkamah*s
4. Ahmad al-Sayyid al-Fil	Inspector of *mahkamah*s
5. Abu al-Qasim Ahmad Hashim	President, Board of *'Ulama*
6. Abu Shamah 'Abd al-Mahmud	Qadi, Khartoum province
7. 'Abd al-Rahman al-Sayyid al-'Awad	*'Umda*, Omdurman
8. 'Abbas Rahmatallah	*Shaikh* of the Ja'aliyin in Omdurman
9. Sadiq 'Isa Sa'ad	Merchant and property-owner, Omdurman
10. Muhammad Qambur	Leading merchant, Khartoum
11. Babiker al-Haj al-Shafi'	Leading merchant, Omdurman
12. Muhammad 'Ali Karamallah	Leading merchant, Khartoum
13. Husain Sharif	Editor of *al-Hadarah* newspaper
14. Hamad Muhammad Bairaqdar	Merchant and property-owner, Omdurman
15. Al-Hajjaz Sulaiman	School headmaster
16. 'Ali Abu Qisaisah	Gordon College teacher
17. 'Ali al-Mahdi	Eldest living son of the Mahdi
18. Qariballah Salih	Leader of the Sammaniyyah *tariqah*
19. 'Uthman Salih	Leading merchant, Omdurman
20. Muhammad al-Mubarak 'Abd al-Mahmud	Religious notable, descendant of the Mahdi's first teacher
21. 'Abd al-Aziz 'Uthman al-Qabbani	Merchant and property-owner, Omdurman
22. Abu Bakr 'Abdallah	School headmaster
23. Muhammad al-Amin al-Qurashi	*Qadi*, Hassaheisa. Religious notable.
24. Haj al-Khidir 'Ali Kamair	Leading merchant, Khartoum
25. Babikir Badri	Inspector of Education
26. 'Ali Muhammad al-Mardi	*'Umda*, Khartoum
27. Ahmad al-'Uthman Dulaib	*Khalifah* of the Dowalaib of Kordofan in Omdurman
28. Ahmad Ibrahim	*'Umdah* of Tuti island
29. Babikir Jamail	*'Umdah* of the Danagla in Omdurman
30. Hamid 'Uthman Ibrahim	*'Umdah* of Khartoum North
31. Muhi al-Din al-Amin	*Khalifah* of the Shaikh Khojali mosque in Khartoum North
32. 'Abd al-Qadir 'Umar	Notable, member of Khartoum North municipal council

Table 5.1 continued

33. 'Uthman Wanni	Leading merchant, Omdurman
34. Ahmad al-Badawi	Membe. of the Board of *'Ulama*
35. Bashir Nasr	*'Umdah*, in Khartoum Province
36. Ahmad Hasan 'Abd al Mun'im	Leading merchant, Omdurman
37. Salih Jibril	Merchant and property-owner, Omdurman
38. Ahmad Siwar al-Dahab	Merchant and property-owner, Omdurman

Source: Sudan Government Archives, Palace/4/10 File no. 705.

further the role of the tribal leaders, in an attempt to limit the employment of politically unreliable graduates in local administration. Support for the three *sayyids* remained strong, for most of the time, but government policy no longer reserved for them the pre eminent attention which had been their due before 1924. The balance of government attention, in short, swung away from the *sayyids* and towards the tribal leaders.[44]

Some unease, moreover, began to creep into the relationship between Sayyid 'Abd al-Rahman al-Mahdi and the government Government officials had become aware that the powerful economic and political position which the *sayyid* now enjoyed could in time constitute a threat to the government. Backed by a strong and militant following, he might be tempted to launch a bid for national leadership. The encouragement which the government had given and continued to give, to the expansion of Sayyid 'Abd al-Rahman' economic undertakings had been intended to transform a potential political leader into a businessman.[45] Instead, the economic under takings, ably and profitably managed by the *sayyid*, were buttressing his political influence.

Although Sayyid 'Abd al-Rahman continued to constitute a key part of the collaborative establishment, there were periods when government policy towards him became distinctly cool. In 1935, for example, the *sayyid* established a new newspaper, *al-Nil*, which took a critical line towards some aspects of Condominium policy: the Gezira scheme was attacked as a 'foreign enterprise', and the govern ment was criticised for permitting the commercial sector to fall under foreign domination.[46] The publication of *al-Nil* seems to have con vinced the government of the need for urgent action to limit the *sayyid*'s wealth and influence. This objective was pursued with some determination over the three years which followed. The cooperative assistance which government bodies had previously extended to Sayyid 'Abd al-Rahman's economic undertakings was withdrawn, and the government even attempted to deprive him of some of the *durah*-growing land which he had previously been allocated. Douglas Newbold, then Governor of Kordofan, contrasted the 'fundamental loyalty' of the Khatmiyyah *tariqah* with the 'fundamental disloyalty' of the Mahdists. The *sayyid*'s network of *manadib* and *khulafa* in the rural areas was closely watched.[47]

Such attempts as the government did make after 1935 to limit Sayyid 'Abd al-Rahman's wealth and influence, however, were too little and too late seriously to affect the *sayyid*'s position. By 1926 the income from his economic undertakings was already running at some £E10 000 per annum. In 1935, strengthened economically by the new opportunities made available to him by the government in the intervening years,[48] Sayyid 'Abd al-Rahman's income exceeded £E30 000.[49] He could also dispose, albeit not to his personal material benefit, of the monies which were accruing to him through *zakat*.[50]

This, then, is the background against which coteries developed around Sayyid 'Abd al-Rahman and Sayyid 'Ali (and to a lesser extent Sharif Yusif) in the late 1920s and early 1930s. Sayyid 'Abd al-Rahman, attempting to spread his influence among educated Sudanese, was the first to establish a coterie. The *sayyid* had developed some contacts among senior graduates prior to 1924, and had used Husain Sharif (his nephew) and *al-Hadarah* newspaper as instruments through which to dissuade graduates from supporting the White Flag League. It was, however, the impact of the 1924 disturbances which convinced him of the likely future political significance of the graduate grouping. Moving with considerable caution, due to the inevitable suspicions which any overt attempt by the *sayyid* to win support among graduates would raise in government circles, Sayyid 'Abd al-Rahman began in 1926 to establish wider contacts among educated Sudanese. In part this was done by supporting activities and institutions favoured by graduates:

> He made donations to charity funds and to schools . . . Donations included a daily gift of one hundred loaves to the Omdurman Mosque School (the Mahad) and £150 to the Ahfad School of Sheikh Babikr Bedri . . . He made plans for the foundation of a public library in Omdurman and for a lodging house for students at the Omdurman Mosque School.[51]

In part it was done by fostering cordial relations with the Graduates
Club in Omdurman. Muhammad 'Ali Shawqi, who held the club's
presidency for most of the late 1920s and early 1930s, seems to have
constituted a conduit through which many prominent graduates were
drawn into Sayyid 'Abd al-Rahman's coterie.

A security report, written in December 1934, attested to the strong
position which the *sayyid* had by then built up among the graduates:

> . . . to the graduate class, Sayyid 'Abd al-Rahman is a political
> leader, pure and simple . . . [he] has been adopted, at least for the
> time being, by a certain section of the instructed (intelligentsia) as
> their candidate for recognition as the leading Sudanese notable.[52]

The district commissioner of Omdurman in 1935 described the techniques whereby the educated were enticed into the coterie:

> He ['Abd al-Rahman] entertained them [the educated] whenever
> occasion offered, subscribed generously to their studies and chari-
> ties and put government hospitality in the shade with his splendid
> receptions at religious and national festivals. He held court like an
> Abbasid Khalif.[53]

The coterie around Sayyid 'Ali al-Mirghani grew up in direct
reaction to Sayyid 'Abd al-Rahman's activities. Sayyid 'Ali had
grown increasingly resentful of Sayyid 'Abd al-Rahman's expanded
influence, and of the manner in which his own role was now overshad-
owed by that of Sayyid 'Abd al-Rahman. With memories of his
pre-eminence in the early years of the Condominium, at a time when
Sayyid 'Abd al-Rahman had been relegated to obscurity and insignifi-
cance, he viewed the new state of affairs with an edge of embitterment. The first open break between the two men appears to have
occurred when Sayyid 'Abd al-Rahman took a lead in organising the
'Petition of Sound Elements' in 1924. Sayyid 'Abd al-Rahman had, in
Sayyid 'Ali's eyes, usurped the initiative, depriving Sayyid 'Ali of a
prerogative which had been his since the outset of the Condominium.[54]

It was, however, not until 1932 that Sayyid 'Ali, conscious now of
the extent of Sayyid 'Abd al-Rahman's influence among the graduates, began actively to create a graduate clientele of his own. The
opportunity for him to move in this direction arose when political

levelopments led to there being an acute division in graduate
opinion. The impact of the world depression, together with a decline
n cotton production brought on by drought conditions and locust
plagues, caused the government to retrench expenditure. The
monthly salaries of newly employed graduates in government service
were cut from £E8 to £E5½. As the salaries of intermediate
school-leavers[55] and of non-Sudanese had not been cut, however,
most graduates were convinced that the government's action was not
motivated by economic considerations alone. Governmental suspicion of the graduates' political allegiances was deemed to have played
a role. The response of graduates to the government's action engendered a deep and lasting division in graduate ranks.

In June 1931 the Omdurman Graduates' Club established a Committee of Ten to negotiate on the graduates' behalf with the
government.[56] By November, however, the Committee of Ten had
achieved little. Students at Gordon College then went on strike, possibly with encouragement from some graduates. The Condominium
authorities, eager for mediation to diffuse the growing discontent but
unwilling to recognise the committee as a representative body, drew
in individual committee members for talks – but refused to negotiate
with the whole committee. Presumably by design rather than by
accident, the government's 'confidential talks' with committee members sowed seeds of discord. Different committee members came to
adopt different negotiating positions. Muhammad 'Ali Shawqi, supported by the Mahdi coterie to which he was affiliated, proposed a
'compromise salary' for newly employed graduates of £E6½. Ahmad
al-Sayyid al-Fil, drawing support from some younger graduates,
opposed the compromise. Whereas the graduates had initially approached the salary-cuts issue with some measure of unity, they were
soon split into two mutually suspicious groupings. Each suspected
that the other was engaged in a secret deal with the government.[57]

Over the years which followed, the graduate community was rent
by a continuing conflict between 'Filists' and 'Shawqists' – the two
groupings which, deriving their names from the patronymics of their
leaders, had taken shape during 1931.[58] The conflict revolved around
control of the Omdurman Graduates' Club. In the 1932 club elections
supporters of Ahmad al-Sayyid al-Fil sought to secure the latter's
election as club secretary in place of Muhammad 'Ali Shawqi.
Shawqi, however, emerged victorious, both in the 1932 and 1933
elections. The Filists, in protest at the Shawqist predominance,

resigned *en masse* from the club in 1933. Between 1933 and 193(Muhammad Salih al-Shinqiti (a Shawqist) held the club secretary ship, and between 1936 and 1938 Isma'il al-Azhari (also, at that time a Shawqist).[59]

The sharp division among the graduates, and the emergence of a group of graduates who were antipathetic to Sayyid 'Abd al Rahman's Shawqist coterie, gave Sayyid 'Ali the opportunity he had been seeking. From 1932 onwards he made public his support fo Ahmad al-Sayyid al-Fil.[60] The Filists were then drawn into a graduate coterie around Sayyid 'Ali. Just as Sayyid 'Abd al-Rahman had patronised the activities of one section of educated Sudanese, so also now did Sayyid 'Ali.

By 1932, therefore, Sayyid 'Abd al-Rahman and Sayyid 'Ali had surrounded themselves with coteries of graduates. The activities o the graduates in each coterie were supported and patronised. The relationship between the religious leader and the graduates in hi coterie was one from which both sides drew strength. While Shari Yusuf al-Hindi also had links with educated Sudanese, no cohesive coterie developed around him. The coteries were, as stated earlier instruments through which the interests and objectives of graduate were shaped and influenced by the two most prominent religiou leaders – who themselves formed a central part of the commercia establishment. These quasi-political groupings were to have a stron; impact on the nationalist movement which developed in the lat(1930s.

V THE LITERARY STUDY GROUPS, LATE 1920s AND 1930s

The formation of literary study groups in the late 1920s and earl 1930s was also significant to the form taken by Sudanese nationalisr when it re-emerged after 1938. The restrictive policy which th Condominium government pursued towards educated Sudanese afte the 1924 disturbances inevitably curtailed the possibility of an overtly political activity among graduates – at least until after th Anglo–Egyptian Treaty of 1936. Graduates, therefore, adopted low profile and limited themselves to activities which could not b deemed provocative. Reading, discussion and literary study group were formed, where a small circle of friends could examine a book newspaper articles or possibly (in the later stages, when confidenc grew) contemporary political issues. Afaf AbuHasabu describes accurately the manner in which literary and political concerns impinged on one another:

> Politics in the immediate post-1924 era was confined to reading, secretly, Egyptian newspapers, or to strictly limited discussions with intimate friends. It was only later, after 1934, that topics of national interest were openly discussed by reading groups and that the groups began to represent distinct political attitudes. In the meantime the activities remained literary and cultural in nature, exploiting literature to refer only vaguely to suppressed national aspirations. In poems, songs and plays which the intelligentsia performed, the concentration was on the glories of the Islamic dynasties and of Arabic culture; or it revolved around the history of Sudan itself and the greatness of ancient Sudanese kingdoms and ancestors.[61]

A large number of these study groups were formed over the decade which followed 1924, in provincial towns as well as in Khartoum and Omdurman. Most were of importance only to the graduates who participated in them. Two, however, were to be of wider political significance: the Abu Ruf and al-Fajr groups.

Previous writing on the Abu Ruf and al-Fajr groups has focused on the issues which allegedly divided them. It is more important for our purposes, however, to emphasise the aspects of similarity. The constituent members of both groups were part of a new generation of graduates. Their generation had not been active in the events of 1924 (most had been still at school or university) and they were intent on learning from the mistakes – as they saw them – of their elders. They were hostile to sectarianism, believing that it had a divisive and deadening impact on Sudanese society, and were determined not to allow sectarian feelings to divide the rising generation of educated Sudanese. They were critical of the senior graduates, whose petty ambitions they blamed for the interminable personal wrangling in the Omdurman Graduates' Club. Their intellectual inspiration was drawn from both European and Arab sources: they read and discussed the books and pamphlets of left-inclined European authors (making ample use of Fabian Society and Left Book Club publications), as well as Egyptian journals and the works of Arab scholars.[62] The activities of these groups involved, in fact, a remarkable flowering of intellectual interest and pursuit in Sudan, such that the intellectual ardour of younger graduates contrasted sharply with the sterile conflicts which dominated relations among senior graduates.

Socialistic and egalitarian-oriented perspectives were inherent in the views expressed by members of both groups. They talked passionately of the need to raise the standards of living of the mass of the population, to spread education, and to modernise techniques of production in industry and agriculture. Their analyses of Sudan's problems, moreover, made frequent reference to the role of different social classes and to the oppression of the population by international capitalism.[63] Both groups, however, maintained an elitist attitude to the means whereby such change could come about. The educated, and specifically the new generation of well-educated graduates, should take the lead and guide Sudanese society towards a more enlightened future. The backwardness and traditionalism which characterised Sudanese society would be eliminated through the spread of education. An article written by members of the al-Fajr group in the mid-1930s – when the public expression of political views was becoming possible – reveals an attitude which both groups shared:

> . . . we definitely wish to stand for a new order of intelligent reform, and a steady progressive life, along our own lines . . . We wish to see the young enlightened generation taking an active part in the affairs of this country . . .
>
> We young men of this generation are sons of the soil, the fruits of a new order that is to link the Sudan with the rest of the world. Both the rudiments of human loyalty, and the sense of communal duty demand that those who hold the good fortune to know slightly better than their fellow-men should put whatever knowledge they have to the service and orientation of those with whom their fathers, themselves and their sons move, live and have their being . . .[64]

While members of the two groups were critical of the senior graduates, the sectarian religious leaders and indeed the Sudanese establishment as a whole, they were neither totally alienated from, nor quite separate from, these strata. Members of the two groups were mostly 'of good family'. Many, indeed, were the sons or relations of senior establishment figures. The divisions between, and manoeuvres among, establishment figures therefore inevitably ha some influence upon them – if only by setting the context within which bonds of friendship among the younger generation formed. The nature of Sudanese towns, and the fact that the composition of study groups was largely determined by place of residence, were bound to give the groups particular 'sectarian connections'. Sudanese towns were constituted by clusters of communities, where each community shared some common ethnic and religious affiliations. Place of residence, therefore, had both ethnic and sectarian connotations. However great the intellectual hostility which the younger graduates harboured towards sectarianism and the Sudanese establishment, then, the bonds of family and residence could still give their activities a sectarian colouring.

The Abu Ruf group was named after the area of Omdurman where most of its members lived. Two brothers, Hasan and Husain al-Kid, appear to have constituted the pole around which the group was formed. Among the group's most prominent members, who began gathering for discussions at the al-Kid family home in the course of 1927, were Khidir Hamad, 'Abdullah Mirghani, al-Nur 'Uthman, Makkawi Sulaiman Akrat, Isma'il al-Atabani, Hasan 'Uthman, Husain 'Uthman, 'Amin Babikir, al-Hadi Abu Bakr Ishaq, Ibrahim Anis, Ibrahim Yusif Sulaiman, Hammad Tawfiq, Ibrahim 'Uthman Ishaq, Hasan Ziadah, 'Abd al-Halim Abu Shamah, and al-Tijani Abu Qurun.[65] Most of the above-named came from *khatmi* families. In the early 1930s, a branch of the Abu Ruf group was established in Wad Medani. The Wad Medani branch, led by Ahmad Khair, was composed mainly of Abu Ruf members who had been transferred on government service to Wad Medani.

The al-Fajr group, also formed in the late 1920s, was initially known as the Awlad al-Mawradah – referring, again, to the area of Omdurman where most of its members lived. When the group became involved in producing the *al-Fajr* magazine after 1934, however, the name of the magazine attached itself to the group. As with the Abu Ruf group, two brothers took a lead in bringing the group together: 'Abdallah and Muhammad 'Ashri. A key role from the early 1930s was played by 'Arafat Muhammad 'Abdallah, who was to become editor of *al-Fajr* magazine.[66] Other prominent members at the outset were Muhammad Ahmad Mahjub, Yusif al-Tinai, 'Abd al-Halim Muhammad, and Yusif Ma'mun.[67] While most members of the al-Fajr group did not come from families traditionally associated with Mahdism, a number were related to senior establishment figures close to Sayyid 'Abd al-Rahman al-Mahdi. The Hashimab family, descendants of the first *mufti* of Sudan under the Condominium, was well represented in the group.

Such ideological differences as there were between the two groups were more a question of emphasis than of principle. The Abu Ruf group was perhaps more imbued with anti-imperialist perceptions and rhetoric, more interested in cooperative links with Egypt,[68] and more inclined towards Arabism than was the al-Fajr group. The al-Fajr group was possibly more optimistic that Condominium rule could permit the eventual emergence of a free and independent Sudan. These, however, did not constitute unbridgeable differences of policy. Each group was held together much more by links of friendship, shared experience and shared discussion than by a clear ideological direction exclusive to its members. In the Graduates' Club elections, family links seem to have been more significant than ideological principle in determining how the al-Fajr and Abu Ruf groups aligned themselves on the Shawqist–Filist division. The al-Fajr group supported Shawqist candidates, while the Abu Ruf group supported Filist candidates.

One issue which did divide members of the two groups and which did perhaps reflect differing ideological perceptions, concerned the links which the al-Fajr group maintained with Edward 'Atiyah, the Syrian-born intellectual who served the Condominium government as an intelligence officer. On the only occasion when, in 1933, members of the two groups sought to join together in a 'Society for Arts, Crafts and Debates', it was Abu Rufian suspicion of 'Atiyah's involvement which aborted the project.[69]

One other group, formed in this case in the mid-1930s, is worthy of mention: the mid-Omdurman group, usually known as the Ashiqqah. The central role in creating the mid-Omdurman group was played by three sets of *ashiqqah* (blood brothers): Yahia and Mahmud al-Fadli, Ahmad and Hasan Yasin, and Hasan and al-Haj Awadallah. Other prominent members were Babikir al-Qabbani, 'Ali Hamid, and Yas'a Khalifah.[70] Members of the mid-Omdurman group tended to be younger, and of a less intellectual and literary bent, than were the members of the Abu Ruf and al-Fajr groups. Their initial activity was focused on political manoeuvring within the Graduates' Club, where they supported the Shawqist faction and established a strong relationship with a more senior graduate, Isma'il al-Azhari. The mid-Omdurman group of the 1930s could best be described as a collection of highly-skilled political activists and manipulators, who had not yet found a suitable arena or framework for their political ambitions. Their political ideas remained inchoate.

VI THE RE-EMERGENCE OF A NATIONALIST MOVEMENT: THE GRADUATES' CONGRESS AND THE DEVELOPMENT OF POLITICAL PARTIES, 1938–46

A number of events and developments in the mid-1930s, both internal and external to Sudan, made possible the re-birth of a nationalist movement. This initially took the form of an organisation whose primary concern was the promotion of graduate interests. The more relaxed attitude which the Condominium government took towards educated Sudanese after Sir Stewart Symes became Governor-General in 1934,[71] and the need to strengthen popular acceptance of the Condominium regime at a time of expanding German and Italian influence in the area, both help to account for the government's preparedness to accept a new form of graduate organisation. More important than either of these factors, however, were the direct and indirect effects of the 1936 Anglo–Egyptian Treaty.

The Anglo–Egyptian Treaty of 1936 stipulated that the primary aim of the Anglo–Egyptian administration in Sudan should be 'the welfare of the Sudanese'; that Egyptian troops could once again be stationed in Sudan; that unrestricted Egyptian immigration into Sudan be permitted, subject to 'reasons of public order and health'; and that 'suitable candidates of British or Egyptian nationality' would be appointed to official positions where no qualified Sudanese was available. On the one hand, British officials were now impelled to offset the danger posed by greater Egyptian involvement in Sudan. More Sudanese needed to be trained for government service at all levels, so as to avoid the necessity of employing Egyptians. The risk that an alienated class of graduates might turn to Egypt for support had to be countered by conciliating the graduates and drawing them into a closer relationship with government. On the other hand, graduates now had a new incentive to ensure that their interests were known and respected. The conclusion of a treaty which covered the future of Sudan, without either party to the treaty seeing fit to consult the Sudanese, was deemed deeply humiliating. There was, therefore, disillusionment with both of the Condominium powers and a determination not to allow such a situation to arise again. An organisation was needed which could insist on a role in any future negotiations.

Before turning to the detailed events which surrounded the formation and development of the Graduates' Congress, the central theme pursued here will be explained. The Congress was largely the creation of the younger generation of graduates – mainly those who had been active in the al-Fajr and Abu Ruf groups. These younger graduates were intent on establishing an organisation which, while starting as a vehicle for the expression of graduate interests, would in due course develop as a national movement with wide popular support and involvement. The new organisation, then, would provide a framework within which the graduates would lead the Sudanese population towards playing a more significant role in the government of their own country, and possibly to self-determination. The religious leaders and other senior establishment figures would be given respect, but they would remain on the sidelines while the educated Sudanese wrested increasing power from the British.

What actually happened was quite different. The emergence of conflicting tendencies within the Graduates' Congress induced groups of graduates to seek outside support. Such support was sought, at least in the first instance, not from the population directly but from elements within the Sudanese establishment. The two most prominent religious leaders, and the circles of establishment figures who surrounded them, constituted the primary source from which immediate practical support could be, and was, forthcoming. Although the political parties which emerged from the Congress developed strong political followings, then, these followings were mediated through the involvement of senior establishment figures. It was the religious leaders who, making use of their substantial influence, brought in their followers to join the parties, rather than the parties which succeeded in mobilising the people on the basis of new forms of allegiance.

Turning for support to Sayyid 'Abd al-Rahman and Sayyid 'Ali was in many ways an easy option for the graduate leaders of the new political parties. The influence which the two *sayyids* had established among senior graduates through their coteries, the economic resources which they had at their disposal, and the respect which they commanded at the popular level all combined to make them desirable allies. The search for 'easy support' also led the new political parties to align themselves, whether openly and directly or covertly and indirectly, with one or other of the two co-domini. The justification for such alignment was that the co-dominum in question could hasten the achievement of Sudanese self-determination.

The perspectives and objectives of the political parties which emerged from the Graduates' Congress were inevitably influenced by the sources from which they drew support, both internal and external. The divisions among graduates, the strength and vitality of the Sudanese establishment (or at least some parts of it), and the partiticular dynamics which followed from the role of the two co-domini, therefore, shaped the post-1938 Sudanese nationalist movement into a very different form from that which the founders of the Graduates' Congress had envisaged.

We will now examine the events which led from the early hopes of the younger graduates to the eventual disappointment of these hopes. While different individuals have claimed paternity of the Graduates' Congress idea,[72] there can be little doubt that the actual formation of the Congress was spearheaded by members of the Abu Ruf group (especially Ahmad Khair and his Wad Medani branch), strongly supported and encouraged by members of the al-Fajr group. The first formal exposition of the Graduates' Congress idea, in fact, came in lecture entitled 'Our Political Duty after the 1936 Treaty' which Ahmad Khair delivered in Wad Medani. The text of the lecture was published in *al-Fajr* magazine on 16 May 1937. Ahmad Khair's exposition reflected clearly the conceptions of the younger generation of graduates as a whole:

> The Sudan at this early stage of its modern history needs leadership and planning. The conclusion then is that today's call is directed to the *literati*, to the enlightened Sudanese, to the graduate . . . How could the graduates perform their duty when they are a non-existent body? . . . Their first duty is to achieve intellectual unity . . . by this is meant the organising of the enlightened section in an association that would exploit the country's sources of strength.[73]

Ahmad Khair warned that 'enlightened opinion should become independent of disgraceful traditions; it should free itself from personal cults'. The Indian Congress, Ahmad Khair contended, should constitute the model which Sudanese graduates should seek to copy. The full implications of this were not spelt out, nor did they need to be: the Indian Congress had developed from being a government officials' union into a nationalist movement. While the Condominium government and most of the senior graduates saw the congress simply as a body which would give expression to the interests and views of educated Sudanese, then, the younger graduates saw it as the basis on which a new Sudanese nationalist movement could be constructed. The need to obtain government consent, nevertheless, required them to adopt a gradualist approach.[74]

The founding conference of the Graduates' Congress was convened, under the chairmanship of the Graduates' Club president Isma'il al-Azhari, on 12 February 1938. Some 1180 graduates attended the meeting. The constitution which the founding meeting ratified specified that membership was 'open to all graduates of educational institutions of a standard higher than the elementary', and that the aims of the congress were 'to promote the general welfare of the country and the graduates'.[75] An annual general assembly, to be held on the second day of the Kurban Bairam, would 'hear the reports and elect a Council of 60'. The Council of 60, meeting several times every year, would set the overall guidelines for congress policy. The actual day-to-day conduct of congress affairs would be the responsibility of a Committee of 15, elected by the Council of 60. Besides the congress presidency, which would rotate on a monthly basis among the Committee of 15, there would be three official posts held by members of the latter committee: general secretary, treasurer and assistant secretary.

Between 1938 and the end of 1941, senior graduates maintained a predominant position in the leadership of the Graduates' Congress, as constituted by successive Committees of 15. These senior graduates were intent on pursuing the essentially moderate path which had been mapped out with the government's understanding. International conditions, in any case, gave them little alternative: the onset of the Second World War, and the severe threat which the Condominium regime faced from Italian forces in Ethiopia and Eritrea, severely limited any possibility of pursuing an active political campaign.

Congress policies over the initial four years were therefore essentially cautious, focusing on matters which were of specific concern to graduates. A study was undertaken of the Sudanese educational system and recommendations were made to the government on how this could be expanded; a memorandum was prepared on the possible future development of the Ma'had al-'Ilmi (the Islamic Institute); literary festivals were held to stimulate wider interest in education; and a petition relating to the leave regulations of government servants was presented to the civil secretary.[76]

While differences did arise between the congress and the government over this period, the general tenor of relations between the two remained relatively cordial. The government was not prepared to allow the congress to project itself as a trade union for government servants, as it was accused of doing on the issue of leave regulations. Nor was the government pleased when the congress presented the

Egyptian prime minister, 'Ali Mahir, with a memorandum calling for greater Egyptian cultural, philanthropic and commercial involvement in Sudan, during the latter's visit to Sudan in February 1940.[77] Differences also arose over congress cooperation with the Omdurman Broadcasting Service. These, however, were individual issues which did not terminate the government's approval of the whole undertaking.

The continued predominance of the senior graduates between 1938 and the end of 1941 did not stem from any immobilism in the congress's internal political dynamics. Change did occur in the identity of the senior graduates who sat on the Committee of 15. Between 1938 and August 1940, in fact, the congress's internal political dynamics were distinctively different from what they were to be between August 1940 and December 1941.[78]

Over the first two years of the congress's existence, the membership of the Committee of 15 was fairly evenly balanced between graduates associated with Sayyid 'Abd al-Rahman's coterie and graduates associated with Sayyid 'Ali's coterie. A group of 'neutral' and largely anti-sectarian younger graduates, mostly Abu Rufists, helped to render partisan divisions muted and non-antagonistic. While congress elections witnessed competition between Mahdist-oriented and Mirghanist-oriented blocks, the general consensus was that partisan differences should be subordinated to the interests and objectives which graduates shared. It was no coincidence that the posts of general secretary, treasurer and assistant secretary over these years were consistently held by individuals who were deemed, at that time, to be neutrals. Table 5.2 provides evidence of this.

Between August 1940 and the end of 1941, however, the subordination of partisan differences gave way to open competition. The congress leadership fell under the control of a three-cornered alliance, dominated by senior members of Sayyid 'Abd al-Rahman al-Mahdi's coterie. Besides the Mahdi coterie, the other two partners in the alliance were the Ashiqqah group and Isma'il al-Azhari. Members of the Mirghani coterie and the Abu Ruf group were squeezed out of the congress leadership.

Each of the three partners in the alliance had much to gain from a supportive and cooperative relationship with its new allies. The Mahdi coterie had from the outset sought a leading role in the Graduates' Congress. They now had the means to achieve this objective. Working together with Isma'il al-Azhari and the Ashiqqah, they were able to displace both the Mirghanists and the Abu

Table 5.2   *Holders of Official Posts in the Graduates' Congress, 1938 to July 1940*

	1938	1939	1940
General Secretary	Isma'il al-Azhari[*]	Isma'il al-Azhari	Hammad Tawfiq
Treasurer	al-Dardiri Nuqud[**]	'Abdallah Mirghani[++]	Khidir Hamad[§]
Assistant Secretary	—	Hammad Tawfiq	'Abdallah Mirghani
Accountant	Hammad Tawfiq[+]	—	Ibrahim Yusif Sulaiman[§§]

[*]   President of Graduates' Club. Respected neutral senior graduate.
[**] Al-Fajr group.
[+] Abu Ruf group.
[++] Abu Ruf group.
[§]   Abu Ruf group.
[§§] Abu Ruf group.

Source: Information compiled by the writer.

Rufist neutrals from the Committee of 15. The Ashiqqah, who had not previously been strong enough to achieve representation on the Committee of 15, could now assure themselves of a prominent role in the congress leadership. With a respected senior graduate as their figurehead leader, and the concerted backing of the Mahdi coterie (with which they had loosely been associated prior to 1938), their position was transformed. Al-Azhari, too, achieved a stronger stake in the congress leadership. His authority within the congress had previously rested on his reputation for neutrality and non-partisanship. In the January 1940 elections, however, he had been forced out of the secretaryship; all of the official positions had fallen to Abu Rufists. He now gained a caucus of support which would enable him to re-capture a key official position.

In the course of 1940, then, the new alliance mounted a challenge to the Committee of 15 which had been elected in January 1940 and succeeded in forcing its resignation.[79] As an instrument for mobilising graduate opinion against the existing committee, the alliance raised an issue which struck a chord among younger graduates. The committee was criticised for being prepared to cooperate with the Omdurman Broadcasting Service unconditionally – i.e. without insisting first that the congress be permitted to transmit its views. In August 1940 the committee was forced to resign and was replaced, through election by the Council of 60, by a new committee in which the alliance was predominant. The only two Abu Rufists who had been elected to the committee immediately resigned in protest against the imbalance in representation and were replaced by Ashiqqah members. The new committee abandoned the previous practice of rotating the presidency every month and appointed Isma'il al-Azhari president for the remainder of the year.

Once the alliance had gained preponderant control of congress in August 1940, the Ashiqqah launched an extensive campaign aimed at strengthening and extending that control. Younger graduates favourable to Ashiqqah viewpoints were actively recruited into congress membership and an attempt was made to influence the attitudes of existing members. When new congress elections were held in January 1941, the alliance retained control of the Committee of 15. Al-Azhari remained president.

While the success of the three-cornered alliance depended much on the inherent strength of the parties involved, and the skill which the Ashiqqah employed in manoeuvring, it also drew on a rising feeling of dissatisfaction among younger graduates. The latter were becoming frustrated by the congress's absorption in matters they deemed minor, to the exclusion of wider nationalist objectives. The Ashiqqah, whose support was strongest among those who had graduated most recently, appealed to this emotion. The new committee, however, was in no position to respond to the wishes of younger graduates. Despite the Ashiqqah participation, senior graduates committed to a cautious approach still formed the majority on the committee. The policy of moderation, restricting the congress to issues of graduate interest alone, continued.

From December 1941, when elections for the 1942 Committee of 15 were held, the congress entered a new stage in its development. For the first time, younger graduates constituted a clear majority on the 1942 committee. Only three senior graduates (Isma'il al-Azhari, Ibrahim Ahmad and 'Abdallahi al-Fadil), in fact, were elected. Members of the Abu Ruf and al-Fajr groups took all of the remaining twelve seats on the committee. Fears aroused by the success of the three-cornered alliance in the August 1940 and January 1941 elections account for this radical change in the congress leadership. The predominance within the congress of a partisan alliance with sectarian overtones threatened to recreate the Mahdi–Mirghani divisiveness which had bedevilled the Graduates' Club. Abu Rufist and al-Fajr adherents came together in a concerted attempt to re-assert the nationalist and anti-sectarian ideals which had inspired them to initiate the congress. The two groups campaigned actively for support during 1941, recruiting new members to the congress who could be counted on to oppose the Mahdi coterie/Ashiqqah/al-Azhari alliance. As recruitment campaigns were being conducted not only by the al-Fajr and Abu Ruf groups but also by the Ashiqqah, the membership of the congress grew rapidly in 1940 and 1941. Most of the new recruits were young graduates, committed to more radical policies than those acceptable to senior graduates. In campaigning against the three-cornered alliance, then, the Abu Ruf and al-Fajr groups created the dynamics which led to the displacement of both the alliance and the senior graduates from the congress leadership.

Out of respect for a senior graduate, the presidency of the 1942 Committee of 15 was given to Ibrahim Ahmad, a member of Sayyid 'Abd al-Rahman's coterie. Despite this, however, the senior graduates had clearly lost their ability to direct and control the congress. This ability now rested with the younger generation, specifically the Abu Ruf and al-Fajr groups, whose nationalist aspirations had given birth to the congress. Wider conditions within and outside Sudan, moreover, were such that a more distinctly nationalist programme for the congress could now be envisaged. The Italian threat to Sudan had effectively disappeared with the defeat of the Italian forces at the battle of Keren in March 1941. Montgomery's victory over Rommel at El Alamein in July 1941 had turned the tide against Germany in North Africa. The Sudan Defence Force had played a critical supportive role in both of these theatres, earning considerable goodwill from the British, and Sudanese intellectuals believed that the noble principles enshrined in the Atlantic Charter heralded a new approach to colonised peoples. An appropriate time appeared to have arrived, therefore, for the congress to put forward national demands.

The more political role which the 1942 committee intended to play was heralded by a telegram which the committee despatched to the Governor-General in January 1942. Following a reference to allied successes in the war, 'in which imperial and Sudanese forces participated', the telegram went on to express 'the hope of the members of Congress that when victory is attained the rights of Sudanese and their welfare as well as those of the Arab nations will be recognised'.[80] The main political initiative which the new committee undertook, however, was the formulation and despatch to the Governor-General of a memorandum calling for Sudanese self-determination. Among the demands made in the memorandum were the following:

1. At the first possible opportunity the British and Egyptian governments should issue a joint declaration granting the Sudan in its geographical boundaries the right of self-determination directly after the war. This right to be safeguarded by guarantees assuring full liberty of expression in connection with this, as well as guarantees assuring the Sudanese the right to determine their national rights with Egypt in a special agreement between the Egyptian and Sudanese nations;
2. The formation of a representative body of Sudanese to approve the budget and the ordinances.[81]

The Condominium authorities had themselves been considering the means whereby Sudanese could be associated more closely with government. The memorandum, nonetheless, drew an uncompromising rebuke from the government. The congress's assumption of a directly political role, implying the right to speak on behalf of the Sudanese population as a whole, was unacceptable. The initial stern rebuke, however, was followed by private talks (similar to the 'individual consultations' which had created divisions among the graduates in 1931) between the civil secretary and some members of the Committee of 15.[82] In these latter talks, the civil secretary expressed some sympathy with the graduates' hopes and expectations, stating that the government had every intention of working gradually towards the realisation of most of the demands which had been put forward.

The government's response to the congress's memorandum faced the Committee of 15 with a dilemma: whether to accept the civil secretary's private assurances that progress would soon be made towards associating Sudanese closely with government (and to cooperate with the government so as to hasten this process), or to pursue a confrontationist policy aimed at forcing the government to accept the congress's demands. On this issue, the Committee of 15 split. Ibrahim Ahmad and members of the al-Fajr group, constituting the majority of the committee, espoused the moderate line.[83] They were prepared to continue contacts with the government. Isma'il al-Azhari, supported within the committee by most of the Abu Rufists and by 'Abdallahi al-Fadil, and outside of the committee by the Ashiqqah, espoused the confrontationist line.[84]

The congress elections for the 1943 council and committee, held in December 1942, deepened and formalised the split within the congress. The confrontationist trend – al-Azhari, the Ashiqqah and the Abu Rufists – won a convincing victory. Al-Azhari regained the presidency. Such moderates as were elected to the Committee of 15 resigned from it and were replaced by confrontationists.

A re-structuring of alliances now occurred. Both Ibrahim Ahmad and al-Azhari had previously benefited from Sayyid 'Abd al-Rahman's support. The *sayyid* now had to choose between his protégés – a choice which would inevitably greatly influence the political balance within the Graduates' Congress. The option of supporting both, although briefly attempted in the early months of 1943, was hardly practicable in the long term.[85] The embitterment of the confrontationist–moderate struggle, and the practical policy differences which followed from it, required a decision one way or the other. Alarmed at the rising extremism of the congress leadership, Sayyid 'Abd al-Rahman eventually gave his full backing to Ibrahim Ahmad and the moderates. 'Abdallahi al-Fadil, the *sayyid*'s nephew and the leader of those members of the Mahdi coterie who had retained their alliance with the Ashiqqah through the December 1942 elections, was instructed to withdraw from this entanglement.[86]

The severing of the remaining link between the Ashiqqah and the Mahdi coterie impelled the Ashiqqah to turn towards other sources of support. To retain their position in the congress leadership, against the determined campaign now waged by the Mahdi coterie on behalf of the moderates, they needed to draw in new allies. Rather than seeking to strengthen their position through the direct mobilisation of the Sudanese population, which might have been effective in the long term but could have cost them control of the congress in the short term, the Ashiqqah sought a new ally within the Sudanese establishment. This they found in Sayyid 'Ali al-Mirghani. The initiative which led to the Mirghanist–Ashiqqah alliance, indeed, came from Sayyid 'Ali himself. Worried by Sayyid 'Abd al-Rahman's expanding influence and ambitions, and by the Condominium government's apparent support for these ambitions,[87] Sayyid 'Ali was determined to weaken his rival's standing among educated Sudanese. The alienation of the congress confrontationists from Sayyid 'Abd al-Rahman gave Sayyid 'Ali a most welcome opportunity. Despite his own personal preference for Ibrahim Ahmad as against al-Azhari, he decided to lend his support to the confrontationists. Through Ahmad al-Sayyid al-Fil and Muhammad Nur al-Din, he first approached the Abu Ruf group.[88] The latter, however, declined to cooperate, unwilling to compromise their anti-sectarian stand. An approach was then made to the Ashiqqah, who welcomed the proferred support.[89]

The policy of confrontation with the British authorities enabled the

Ashiqqah to draw support from one other quarter: Egypt. Eager to exploit anti-British feeling in Sudan, with a view to using this to promote its own objectives there, the Egyptian government was a ready partner. In 1943 Isma'il al-Azhari undertook an exploratory visit to Egypt, holding talks with a variety of party and government officials. Some Egyptian financial assistance appears to have begun to reach the Ashiqqah after this visit, but the main benefit probably lay in the publicity which the Egyptian media were now prepared to give to Ashiqqah views and activities.

The adoption by the Ashiqqah of the 'Unity of the Nile Valley' slogan in 1944, envisaging Sudanese self-determination under the Egyptian crown, followed naturally from the relationship which developed. At one level the adoption of the union policy was tactical: with the support of the minor co-dominium, the major co-dominium could, it was hoped, be removed. Once self-determination had been achieved, Egypt's claims over Sudan could themselves be rejected. At another level, however, the slogan touched a deeper perception: that Egypt constituted a nationalist pole around which opposition to the British presence in the area could coalesce, and with which Sudan's post-colonial future would inevitably be entwined. While the Ashiqqah's adoption of the union policy may have been motivated largely by the tactical consideration,[90] the adoption of the policy by the other confrontationist groups in the congress probably reflected more the ideologically-based perception. An Arab nationalist dimension had been present in the thinking of the Abu Ruf group ever since the 1920s.[91]

The analysis given here of the divisions in the Graduates' Congress between 1938 and 1943 may appear over-detailed. The events which occurred over these years, however, were of critical importance. The shape and form taken by Sudanese politics between 1943 and 1969 were set by these events. They determined the nature of the political parties which fought for and gained the country's independence, and the political regimes which followed independence. By the end of 1943, the character of the political parties which were to take the centre of the political stage was already effectively determined. The crucial alliances which were to underlie these parties, between establishment figures and groups of graduates, had been formed. Rather than the graduate elite mobilising the populace into a national movement, the new party leaders' primary political constituencies were within the Sudanese establishment.[92] The relationships between establishment patrons and party leaders at times underwent stress, especially on the Khatmiyyah/Ashiqqah side, but the dynamics of mutual dependence would generally bring them together again.

The alliances which the graduate political leaders formed with establishment patrons were, between 1943 and 1956, complemented by the cooperative relationships which they developed with one or other of the two co-domini. The confrontationist groups maintained, as has already been mentioned, a cooperative relationship with Egypt. Adopting a policy favouring union (however defined) with Egypt, they became known as 'unionist' parties. The moderates maintained a cooperative relationship with the British authorities in Sudan. They called for an independent Sudan and deemed the representative institutions created by the Condominium government suitable channels through which to press the claim for self-determination.

The increasingly polarised state of opinion within the Graduates' Congress between 1943 and 1945 provided the impetus which led to the actual formation of political parties. Following a strong campaign waged by the Mahdi coterie, the moderates were able to gain control of the 1944 Committee of 15. Ibrahim Ahmad resumed the presidency. The moderates' position, however, was tenuous. Lacking sufficient support in the Council of 60, they were unable to change congress policy towards the newly-instituted Advisory Council of Northern Sudan. The policy remained one of non-cooperation.[93] In the elections for the 1945 council and committee, the confrontationists won a resounding victory. The Ashiqqah gained a clear majority of the seats on the Committee of 15. For the remaining years of the congress's existence (formally, until 1952), the Ashiqqah retained a controlling position in both the Council of 60 and the Committee of 15, with al-Azhari serving as president. Most of the moderates, intent on establishing separate political organisations, resigned from the congress in the course of 1945. The congress became, in effect, the organisational structure of the Ashiqqah Party.

Of the various political parties formed on the confrontationist/unionist side in the mid-1940s, the Ashiqqah Party was without doubt the largest and most significant.[94] With the backing of Egypt and Sayyid 'Ali, and able to recruit new members both through the Khatmiyyah network and through the Graduates' Congress organisation and branches, it soon constituted a substantial political movement. Contributions from *khatmi* merchants strengthened its financial base. It advocated the establishment of 'a democratic Sudanese government in union with Egypt under the Egyptian crown'.[95]

Among the smaller unionist parties, the Ittihadiyyin (Unionists) probably carried most influence, albeit only among the more intellectual elements of Sudanese society. Formed by members of the old Abu Ruf group in October 1944, the party favoured the establishment of a free and democratic Sudanese government which would enjoy dominion status under the Egyptian crown. Such an arrangement would not imply Egyptian domination of Sudan but would, the party programme stated, enable both Egypt and Sudan to 'enjoy equal rights and sovereignty'.[96] Although party members tended to come from a *khatmi* background, the party maintained a firmly anti-sectarian line. The somewhat elitist intellectualism inherent in the party's approach inhibited the development of a mass popular following. Among the founders of the party were Khidir Hamad, 'Abdallah Mirghani, Ahmad Khair and Hammad Tawfiq.

The Ahrar (Liberals) advocated a confederal relationship between Egypt and Sudan. In 1946, however, the party split and one section of it (the Liberal Secessionists) transferred its loyalties to the pro-independence camp, ultimately merging into the Umma Party. Those who remained on the unionist side re-named their party al-Ahrar al-Ittihadiyyin (the Liberal Unionists). Most of the principal figures involved in the al-Ahrar al-Ittihadiyyin later joined the Sudanese Communist Party. In 1946 one other unionist party, the Unity of the Nile Valley Party, was formed. The latter grouping, led by Dardiri Ahmad Isma'il, sought the integration of Sudan into a unitary Egyptian state.

While the unionist parties tended to act in concert when confronting the Condominium government, it was not until 1952 that they all came together within one political party: the National Unionist Party.

In the independence camp, supporting the 'Sudan for the Sudanese' slogan, only one significant party developed prior to 1950. The moves which led up to the formation of the Umma Party began with the registration in 1944 of a Qawmiyyin 'club' among graduates. The Qawmiyyin were members of the al-Fajr group, led by Ahmad Yusif Hashim and Muhammad Ahmad Mahjub. Their programme called on Egypt and Britain to set a transitional period for Sudan's self-determination, during which power would gradually be transferred from the Condominium government to the Sudanese. In 1945, however, when the Mahdi coterie instituted the Umma Party, the Qawmiyyin merged into the new party. Whereas the Qawmiyyin had judiciously and cautiously distanced themselves from Egyptian claims over Sudan, the Umma Party was more forthright and overtly hostile in its attitude to the junior co-dominum. Among those who helped found the Umma Party were Ahmad 'Uthman Al-Qadi, 'Abdallah Khalil, Muhammad 'Ali Shawqi, Ibrahim Ahmad, Muhammad al-Khalifah Sharif, Muhammad 'Uthman Mirghani and Ahmad Yusif Hashim.

Although attempts were made to re-unite the divided Sudanese nationalist movement,[97] the divisions persisted.

VII   THE RISE OF A RADICAL NATIONALIST MOVEMENT, 1945–56

As has been shown in the previous section, the Sudanese nationalist movement emerged into the mid-1940s in a divided condition. The major political parties were closely associated with patrons within the Sudanese establishment, and with one or other of the co-domini. The objectives of these parties were inevitably shaped and moulded by establishment interests. Their main concern was with Sudan's political future, whether independent or in union with Egypt, rather than with social or economic change. The policies they put forward in social and economic fields purveyed a generalised desire for development and the common welfare. Evidently the intention was to dismantle the political structures of Condominium rule while retaining intact its principal social and economic structures.

The reluctance or perhaps inability of the main political parties to envisage radical change outside the purely political field, laid the basis for the emergence of a new 'radical nationalist' movement – composed of political groupings committed to the kind of wide-ranging programmes of social and economic transformation eschewed by the main parties. Given the poverty experienced by so much of the population, and the unequal distribution of wealth and social influence (as described in Chapter 3), there were inevitably parts of the population whose discontent with existing conditions made such programmes attractive. Although the rural poor and some of the urban poor were neither sufficiently politically conscious to respond, nor practically capable of responding, to a call for social and economic transformation, the programmes put forward by radical nationalists could find a response among the intermediate strata and urban workers.

The task confronting radical nationalists in putting their programmes before the population was facilitated by the development at this time of associations defending the sectional interests of particular parts of the population (workers, students, women, etc.). As shown in Chapter 4, a close and mutually supportive relationship developed between these associations and radical nationalist groupings. Often, indeed, the associations were directly created by the political groups, although the membership of the former would be considerably more catholic in political complexion than the latter. A shared concern with social and economic matters created a natural sense of common purpose between the associations and radical nationalists. Through their influence on trade unions, women's unions, students' unions and tenants' unions, therefore, radical nationalist groupings could play a more substantial political role than their relatively limited memberships would seem to have justified.

The Sudanese Movement for National Liberation (SMNL), later to become the Sudanese Communist Party, was by far the most important of the radical nationalist groupings which emerged at this time.[98] Two separate circles of Sudanese communists came together to form the SMNL. The first circle had developed among Sudanese students in Cairo, who were drawn into the Egyptian Movement for National Liberation (EMNL). As early as 1944 this circle began publication (in Egypt) of a magazine, *Umdurman*, aimed at influencing Sudanese opinion. The second circle emerged within Sudan, largely through contacts between British communists, serving in Sudan as soldiers and officials, and Sudanese students and young graduates.[99] The SMNL formally came into existence early in 1946.

The SMNL's development over the 1946–56 period may be divided into three stages: 1946–7, 1947–9, and 1949–56.[100] Between its inception and July 1947, the movement was led by 'Abd al-Wahab Zain al-Abdin,[101] who held the post of organisation secretary. Under 'Abd al-Wahab's leadership the movement operated in a highly secretive manner, concealing its existence both from the Condominium authorities and from other nationalist parties and movements. Its principal objective at this time seems to have been to exert a radicalising influence on the Ashiqqah. This concentration on, and involvement with, the Ashiqqah ultimately led to a change in the movement's leadership. Accused of being a 'royalist communist' (presumably because he accepted the Ashiqqah objective of Sudanese self-determination under the Egyptian crown) 'Abd al-Wahab was forced to cede the post of organisation secretary in July 1947 to 'Awad 'Abd al-Raziq.[102]

Between July 1947 and early 1949 the SMNL adopted a more open role. Rather than seeking to radicalise the Ashiqqah from within, the movement now sought to mobilise the population directly. The movement's Marxist ideology was actively diffused and a campaign to attract new recruits, mainly among students and workers, was undertaken. Considerable attention was given to establishing and maintaining SMNL influence within the associations representing sectional interests. SMNL members were prominent among those who formed the Workers' Affairs Association (1946) and the Women's Association (1947), retaining key positions in both associations. In 1947 the movement set up a front organisation for Sudanese youth, the Youth Conference,[103] and in that same year SMNL members won control of the University College Students' Union. With strong support among students, and the ability to mobilise opinion elsewhere in the urban population, the SMNL was able to play an important part in the 'boycott movement' of 1947–8. The latter movement, involving nationwide demonstrations organised initially by the unionist parties to protest against the 1948 Legislative Assembly elections, gave the SMNL the opportunity both to display and to strengthen its support. The militancy of the demonstrations and the sharpness of the confrontation with the Condominium authorities[104] owed much to the SMNL's role.

The attitude which the SMNL adopted towards the Ashiqqah over this period was two-sided. On the one hand, the Ashiqqah and other unionist parties were vilified for defending the interests of the Egyptian bourgeoisie, just as the Umma Party was condemned for protecting British interests.[105] On the other hand, the Ashiqqah's confrontationist campaign against the Condominium authorities was seen as complementary to that waged by the SMNL. Cooperation between the two could be of mutual benefit. 'Awad 'Abd al-Raziq maintained, furthermore, a Menshevik attitude towards the prospects for revolution in Sudan: bourgeois parties would inevitably take the lead in the democratic revolution, and only thereafter could a socialist party hope to gain power. The movement did, however, now distance itself from the Ashiqqah's unionist policy, stating its immediate policy simply as the liberation of Sudan and the institution of a democratic regime.

Early in 1949, 'Awad 'Abd al-Raziq was removed as party leader. His place was taken by 'Abd al-Khaliq Mahjub, who retained this position through to his execution in 1971. Subsequent publications of the Sudanese Communist Party have given a number of reasons for 'Awad's removal. He is criticised for having imposed his personal wishes on the movement, rather than abiding by party rules, and for 'flirting with bourgeois parties'.[106] The nature and extent of his cooperation with the Ashiqqah evidently lay behind the latter criticism. In October 1951 'Awad 'Abd al-Raziq and some supporters sought, in the course of an SMNL congress, to re-capture the leadership. They charged 'Abd al-Khaliq with seeking to skip a stage in socio-political development, and pressed the view that Sudan needed to pass through a democratic revolution under bourgeois leadership before it was possible to organise directly for socialist revolution. The dissenters were defeated and subsequently left the SMNL, forming a new organisation, the Sudanese Democratic Movement, which itself ultimately split and withered away.[107]

Under its new leadership the SMNL, between 1949 and 1956, pursued an intensified campaign to mobilise workers, peasants and students in the anti-colonial struggle. While the movement was still prepared on occasion to cooperate with the unionist parties, when the conditions of that cooperation were clearly specified, the general attitude towards these parties was more critical than before. Greater emphasis was placed on the SMNL's separate identity. The movement's achievement over this period is ably depicted by Mohamed Nuri El-Amin:

> The SMNL under 'Abd al-Khaliq thus became what the more influential amongst its founders and supporters . . . had from the start wanted it to be: professedly communist, staunchly anti-imperialist, unashamedly anti-bourgeois political parties, proudly independent, and extremely combative. As such it quickly came to pose a major threat to the authorities, to the big national parties who had long taken it for granted that they were the sole representatives of the Sudanese nation, and to the more moderate communists who had always harboured some doubts as to whether the new line was the best way of realising the objectives of the party. As for the authorities, by 1950 the Government fully realised that communism was not the transitory phenomenon it had first thought it to be; and also that if its tide was to be stemmed, a much tougher approach was surely needed.[108]

In 1953 the SMNL, while not itself seeking registration as a political party, established a public organ – the Anti-Imperialist Front – to compete in the elections for the constituent assembly. The Front succeeded in winning one seat in the assembly.[109]

As Sudan moved towards independence, then, the political scene was dominated by parties linked to establishment interests, but radical nationalists had achieved positions of influence within some critical sectors of the population. It should be admitted, however, that the dichotomy between establishment-linked nationalism and radical nationalism presented here does not fit as neatly as has so far been suggested. Most of the unionist parties had radical nationalist wings: members whose objectives were not limited to the dismantlement of political structures alone, and whose social and economic concerns drew them into involvement with trade unions, tenants' unions and other associations. The youth movement of the Ashiq-qah, for example, falls clearly into the radical nationalist classification. A continuing struggle between establishment-linked nationalism and radical nationalism, in fact, occurred within the Ashiqqah and subsequently within the National Unionist Party.

VIII   THE TRANSITION TO INDEPENDENCE

The dynamics of the divided Sudanese nationalist movement as it passed through the transition to independence stayed within the mould set by the events of the early 1940s: the Umma Party pressing for independence, and prepared to cooperate to this end with the Condominium government; the unionist groupings, which came together in 1952 to form the National Unionist Party, pressing at least until 1954 for union with Egypt; and the radical nationalists, in the background, beginning to raise a challenge to the establishment-oriented nature of both of the major political tendencies. The Umma Party's increasing enthusiasm for early independence led some of the non-Mahdist tribal leaders to distance themselves from Sayyid 'Abd al-Rahman and, joining together with a small number of intellectuals, to form the Socialist Republican Party. It seems probable that Condominium officials encouraged the latter development.

The intricate interactions between the British and Egyptian governments, and between the various Sudanese nationalist groups and the two co-domini, have been examined in detail elsewhere.[110] Here they will only be summarised. The pace of progress towards Sudanese self-determination was set as much by the desire of each co-dominum to out-manoeuvre the other as it was by developments within Sudan. The creation by the Condominium government of the Advisory Council for Northern Sudan (1943–8), and of the Legislatve Assembly (1948–52), in part reflected the desire of the British to retain the initiative. The pressures which followed from the Egyptian government taking the Sudan issue before the United Nations, linking the issue with a satisfactory understanding over the British military presence on the Suez canal, and ultimately abrogating the 1898 and 1936 agreements, all forced the pace towards a more significant role for Sudanese in government.

When the Egyptian monarchy was overthrown in July 1952 and the new Egyptian government indicated its willingness to allow the Sudanese to choose between union or independence, the way was open for an agreement. Discussions between the principal Sudanese parties and the Egyptian government led to an agreed framework for self-determination being reached on 10 January 1953. Agreement between the British and Egyptian governments followed on 12 February. Elections for Sudan's first parliament took place in November and December 1953, with the National Unionist Party winning a large majority (see Table 6.1, p. 208). Isma'il al-Azhari assumed office as prime minister in January 1954. Early in 1955 it became apparent that al-Azhari and the majority of his ministers were intent on leading Sudan towards independence, not union with Egypt. Given the tactical reasons which had originally caused the confrontationist groupings to adopt the 'Unity of the Nile Valley' policy, it should not cause surprise that the overall strategy could now change. The reality of Britain's impending withdrawal made union with Egypt unnecessary.

6 The Dynamics of Post-independence Politics, 1956–69

I PERSPECTIVE

The political history of the 1956–69 period was dominated by one central characteristic: political influence and authority rested with those social groupings which had benefited from the distribution of resources under the Condominium. As might be expected, therefore, those who framed government policy were not inclined to undertake a radical reformation of the country's socio-economic structure. The two kinds of imbalance or inequality which had become prominent under the Condominium – differentiating both regions of the country and social groupings within it – continued and, indeed, became more marked.

This is not to say that politicians were unaware of the imbalances, or of the desirability of pursuing policies which sought to rectify them. Most party programmes in the 1950s and 1960s pledged the party concerned to foster development in the less developed provinces and to improve conditions for the less privileged elements in society. The state, however, lacked the dynamic to turn such pronouncements into a reality. Political parties achieved, and maintained themselves in power, by their alliances with those senior establishment figures whose social influence (whether based on tribal, religious or economic pre-eminence) enabled them to sway the voting inclinations of the population. Their hold on power, therefore, did not depend on the pursuit of policies whose economic, social or political content attracted popular support.

The political dynamics of the 1956–69 period stem from this aspect. Those who ruled Sudan over these years sought to develop the country within the socio-economic structure which they had inherited from the Condominium era, with minor changes. The interests of the incipient bourgeoisie found expression in the framework set by the Sudanese establishment. Ever-deepening problems arose, however, as a result of the perpetuation and intensification of the two critical imbalances in the system. Political movements based on those who were regionally or socially disadvantaged grew in strength, posing a threat to the stability and coherence of the polity – or at least to the ability of the establishment and the incipient bourgeoisie to retain the leading role. Radical political parties, free officer groups in the army, trade union and occupational organisations based on the intermediate strata or possibly the urban and rural poor, regionalist parties and regionalist/secessionist guerrilla movements all formed part of this response to a system of rule which perpetuated and intensified social and regional imbalances. The radical nationalist and regionalist organisations which had sprung up in the late 1940s and early 1950s naturally formed the basis of this opposition.

The threat to the establishment-dominated Sudanese polity from radical and regionalist elements grew stronger as the years passed and the imbalances persisted. The growing strength of the radical/regionalist threat produced three different types of reaction among establishment/bourgeois circles. First, there were those who were confident that the threat could be contained without necessitating major change. Such elements concentrated their attention on devising legislation which limited extra-parliamentary radical activity (e.g. laws restricting the right of workers to strike, outlawing 'subversive organisations', narrowly defining the permitted role of trade unions, etc.), and on ensuring that the division of parliamentary constituencies gave due weight to parts of the population imbued with conservatism (e.g. the 1958 electoral laws).

Second, there were others who favoured reliance on the military – whether as an instrument to be used against the regionalist groups who threatened the state's integrity (particularly with respect to southern Sudan), or else as a force which would take over the functions of government (i.e. the 'Abbud regime). The role of the military in the latter case would bear no resemblance to that of the free officers in Nasser's Egypt. The army generals would maintain the country's existing socio-economic structure, not seek to reform it.

Third, others again began to move away from the establishment/bourgeois reluctance to envisage significant change. An inclination was exhibited towards reforms which might begin to rectify the country's regional and social imbalances. The political groups which adopted this view wanted the state to play a more active role in managing the economy and distributing the benefits of production. The failure of the existing system to solve the country's problems was blamed on the traditionalism of parts of the establishment, whose influence over the state should therefore be reduced. The more modern state machine which would then emerge would be able to deal with the country's problems more effectively, making greater use of the knowledge and expertise of trained and educated Sudanese.

The development of these latter notions accounts for the new direction taken by the National Unionist Party between 1956 and 1958, the split in the Umma Party after 1966, and the dissension within the Democratic Unionist Party in 1968–9 (when a group of Democratic Unionist members of parliament, led by Musa Mubarak, pursued a critical line towards their party leadership). It was, not surprisingly, the more educated members of the political elite who tended to take this approach, gaining support more from the commercial sector of the bourgeoisie than from the agrarian landowners or pump-scheme operators.[1] The significance of these reforming groups within the political system, however, should not be exaggerated. Their reformist inclinations tended to be strongest when they had no stake in government, and in some cases seemed to be motivated more by tactical considerations than by deep-rooted commitment.

One positive aspect of the pre-1969 independent Sudanese state, at least over the two parliamentary periods (1956–8, and 1964–9), was the degree of political freedom which it offered its citizens. No doubt this freedom could only be fully appreciated and utilised by a fairly small elite, but the atmosphere of open and unfettered debate which occurred within the parliament, the press and the institutions of higher education encouraged a high degree of intellectual sophistication within this elite.

What follows in this chapter is not intended to constitute a detailed account of politics and policies pursued between 1956 and 1969, but focuses rather on aspects which highlight some of the key dynamics.

II 1956–8: THE FIRST PARLIAMENTARY PERIOD

(a) The emergence of the National Unionist Party as a secular nationalist movement

The experience of the National Unionist Party (NUP) between its substantial victory in the 1953 elections (winning 46 of the 92 seats in the constituent House of Representatives) and the 1958 coup, is indicative of the manner in which the Sudanese establishment (spe cifically the two main religious leaders) controlled and manipulated political authority at this time.

The NUP had been formed in 1952. It was the Egyptian government which had taken the initiative in bringing together the formerly divided and diverse unionist groupings, under the patronage of Sayyid 'Ali al-Mirghani. Isma'il al-Azhari was made party president, heading a national executive composed of elements from each of the erstwhile groups. From the outset, the NUP had a radical nationalist wing, distrustful of the party's links with establishment figures and eager to prevent such figures controlling party policy. The radical nationalist wing was based mainly on young members of the Ashiqqah, many of whom had served as secretaries of Ashiqqah residential area committees prior to 1952. These radical nationalists briefly formed an Ashiqqah Revolutionary Council in 1952 to oppose the allegedly reactionary elements which had gained key positions in the new party's leadership (the reference here was primarily to Mirghani Hamzah and Khalafallah Khalid, both of whom were closely associated with Sayyid 'Ali).[2]

The commanding position which the NUP enjoyed in the House of Representatives following the 1953 elections (see Table 6.1) would seem to have given Isma'il al-Azhari, as prime minister of the internally autonomous government which assumed power in January 1954, some freedom of manoeuvre. As the NUP's success in the elections was in part attributable to the charismatic following which al-Azhari had begun to attract, and to the organisational skill shown by his ex-Ashiqqah associates, the new prime minister appeared to have a strong basis on which to pursue his own policies – irrespective of the wishes of the NUP's religious patron. It was not Sayyid 'Ali's influence alone which had made success possible. Once al-Azhari began to show some independence of the religious patron, however, he countered a sustained and ultimately successful attempt to remove him from power. Sayyid 'Ali al-Mirghani and Sayyid 'Abd al-Rahman al-Mahdi, arch-rivals since the 1920s, came together to ensure the preservation of their political influence into the independence era.

Three developments appear to have convinced Sayyid 'Ali of the potential threat to his own political influence. First, in December 1954 three of the *sayyid*'s closest associates (Mirghani Hamzah, Khalafallah Khalid and Ahmad Jaili) were dismissed from al-Azhari's government, on grounds of failing to respect the cabinet's collective responsibility.[3] While al-Azhari had in fact sought and

Table 6.1   Seats Gained in the 1953 Elections for the House of
Representatives, by Province (Territorial Constituencies only)

Province	NUP	Umma	Socialist Republicans	Southern Party	Others	Total No. of Seats
Blue Nile	6	10	2	0	0	18
Darfur	2	6	1	0	2	11
Kordofan	11	6	0	0	0	17
Bahr el Ghazal	1	0	0	2	4	7
Equatoria	0	0	0	5	2	7
Kassala	6	1	0	0	1	8
Upper Nile	4	0	0	2	2	8
Khartoum	9	0	0	0	0	9
Northern	7	0	0	0	0	7
Total	46	23	3	9	11	92

Source: Sudanese Elections Commission, *Final Report on the 1953 Elections* (Government Printer, Khartoum, 1954), p. 27.

obtained Sayyid 'Ali's consent before taking this action,[4] the incident demonstrated al-Azhari's determination to maintain his own authority. Second, in June 1955 al-Azhari dismissed from his cabinet another senior *khatmi* minister, Muhammad Nur al-Din, despite a specific request from Sayyid 'Ali that this minister retain his government position.[5] Muhammad Nur al-Din had remained faithful to his unionist convictions while al-Azhari and other NUP leaders had changed tack and were now intent on independence. Third, in August–September 1955 Sayyid 'Ali sought to persuade al-Azhari's government to allow the issue of Sudan's future status (independence or union with Egypt) to be determined by a popular plebiscite. Al-Azhari insisted that the decision should rest with the parliament alone. The differences on this issue appear to have provoked considerable bitterness – possibly because Sayyid 'Ali saw the plebiscite as a means of avoiding any impairment to his relations with the Egyptian government.

From early in October 1955 Sayyid 'Ali began to move toward seeking al-Azhari's downfall. One final incident strengthened the *sayyid* in his resolve. Al-Azhari, concerned to ensure that he retained the parliamentary support necessary to counter the proposal for a plebiscite, began to open up contacts with associates of Sayyid 'Abd al-Rahman al-Mahdi. The possibility of an Umma–NUP coalition was mooted. Sayyid 'Ali, learning of these contacts, promptly an ranged to meet Sayyid 'Abd al-Rahman himself (the first meeting between the two arch-rivals for 20 years).[6] The understanding reached by the two religious leaders at the latter meeting, held on 10 October 1955, made possible a joint effort to displace al-Azhari.[7]

On 10 November 1955 some of Sayyid 'Ali's ex-NUP followers in parliament (now characterised as the Independent Republican Party) sided with Umma Party MPs in voting against al-Azhari's government on the budget issue. The expectation was that Mirghani Hamzah would become prime minister, heading an Umma–*khatmi* coalition government. The two religious leaders, however, had misjudged the popular mood. Violent street demonstrations broke out in support of al-Azhari. When the House of Representatives reassembled on 15 November, al-Azhari had regained majority approval. His displacement would have to await further developments.

Following the failure of the initial attempt to remove al-Azhari from power, Sayyid 'Ali adopted a new strategy. He called for the establishment of a 'national government':

> All Sudanese political parties should form a national government, so that our national objectives and strategies should be realised in an atmosphere of political tranquillity and mutual understanding.[8]

Such a government would at least reduce al-Azhari's freedom of action and might make possible the selection of a new prime minister. Sayyid 'Abd al-Rahman and the Umma Party lent their support to this initiative. While al-Azhari's position was strong enough to enable him to guide through parliament on 23 December the declaration of Sudanese independence, which became effective on 1 January 1956, he had by the end of January lost the ability to resist the call for a national government. Apparently under instructions from Sayyid 'Ali, a group of *khatmi* ministers who had remained within the NUP made clear during January their preference for a national government. The latter group was led by Shaikh 'Ali 'Abd al-Rahman.[9] On 2 February 1956 al-Azhari duly formed a new cabinet, drawing into the government elements from all of the major political parties and groupings.

The formation of the 'national government' in February 1956, however, only brought al-Azhari a temporary respite. In May of that year a new political party was formed, the People's Democratic Party (PDP). The new party, which benefited from Sayyid 'Ali's blessing, drew together the three groups of ex-NUP *khatmi* MPs who had (for

different reasons) opposed al-Azhari: Mirghani Hamzah's Indepen
dent Republicans, Muhammad Nur al-Din's unionists, and the
grouping led by Shaikh 'Ali 'Abd al-Rahman. At the end of June
1956 the PDP and the Umma Party succeeded in forcing al-Azhari'
resignation. On 5 July an Umma–PDP coalition government wa
formed, headed by 'Abdallah Khalil. Over the remaining two year
of the first parliamentary period, the NUP was excluded from power

Despite the confrontation with Sayyid 'Ali, Isma'il al-Azhari and
his associates should not be deemed to have adopted a position
antipathetic to the Sudanese establishment as a whole – only to one
part of that establishment (albeit a very important part). It is signifi
cant, indeed, that many prominent tribal leaders rallied to al
Azhari's support, including Muhammad Ahmad Abu Sin (*nazir* o
the Shukriya), Ibrahim Farah (*nazir* of the Ja'aliyin) and Muhammad
Siddiq Talhah (*nazir* of the Butahin).[10] Similar support was forth
coming from the leaders of many of the smaller sufi orders, and even
from some of the local *khatmi* dignitaries (*khulafa*). One of Sayyid
'Ali's nephews, Hasan al-Mirghani, disassociated himself from hi
uncle's predilections.

Nonetheless, having been forced into opposition, the NUP de
veloped a more radical posture than that to which it had previously
adhered. The emphasis was now placed on the party's 'secula
nationalism', and one of the main slogans used by the party in the
1958 elections was '*la qadasah fil-siyasah*' (literally 'no holiness i
politics'). Stronger links were forged with those trade unions, pro
fessional associations and radical nationalist groups which were con
fronting the Umma–PDP government, such that in October 1958 a
national front was formed comprising the Sudanese Communis
Party, the Sudan Workers Trade Union Federation, tenants' and
farmers' unions, student unions, the (southern) Federal Party and the
NUP. The charter of the front called for the abolition of law
restricting basic freedoms, the cancellation of the aid agreement with
the United States, the assertion of positive neutrality in Sudan'
foreign policy, the normalisation of relations with Egypt, and the
adoption of a national democratic constitution.[11] The NUP gave it
support to the strike organised by the SWTUF on 21 October 1958 i
protest against the government's denial of legal recognition to the
SWTUF.

(b) Changing electoral rules and the 1958 elections

Having gained power, the Umma–PDP coalition government sought to improve its chances of retaining power in the elections scheduled for 1958 by adapting the electoral framework. A concerted attempt was made to ensure that the electorate was structured in such a manner that the more conservative political forces gained increased representation. Greater 'representation', therefore, was given to those parts of the population where tribal and religious allegiances remained strong and where the electors would vote loyally for whoever their tribal or religious leaders nominated.

Some of the measures taken, although geared towards short-term political manipulation, were legitimate and to some extent justified. These measures included:

(i) Dropping the educational requirement for electors in the senate constituencies. Education had been the sole qualification for such electors in the 1953 elections. Now every Sudanese male above the age of 30 was permitted to vote.

(ii) Loosening the nationality provisions, such that some of those individuals previously excluded from voting on nationality grounds could now vote. More than 50 per cent of the 6264 people who gained Sudanese nationality before the 1958 elections (under the 1957 Nationality Bill) were Fellata, of West African origin. The Fellata, having been influenced by Mahdism, supported the Umma Party.

(iii) Introducing mobile polling units in nomadic areas, so as to increase voting among the nomadic population.[12]

Other measures, while still legitimate, involved a more direct attempt to change the parliamentary balance. The five graduates' constituencies which had existed in the 1953 elections were abolished. Four of the graduates' seats had been won in 1953 by the NUP, and one by the Anti-Imperialist Front. Of even greater significance was the re-ordering of territorial constituency representation, which involved increasing the number of House of Representatives constituencies from 92 to 173. The rural areas were the beneficiaries of the new distribution of constituencies. While this could be justified on grounds of equalising the size of the population units within different constituencies (in 1953 urban constituencies had comprised about 43 000 people, whereas rural constituencies had comprised about 120 000), the major increases in constituency numbers occurred in provinces where the PDP and Umma Party held predominant influence (see Table 6.2).

Yet other measures constituted illegitimate devices to strengthen the position of the ruling parties. Bechtold's analysis of the 1958 elections shows that the territorial delimitation of nine constituencies was gerrymandered in order to improve the prospects for the PDP or Umma Party. It should be noted that whereas the delimitation of constituencies in 1953 was determined by an international commission, and in 1965 would be undertaken by a non-partisan committee, in 1958 the government retained control over this matter. In some cases constituencies were created comprising non-contiguous parcels of territory.[13] The Umma or PDP candidates won in eight of the nine gerrymandered constituencies.

While the victory of the Umma–PDP alliance in the 1958 elections was not wholly the result of changes in the electoral framework, these changes certainly constituted a significant element in that victory. As indicated in Table 6.3, the NUP won about 340 400 votes in the 1958 elections (northern provinces) but only gained 40 seats; whereas the Umma Party won about 310 000 votes and gained 62 seats. The PDP, winning about 147 000 votes, gained 26 seats. In this way the strength of the threat posed to the political influence of the major religious leaders by the NUP's secular nationalism was diminished.

(c) The South

Over the period between 1953 and 1958 the political dynamics of self-determination and independence impinged adversely on southern Sudan. The most critical factors which shaped events stemmed from the South's severe underdevelopment and experience of political isolation (as described in Chapter 4). Lacking coherent political organisations through which southern interests could be articulated and defended, the views of southerners could easily be disregarded (or deliberately overlooked) by the northern political elite.

The 1953 elections constituted no basis on which an organised political movement representing southern interests could be built. Most of the successful candidates described themselves as belonging to the 'Southern Party', but this 'party' had neither programme, nor organisation, nor accepted leadership. The fluid and insubstantial nature of the political allegiances of the new southern MPs was

Table 6.2 Increases in Constituencies in Northern Sudan Between the 1953 and 1958 Elections, by Province

Province	Number of Constituencies in 1953	Number of Constituencies in 1958	Percentage Increase	Political Complexion of Province
Northern	7	16	128.0	PDP stronghold
Kassala	8	16	100.0	PDP/Umma stronghold
Darfur	11	22	100.0	Umma stronghold
Blue Nile	18	35	94.4	Umma/NUP mixed
Kordofan	17	29	76.6	NUP/Umma mixed
Khartoum	9	9	0.0	NUP stronghold

Source: Figures taken from el Fatih Abdullahi Abdel Salam, 'The Umma Party 1945–69', unpublished MA thesis, University of Khartoum, 1979, p. 120.

Table 6.3 Votes Won and Seats Gained in the 1958 House of Representatives Elections, by Province (Northern Sudan only)

Province	Umma Party		NUP		PDP		Others	
	Votes won (thousands)	Seats gained	Votes won (thousands)	Seats gained	Votes won (thousands)	Seats gained	Votes won (thousands)	Seats gained
Khartoum	—*	—	45.6	8	23.9	1	2.2	0
Blue Nile	139.2	17	129.9	16	27.7	2	9.0	0
Northern	6.2	2	38.1	2	46.2	12	3.9	0
Kassala	20.5	5	21.3	1	36.6	10	10.8	0
Kordofan	86.5	19	72.0	10	9.5	0	16.3	0
Darfur	57.4	19	24.0	3	2.7	0	10.3	0
Total	310.0	62	340.4	40	147.0	25	53.3	0

* Under its alliance with the PDP, the Umma Party put up no candidates in Khartoum.

Source: Compiled from statistics given in Sudanese Elections Commission, *Report on the 1958 Elections* (Government Printer, Khartoum, 1958).

Table 6.4 Overall Result of the 1958 Elections

Party	House of Representatives	Senate
Umma	63	14
NUP	44	5
PDP	26	4
Southern Liberals	40	7
Total	173	30

Source: Peter K. Bechtold, *Politics in the Sudan Since Independence* (Praeger Publishers, New York, a division of Greenwood Press Inc., 1977), p. 190. Copyright © 1977 by Praeger Publishers. Used with permission.

reflected in frequent changes of allegiance over the parliamentary period. On the boat which carried most of the southern members of parliament to Khartoum, the decision was taken to constitute themselves as the Liberal Party but, as Howell states, 'the Liberal Party never became very much more than a parliamentary number . . . almost continually divided by disputes over policy and leadership'.[14] Although some five of the southern MPs had run for election under the banner of the NUP, this did not reflect a long-term commitment to that party. The 'assistance' which northern politicians could offer to their southern counterparts once they arrived in Khartoum inevitably swayed parliamentary votes and loyalties.

Both before and after independence, then, the South's political interests could be, and were, subjected to the overriding concerns of the northern political elite. No southerner had been invited to take part in the discussions which the northern political parties had held with the Egyptian government prior to the 1953 Anglo–Egyptian agreement. Southerners remained peripheral to the debate over independence arrangements during 1955, except when their votes were needed in parliament. Such attention as the major northern political parties did give to southern Sudan, moreover, was motivated by short-term political interest and often had destructive consequences. Promises were made by northern politicians in the course of the 1953 elections which bore little relation to what these politicians intended, or were able, to do. The NUP's 'Manifesto on the Southern Sudan', for example, stated that

. . . not only shall priority be given to southerners in the South but also shall the employment of southerners be greatly fostered in the North, especially in the higher ranks of the central government.[15]

Yet the Sudanisation commission, which held responsibility for the allocation of posts formerly occupied by non-Sudanese, operated according to standard civil service criteria, making appointments on the basis of seniority, experience and qualifications. Far from southerners being 'given priority in the South' or gaining posts in the 'higher ranks of the central government', southerners benefited little from Sudanisation. The outgoing British officials were mostly replaced by northern Sudanese counterparts.

The disappointment over broken promises, the resentment at the constant overlooking of the South's political interests, and the alienation brought on by instances of insensitivity shown by inexperienced northern officials drafted to the South, all created a growing spirit of unrest in southern Sudan in 1954 and 1955.[16] The involvement in the area of Christian missionaries and the meddling of the Egyptian government (seeking to undermine the position of al-Azhari and force the NUP back towards a unionist policy) added strength to this spirit. In August 1955 the Equatorial Corps of the Sudan Defence Force mutinied. Some 261 northern Sudanese and 75 southerners were killed in the disturbances which followed.

From independence through to the overthrow of the first parliamentary regime, the major northern political parties and the southern political elite saw the issue of southern Sudan in fundamentally different ways. While both traced the growing problem of unrest in the South to the cultural, linguistic and religious differences between the South and North, and recognised that Condominium policies had emphasised if not created these differences, the conclusions they drew differed radically. The northern political parties set out to undo the disintegrative effects of Condominium policy: abolishing the southern command of the Sudan Defence Force (now transformed into the Sudanese Armed Forces), introducing Arabisation into southern education, bringing the mission schools under government control, and encouraging human contacts and exchanges between South and North. A coherent rationale underlay this policy, yet it neglected the negative impact which these moves would have on an already-suspicious and defensive population.

The southern political elite, on the other hand, sought the adoption of a constitutional framework which would give some protection to the South's particularistic interests. Increasingly, this took the form of demands for a federal arrangement. The support of southern MPs for the declaration of Sudanese independence was given only after the House of Representatives had resolved on 19 December 1955 that 'the claims of the southern members of parliament for a federal government for the three southern provinces be given full consideration by the constituent assembly'.[17] When the assembly's constitutional committee, which contained only three southerners among its 43 members, in due course gave consideration to this matter and rejected federation, the southern political elite became embittered. The 1958 elections saw a more hard-line group of MPs, organised as the Federal Bloc, returned to parliament from southern Sudan.

III   1958–64: THE 'ABBUD REGIME

(a) The assumption of power by the military

The military coup which occurred on 17 November 1958 was more a civilian handover of power, instigated by the then prime minister 'Abdallah Khalil, than a military seizure of power. The role which 'Abdallah Khalil played in prompting the military action is amply documented in the evidence which General 'Abbud and others subsequently presented to the 1964 committee of enquiry into the events of November 1958. General 'Abbud stated:

> Ten days before the opening of parliament 'Abdullah Khalil visited me and reiterated his view that the political situation in the country was deteriorating progressively. He argued that only the army could save the country from this state of anarchy and indecision. A few days later he sent Zain al-'Abdin Salih to me with a similar message. Three days later 'Abdallah Khalil visited me again. This time I assured him that the Y-day would be before parliament re-opened. He replied: 'May God assist you' . . .
> I did not ask him for any written orders, because we were not used to that in the army. 'Abdallah Khalil's orders were the orders of a superior to his subordinate. I accepted them on that basis and I carried them out accordingly . . .
> 'Abdallah Khalil was the mastermind of the coup idea . . . Had he asked us to stop staging the coup, we would have done that immediately.[18]

'Abdallah Khalil had hoped and believed, it would seem, that the intervention of the military would enable him to remain in government.

The coalition Umma–PDP cabinet which he headed was disintegrating due to differences over the acceptance of American aid, with the Umma Party favouring acceptance and the PDP opposed. Contacts over the formation of an alternative coalition government had begun. A meeting in Cairo between al-Azhari and Shaikh 'Ali 'Abd al-Rahman in October had suggested that an NUP–PDP alliance was envisaged, but in fact discussions between senior members of the Umma Party and the NUP were proceeding at the same time. Under either of the possible coalitions 'Abdallah Khalil would, it seems, have been forced to relinquish the premiership. On the evening of 16 November agreement was reached on the formation of an Umma–NUP coalition; the announcement was to be made at the re-opening of parliament the following day. The military had by then, however, assumed power.

The role which 'Abdallah Khalil had envisaged for the military is evident from his remarks to colleagues on the morning following the coup:

> Nothing has changed. Politics will go on as they are. Tomorrow you will hear on the radio that there will be a new government, and a new council of ministers . . . The new government will include eight ministers from the Umma Party, and perhaps four from the NUP, and one or two from the PDP.[19]

Such may also have been the conception of the army generals when they took power. By 19 November, however, they had decided to involve the military more deeply in the political process. The formation of a Supreme Council of the Armed Forces (SCAF) was announced, composed of thirteen senior army officers. The SCAF then proceeded to nominate the members of the new council of ministers. Seven of the senior army officers on the SCAF were given ministerial portfolios.

General 'Abbud's 'broadcast to the nation' on the morning of 17 November both expressed, and was geared to cater to, the fears and concerns of the Sudanese establishment – over the parliamentary government's weakness in the face of an increasingly strong radical movement, the disruption caused by the trade unions, and the deteriorating economic situation. The new regime would, General 'Abbud assured the Sudanese population, restore order to a situation of spreading anarchy:

. . . All of you are aware of the state of deterioration, chaos and instability which prevailed throughout the country. This corruption and chaos was extended to the governmental and public institutions. All this was due to the strife among political parties, each of which sought gains for itself by various means, legal and illegal, and through the exploitation of some papers and the contact with foreign embassies.[20]

The general announced the dissolution of all political parties; the prohibition of gatherings, processions and demonstrations in all the provinces; and a ban on all papers 'until further notice is issued by the minister of the interior'.

Over the six years which followed the November 1958 coup, the senior army officers who now held power benefited from the active support of significant parts of the Sudanese establishment. This, indeed, constituted the regime's social base. The rivalries within the establishment, however, were such that the regime's close relationship with one part of the establishment could adversely affect its relationship with other parts. The failure of some establishment circles to attract the favours of the regime, therefore, could impel them – at least temporarily – towards adopting an opposition posture.

This process is best illustrated with respect to the Mahdist leadership. Two days after the coup, Sayyid 'Abd al-Rahman al-Mahdi issued a pronouncement which strongly supported the action which the army leadership had taken. It is interesting that the themes pursued in this pronouncement directly echoed those which General 'Abbud had propounded in his broadcast. The *sayyid* stated:

It grieves me greatly to say that the politicians who have led the political parties have all failed. None of the four governments which followed one another in the seat of power proved successful . . . The Sudanese people became disillusioned . . .

This now is a day of release. The men of the Sudanese army have sprung up and taken matters in their own hands . . . They will not permit hesitation, anarchy or corruption to play havoc in this land . . .

God has placed at our disposal . . . someone who will take up the reins of government with truth and decisiveness . . . Rejoice at this blessed revolution and go to your work calmly and contentedly, to support the men of the Sudanese revolution.[21]

Sayyid 'Abd al-Rahman's early enthusiasm reflected the close ties which linked the new regime to Mahdist circles: the possibility of military involvement in government had in fact first been mooted in discussions between Siddiq al-Mahdi (Sayyid 'Abd al-Rahman's son) and General 'Abbud in September 1958;[22] the coup itself had been instigated by the Umma Party prime minister; two prominent members of the Umma Party were appointed to the new council of ministers; and the new regime's initial 'strongman', General Ahmad 'Abd al-Wahab, had been known as a strong Umma Party supporter.[23] It seems possible, moreover, that 'Abdallah Khalil had indicated to Sayyid 'Abd al-Rahman that the new regime might bestow on the *sayyid* the title of President-for-life.[24] The carry-over of policy from the Umma Party to the new regime was demonstrated most clearly when General 'Abbud confirmed his government's acceptance of the American aid agreement.

From March 1959, however, the Mahdist establishment began to take a rather more critical view of the regime. This followed changes within the regime leadership. Two senior army officers who were not on the SCAF, Brigadier 'Abd al-Rahim Shannan (commander of the northern areas) and Brigadier Muhi al-Din Ahmad 'Abdallah (commander of the eastern areas) moved their troops to Khartoum and demanded the reconstitution of the SCAF. The former officer was known to have had links with the PDP, and the latter with the NUP. Their major objective seems to have been to counter the ascendancy of General Ahmad 'Abd al-Wahab. In the events which ensued, the SCAF was indeed reconstituted (with the inclusion of the two brigadiers) and Ahmad 'Abd al-Wahab was dismissed.[25] Although the two brigadiers were themselves subsequently dismissed from the SCAF, when they sought in May 1959 to remove another senior Umma-connected officer (Hasan Bashir Nasr) from the leadership, the departure of Ahmad 'Abd al-Wahab loosened the links between the regime and the Mahdist establishment.

The measure of disillusionment brought about in Mahdist circles by personnel changes in the regime laid the basis for Siddiq al-Mahdi, who became *imam* of the *ansar* following Sayyid 'Abd al-Rahman's death in 1959, to adopt an oppositionist role. Political principle may also have helped set the new direction: while the new *imam* had not opposed 'Abbud's assumption of power, he wanted the military role in government to be limited both in time and extent. Siddiq, therefore, participated in the establishment of a national front in 1960, grouping together some former politicians who were committed to the restoration of civilian rule. The memorandum which the front presented to the government in November 1960 called for the return of the army to its barracks, the formation of an interim civilian government, and the holding of elections for a constituent assembly.[26] With Siddiq's untimely death in 1961, however, the Mahdist leadership adopted a more complaisant attitude to the regime. Al-Hadi al-Mahdi, who now assumed the imamate, used the occasion of his first pronouncement as *imam* to conciliate the regime.[27]

The Khatmiyyah establishment, meanwhile, moved from a cautious welcome of the military regime to active participation in its institutions. Sayyid 'Ali's initial reaction to the military takeover was considerably more circumspect than was that of Sayyid 'Abd al-Rahman. While this may in part have reflected Sayyid 'Ali's customary disinclination for the expression of forthright views, the suspicion that the new regime constituted a military extension of the Umma Party also caused restraint. The *sayyid*'s message to the Sudanese population stated:

> We have heard that the Sudanese army . . . has taken over the reins of power in our country. We trust that the army's efforts and intentions instil assurance in people and instil security and stability in the realms of the country.
>
> We also ask God that what has happened may lead to the prosperity and success of the country, and that he may inspire those who have taken responsibility.[28]

With the removal of Ahmad 'Abd al-Wahab from the SCAF, the Khatmiyyah began to draw closer to the regime. Policy grounds were later used, with some degree of credibility, to justify the strengthening Khatmiyyah alignment with the regime. Once Ahmad 'Abd al-Wahab had been forced off the SCAF, it was contended, the regime had been able to pursue a more genuinely non-aligned foreign policy, to establish a close and mutually beneficial relationship with Nasser's Egypt, and to conclude the 1959 Nile waters agreement.[29] The support of the Khatmiyyah establishment became crucial to the regime's survival (or at least to its retention of any claim to legitimacy). When the national front put forward its demand in 1960 for the restoration of civilian rule, the Khatmiyyah establishment took a lead in preparing a 'Memorandum of Honourable Citizens', pledging allegiance to the regime. Among those who signed the memorandum were most of the principal PDP leaders, including Shaikh 'Ali 'Abd al-Rahman and Muhammad Nur al-Din.[30] These same elements played an active role within the political institutions created by the regime in 1963.

(b) Civilian representation

In August 1959 General 'Abbud formed a committee, headed by chief justice Abu Rannat, to 'raise recommendations on the best way to make the people participate in their government', as a first step 'towards a final constitutional set-up which suits the Sudanese environment and protects it against hurriedly imported systems'.[31] The committee in due course recommended a three-tier system. Directly-elected local councils would send delegates to sit on province councils, which in turn would send six delegates each to the central council. The 54 provincial delegates in the central council would be complemented by 18 members nominated by the president. Government ministers would also sit on the council, *ex officio*. The central council's principal roles were to 'formulate legislation' and to 'draw up a constitution'.[32]

The full structure, as recommended by the Abu Rannat committee, was not brought into being until 1963, when elections for the local councils were held. The central council was inaugurated in November of that year. Such formalised civilian representation as the 'Abbud regime did arrange at the national level, therefore, covered only the eleven months prior to the regime's overthrow. The controlled and contrived nature of this representation – where parties were banned, and candidates could only seek election on their individual merits – gave the central council limited political significance. Government policies were tamely applauded.

The structuring of the elections ensured that those who won election to the central council came yet more exclusively from establishment backgrounds (tribal leaders, religious leaders, major merchants or professionals/senior administrators) than did the members of the 1953 and 1958 parliaments. Table 6.5 below classifies the council members according to their social backgrounds. Such 'farmers' and lower civil servants as gained membership mostly represented the southern provinces. The six members from Khartoum province consisted of three well-established merchants, two senior government officials, and one professional. The six from Kassala province comprised three tribal leaders, two senior government

Table 6.5   Occupational/Social Backgrounds of Central Council Members,
1963

Occupation/Social Background	Number	Percentage
Tribal leaders	22	31
Administrators	16	22
Merchants	15	21
Farmers	10	14
Religious leaders	9	12

Source: Hassan Saad el-Din Hassan, 'The Central Council of the Abboud
Regime', unpublished dissertation, Department of Political
Science, University of Khartoum, 1976, p. 28.

officials and one religious leader. The tribal leaders and religious
leaders all owned substantial agricultural schemes.[33]

(c) The South

Unrest in the South was to grow in intensity under the 'Abbud
regime, ultimately leading to the outbreak of the armed insurgency in
1963.[34] The critical interactions which led towards civil conflict can be
explained simply.

The conviction that the South's interests could only be adequately
protected if Sudan adopted a federal constitution had, by 1958,
become the apex around which the southern political elite revolved.
The assumption of power by the military extinguished hope for the
achievement of this objective. A series of speeches by the military
officers who had been appointed provincial governors in the South
brusquely ruled out political concessions.[35] The belief spread within
the southern political elite that the military take-over was a 'northern
plot', intended to extricate the northern political parties from a
situation where they had become less capable of resisting southern
demands.[36] The belief was mistaken, although it was true that the
greater unity and determination of the bloc of southern MPs elected
in 1958, and the divisions among the northern parties, had given the
South more opportunity than before of winning concessions.

The military regime's response to the political demands of southerners was to step up attempts to eliminate the South's particularism –
those aspects of language, culture and religion which formed the

basis of southern demands for separate treatment. When the measures which were taken towards this end encountered and engendered opposition, force was used to ensure acquiescence and to impose respect for 'law and order'.

The violence employed by the police and armed forces in suppressing dissent caused growing numbers of southern civilians to escape from government control, either by fleeing into exile or by absconding into the bush. The former were, in the initial stage, predominantly southerners who had completed their secondary (or higher) education and had held administrative or teaching posts. They came to constitute the core of the exile southern political leadership, forming the Sudan African Closed Districts National Union (SACDNU) in February 1962, which changed its name in April 1963 to the Sudan African National Union (SANU).[37] The political objective was now independence for southern Sudan. Those who absconded into the bush were more likely to be 'semi-educated' – former secondary school students who had abandoned (or been forced to abandon) their studies, or else very junior government employees with only elementary – or possibly intermediate – level education. Of greatest significance in the latter grouping were prison warders, NCOs and policemen.[38] These were to join up with some of the 1955 Equatorial Corps mutineers and to form bands of guerrilla fighters: the Anyanya.[39] A loose and secretive organisation emerged among educated southerners in Khartoum, to surface after October 1964 as the Southern Front.

While the military regime did examine possibilities of forwarding economic development in southern Sudan,[40] the main concern of government policy lay in Arabisation and Islamisation. Koranic schools were established in different parts of the south, intermediate Islamic institutes were established in six southern towns, and a secondary Islamic institute was set up in Juba.[41] In 1960 it was decreed that Fridays would replace Sundays as the day of rest in the South. Arabic replaced English as the medium of instruction in intermediate-level southern schools. In 1962 the Ministry of Interior promulgated a Missionary Societies Act, stating that because it had become 'clear that missionary organisations have directed most of their internal and external effort against the national government', it was necessary to 'regularise the work of the missions by limiting them to religious functions'.[42] In February 1964 the 335 Christian missionaries working in southern Sudan were expelled.

The policies pursued by the military regime in the South should not be construed as irrational, nor deemed to have been motivated by antipathy to Christianity. The military rulers saw themselves as waging a concerted campaign to counter the divisive effects of the Condominium's southern policy. The insensitive manner in which they pursued this objective, and the degree of violence which they were prepared to inflict on supposedly dissident parts of the population, however, simply strengthened southern consciousness of the North's domination.

The southern political elite began fleeing abroad in 1960. Major demonstrations against government policy occurred in southern schools in 1960 and 1962, followed by tough reprisals by the army. Anyanya activity began over the last five months of 1963, and by early 1964 Sudan was rent by civil war.

IV   1964–9: THE SECOND PARLIAMENTARY PERIOD

(a) The rise and fall of the transitional government, and subsequent developments

For a brief time, between October 1964 and February 1965, it looked as if the hold of the establishment over the political system was threatened. The overthrow of the 'Abbud regime was largely the work of radical political forces. Elements favourable to these radical political forces enjoyed predominant influence in the transitional government which was formed on 30 October 1964, under the leadership of Sirr al-Khatim al-Khalifah. The four months which followed saw a determined struggle by the establishment, working through the old political parties, to regain control over the political system. In the later part of February 1965 the transitional government was forced to resign.

It was the combined effect of massive popular demonstrations and a general strike, reinforced by indications that junior and middle-ranking army officers could not be relied upon to support the SCAF, which finally brought down the military regime. The discontent which had built up over the years was unleashed in reaction to the violence employed by the army in breaking up a students' meeting convened to discuss the situation in the South. One student was shot dead in the course of this confrontation, which occurred on 21 October, and another died in hospital the following day. A spontaneous protest demonstration by students in Khartoum on the morning of 22

October was joined by some 30 000 people. Sporadic incidents occurred in the Three Towns area through 22 and 23 October, with crowds gathering and attacking police vehicles. The government imposed a curfew at 2 p.m. on the afternoon of 23 October.[43]

While the demonstrations had begun in a sporadic and spontaneous fashion, the campaign against the military regime became more organised and concerted from 23 October. On that day a meeting of Sudanese members of staff in the university drew up a memorandum calling for a return to civilian rule, with the signatories simultaneously submitting their resignations from their university posts. Similar meetings were soon being held among teachers, doctors, lawyers, judges and civil servants, with similar memoranda being produced. Coordination among these groups led to a procession forming outside the judiciary building in Khartoum on the morning of 24 October, from where statements calling for the return of civilian rule were to be carried to the republican palace. When soldiers prevented the procession from moving, the groups which had organised it drafted a common call for a general strike:

> Masses of our great people, from workers, peasants, merchants, and civil servants to professionals, the professions that have signed below call upon you to carry out a general strike until the overthrow of the cursed military regime.[44]

The nature of the movement now brought workers and rural tenants into the forefront of the anti-regime campaign. On 25 October workers' and tenants' representatives came together with representatives of lawyers, doctors, teachers, etc. to form the national professionals' front. The general strike, which the front now coordinated, began on 26 October, with devastating effect:

> The general strike ground the towns to a standstill. It halted all internal communications, emptied the administration of its civil servants, cut the army in the South from its supply lines and reinforcements, and drew massive popular demonstrations up and down the country. The towns were rising in slightly slower sequence than the capital, but they were rising all the same, at Port Sudan, Medani, El Fasher and Atbara . . . In the Gezira, delegates of 60 organisations, watched over by a continuous audience of 3000, held a conference for the duration of the strike to hammer out new policies for the country.[45]

On the evening of the first full day of the strike, free officer elements within the army brought in troops to surround the republican palace, impressing on the members of the SCAF (who were meeting within) the weakness of their position. By the morning of 27 October, the SCAF had dissolved itself and the council of ministers, leaving General 'Abbud with executive and legislative powers pending the formation of a transitional national government.

The ousting of the SCAF, to be followed on 15 November by that of General 'Abbud was the achievement of groups which were not dependent for support on the Sudanese establishment. While the university teachers, lawyers, doctors and other professionals who helped initiate the movement enjoyed a high status within Sudanese society, they pursued their campaign not by drawing in the religious leaders, tribal leaders and big merchants, but by seeking to mobilise the urban workers and intermediate strata. A number of those who were active in the professional groups which formed had been associated with the Sudanese Communist Party. The social and economic programmes which began to emerge from the professionals' front, once the SCAF had been removed, incorporated radical demands for a state monopoly of foreign trade, and for the nationalisation of foreign banks and companies and of the private cotton estates.

The old political parties, meanwhile, had created an organisation of their own. The NUP, PDP and Umma Party, joined now by the Islamic Charter front (Muslim Brothers), came together in a united parties front. Negotiations between the latter front and the national professionals' front were arranged in the last days of October, so as to determine the composition of the transitional government. The leading role played by the national professionals' front in the overthrow of military rule was reflected in the composition of the new council of ministers, which was announced on 31 October. It comprised seven leading members of the national professionals' front (including the secretary of the trade union federation, and the secretary of the Gezira tenants' union), two southerners, and one member each from the Umma Party, NUP, PDP, Islamic Charter front and Communist Party.[46] As the members from the national professionals' front tended to ally themselves with the communist member, the council had a strongly radical tendency.

Over the months which followed, the transitional government set out in the direction of radical change, with respect to both domestic and foreign policy. A committee was set up to prepare recommendations on the phasing out of 'native administration'; an illegal enrichment court was established to investigate charges of corruption and suspect economic deals; the decision was taken to grant women the vote in all future elections; a commission was appointed to advise on agricultural reform; an economic strategy was devised which would involve assisting Sudanese companies to take over import–export trade from foreign companies, and generally helping Sudanese national capital to compete with foreign capital; much of the restrictive legislation which the 'Abbud regime had introduced was repealed, especially that relating to trade union rights; arrangements were made for boosting trade with Eastern Europe; and an active policy of support for liberation movements in the Middle East and Africa was adopted.

A number of these measures raised serious concern within the establishment. There was a strong suspicion that the illegal enrichment court would be used as an instrument with which to purge the civil service of rightist elements – not just of corrupt people. Of greater concern, however, was the proposal which emanated from the professionals' front, that 50 per cent of all seats in the new constituent assembly should be allocated to workers' and peasants' representatives. It was becoming apparent, moreover, that the professionals' front was seeking a long-term role in the country's policies. Branches of the front were being established in different parts of the country, and it seemed possible that the front would engage as one unit in forthcoming elections.

The united parties front centred their campaign against the dominant elements in the transitional government on the demand for early elections. This goal was pursued with increasing vituperation. The traditionalist followings of the establishment leaders were used to counter the transitional government's support among the urban populace. On 18 February the prime minister, Sirr al-Khatim al-Khalifah, tendered his government's resignation. Six days later he formed a new government, composed of ministers from the Umma Party, the NUP, the Islamic Charter front and the Southern front. The radical experiment was over.

The April 1965 elections, which were only held in northern Sudan due to the state of insecurity in the South, resulted in the Umma Party and the NUP emerging once again with strong parliamentary support. While politics had in many ways reverted to the 1956–8 pattern, however, there were some significant differences. These differences can best be appreciated with reference to Tables 6.6 and

Table 6.6   *Distribution of Seats after the 1965 Elections*

Party	Territorial constituencies	Graduates' constituencies	Total
Umma	76	—	76
NUP	52	2	54
ICF	3	2	5
PDP	3	—	3
Communists	—	8	8
Communist 'sympathisers'	—	3	3
Independents (including Beja Congress)	24 (10 Beja)	—	24
Total	158	15	173

Source: Peter K. Bechtold, *Politics in the Sudan Since Independence* (Praeger Publishers, New York, a division of Greenwood Press Inc., 1977), p. 232. Copyright © 1977 by Praeger Publishers. Used with permission.

6.7, which give details of the results of both the 1965 and 1968 elections. Regionalist parties in the second parliamentary period had become active in northern Sudan. The strongest of these was the Beja Congress, which won ten seats in 1965, and three in 1968, but in western Sudan, also, regionalism was becoming stronger. The growing number of votes attracted by independents and by a multiplicity of small organisations (many on the left), moreover, showed that the hold of the old political parties was beginning to weaken. The major new factor which was to influence the composition of governments, however, was the split in the Umma Party, with a modernist wing headed by Sadiq al-Mahdi, and a traditionalist wing headed by the *imam* al-Hadi al-Mahdi.

This, then, provided the framework within which a series of governments succeeded each other over the 1965–9 period. Between May 1965 and June 1966 Muhammad Ahmad Mahjub headed an Umma–NUP coalition; from June 1966 to May 1967 Sadiq al-Mahdi headed a coalition between his wing of the Umma Party and the NUP; from May 1967 through to the May 1969 coup, Mahjub returned at the head of a coalition between the *imam*-wing of the Umma Party and the NUP.

Despite the holding of a Round Table Conference in March 1965, bringing some of the exiled southern political leaders into negotiation with representatives of northern political parties, the conflict in the South continued.

Table 6.7   Official Election Results, 1968

Party	Votes	Percent	Number of candidates	Number of constituencies contested	Seats won
DUP	742 236	40.80	299	196	101
Umma–Sadiq	384 986	21.15	221	148	36
Umma–Imam	329 952	18.13	168	119	30
Independents	70 047	3.85	72	59	9
SANU	60 493	3.32	55	37	15
ICF	44 552	2.45	26	26	3
Umma	43 288	2.38	45	33	6
Southern Front	39 822	2.19	43	40	10
Socialist Front	21 814	1.20	5	5	—
Socialists	19 690	1.08	12	12	—
Beja Congress	15 382	0.85	11	10	3
NUP	10 159	0.56	3	3	—
Not Identified	8 264	0.45	2	2	1
Tenants' Union	6 661	0.37	8	8	—
Workers' Force	5 204	0.28	1	1	1
Nuba Mountain Federation	3 171	0.17	2	2	2
Nile	2 704	0.15	5	5	1
Free	1 844	0.10	7	7	—
Islamic	1 772	0.096	1	1	—
Western Sudan Union	1 695	0.093	3	3	—
Communists	1 652	0.091	2	2	—
Democratic South	1 535	0.084	3	3	—
Unity	1 478	0.081	4	4	—
Workers' Federation	668	0.037	1	1	—
Peace	387	0.021	4	4	—
Social Democrats	220	0.012	1	1	—
NUP–Sadiq wing	63	0.003	1	1	—
Congress of New Forces	33	0.002	1	1	—
Total	1 819 772	100	1 006		218

Note: The Communist Party, having been banned in 1966, was not formally allowed to compete in the 1968 elections.

Source: Peter K. Bechtold, *Politics in the Sudan Since Independence* (Praeger Publishers, New York, a division of Greenwood Press Inc., 1977), p. 248. Copyright © 1977 by Praeger Publishers. Used with permission.

V THE ECONOMY

Economic policy over the 1956–69 period was geared mainly towards expansion within the framework established prior to 1956. Such productive investment as there was in the private sector tended to go either into pump schemes or into mechanised dry farming. Table A.5 in the Appendix indicates that the expansion of pump schemes between 1956 and 1960 was maintained at much the same rate as between 1951 and 1955. After 1960, however, the rate of expansion declined. The falling price of cotton on the world market made many of the schemes uneconomic, such that the flow of private investment into this field virtually ceased after 1962. Private investment in mechanised dry farming, on the other hand, continued at a steady pace throughout the 1956–69 period. By 1969 some 500 mechanised dry farming schemes were in existence, covering in all about 1.8 million feddans.

The promotion of industrial development was given considerable emphasis in government policy-statements, although it was the private sector which was expected to take a lead. A paper produced by the Ministry of Commerce, Industry and Supply in 1956 stated that government participation in industry was to be restricted to the provision of public utilities, and to those fields 'where private initiative and knowledge are wanting and private capital is either shy or not forthcoming'.[47] In fact no such direct participation took place until 1959. Over the 1959–69 period the state invested some £S23 million in establishing nine factories: three canning factories, two sugar factories, a milk dehydration factory, an onion dehydration factory, a tannery and a cardboard factory. The creation of these factories did not indicate that government policy was shifting towards favouring state control of industry. The government hoped that private investors would in due course take a share in, or purchase ownership of, the factories.[48] Such hopes did not materialise. Private investment in industry as a whole remained very light.

The only development plan produced over the 1956–69 period was the 'Abbud regime's Ten Year Plan of Economic and Social Development, 1961/2–1970/1.[49] Although the subsequent parliamentary governments formally eschewed the plan, it seems to have continued to provide a framework for economic decision-making through to 1969. The plan gave emphasis to expanding the 'modern sector', in terms of concentrating planned investment in this capitalist-oriented sector; promoting import substitution; and fostering private investment.[50] Of the £S565.4 million investment total envisaged for the ten-year period, £S228.4 million was expected to come from the private sector.

Foreign trade remained closely linked into the Western economies, and the bulk of economic aid came also from this quarter. Overall figures for the growth of Sudan's GDP between 1956 and 1969 can be found in Table A.10 of the Appendix.

7 Politics and Economy under the Nimairi Regime, 1969–85

I THE OVERALL PATTERN

The Sudanese state which emerged after the coup carried out by free officers on 25 May 1969 was substantially different from that which had existed prior to that date. This is not to say that the 'May revolution' was a genuine revolution. The changes instituted in the country's economic and social structure were, ultimately, insufficiently significant to justify using the term 'revolution'. The political dynamics of the post-1969 state, however, were quite different from those of the pre-1969 state – not just in an institutional sense, but in the manner in which political authority related to the country's social forces.

As has been shown in Chapter 6, the pre-1969 Sudanese state enjoyed only limited autonomy. It was controlled fairly directly by the 'incipient bourgeoisie', through the influence which the Sudanese establishment could exert on the main political parties and on the military leadership. After 1969 the state achieved, at least for a time, greater autonomy. No longer was political authority beholden directly to the interests of the incipient bourgeoisie. The massive nationalisations of 1970 damaged the interests of a wide range of Sudanese and foreign entrepreneurs, demonstrating the regime's greater autonomy of these elements. The Sudanese state now seemed capable of pursuing policies inimical to capitalist patterns of development. Even if development did proceed along capitalist lines, moreover, it appeared that a more coherent development programme than before could be pursued. The centralised authority of the state could be used to intensify the development effort and bring benefits to a wider cross-section of the population.

Such hopes were not realised. Over the sixteen years of the Nimairi regime, Sudan's economy became in many respects more dependent on the advanced capitalist world and less balanced in its distribution of benefits than it had been before. This chapter focuses on the reasons why events took this turn.

233

The central themes pursued in this chapter may be summarised as follows. The implementation of a development programme satisfying non-capitalist objectives could only be realistically undertaken if the regime's military leadership depended on, and benefited from, the organised support of those social groupings which stood to gain most from an egalitarian economic policy. Without such organised support, the opposition of those who stood to lose by the policy could deflect or frustrate the strategy. Given the history of political organisation in Sudan, the Communist Party was bound to play a critical role in mobilising the necessary support. The influence which the party carried in trade unions, tenants' unions, students' unions and professional associations would be crucial. Once the initial cooperation between the military leadership and the Communist Party had given way to recriminations, conflict and ultimately suppression, the possibility of pursuing a distinctively non-capitalist path of development disappeared.

The abandonment of attempts to steer the economy away from capitalist patterns of development, however, did not necessarily mean any lessening of the focus on economic development. The regime could still hope to use the more centralised authority of the post-1969 state to undertake an ambitious development programme, carried out within a free enterprise framework but involving an active role for the state. This was the strategy which the regime adopted in the early 1970s. The pursuit of this policy, however, ultimately drew the regime into a dependent relationship with external capital. Having started by breaking the control of the incipient bourgeoisie over the state, therefore, the regime eventually created a situation where the state's autonomy was increasingly eroded by the requirements of foreign investors and creditors.

II THE FREE OFFICERS' MOVEMENT AND THE SEIZURE OF POWER

The detailed attention given in this section to the background and origins of the free officers' movement may seem excessive. A clear idea of the perceptions, experience and objectives of those who took power in May 1969, however, is essential to an understanding of the regime which they established – and of the reasons for its ultimate failure. The opprobrium which has rightly been cast on Ja'afar Muhammad Nimairi since his overthrow may obscure the nature of the movement from which he emerged: a group of radically-oriented young army officers who believed they could liberate the Sudanese people from the domination of a traditionalist establishment linked to international capitalism.

(a) Origins of the free officers' movement: the 1950s

The origins of the Sudanese free officers' movement go back to the early 1950s. A few months after the July 1952 coup in Egypt, some young officers in the Sudan Defence Force, referring to themselves (privately) as 'free officers',[1] established a loose organisation committed to 'copying the Egyptian experience'. At the centre of this organisation were two brothers: Ya'qub Kibaidah, an officer in the Eastern Arab corps, and 'Abd al-Rahman Kibaidah, an officer in the Western Arab corps.[2] As Sudan was still under Condominium rule, with an important part of the Sudanese nationalist movement calling for union with Egypt, it is not surprising that these early free officers espoused a unionist line. It is even possible that the idea of organising a free officers' movement in Sudan may have been suggested to Ya'qub Kibaidah by the Egyptian military commander in Sudan, with whom Kibaidah enjoyed good personal relations.[3] Such unionist inclinations as the early free officers may have had, however, seem to have been abandoned as Sudan moved to independence in 1956.

The movement led by the Kibaidah brothers in the 1950s was in fact little more than a network of friendship and contact among like-minded individuals. The aims of the officers who composed the network, moreover, centred (after 1956, at least) on improving the efficiency of government not on instituting any fundamental change in Sudan's economic and social system. Believing that the post-independence parliamentary institutions had brought to power leaders who were incompetent and corrupt, they wished to provide the country with a more capable leadership. The regime which they hoped to introduce would be unashamedly military. For a period of at least five years, army officers would run the country directly, albeit seeking the cooperation of 'trustworthy and honest civilians'.[4] Political parties were seen as divisive and corrupting. They would not be permitted.

The Kibaidah group planned their seizure of power for 14 June 1957. Officers in the Khartoum area, led by Major 'Abd al-Rahman Kibaidah, were to mobilise their troops and take control of government buildings. On 11 June, however, Major Kibaidah was arrested together with a number of fellow conspirators.[5] Although the failure of the coup and the subsequent arrests constituted a severe blow to the free officers, the movement survived. The authorities were unable to lay bare the whole network of contacts which had been established, and even some of those arrested had later to be released due to lack of evidence.

General Ibrahim 'Abbud's assumption of power in November 1958 did not deflect the free officers from their own plans for a military-based government. The army leadership which had taken power was regarded as being as effete and corrupt as the civilian politicians, embodying many of the divisive social attitudes which had discredited the parliamentary government. The movement was lightly involved in the military actions led by Brigadiers 'Abd al-Rahim Shannan and Muhi al-Din 'Abdallah in March and May 1959,[6] intended to turn the regime in a more radical direction.[7] The frustration of these latter actions led the free officers to involve themselves in a full-scale coup attempt, under the leadership of Colonel 'Ali Hamid, in November 1959. When this attempt failed, largely through mismanagement,[8] General 'Abbud struck back strongly: the five main instigators were executed (including 'Ali Hamid and Ya'qub Kibaidah) and a large number of officers suspected of complicity were dismissed from the army. The free officers' movement of the 1950s was effectively destroyed.

(b) Development of a new free officers' movement in the 1960s and the 1969 coup

The free officers' movement which developed in the early 1960s had little in common with, and owed few debts to, the earlier movement. Among those officers who achieved prominence in the post-1960 movement, only two had played any role in the pre-1960 movement: Ja'afar Muhammad Nimairi and Faruq Hamadallah.[9]

Of critical importance among the factors which gave birth to the new free officers' movement was the role of the Sudanese Communist Party. On the one hand, the party's resolute opposition to the 'Abbud regime, since the latter's inception, made Sudanese communists the natural allies of those who, like the free officers, were inimical to the regime. On the other hand, the party appears to have deliberately sought a presence within the army. The value of such a presence was as a safeguard: to frustrate attempts by the authorities to use the army against the party. There came to be a considerable number of soldiers and army officers, therefore, who were associated, whether closely or loosely, with the Communist Party.[10] The officers among this number constituted the nucleus around which the new free officers' movement was formed. A broader cross-section of progressively-inclined officers, not always aware of their colleagues' links with the Communist Party, gathered around this nucleus.[11] As might be expected, the new brand of free officer was committed to a more radical re-structuring of Sudan's social and economic system than that envisaged by the pre-1960 free officers. They did not, however, necessarily envisage the army playing a leading role in this process.

The initial links which brought the new free officers' movement into existence seem to have been forged in the course of 1960 and 1961. Although still small and loosely organised, the movement began publication during 1961 of an underground news-sheet entitled 'The Voice of the Armed Forces'. The news-sheet, printed on the underground presses of the Communist Party, dealt in part with issues specific to army organisation and in part with national issues. Through this publication the free officers expressed their intention of 'working with the popular movement to ensure the regime's overthrow'.[12]

By 1964 the free officers' movement had established sufficient influence within the army to play a limited role in the events which terminated 'Abbud's rule. While it was civilian political organisation and action which revealed the regime's lack of legitimacy and thereby undermined its credibility and morale, 'Abbud's options were severely restricted by doubts as to the army's reliability. Free officers helped to ensure that 'Abbud did not obtain the support he needed to crush the civilian resistance, and were active in dissuading officers from ordering, and soldiers from carrying out, the shooting of civilian demonstrators. At one stage free officers headed an action which brought troops in to surround the republican palace, thereby increasing the pressure on 'Abbud to dismantle his military government.[13]

Over the four years which followed 'Abbud's overthrow, the free officers' movement adopted a low profile. The general trend of political developments was not to their liking. The radically-inclined transitional government which took power on 1 November 1964 was forced to resign on 18 February 1965. To the free officers, the unstable succession of governments which followed represented a betrayal of the hopes engendered by the October revolution.

Government was again in the hands of an establishment which saw no need to undertake structural social and economic reform; the war in the South continued, imposing an unwelcome burden on the armed forces; and the political scene appeared to be dominated by petty divisiveness and sectarian wrangling, rather than by an attempt to confront the country's real problems. The Arab defeat in the 1967 war added a new layer of humiliation. Nevertheless, conditions did not favour free officer intervention in politics. After the experience of 'Abbud's military dictatorship, the civilian population remained suspicious and distrustful of politically motivated soldiers. Moreover, as a result of a mutiny among army officers serving in southern Sudan in December 1965,[14] and an apparent coup attempt in December 1966,[15] army intelligence was alive to the dangers posed by some of the younger officers. Officers suspected of dissident inclinations were posted to Sudan's outlying provinces, on the assumption that coups could only be mounted in Khartoum.

The main focus of activity by the free officers' movement over these years, therefore, was on the recruitment of new members to the movement. The process of recruitment began by addressing a question to prospective recruits: 'Do you think the independence of our country involves economic liberation as well as political liberation?' Officers who responded affirmatively would gradually be drawn into the web of contacts which constituted the framework of the free officers' movement. With Colonel Nimairi, a senior member of the movement, holding the post of commander of the Gebeit training school between 1967 and 1969, contacts between free officers and newly commissioned officers were easy to arrange.[16]

Such overall organisation as was necessary at this stage was handled by a committee of officers based in Khartoum.[17] It was this committee which, in October 1968, convened a meeting of some 15–20 leading free officers to discuss the movement's future strategy. A majority of those who attended the meeting favoured a strategy geared towards the seizure of power. The minority, largely comprising officers associated with the Communist Party, opposed this view. Agreement was reached that plans for the overthrow of the existing regime should be drawn up, but that any decision on the implementation of such plans should await consideration at a later date.[18]

In the months which followed the October 1968 meeting, the core of free officers in Khartoum proceeded to formulate the required plans. Primary consideration was given to the nature of the regime which would be established. Following the Egyptian experience, it was decided that sovereign authority would be vested in a Revolutionary Command Council. A civilian Council of Ministers would be responsible for the day-to-day running of government business. The Revolutionary Command Council would ensure that government policies were indeed geared to that transformation in the economic and political system in which the free officers believed. Despite an early predilection for appointing a figurehead leader[19] – an individual well known to the Sudanese public, who could help legitimise the regime but would carry no effective power – the free officers eventually rejected this option. It was decided that Colonel Nimairi, the most senior ranking member of the movement, would head the Revolutionary Command Council.

Attention was also given to the means whereby civilian support could be drawn in to buttress the position of the new regime, as early as might be practicable following the seizure of power. It was deemed important for the new regime not to present a purely military face, not even at the outset. The free officers needed to assure themselves before the coup, therefore, of the cooperation of one or more eminent civilians, whose mere presence among those leading the new regime would indicate to the expectant population the character of the regime. The decision was taken to approach Babikir 'Awadallah,[20] who had gained national respect through the role he had played in the anti-'Abbud professionals' front, and whose resignation as chief justice in protest against legislation banning the Sudanese Communist Party in 1967 had won him a particularly strong standing on the left. When approached in December 1968, Babikir 'Awadallah duly agreed to cooperate: he would enjoy membership of the Revolutionary Command Council once it was established following the coup, and would head the Council of Ministers. While not made privy to the military aspects of the takeover, he was expected to give advice on the composition of the Council of Ministers to be established immediately after the coup, and subsequently to organise the new regime's relations with favoured civilian groupings. By his membership both of the Revolutionary Command Council and of the Council of Ministers he would form an effective link between these two bodies.

The mechanics of the takeover of power were considered early in 1969. Information that the armoured school would be sent on manoeuvres in May at Khor 'Umar – a short distance to the north of Omdurman – provided the basis around which the projected coup was planned. The strong free officer presence among the training staff of the armoured school[21] meant that these officers would have the opportunity, in the relative seclusion of Khor 'Umar, to prepare the school's 200 trainee soldiers for the takeover. Two companies of paratroops, among whom the free officers were equally strong,[22] would join the armoured school troops at Khor 'Umar. There were other reasons why the month of May constituted a suitable time to act. Many senior officers, escaping Sudan's summer heat, would have found reasons for travelling abroad. Colonel Nimairi, however, would be on vacation in Omdurman at that time.

By the end of March 1969, therefore, a plan had been formulated covering both the seizure of power and the form which the subsequent regime would take. In the middle of April a meeting was convened to determine whether or not the plan would actually be implemented. On this occasion a majority of those who attended the meeting opposed the projected coup. Seven out of the thirteen officers present took this stand arguing that the popular forces were not sufficiently well organised to make use of the situation created by the seizure of power, that the existing regime (as opposed to the individual politicians who wielded power) still enjoyed some respect among the population; and that there would be a damaging reaction against all progressive forces if the attempted seizure of power failed. Most, but not all, of the officers in this majority grouping were associated with the Communist Party.[23] The minority of six officers who favoured the plan's implementation argued that the time for a change of regime was indeed ripe and that so good an opportunity for seizing power might not recur in the near future. The decision was taken not to proceed with the plan but to re-consider the possibility of a coup at a later date.

Following the decision taken at the free officers' meeting in mid-April, two separate strands of action (or inaction) developed within the movement's leadership. For the seven officers who formed the majority block, any possibility of the movement carrying through a coup in May 1969 was now abandoned. The minority of six, however, determined to proceed with the plan and to seize power, without allowing their erstwhile colleagues to know of their intentions. These six officers were Colonel Ja'afar Muhammad Nimairi, Major Khalid Hasan 'Abbas, Major Abu al-Qasim Muhammad Ibrahim, Major Ma'mun 'Awad Abu Zaid,[24] Faruq Hamadallah[25] and Major Zain al-Abdin 'Abd al-Qadir. As these officers held the key positions in the armoured school and paratroops necessary for the plan's implementation, they were well placed to go ahead on their own.

The final planning for, and actual implementation of, the coup which occurred on 25 May 1969, therefore, was undertaken within a framework originally set by the central leadership of the free officers' movement, but ultimately without the involvement or knowledge of the majority block of free officer leaders.[26] Babikir 'Awadallah agreed to play the same role as previously envisaged, in cooperation with the narrower group of officers who were now involved. By 4.00 a.m. on the morning of 25 May the key installations in the Three Towns area had been occupied and the leading army generals present in Sudan had been placed under arrest. At 7.00 a.m. Radio Omdurman broadcast recorded speeches by Ja'afar Nimairi and Babikir 'Awadallah. Later in that morning the names of those appointed to the new Council of Ministers were broadcast. The list of ministers had been agreed between Babikir 'Awadallah and the six officers at a meeting held on 23 May.

At the outset of the military action on 25 May the intention had been to form a Revolutionary Command Council composed of the six officers and Babikir 'Awadallah. Events which occurred during the course of that day, however, led to a widening of the membership. While Faruq Hamadallah, Ma'mun 'Awad Abu Zaid, Khalid Hasan 'Abbas, Abu al-Qasim Muhammad Ibrahim and Zain al-Abdin 'Abd al-Qadir spent the day visiting critical army units and security organisations so as to ensure their support for the new regime, Ja'afar Nimairi became involved in discussions with two of the free officers who had voted against the coup plan at the April meeting: Lieutenant-Colonel Babikir al-Nur and Major Abu al-Qasim Hashim. The former was the most senior army officer associated with the Communist Party, and the latter maintained links with civilian Arab Nationalist or Nasserist circles. It was evident that the new regime's basis of support could be strengthened if such elements were drawn on to the Revolutionary Command Council. The decision to include these two officers and one other – Hashim al-'Ata, also associated with the Communist Party – on the Revolutionary Command Council was taken by Nimairi alone, without consulting his colleagues.[27] The ten-member Revolutionary Command Council whose composition was announced on the evening of 25 May, therefore, brought in not only those individuals who had carried through the coup but also some of the majority block in the free officers' movement which had originally opposed the projected coup.

III PROGRAMMES FOR SOCIAL AND ECONOMIC CHANGE, 1969–71

The Council of Ministers established following the May 1969 coup appeared well suited to bringing about significant changes in Sudan's economic and social system. The members of the council came from a variety of different backgrounds, but most had either been members of radically-inclined political movements or parties (the Communist Party, the Arab Socialists,[28] the Arab Nationalist grouping[29]), or else were independent and unaffiliated radical intellectuals. Many of the latter had been active in the professionals' front which had mobilised opinion against General 'Abbud in 1964, and some had served as ministers in the subsequent short-lived transitional government. Programmes for social and economic change would, it seemed, enjoy the support of the Revolutionary Command Council (RCC). The broadcast speeches on 25 May of both Ja'afar Nimairi and Babikir 'Awadallah raised the prospect of substantial change. That of Babikir 'Awadallah was the most specific:

> The revolutionary government fully recognises that our economic and financial catastrophes are due to the fact that the country adopted a capitalist path of development based on foreign control and influence . . . A big portion of our national income is draining away in improper and extravagant government spending, particularly at the top of the pyramid . . .
> We believe that increasing the national income and the volume of investment can be achieved by the following measures:
> 1. Strengthening and extending commercial and economic relations with socialist and Arab countries through bilateral agreements.
> 2. Extending the public sector base, particularly in the industrial sector of our economy where it should replace foreign capital, with the state taking the monopoly of principal import and export commodities and setting up special corporations for the marketing of principal exports.
> 3. Encouraging national private capital which has no relations with imperialism and protecting it against foreign competition.
> 4. Changing the present government foreign credit policy. Foreign loans should only be borrowed at cheap rates for long terms, and only to finance development projects.[30]

The programmes and policies put forward in the immediate after-math of the May 1969 coup will not be covered in detail here, partly because many of them were barely initiated when political changes forced their abandonment. By listing the major initiatives which were taken, however, some indication can be given of the new directions in which government policy was now able to develop. The relative autonomy of the new regime – its ability to adopt policies which prejudiced the interests of the previously dominant Sudanese establishment and bourgeoisie – was reflected in these initiatives.

The attempt to strengthen state control of the economy, and to restrict the private sector's freedom of action, was begun at an early stage. On 16 October 1969 the establishment of two state companies to control key sectors of international trade was announced. One was to enjoy monopoly rights over the import of jute, sugar, chemicals and insecticides, and the other would import all government require-ments of cars, tractors and medicines.[31] In May 1970 the government initiated a series of confiscations, sequestrations and nationalisations of privately owned trading companies, industrial undertakings and financial institutions. The sequestrations, mainly of trading compa-nies, were carried out under the Sequestration Act of 9 May 1970, which authorised the RCC to:

> place under sequestration the property of any person or corporate body that in its opinion is carrying on business or other activities against the public interest or the economic interest of the state.[32]

The companies owned by the prosperous 'Uthman Salih and Sons group were sequestered on 14 May,[33] and a further sixteen companies suffered the same fate on 4 June. The latter were the African Company for Trade, Oil and Confectionery (Bittar group); Tsakiro-glou and Company; Contomichalos and Sons; Morhig Company; Sarkis Izmirilian Company; Joseph Kahwati and Sons; Sadiq Abu'Agla Company; Licos Ma'louf Products; 'Aziz Kafouri Com-pany; George Doptoglon Company; Hafiz al-Barbari Company; Trucco and Company; and the Sudan Tobacco and National Ciga-rette Company.[34]

The first major acts of nationalisation were announced by Ja'afar Nimairi in a speech on the first anniversary of the seizure of power.[35] All banks were declared nationalised with immediate effect, as also were four British-owned companies. The banks in question were the

24 branches of Barclays; the six branches of Bank Misr; the four branches of National and Grindlays; the three branches of the Arab Bank; the single branch of the Commercial Bank of Ethiopia; the Sudan Commercial Bank; and the Al-Nilein Bank. The latter two banks had both been established and run by Sudanese investors. The four British-owned companies nationalised at this time were Mitchell Cotts and Company, Gellatly Hankey and Company, the Sudan Mercantile Company and Imperial Chemical Industries (Sudan). On 4 June the Sudan Portland Cement Company was nationalised, on the grounds that cement was a 'strategic commodity', and on 14 June there followed the nationalisation of five other major companies: the Blue Nile Brewery, the Bata Shoe Company, the Red Sea Stevedoring Company, the National Cash Register Company (Sudan), and the Sudanese Packing Company. A further 27 smaller companies were nationalised on the same day. On 21 June the Pepsi Cola Company (Sudan) was nationalised. By the end of June 1970, then, the state had taken control of almost all the import–export undertakings and financial institutions in the country, as well as the major manufacturing operations. Compensation offered was in the form of Sudanese bonds, bearing an interest rate of 4 per cent and a value equivalent to the assessed value of the properties seized. Repayment would begin in 1980, continuing through to 1985. *The Times* described the compensation arrangements as 'neither fair, prompt nor effective'.[36]

The Five Year Development Plan which the RCC passed on 20 March 1970, for implementation to begin in July of that year, constituted another means whereby the regime sought to involve the state more closely in the economy. The plan, drawn up by a team of Sudanese economists supplemented by fourteen Soviet experts,[37] envisaged the state sector accounting for £S215 million out of a planned investment total of £S385 million over the 1970–5 period. Gross national product would rise by 8.1 per cent per annum, as against an average of 4.7 per cent over the previous five years. The plan contained few large projects. Much of the expected rise in production would come from improved productivity, unleashed in part by a more rational use of existing resources. Emphasis was placed on productive investment rather than on infrastructure. Between 1965 and 1970 productive investment had accounted for only about 41 per cent of total public investment. Over the Five Year Plan period this share was to rise to some 55 per cent.[38]

Some of the regime's early measures confronted directly that Sudanese establishment which had stood behind former regimes. On

28 June 1969 the Council of Ministers announced the abolition of 'native administration' in Khartoum province, Northern province and the irrigated parts of Blue Nile province.[39] The posts of *nazir*, *shaikh* and *'umda* ceased to exist in these areas. Elsewhere in the country the government would work towards phasing out native administration in a more gradual fashion. On 17 August 1969 the government took action to recover monies owed to the treasury by the Mahdi and Mirghani estates in tax arrears. The Rabak ginning factory and oil mill belonging to the Mahdi estate were appropriated, as also were all lands owned by the Mirghani family in Khartoum North.[40] The adoption of the Political, Administrative and Press Corruption Act on 11 July 1969 seemed evidence of the regime's determination to break with the corrupt practices of the past – practices which, in the regime's view, had enabled the establishment to control and distort government decision-making.[41] Tribunals were established under the act to try some of the political leaders of the ousted regime.

On social policy, the new government acted quickly to revise labour laws. An 82-member council was formed to make recommendations on unified labour legislation. The council was chaired by Shafi' Ahmad al-Shaikh, secretary-general of the Sudan Workers' Trade Union Federation, and included representatives of most of the main trade unions and employees' associations. At the council's first meeting, on 26 June 1969, the Minister of Labour, Dr Taha Ba'ashar, called for legislation which 'would emerge from socialist concepts . . . based on the concept that work is an honour'.[42] Two pieces of legislation ultimately emerged from the council's deliberations: the Unified Labour Law and the Workers' Culture Law, both gaining the RCC's ratification on 24 November 1970.[43] Other attempts at directly shifting the balance of economic advantage among Sudan's social groups were the decree on 7 September 1969 ordering an immediate reduction by 25 per cent in the rents charged for smaller houses;[44] the Council of Ministers' decision on 14 June 1969 to write off the £S7 million accumulated debts of the Gezira tenants;[45] and the instructions which were issued in June restricting the use which civil servants and government ministers could make of government houses and government cars. The emphasis now placed on social services catering to popular needs was reflected in the announcement on 21 June 1969 that the intake of intermediate schools would be raised from 24 000 to 37 500 for the next academic year, and the intake of secondary schools raised from 7000 to 10 400.[46]

Foreign policy also underwent a radical change. The change was in part linked to the new direction taken in economic policy. The attempt to pursue a development policy geared towards greater self-sufficiency and a more egalitarian distribution of rewards required, so it was believed, a re-orientation of foreign trade. The development of stronger economic relations both with some neighbouring countries and with communist countries could help Sudan break out of its dependent relationship on the advanced capitalist world – a relationship which had distorted Sudan's economy under previous regimes.

To the outside world, it was the new links with communist countries which attracted most attention. On 4 June 1969 diplomatic recognition was extended to the German Democratic Republic,[47] followed shorty thereafter by the visit of a high-ranking GDR delegation to Sudan. Over June and July, Sudanese trade and finance delegations visited most of the capitals of Eastern Europe, and Eastern European delegations arrived for talks in Khartoum. In a survey of the outcome of these negotiations, the Sudanese Minister of Finance spoke on 6 August of a wide array of industrial and agricultural projects which could be expected to benefit from East European assistance.[48] The Bulgarian government announced a £6 million loan for Sudan on 18 June 1969; the Czech government a $10 million loan on 5 November 1969; the GDR government a £4 million loan on 14 November 1969; the Soviet government a £4 million loan on 28 November 1969; and the Hungarian government a $10 million loan on 7 July 1970.[49] Sudanese ministers described these loans as being offered on more favourable terms than loans from Western countries – bearing lower rates of interest, with repayment over a longer period. That some of the loans were repayable through sales of Sudanese products was also deemed advantageous. Trade agreements concluded with Eastern European countries at this time raised the prospect of a major re-direction in Sudanese trade. On 29 September 1969 the government announced that most of Sudan's imports would henceforth be drawn from countries whose trading relationships with Sudan were bound by trade agreements.[50]

Despite the publicity which Sudan's relations with communist countries attracted in Western countries, the development of cooperative relations with Egypt and Libya probably figured more prominently in the concerns of the Sudanese government itself. On 30 July 1969 a communiqué, issued following the visit of a Sudanese delegation to Egypt, announced the formation of a joint economic committee to prepare recommendations on economic cooperation between the two countries.[51] The committee's deliberations led to the conclusion of a Sudan–United Arab Republic Economic Integration Agreement on 2 September of that year. The latter agreement envisaged the gradual lifting of customs barriers between the two countries, and the lifting of restrictions on the free movement of labour and capital. Sudan and the United Arab Republic would, through joint ministerial meetings and committees, coordinate their policies on planning and economic development, foreign trade, agriculture, industry, labour and social affairs.[52]

Following the overthrow of the Libyan monarchy at the beginning of September 1969, the scope for cooperation among the states of north-east Africa widened. The radically-oriented regime led by Mu'ammar al-Qadhafi which had assumed power in Libya proposed Libya's inclusion in the cooperative framework established between Sudan and Egypt. The form of cooperation now began to become more politicised, with greater emphasis on institutional structures. The Tripoli Charter, concluded between the three countries on 28 December 1969, envisaged cooperation on defence and foreign policy as well as on economic matters.[53] The need for unity and the intention to work towards unity was agreed, but the form of that unity would be subject to further consideration. A Tripartite Economic Agreement, signed on 20 April 1970, followed the same lines as the Sudan–UAR Economic Integration Agreement, but included provisions for the establishment of a council of economic integration. The latter body would be headed by the economics ministers of the three countries and would be based in Cairo.[54]

In November 1970, a meeting between Nimairi, Qadhafi and Sadat (who had assumed the Egyptian presidency following the death of Nasser in September of that year) established a 'unified tripartite leadership' to speed up the strengthening and promotion of cooperation between the three countries. The three leaders would meet regularly with a view both to coordinating policy and to planning the eventual establishment of a federation between their countries. A higher planning committee, a national security council and a follow-up committee were also created.[55] The discussions which occurred at this time, however, brought out some differences of approach between the three governments. The Sudanese government favoured a gradualist approach to integration. Emphasis was placed on laying a firm basis for integration by cooperation in the relatively non-controversial economic field before moving on to more politically-charged domains. Careful and extended study should be given to selecting the most appropriate[56] process of integration before integrative institutions were created. The Libyan government with some support from President Sadat, however, advocated immediate measures to form a common political organisation and pursue a unified foreign policy. The delimitation of a transitional period for the move to a Federation of Arab Republics was proposed.[57] In April 1971, when the Tripoli Charter partners (now joined by Syria) announced their intention of proceeding with the creation of federal institutions, the Sudanese government declined to participate in the undertaking 'until a later date'.[58]

The distinctive nature of the new regime's attitude to the issue of southern Sudan became apparent at an early stage. On 9 June 1969 Ja'afar Nimairi issued a 'Declaration on the Southern Question' which recognised the right of the peoples of southern Sudan to regional autonomy within a united Sudan. Before any measure of regional autonomy could be introduced, however, it was necessary to build:

> a broad socialist-oriented democratic movement in the South, forming part of the revolutionary structure in the North and capable of assuming the reigns of power in that region and rebuffing imperialist penetration and infiltration from the rear.[59]

To indicate the regime's goodwill and to lay the basis for progress towards regional autonomy, a number of immediate measures were taken: the creation of a Ministry of Southern Affairs; the continuation and further extension of the amnesty law; the allocation of new funds for economic, social and cultural development in the South; and the institution of training programmes for southern personnel. Perhaps of greater importance than either the proclaimed intention to introduce regional autonomy or the immediate measures, however, was the new government's preparedness to recognise 'the historical and cultural differences between the North and the South' and the southern peoples' 'right to develop their respective cultures and traditions'.[60] The extent to which these pronouncements and policies actually contributed to the eventual termination of the southern Sudan conflict will be considered later in this chapter.

While these new social, economic, regional and foreign policies were being initiated, the political framework was rent, as will be explained below, by sharpening divisions among the individuals who, and groupings which, had achieved a presence within the RCC and the Council of Ministers. It had been intended that the elaboration of a National Charter, which would define the regime's policy objectives and perspectives, would provide an agreed basis for cooperation. The committee charged with drafting the proposed charter was formed on 13 July 1969.[61] The prepared draft was in due course passed on for discussion to a broadly-based National Charter Committee, which was convened for the first time on 15 June 1970.[62] The divisions, however, proved too deep for a lasting basis for cooperation to be established. They stemmed not simply from differing perceptions on policy, but from fundamental differences of interest and belief on the form of political organisation which was desirable. Meanwhile, outside the circle of participants in government, the *ansar* uprising on Aba Island in March 1970, led by Imam al-Hadi al-Mahdi, posed a severe threat to the regime's survival.

IV THE FAILURE TO MAINTAIN THE PROGRESSIVE ALLIANCE, 1969–71

The policies of social and economic change which were adopted following the May 1969 coup were not pursued for long – at least not in the form in which they had originally been conceived. Despite the initially strong commitment to radical change, and despite the regime's evident autonomy of that Sudanese establishment which had previously blocked such change, the attempt at radically transforming Sudan's society and economy was abandoned. The regime itself gradually changed its character. For an understanding of what happened, and why, attention must be given to the divisions which emerged within the 'progressive alliance'.

The central issue around which the differences emerged was that of political organisation. The perceptions on this matter held by the secretary-general of the Communist Party, 'Abd al-Khaliq Mahjub, were effectively incompatible with those held by the free officers who had seized power on 25 May. To 'Abd al-Khaliq and his associates, the Communist Party constituted the kernel of the Sudanese progressive movement. The fruit of years of work by the party in trade unions, tenants' unions, professional associations and women's and students' groupings had been the development of a broadly-based popular movement. Through its members working in these bodies, the party had been able to mobilise wide sections of the population –

holding varying political allegiances – to resist the oppression they had suffered under previous regimes. To the extent that the former regime had lost much of its credibility and legitimacy, this was the achievement of the Communist Party. The future of the Sudanese progressive movement should not be entrusted blindly to the safe-keeping of a group of petit-bourgeois army officers, however radical their declared intentions. If the new regime was to maintain its progressive policies and outlook, therefore, it was essential for the Communist Party to retain its independent existence and an ability to criticise the regime where it felt necessary. Political authority should rest with a national democratic front, grouping together those parties, unions and associations which accepted the radical objectives laid down in the National Charter. The parties, unions and associations would cooperate together and act together on agreed policies, but would retain the freedom to express distinctive views and opinions.

The perceptions of the free officers who had carried through the coup, however, were markedly different. They regarded themselves as authentic revolutionaries, the instigators not of a coup but of a revolution. Power had been wrested from the hands of a traditionalist Sudanese establishment linked to Western imperialism, and would now be used to serve the interests of the mass of the population. While these officers respected the Communist Party's past record in resisting oppression, favoured most of the policies espoused by the party, and were prepared to allow the party some short-term latitude in adapting itself to the new situation,[63] they saw no reason why the party should in the long term retain an independent position or even an independent existence. Now that a progressive regime was in power, communists should, they believed, join the single political oganisation which would be established, and seek as individual members of that organisation to achieve the social and economic objectives in which they believed. Previously-existing parties, unions and associations would all be dissolved and replaced by a unified structure of organisation and participation, committed to socialist objectives. The new regime was not 'the property of any one political grouping', but was 'open to all who accepted its principles', even to 'the members of the defunct political parties who had been misled by corrupt leaderships'.[64] The idea of a national democratic front was rejected: in part because any organised 'independent criticism' (as distinct from criticism by individuals) was seen as disruptive to regime unity, and in part because the formation of such a front would inevitably shift power from the RCC to the Communist Party. The predominant influence held by the party in those unions and associations which would join the front would, it was believed, ensure that outcome.

The Communist Party's attitude towards the regime can only be fully understood in the context of a debate which had raged within the party leadership during the 1960s. The debate concerned the role of armed force in forwarding the party's political objectives. Some of the divisions engendered by this debate were to have an impact on events after 25 May 1969. The issue first arose in the context of the elections held for the central council established by General 'Abbud in 1963. Whereas the party leadership encouraged participation in these elections, on the grounds that they offered an opportunity for political mobilisation, some party members rejected this line. The latter members split away from the party and formed a new organisation, the Communist Party Revolutionary Leadership (CPRL), headed by Yusif 'Abd al-Majid. The CPRL advocated the adoption of guerrilla war tactics. Under the parliamentary regime which followed 'Abbud's overthrow the CPRL maintained its rejection of electoral politics and continued to advocate methods of revolutionary violence. The CPRL, however, never gained any substantial popular backing and gradually dissolved when further splits truncated its already small membership.[65]

Even after the supporters of guerrilla struggle had broken away, there remained differences within the Communist Party as to the methods whereby the party's objectives could best be pursued. In the face of government attempts in 1966–7 to deprive the party of its legal existence and to suppress its activities, some party leaders were more eager than others to envisage violent resistance. 'Abd al-Khaliq Mahjub, however, opposed the use of violence, fearing that such action would provoke strong and crippling reprisals.[66] The emphasis placed by 'Abd al-Khaliq on mobilising popular support by patient political work among the masses, rather than on direct action against the regime, was given clear expression in the report accepted by the 4th party congress in October 1967:

The popular struggle alone can mobilise the people's forces and prepare the necessary conditions for the ripening of the revolutionary crisis. Only by working among the people in their daily struggle can we convince the people that life under reactionary rule is unbearable; and only in this way can the working class and peasantry raise their ability to sacrifice and reach a level where they can achieve the duties of the democratic revolution.[67]

Following 'Abd al-Khaliq's line, therefore, party policy rejected 'adventurist undertakings'. The attempt to pursue an open political role at a time when the government was seeking to proscribe any Communist Party activities, led the party in 1967 to support the formation of a Socialist Party, headed by Amin al-Shibli.

In December 1968 a new divergence over tactics emerged within the party leadership. The divergence stemmed from an article which a member of the party's political bureau, Ahmad Sulaiman, wrote in *al-Ayyam* newspaper on 8 December. Analysing the reasons why the progressive forces which had engineered 'Abbud's downfall had failed to maintain a leading role under the regime which followed, Ahmad Sulaiman attributed the failure to the lack of sustained cooperation between progressive army officers and leftist civilian movements. It was, he claimed, the cooperation between these two elements which had led to the overthrow of the former regime. The absence of any subsequent cooperation between them had enabled the right-wing parties to regain power. He drew the conclusion that any future prospect for the establishment and maintenance of a socialist-oriented regime in Sudan depended on progressive army officers playing a prominent role. They should help maintain in power a government based on leftist civilian movements.[68]

Ahmad Sulaiman's writing attracted strong criticism from other leading members of the party. At a meeting of the party's central committee in March 1969, Ahmad Sulaiman and four members of the central committee who had supported his views were censured for having 'failed to abide by policies adopted at the 4th party congress'.[69] In a central committee report entitled 'For an Improvement in the Direction of Work, One Year after the Congress', which was issued after the meeting, Ahmad Sulaiman's views were rejected in strong terms: 'the putchist tactic instead of mass action represents the interests of the bourgeois class and of the *petite bourgeoisie*'.[70]

The cautious attitude which 'Abd al-Khaliq Mahjub and the majority of Communist Party political bureau members took towards the seizure of power by free officers in May 1969, therefore, was consistent with party policy as it had developed through the 1960s. The statement issued by the party on the afternoon of 25 May emphasised the *petit-bourgeois* social character of the action which had been taken and of the officers who had taken it. Later statements, nonetheless, pledged Communist Party support for the new regime provided the progressive policies proclaimed were indeed pursued, and provided the party was permitted to operate freely.

'Abd al-Khaliq Mahjub's initially grudging acceptance of the coup opened up a new and ultimately more serious division within the party. An influential minority within the central committee, led by Mu'awiyah Ibrahim, criticised the limited and conditional nature of the support offered to the new regime. As the coup had removed from power a government dominated by traditionalist forces and linked to imperialism, Mu'awiyah Ibrahim and his associates (who included Ahmad Sulaiman) contended that an immediate and out-right expression of support would have been in order. Given the new regime's progressive direction and its preparedness to appoint com-munists to the Council of Ministers, 'Abd al-Khaliq's caution was deemed churlish.

The division which had opened up was to grow steadily deeper over the two years which followed. On the one side, 'Abd al-Khaliq and the majority of political bureau members contended that the party's support for the regime should be conditional on progress towards establishing a national democratic front; that the army consisted of different social classes and would not necessarily provide a long-term basis of support for progressive policies; and that the 'collapse of the reactionary authority and rise of a progressive na-tional authority' could indeed benefit the popular movement, but only if there was 'a democratisation of state institutions', and if the 'rights of expression and organisation of revolutionary bodies' were respected.[71] On the other side, Mu'awiyah Ibrahim and his associates argued that the full revolutionary potential of the new regime should be recognised and exploited. By involving itself unconditionally in the regime's activities and institutions, the party could help to achieve a rapid transformation in Sudan's economy and society.[72] Ultimately this position led the Mu'awiyah Ibrahim section to accept the party's dissolution and its replacement by the unitary organisational frame-work favoured by the RCC.

The political struggle which occurred between 1969 and 1971 was, therefore, in part a contest for power and influence between the RCC and the Communist Party, and in part a contest between different tendencies within the Communist Party. The further the struggle advanced, the closer was the Mu'awiyah Ibrahim group's association with the RCC. The central Communist Party leadership moved from involvement with the regime to opposition.

The development of the political struggle over these two years falls into five phases. From May to October 1969, relations between the Communist Party and the RCC were marked by overt cooperation. Points of tension did exist: the Communist Party leadership maintained that the nomination of communists to serve in the government should have emanated from the party and not the RCC; and the party objected to the RCC's banning of the 'revolutionary committees' which it was seeking to form.[73] Different perspectives on future political organisation were also becoming apparent. Nonetheless, relations retained a cooperative tenor.

Between October 1969 and March 1970, the relationship began to lose some of its cordiality. Differing perceptions of the Communist Party's role in the new regime were evident from an incident which occurred early in October. On a visit to East Berlin, prime minister Babikir 'Awadallah was reported as saying that 'the May Revolution cannot give up the communists'.[74] An RCC pronouncement the following day stated that Babikir 'Awadallah had been expressing a personal viewpoint and that:

> This revolution is all the people's revolution without any prejudice to former political colours . . . [it is] an original popular revolution based on the beliefs, morals, ideals and traditions of the people . . . The doors are open for all patriotic and socialist elements who condemn the former parties' regime.[75]

On 28 October the RCC announced a government re-shuffle. Babikir 'Awadallah lost the prime ministership, which was assumed by Ja-'afar Nimairi. A number of RCC members were given ministerial positions, such that the RCC became more directly involved than before in the actual conduct of government. Four of the five ministers who left the government in this re-shuffle had been associated with the Communist Party. Some party members, however, retained their ministerial posts.[76]

From April to November 1970 the RCC (or at least the majority element within it) exerted strong pressure on the Communist Party in an attempt to gain the party's acceptance of a 'single political organisation'. Ja'afar Nimairi had already announced, on 4 January, that a Sudan Socialist Union would be established and that political participation would be limited to this framework.[77] The RCC's pressure intensified the dissension within the party between Mu'awiyah Ibrahim's 'cooperators' and 'Abd al-Khaliq's conditionalists'. The arrest of 'Abd al-Khaliq in April 1970, followed by his banishment to Egypt for three months,[78] appeared designed to strengthen the position of the cooperators. At a Communist Party consultative conference convened in August to discuss the divergent views on strategy, however, 'Abd al-Khaliq secured majority support for his position. By mid-November it had become clear that the party leadership was not likely either to change or to adapt its policy. The stage was set for open confrontation.

On 16 November 1970 the majority element within the RCC dismissed from this body the two members who were associated with the Communist Party (Babikir al-Nur and Hashim al-'Ata) and one member who had shown sympathies with the party's critique of the regime's performance (Faruq Hamadallah). In the period through to February 1971 the RCC, now less subject to the inhibiting effects of policy differences among its members, began a purge of 'hostile elements' within the regime's institutions. Communists who adhered to the views of 'Abd al-Khaliq Mahjub were dismissed from positions of influence in the government, army and administration. 'Abd al-Khaliq himself was imprisoned, together with some of his senior associates.

On 8 February 1971 a speech by Ja'afar Nimairi initiated a new and more concerted attempt to crush the main part of the Communist Party, while the regime pressed ahead with arrangements for the establishment of the Sudan Socialist Union and for unitary organisations representing sectional and occupational interest groups. The Communist Party was accused of 'treading on all our people's values and morals', of 'hastening to oppose any noble objective irrespective of what it is so long as it was not sponsored by the party', of 'sabotaging production', of 'spreading insidious views on the regime through leaflets and demonstrations', and of 'exercising the personality cult'.[79]

Between February and July 1971, then, the RCC sought not just to purge from the regime's institutions those communists who adhered to the party leadership's line, but to dismantle and destroy the Communist Party itself. Key figures in Communist Party organisation throughout the country were arrested. The only party member loyal to the central party leadership who retained a ministerial position was Joseph Garang, Minister of Southern Affairs.[80] Supporters of Mu'awiyah Ibrahim's line, meanwhile, remained within the government.

The severity of the RCC's crackdown appears to have set in train the events which brought the RCC–Communist Party struggle to its final *denouement*. On 19 July 1971, officers associated with the Communist Party briefly succeeded in seizing power. While 'Abd al-Khaliq Mahjub probably knew of the intended seizure and failed to prevent it,[81] most members of the political bureau and central committee had neither given their prior approval to, nor were complicit in, the action.[82] A counter-coup on 22 July restored Nimairi to power. 'Abd al-Khaliq Mahjub, Joseph Garang and Shafi' Ahmad al-Shaikh (the trade union leader) were among those executed following the counter-coup, as also were the officers who had planned the 19 July coup: Hashim al-'Ata, Babikir al-Nur and Faruq Hamadallah.[83]

V THE POLITICAL INSTITUTIONS OF THE REGIME, POST-1971

The conflict, and ultimately the break, with the Communist Party had a decisive impact on the character of the Nimairi regime. When the free officers first seized power, they had proclaimed a radical overall objective: the transformation of Sudan's society and economy. The effective implementation of a policy of this nature, however, required the cooperation and involvement of radical civilian Sudanese – among whom the Communist Party had played a core role for some 20 years. Once the regime had broken with the Communist Party, much of the momentum and support which would have been needed to achieve radical transformation, and which initially gave government policy a radical direction, was lost to the regime. The transformation of Sudan's society and economy no longer appeared either feasible or desirable.

The relative autonomy of the Sudanese state as it had emerged after the May 1969 coup enabled the regime to change tack with little difficulty. The transformationist perspectives of 1969–70 were replaced by an emphasis on national unity and economic development.[84] These issues now came to constitute the focus around which the regime sought to build up its claim to legitimacy. The aim of the 'May revolution', it was now said, had been to establish Sudan's national unity – bringing Sudanese people together under a government which would truly 'reflect the interests of all Sudanese'. Such a government would have the strength and the technical ability to implement ambitious development programmes, unencumbered by the political in-fighting and the traditionalist hindrances which had frustrated the development effort under previous regimes.

The practical achievements of the post-1971 regime will be examined later. The concerns of this section, and the subsequent one, are to describe the institutional structures through which the regime operated, and the political dynamics which determined the form taken by the institutions. A fundamental paradox underlay these institutions. They were conceived at a time when the regime retained a radical perspective, and were thus shaped as instruments for the transformation of Sudan's economy and society. Yet their principal development occurred after the regime's perspectives had changed. The institutions were purveyed, therefore, more as representative channels through which the Sudanese population as a whole – regardless of class, social group or previous political allegiance – could determine the policies through which, and the people by whom, they were governed.

This paradox accounts for the weakness of the institutions. On the one hand, while possessing the top-heavy, centre-led attributes of political institutions in 'revolutionary-centralising' single party regimes, they did not encourage that dynamic interaction with the population normally sought by institutions designed as instruments for change. On the other hand, while claiming to constitute the channels through which the Sudanese population achieved representation, they were in practice subject to regime manipulation and control. Intended to be instruments for change, the institutions were structured such that authority and initiative remained at the centre.

The political system instituted by the Nimairi regime comprised six elements, mentioned here in the order in which they were introduced.[85] First, the National Charter: the document which, providing a blueprint for the kind of society and polity to be created and the means to be used to that end, was supposed to guide the actions and aims of all the governing institutions. The committee responsible for drawing up the charter finished a first draft in November 1969. It was then discussed by the RCC and the Council of Ministers, and debated (as mentioned earlier) by a people's committee specially constituted for this purpose, between November 1970 and April 1971. After further amendments made by a 'revision committee', the charter was ultimately ratified as 'the basic philosophy of the Revolution' at the founding congress of the Sudan Socialist Union in January 1972. Over the years which followed, the practical importance of the document steadily declined. While the charter was never formally abandoned, the vision it portrayed of a transformed Sudanese society ceased to be relevant.

Second, the 'popular and functional organisations'. 'Functional organisation' referred to a union or association based on a profession or type or work: farmers' unions, teachers' unions, workers' unions, etc. 'Popular organisation' referred to a body which grouped people together on any other basis: the youth union, the women's union, village development committees, etc. A number of the unions and associations which now came under the regime's 'popular and functional organisations' structure had been in existence prior to May 1969. These were, however, generally re-organised so as to ensure compatibility with the new institutional framework and, effectively, agreement with government policy. Some new popular and functional organisations were established during 1969: the initial village development committees and units of the Sudan Youth Union (then known as the *kata'ib mayu*). The overall structure of popular and functional organisations, however, was not completed until the end of 1973, when the merchants' union and the re-modelled teachers' union held their founding congresses.

Third, the people's local government councils. The People's Local Government Act of November 1971 created a pyramid structure of councils. At the base were the councils in every village, town section, market area, industrial area and nomadic encampment. The original intention was that the popular and functional organisations would have the sole right to nominate candidates for election to these councils – although the population as a whole within the council area would vote in the elections themselves.[86] In actual practice, however, few restrictions were placed (openly, at least) on the nomination of candidates. Above the 'base councils', in an ascending order, were rural and town councils, sub-province area councils, and province executive councils. Each council above the base level consisted mainly of representatives from the level below, but in some cases seats on the council were also allocated to local representatives of popular and functional organisations and to representatives of ministries active in the area. The whole scheme was intended, by placing local authority in the hands of this web of councils, to draw the population into more active involvement in the regulation of local affairs.

The process of creating local government councils began at the base level in 1971, but it was not until the latter part of 1973 that the whole structure had been completed. At the beginning of February 1974, the Minister of Local Government reported the existence of 3993 village councils, 737 town section councils, 281 nomadic encampment councils, 78 market councils, 15 industrial area councils, 228 rural councils, 90 town councils, 35 sub-province area councils and 10 province executive councils.[87] Many of these councils, especially those at the base level, however, had little more than a paper existence.

Fourth, the Sudan Socialist Union (SSU) – described in the constitution as the 'sole political organisation'. The intention of creating a single political organisation was first announced within one month of the May 1969 coup, and the name 'Sudan Socialist Union' was first applied to this concept in January 1970. It was not until May 1971, however, that a preparatory committee was established to make arrangements for the formation of the Sudan Socialist Union. The preparatory committee drew up a document entitled 'Basic Rules of the Sudan Socialist Union', which was presented to and passed by a founding congress of the SSU in January 1972. The congress consisted of leading figures in the popular and functional organisations, representatives of the military and security forces, and some 'notable personalities' appointed by the president.

The basic rules laid down a 'democratic centralist' structure for the SSU: at the popular level a network of 'basic units' covering the country, each unit choosing its own committee, and above that a party conference and party committee at the branch, district, sub-province and province levels. The party conference at each level was to consist mainly of representatives from the conference at the level below, and the committee was to be elected by the conference at its own level (see Figure 7.1) The institutions at the national level were the national congress (composed of representatives from the provincial conferences and some presidential appointees), the party presidency (elected by the national congress), the secretariat-general (appointed by the party president), the central committee (one half appointed by the party president and one half elected by the national congress), and the political bureau (elected by the central committee on the nomination of the party president). The SSU structure was duly built up along these lines following the founding congress. In January 1974 the holding of the first national congress marked the completion of the structure. Reporting to the congress, President

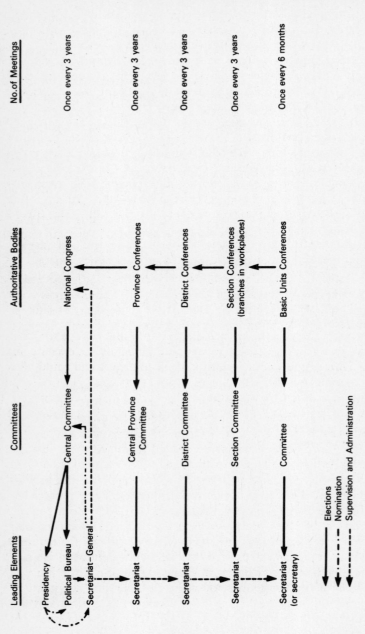

Figure 7.1 Structure of the Sudan Socialist Union, 1975

Note: At the topmost level the secretariat-general could nominate some individuals to the national congress and to the central committee; the party presidency, moreover, presented to the central committee a list of names for the political

Nimairi announced that a total of 6381 basic units, 1892 branch organisations, 325 district organisations, 34 sub-province organisations, and 10 province organisations had been established.

Fifth, the regional autonomy arrangement for the southern Sudan. The Addis Ababa agreement of March 1972 (to be covered in detail in section VIII below) provided for the establishment of an autonomous government in the South – exercising certain specific powers and relying on specified sources of financial support. Executive authority within the region would rest with a higher executive council, and legislative authority with a regional people's assembly. Elections for the assembly were duly held in November 1973. As the emergence and implementation of the regional autonomy arrangement was affected by different considerations from those affecting the other five elements in the governing system, further analysis of the operation of regional autonomy will be postponed until section VIII below.

Sixth, the central government institutions, as laid down in the permanent constitution. The permanent constitution itself came into force in April 1973, following six months' debate by a constituent people's assembly. The two principal central government institutions defined in the constitution were the presidency and the people's assembly. The powers of these two institutions were in effect interwoven, but with the presidency wielding predominant influence. The president enjoyed the power to appoint ministers to execute his policies. The assembly could question these ministers and could, by a two-thirds majority, force a minister to submit his resignation to the president, but it could not compel the president to accept this resignation. The assembly had no right to censure the president for his policies, although it could compel the president to subject any of his policies to a popular referendum, provided a two-thirds majority of its members approved this action. On the legislative side, the president, besides himself enjoying certain rights in legislation, could annul any bill passed by the assembly. The assembly could, however, overrule the president's annulment if a two-thirds majority in favour of so doing existed.

The constitution specified that members of the people's assembly be elected in such a way that 'geographical areas, administrative units and the alliance of forces of the working people' were represented. This was duly made the basis of the 1973 Election Law. Three separate kinds of constituency were created: geographical constituencies (where the population as a whole could vote); popular and functional constituencies (where each popular and functional organisation could choose its own representatives for the assembly); and local government constituencies (where the members of local government councils could choose their representatives). In addition to the 225 elected members, 25 members were to be appointed by the president. Under this system, the elections for the first people's assembly were carried through in April and May 1974.

The president, under the constitution's provisions, was to be 'nominated by the Sudan Socialist Union in accordance with its Basic Rules'. The basic rules, in turn, laid down that following nomination by the SSU national congress, the nominee for the presidency should submit himself to a national plebiscite. Each presidential term was to last six years. As Ja'afar Nimairi had submitted himself to a presidential plebiscite in October 1971 – when the RCC was formally disbanded and replaced by the presidency – no new plebiscite was needed until 1977. Some 4 million people had voted in the 1971 plebiscite, of whom 98.6 per cent returned an affirmative vote. Voting conditions did not satisfy the requirements of a secret ballot.

VI POLITICAL DYNAMICS AFFECTING THE ROLES OF THE POLITICAL INSTITUTIONS

As mentioned earlier, the political institutions of the Nimairi regime were initially designed as instruments for radical social and economic change, but were actually used for a different purpose. The change of purpose can best be appreciated by considering the nature of the political groupings which wielded influence within the regime in the early 1970s, and by showing how effective influence moved away from some groupings towards others.

Those who conceived and laid the basis for the institutional framework were mostly either former communists (adherents of Mu'awiyah Ibrahim's dissident wing) or else were Arab nationalists. The Arab nationalist grouping was characterised by a socialistic but non-Marxist ideological orientation, an emphasis on strengthening relations with Egypt and other left-inclined Arab countries, and a tendency to advocate patterns of political and economic development based on Egyptian experience. Among the key government leaders in 1970–1 who belonged to the Arab nationalist grouping were Babikir 'Awadallah (first vice-president after October 1971), Muhi al-Din Sabir (Minister of Education), Muhammad 'Abd al-Halim (Minister of Finance) and Abu al-Qasim Hashim (Minister of Youth, and a member of the RCC until its disbandment). Some other members of the RCC (principally Ma'mun 'Awad Abu Zaid and Khalid Hasan 'Abbas) were loosely associated with the Arab nationalists.

From May 1969 until November 1970 the Mu'awiyah Ibrahim communists and the Arab nationalists enjoyed considerable influence within the regime, even though they were facing competition from the main part of the Communist Party and from a small group of Arab socialists. Their influence strengthened further after November 1970, when communists loyal to 'Abd al-Khaliq Mahjub's leadership were purged from government positions. Between November 1970 and the later part of 1971, in fact, they appeared to dominate the political scene, despite being evidently dependent on President Nimairi's favour. It was over this period that the main political structures were planned. Mu'awiyah Ibrahim communists and Arab nationalists played a significant part in drafting and passing the National Charter; they were predominant in the SSU preparatory committee which drew up that organisation's basic rules; they played a central role in the creation of the main popular organisations; and the influence of their ideas can be traced in many of the central themes of the constitution. The People's Local Government Act can not be attributed to them, but the system was one which they fully accepted and believed could be used to fulfil their own objectives.[88]

While the two groupings differed on some issues, they held similar perceptions of the kind of political system which they wanted to create. It may be unwise to over-emphasise the depth and coherence of the socialist ideology they purveyed (at least in the case of the Arab nationalists), but they were both intent on establishing institutions geared towards fundamental social change. At the centre of the system, they envisaged a radically-oriented SSU, seeking to shift the balance of wealth and power in the country away from the traditional establishment which for so long had used its social influence to maintain a grip on economic resources in the country areas. To carry out this role, the SSU would not be open to anyone who formed part of, or represented the interests of, the old establishment, or who had been active in the Umma or Democratic Unionist Parties. While the SSU was intended to be a mass organisation rather than a cadre party,[89] particular emphasis would be placed on drawing into the organisation elements which had shown themselves committed to substantive change. It tended to be assumed that once the influence of the old establishment had been neutralised, the ordinary people as represented in the SSU would inevitably constitute a radical force.

The SSU's structure, as laid down by the two groupings in the basic rules which they drafted, was modelled on the pattern set by other revolutionary-centralising parties – those of Yugoslavia, North Korea, Guinea, Tanzania and Egypt being taken as models. The duties and responsibilities of the various committees and conferences of the SSU followed the democratic centralist principles found in those parties. The introduction to the basic rules describes the SSU as 'a revolutionary socialist vanguard, embracing the forces of our working people . . . to lead the struggle of the masses of our people'. It was stipulated in the basic rules that 50 per cent of any committee or conference of the SSU should consist of workers and farmers.

The two groupings intended the SSU to guide both the central government and local government authorities in bringing about the transformation of society – that transformation which was laid down in the National Charter. The granting of very significant powers to the president under the constitution seems to have been intended to give the president (as the SSU's nominee) the ability to undertake the desired programme. At the local level, the people's local government councils would be continually under pressure from the local branches of the SSU. These branches would always be seeking the selection and election of radical elements on to the councils and the adoption of radical policies by these councils. In this way the balance of wealth and power in the country would be changed. The popular and functional organisations would also help in attaining this objective. It was believed that these organisations would be radical by their nature, because essentially they were interest groups and the interests they sought to satisfy were not compatible with those of Sudan's traditionalist establishment: the women's union would press for equal rights for women, the youth union would call for a role for youth in society, etc. Led by militant elements closely allied to the SSU, the representatives of the popular and functional organisations in the local government councils would lead these bodies in a progressive direction.

The success which the Mu'awiyah Ibrahim communists and the Arab nationalists had achieved in laying down the institutional framework for the Nimairi regime, however, was not mirrored in their ability to retain political influence. In the later part of 1971 and early in 1972, President Nimairi's favour turned away from them and towards a new grouping, to be referred to here as 'technocratic neutrals'. While the latter grouping was even more diffuse and less organised than the Arab nationalists, its members did share common perceptions and tended to act together. Those members of the grouping who attained government office were mostly specialists in the field relevant to their ministries; many had spent a long time outside Sudan working for international bodies; and most had not been associated with any political group or party before.[90] The technocratic neutrals talked less of transforming the nature of Sudanese society, and more of development within the existing framework. They saw the newly formed institutions not as instruments for change but as channels through which the regime could maintain the support and involvement of the population. They were not committed to emphasising the role of radical elements within these institutions, nor to excluding from them the old establishment. Most of the major government ministers who held office in 1972 and in the years which immediately followed, could be classified as technocratic neutrals: Dr Ja'afar Bakhit (Minister of Local Government), Dr Mansur Khalid (Minister of Foreign Affairs), Ibrahim Mun'im Mansur (Minister of Finance), Dr Bashir Abbadi (Minister of Communications), Dr 'Abdallah 'Abd al-Rahman (Minister of Administrative Reform), and Wadi' Habbashi (Minister of Agriculture).

While a variety of different reasons can be put forward to explain how and why the technocratic neutrals were able to displace from influence the two more radical groupings, the most fundamental reason is straightforward. The radically-oriented institutions envisaged by the Mu'awiyah Ibrahim communists and the Arab nationalists could only have come into being if sufficient numbers of radical Sudanese were prepared to work within them. Without the support and involvement of that core of Sudanese radicalism constituted by the Communist Party, however, the institutions benefited from only limited participation by radicals. Moreover, those Sudanese who rallied to the Nimairi regime following Hashim al-'Ata's attempted coup in July 1971 were mostly inimical to radical change. They supported Nimairi because they deemed his regime preferable to a communist-based alternative. The strategy pursued by the two radical groupings, therefore, lacked both realism and political rationale.

The Mu'awiyah Ibrahim communists were the first of the two radical groupings to lose their ministerial positions. After July 1971 pressures arose, especially within the army, to remove communists of whatever type from the government. In Council of Ministers reshuffles in August and October 1971, most of the ministers who belonged to this grouping lost their positions and were replaced by technocratic neutrals.

The newly introduced technocratic neutrals and the Arab nationalists did not make a cohesive team, and in the later part of 1971 and early in 1972 a confrontation developed between them. Besides the differences on the role and functions of the political institutions, there were severe differences on foreign policy issues. The technocratic neutrals tended to favour the restoration of diplomatic relations with the United States (broken since June 1967), to oppose any immediate attempt at improving relations with the Soviet Union (badly damaged by the aftermath of the July 1971 coup), and to oppose any move towards Sudan joining the Egypt–Libya–Syria federation. On each of these issues the Arab nationalists took the opposite stand. Further differences arose over foreign investment, and over the desirability of negotiating a peaceful settlement of the southern conflict with the Southern Sudanese Liberation Movement. Increasingly, President Nimairi gave his support to the technocratic neutrals, and by the end of 1972 all the main Arab nationalists had either resigned or been dismissed from office. The positions lost by Arab nationalists were taken over either by technocratic neutrals or by southern politicians (especially after the March 1972 agreement) who worked in alliance with this group.

By 1973, then, the technocratic neutrals had emerged predominant. This is not to say that no members of the two previous groupings were left in positions of authority, but simply that such members as were still there tended to accept the general lines laid down by the technocratic neutrals.

The three sections which follow below will assess the performance of the Nimairi regime in its 'technocratic neutral' stage: broadly the period between 1972 and 1980. Over these years the regime sought, as indicated earlier, to base its claim to legitimacy on a very different ground to that put forward immediately after the May 1969 coup. The regime was now portrayed as a broadly-based system of effective government – a regime whose institutions were both open to and based on the Sudanese population as a whole. Free of ideological institutions and of the hindrances raised by an imported parliamentary system, the contention was, the regime could achieve those two key objectives which had eluded previous governments: national unity and economic development. Widespread popular participation, through the various institutions which had been established, would both give the regime a firm basis and facilitate the achievement of its objectives.[91] The three areas in which the regime's performance needs to be examined, therefore, are those of encouraging popular participation, effecting national unity, and forwarding economic development.

VII POPULAR PARTICIPATION: THE SUDAN SOCIALIST UNION

The key institution intended to channel and encourage popular participation was the Sudan Socialist Union. Most of the other institutions were supposed to constitute instruments through which ideas formulated within the SSU could be implemented. If the SSU failed to function as a channel for popular participation, therefore, the claim that the regime was founded on a 'popular base', which could help shape government policy, would clearly lack realism. The analysis of popular participation under the Nimairi regime given here will thus focus exclusively on the SSU, and specifically on the activities of the basic units (the level at which the organisation was supposed to be in contact with the majority of the population).

The role of the basic units in their interaction with the population as a whole was defined clearly in the SSU basic rules. The basic unit committee's responsibilities were listed as follows:

1. [The basic unit committee] shall assume revolutionary leadership for cultural activities and action, and lead the unit in contacting the people and working within their ranks.
2. It shall assume political leadership, control daily activities, implement policies and plans contained in the SSU directives issued by the committees of the SSU at a higher level and study monthly and other periodical reports submitted to it according to the regulations.
3. It shall promote socialist thought in conformity with the principles and aims of the May Revolution as laid down in the National Charter and persevere in awakening the working people to take part in national and socialist action.
4. It shall pursue the promotion of the people's social, cultural, economic and spiritual life . . .
5. It shall acquaint itself with, study and solve the needs and problems of the working people in collaboration with all local institutions and organisations and shall raise serious needs and problems to higher levels of the SSU and advocate their solution.

6. It shall mobilise efforts to increase production in all fields.
7. It shall combat all sorts of exploitation and bureaucracy that hinder citizens from the enjoyment of their rights or deprive them from equal opportunities in employment or any other right.
8. It shall convey to the members of the basic unit the policy of the SSU and its plans and programmes, acquaint the people with them and urge their active participation in their implementation.
9. It shall create a positive and organised spirit within the basic unit, ensuring that all members carry out their duties with vigour and that the unit as a whole works towards consolidating national unity and creating a socialist spirit within its sphere such that the practice of a real and popular democracy is possible.
10. It shall urge and help members to join institutions, councils and bodies that exercise political and economic powers and ensure that they help to implement within these spheres the general policy and the political plans of the SSU.[92]

A research project which the writer organised between 1974 and 1977 revealed that only a minority of basic units were active in any sense. Out of 143 basic units covered, in different parts of the country, only 51 had a functioning committee (i.e. one which held regular meetings).[93] Moreover, despite the SSU being the country's 'sole political organisation', and despite the emphasis given in the basic rules and associated documents to the unit committee's political role ('it shall assume political leadership' . . . 'it shall promote socialist thought' . . . 'it shall combat all forms of exploitation and bureaucracy' . . . 'it shall convey to the members of the basic unit the policy of the SSU' . . . 'it shall ensure that the unit as a whole works towards consolidating national unity and creating a socialist spirit in its sphere' . . . etc), the main emphasis in the activities actually pursued by basic unit committees was on schemes for the improvement of local facilities.

Table 7.1 gives details of the activities pursued by the 51 'functioning' committees surveyed in the above-mentioned project. As can be seen, the seven most common activities pursued all fall within the sphere of 'improvement of local facilities': organising consumer cooperatives, campaigns to clean the environment, the supply of commodities, and initiating self-help educational projects, anti-

Table 7.1 Activities Undertaken by Functioning Basic Unit Committees

Activity	Number of committees which undertook activity	Percentage of total
1. Establishment of consumer cooperatives	26	50.1
2 Organisation of a campaign to clean the area, etc.	21	41.2
3 Initiation of self-help educational projects (building classrooms, schools, etc.)	20	39.2
4 Carrying out an anti-illiteracy campaign	19	37.3
5 Arranging the supply of commodities to the population	16	31.4
6 Provision of social amenities other than educational or health (e.g. water supplies, kindergartens, etc.)	15	29.4
7 Initiation of self-help health projects (building clinics, etc.)	10	19.6
8 Submission of monthly reports to higher SSU bodies	10	19.6
9 Organisation of rallies in support of the government (or else arranging for people to attend rallies elsewhere)	10	19.6
10 Organisation of social or athletic clubs	8	15.7
11 Establishment of non-consumer cooperatives (flour mills, agricultural schemes, etc.)	7	13.7
12 Facilitating trade in the area	6	11.8
13 Holding meetings with popular and functional organisations so as to coordinate action	5	9.8
14 Holding meetings intended to direct the activities of people's local government councils	4	7.8
15 Formulation of a plan of action for the area	4	7.8
16 Convening general meetings of unit members at least every 6 months (as required)	4	7.8
17 Holding meetings to convey to the population the principles of the National Charter	3	5.8
18 Studying and discussing reports from higher levels in the SSU, on a regular basis	3	5.8

Table 7.1 continued

19	Promoting socialist thought in the area	2	3.9
20	Carrying out of a survey of the area	2	3.9
21	Discussing general political questions within the committee	2	3.9
22	Discussing methods of increasing production	0	0

Note: The figures given here relate only to the 51 basic unit committee which were functioning (out of a total of 143 surveyed).

Source: Author's research.

illiteracy campaigns and projects for the provision of general soci amenities. Even items 8 and 9 in the table, which do relate to th political structure, are scarcely a reflection of autonomous grassroot political activism. In the case of item 8 the content of reports seem mostly to have been limited to details of new members recruited an of progress on projects under way (i.e. the provision of local facili ties), while in the case of item 9 the holding of rallies in support of th government does not involve a genuine debate on the directions c government policy. The activities where committees were acting as link in a chain of communications between the SSU leadership an the population as a whole, relaying to the people the conceptions c the leadership and channelling popular concerns to the leadership are ranked no higher than 13th in the table. No such activity wa undertaken by more than 10 per cent of even the 'active' basic uni committees. In short, ten of the twelve most common activitie pursued by basic unit committees related to only one of the com mittees' functions as defined by the basic rules ('The committee sha pursue the promotion of the people's social, cultural, economic an spiritual life'), while the ten less common activities pursued covere largely the political realm upon which the basic rules placed primar emphasis.

The view of SSU basic units which emerges, therefore, is o organisations which were functioning (when they were functioning primarily as village or town quarter development committees, an which played only a marginal role in conveying popular concerns t the national leadership or in politicising the population in the manne intended (at least according to the basic rules) by the nationa leadership. This view is given credence by some other aspects of th operation of the basic units. The participation of SSU members and the wider population in the activities of the basic unit was shown, in the research project mentioned above, to depend on the committee's ability to help in the improvement of local facilities and to satisfy immediate needs. When the committee was unable to respond directly to expectations in this field, popular involvement in the committee's activities declined and the committee itself often retreated into inactivity. The initial formation of basic units in mid-1973, in fact, occurred at an unfortunate time: essential commodities came to be in short supply in Sudanese towns in August and September of that year. Some committee secretaries were convinced that the failure of many who had registered for SSU membership in July 1973 to play a part in their units' activities was due to the shortages – and to the evident inability of the committees to help solve this problem. Similarly, where basic unit committees had initiated self-help projects to construct health clinics, classrooms and schools, the government ministry concerned (health or education) was sometimes unable to supply the staff for the new clinic, class or school. This too adversely affected the ability of basic unit committees to remain active.

Among the population as a whole, moreover, there was widespread confusion as to the distinctive role of the SSU, and even the SSU's distinctive existence. Many people were unable to distinguish between SSU basic units, people's local government councils, village development committees and branches of popular and functional organisations – in so far as all of them were concerned with developing the facilities of the village or town quarter, and all were seeking to encourage self-help projects in similar fields. The confusion was compounded by the fact that the same individuals tended to serve on the basic unit committee as were on the people's local government councils, the village development committees, and the branch committees of popular and functional organisations.

While the SSU was not totally moribund at the basic unit level, therefore, it did not constitute an effective vehicle for political communication: either for communication of popular perceptions to the leadership, or of the leadership's perceptions to the populace. Conceived initially as an instrument for change, yet developed (supposedly) as a forum for representation, the SSU ended up being neither. Given the top-heavy nature of the SSU hierarchy, there was little room for any political initiative to emanate from the lower

levels. The disinclination of basic unit committees to play a politica
role probably reflected this reality. While the SSU carried politica
significance at the national level, this significance came from it bein
an arm of the regime. Differences of opinion could certainly exis
within the national congress, the central committee and the politica
bureau, but the opinions expressed within these bodies neither stemme
from, nor were determined by, widespread policy debates among SSU
members. As the SSU had been intended to provide the politica
dynamic and momentum behind the other institutions – the people'
local government councils, the national assembly and the popula
and functional organisations – it is not surprising that the latte
institutions mirrored the SSU's 'arm of the regime' role.

VIII THE PURSUIT OF NATIONAL UNITY: REGIONAL AUTONOMY IN THE SOUTHERN SUDAN

The Nimairi regime's most outstanding success in the 1970s, with
little doubt, was that of achieving a peaceful settlement to the conflic
in the southern Sudan. The significance of this achievement shoul
not be understated. Without it, the intensive development effort o
the mid-1970s could never even have been attempted: the domesti
resources for such an undertaking would have been lacking, as als
the international confidence necessary for raising loans. Nonetheless
the conclusion of the Addis Ababa agreement in March 1972 was a
much the outcome of a fortunate set of circumstances as it was of
well-conceived government policy. While the perception whic
government spokesmen purveyed at the time – that once the regim
had rid itself of the communist element, it could give priority to th
cause of national unity and come to terms with the rebel Anyanya
has some superficial plausibility, the real dynamics which led t
peaceful settlement were more complex.

The most important, yet least discussed, factor which made poss
ible the conclusion of the Addis Ababa agreement relates to change
in political authority within the southern armed opposition. Prior t
1971, the possibility of peaceful settlement to the conflict was im
peded by the absence of any authority within the southern oppositio
which could realistically negotiate a settlement. The scattered an
uncoordinated nature of the guerrilla campaign (with local Anyany
leaders often responsible to no one but themselves), the sever
divisions within the exile political leadership, and the absence of

strong or continuing relationship between the exile politicians and the guerrilla fighters in whose name the politicians claimed to be speaking, meant that no body or institution existed which had the practical authority to negotiate a settlement and ensure that it held.

A number of attempts were made in the late 1960s to weld together a cohesive southern resistance. Most such attempts, however, ended quickly in failure. In mid-1967 some of the younger southern exile politicians, led by Gordon Mortat Mayen and Barri Wanji, launched an initiative to bring the existing exile groups and the Anyanya leaders together in one organisation. At the Angudri convention, held in August 1967, representatives of these various factions agreed to establish a Southern Sudan Provisional Government (SSPG), with Aggrey Jaden as president and Emilio Tafeng as Anyanya commander-in-chief. Tribal, religious and personality differences and competition, however, soon led to the disintegration of the SSPG. A further attempt to create a united leadership for the southern resistance was made at the Balgo Bindi[94] convention in March 1969. A new provisional government was formed, the Nile Provisional Government (NPG), with Gordon Mortat Mayen as president, Marco Rume as vice-president, and Emilio Tafeng once again as Anyanya commander-in-chief. From the start, however, the NPG stood little chance of providing a coherent leadership. A number of the most prominent southern exile politicians held aloof from it, and few of the Anyanya leaders accorded it much respect.[95]

In the second half of 1969, however, authority within the southern opposition began to cohere around the figure of Joseph Lagu, the Anyanya commander in eastern Equatoria. Following the Balgo Bindi convention, Lagu renounced the authority of Emilio Tafeng and proclaimed the establishment of the Anyanya National Organisation, under his own command. Over the 18 months which followed, Joseph Lagu was to emerge as the acknowledged political and military leader of the southern armed opposition. Two factors account for the Anyanya National Organisation's ability to assume the central role in the southern resistance. First, the character of the leadership. Joseph Lagu, a former captain in the Sudanese army, was younger, better educated and more dynamic than Emilio Tafeng and most of the other senior Anyanya officers. Second, the Anyanya National Organisation benefited from access to an ample supply of weapons. This was an indirect effect of political developments in Khartoum. The May 1969 coup, with the reinforcement which it imparted to Arab radicalism, aroused the concern of the Israeli government, which promptly sought to undermine the new regime and distract it from wider Arab causes. The Israeli authorities picked out that section of the Anyanya which seemed to have the most effective leadership – the Anyanya National Organisation – and from September 1969 began supplying it with weapons. Over the last part of 1969 two air-drops of arms per month were made to Joseph Lagu's forces.[96] Paradoxically this action, aimed at intensifying the civil war in Sudan, ultimately had precisely the opposite effect. Access to weaponry enabled Joseph Lagu to unite under his leadership the previously divided and highly uncoordinated bands of the Anyanya, and finally placed him in a position where he could negotiate a settlement of the conflict with the central government.

The 1969–71 period, then, saw the gradual unification of the southern resistance. Emilio Tafeng, despite being recognised by the Nile Provisional Government as Anyanya commander-in-chief, broke away from the NPG in mid-1969 and established the Anyidi Revolutionary Government (together with his chief-of-staff, Frederick Magott). This body, however, only attracted the support of a small part of the Anyanya and, in April 1970, Tafeng acknowledged the overall leadership of Lagu. In June 1970 the NPG lost its remaining support among the Anyanya: Emmanuel Abur, the principal Anyanya leader in Bahr el Ghazal province, renounced allegiance to the NPG and placed himself under Lagu's command. At about the same time Samuel Abujohn, who controlled Anyanya forces in western Equatoria and had sought to establish a separatist state based on the Zande tribe, abandoned his own plans and acknowledged Lagu's leadership. The NPG duly recognised the realities of the situation and, in the later part of July 1970, announced its own dissolution and the handing over of all authority to the Anyanya National Organisation. Lagu spent the remaining months of 1970 strengthening his control over the Anyanya forces and re-organising the guerrilla structure.[97]

By the beginning of 1971 the Anyanya, under Lagu's command, had thus come to constitute a genuinely united fighting force, as opposed to the coalition of disparate bands over which Emilio Tafeng had maintained a nominal command. In the areas it controlled, the Anyanya National Organisation built up a civilian administration. In January 1971 Lagu proclaimed the establishment of the Southern Sudan Liberation Movement, constituting a political leadership 'to act under the control of the Anyanya armed forces'. The exile political elite remained in the picture, therefore, only to the extent that the

Anyanya were prepared to make use of them. There now existed a unified southern resistance movement, which had sufficient power and authority to negotiate an end to the protracted conflict.

It would, however, be unfair to suggest that the Addis Ababa agreement was simply the outcome of political re-structuring within the southern resistance. The central government had begun, by 1971, to re-think its policy towards the conflict in the South. This resulted in part from the evident ineffectiveness of existing policy. The attempt to implement an intensive social and economic development programme in the South, with a view to laying the basis for regional autonomy, could make no progress when the government lacked control over much of the region. Development projects were being destroyed more quickly than they could be constructed. In part the re-thinking of policy stemmed from the changing composition of the central government. The increasing emphasis given to 'national unity' as against 'socialist construction' gave the Nimairi regime a rationale for seeking the most direct route to national reconciliation. The social and economic pre-conditions which had earlier been deemed essential for the effective operation of regional autonomy could now be jettisoned. It should be stressed, nonetheless, that the initial moves towards negotiations were made while Joseph Garang (who retained his commitment to socialist construction) was Minister of Southern Affairs.[98]

Also of importance was the availability of a mediating body which enjoyed the confidence of both sides of the conflict. The All-African Council of Churches (AACC) had shown an interest in promoting a settlement of the southern Sudan conflict from the mid-1960s.[99] In January 1971 the AACC was invited to send a delegation to Sudan to 'review the government's attempts at restoring a state of normality in the South'.[100] Eager to use this opportunity to best advantage, the AACC gave its delegation instructions to raise the possibility of a negotiated settlement. Before the delegation left for Khartoum, its members held talks with a body in Uganda known as the Kampala Committee – a grouping of southerners and non-Sudanese SSLM-sympathisers resident in the Ugandan capital.[101] The parameters of an approach to negotiations were discussed. When the AACC delegation arrived in Khartoum in May 1971, therefore, it was more intent on the pursuit of a negotiated settlement than on reviewing conditions in the South. In talks with government ministers a framework for government–SSLM talks was agreed, comprising the following points:

i.   The government of Sudan is in favour of the (AACC) delegation making contacts with representatives from the South with a view to establishing direct contact for talks on reconciliation.

ii.   Groups to be represented are those who have influence on people in the South and among the refugees.

iii.   Talks could take place anywhere.

iv.   The government would agree to a 'cooling off period' if no security danger is involved.

v.   Details of regional autonomy within one Sudan would be discussed.

vi.   The question of under whose auspices the talks would take place would be discussed later.[102]

Over the months which followed the May 1971 visit to Khartoum, the AACC opened up contacts with the SSLM. Due to the remoteness of Joseph Lagu's headquarters in southern Sudan, and to the dispersal of those Anyanya leaders and exile politicians with whom Lagu wished to consult, the progression towards negotiations necessarily moved slowly.[103] Early in July 1971 three SSLM delegates, speaking on behalf of Joseph Lagu, assured Canon Burgess Carr of the AACC that the SSLM was prepared to negotiate, provided negotiations were held on neutral ground and were sponsored by a mutually acceptable African leader. Preliminary talks, aimed at laying the basis for negotiations, were held between SSLM and government delegations in November at Addis Ababa, under Emperor Haile Selassie's sponsorship. Addis Ababa remained the site for the full negotiations, held in February 1972, between a Sudanese government delegation led by vice-president Abel Alier and an SSLM delegation led by Ezboni Mondiri. Preliminary accord was reached on three texts, which were to constitute the substance of the Addis Ababa agreement:

(i)   An organic law organising regional self-government in the southern Sudan, with an ordinance on items of revenue.

(ii)   A ceasefire agreement.

(iii) Protocols on interim arrangements relating to administration, military affairs, judicial affairs, and repatriation and resettlement.

The month which followed the February negotiations saw much politicking within the SSLM. It seems that Joseph Lagu was initially dissatisfied with some aspects of the draft settlement (despite his own delegation having initialled the texts) and was intent on seeking changes before he ratified any agreement. The Israeli government promised Lagu increased assistance if he should renounce the settlement package.[104] Ultimately, however, a countervailing pressure proved more significant: the Sudanese and Ugandan governments had reached agreement on the expulsion of 'elements hostile to the other state' from their territories.[105] The Libyan government, moreover, succeeded in persuading Iddi Amin, early in March 1972, to sever diplomatic relations with Israel and to expel all Israeli military advisers from Uganda.[106] Unable to use Uganda either as a safe base for organisation, or as a channel through which Israeli military aid could reach the Anyanya,[107] the SSLM would have encountered difficulty in maintaining a strong military campaign. On 18 March, Lagu duly signed the Addis Ababa agreement, comprising the texts agreed in February. The civil war was over.

The implementation of regional autonomy in the southern Sudan duly followed from the Draft Organic Law to Organise Regional Self-Government in the Southern Provinces, as agreed by the two sides at Addis Ababa. Article 7 of the law specified the functions reserved for the central government as follows:

   (i) National defence.
   (ii) External affairs.
   (iii) Currency and coinage.
   (iv) Air and inter-regional river transport.
   (v) Communications and telecommunications.
   (vi) Customs and foreign trade, except for border trade and certain commodities which the regional government may specify with the approval of the central government.
   (vii) Nationality, immigration and emigration.
   (viii) Planning for economic and social development.
   (ix) Educational planning.
   (x) Public audit.[108]

Article 11 specified that the regional assembly in the South could legislate on 'the preservation of public order, internal security, efficient administration and the development of the southern region in cultural, economic and social fields . . .' The article then went on to list some specific areas of regional authority. The regional president was to be 'appointed and relieved of office by the president on the recommendation of the people's regional assembly', and the high executive council was to be 'composed of members appointed and relieved of office by the president on the recommendation of the president of the high executive council'. The members of the high executive council and the regional president were, therefore, directly or indirectly responsible to two authorities: the national president and the regional assembly. The latter body, elected by 'direct secret ballot', constituted the legislature for the region, but the national president could 'veto any bill which he deems contrary to the provisions of the national constitution'. As for arrangements regarding the armed forces, Mom Kou Nhial Arou summarises these concisely:

> The agreement stipulated that there should be a Southern Command . . . composed of twelve thousand officers and men, half of whom would originate in the South, and the other half of whom would come from elsewhere in the Sudan. Most of the troops from the South were expected to be drawn from the former Anyanya army. There was, however, a provision that there should be integration between the two halves; that is, each unit of southern soldiers would receive elements from the old Sudan government forces in the form of an officer to act as second in command, and various technical and administrative personnel.[109]

Over the mid-1970s, the regional autonomy arrangement in southern Sudan operated with a reasonable degree of success. The Anyanya were integrated into the new framework, whether in a civilian capacity or as part of the Sudanese army; the resettlement of southern refugees (who had been resident in neighbouring countries) was carried through effectively; the regional assembly elections of 1973 and 1978 provided the opportunity for a rather more genuine competition among different groupings than was evident in the national assembly elections; the assembly performed a useful role as critic of high executive council policy; and the high executive council managed for a time to contain tribal-based divisiveness.

The ultimate re-emergence of civil conflict in the southern Sudan in the 1980s was due not to any inherent inadequacies in the regional autonomy arrangement, but to the impact of wider policies pursued by the Nimairi regime. This is discussed in section X below. The balance of credit accruing to the regime for its policy in the South, then, can be conveyed as follows: the most critical factors which made settlement possible were to be found not in the regime's high regard for 'national unity' but in changes within the southern opposition; the regional autonomy arrangement implemented by the regime (first proposed on 9 June 1969) proved workable in the short-term and constituted an effective instrument through which civil order was re-established, but it was ultimately undermined by the regime's wider policies.

IX ECONOMIC POLICY AND ACHIEVEMENT

'Development', as stated before, was one of the two key concepts on which the technocratic neutral elements who predominated in the Sudanese government through the mid- and late 1970s laid emphasis. Sudan's development was no longer deemed to require any fundamental change in the social and economic structure inherited from pre-1969, but was seen as dependent on the injection of sufficient capital into the existing structure. The state, it was now envisaged, would concentrate on laying down the necessary infrastructure (communications, electricity supply, etc.), while giving the private sector a leading role in developing the productive sphere. In promoting private investment in the productive sphere, however, the state would enter into partnership with private investors, and would in particular fields (especially sugar and textiles) carry out productive investments which would lead the way for private investors. The attraction of capital, therefore, became the central economic concern of the government. This required the passage of legislation to protect private investment (the Development and Promotion of Industrial Investment Act, 1972; the Development and Encouragement of Industrial Investment Act, 1974; the Development and Encouragement of Agricultural Investment Act, 1976; the Encouragement of Investment Act, 1980), and the pursuit of economic policies acceptable to the International Monetary Fund – so as to give potential investors the necessary confidence.

The adoption of this new policy came at a time when rising oil revenues in the Gulf seemed to offer new prospects to the Sudanese economy. This, indeed, was a factor which helped to shape the perceptions of those who formulated Sudanese economic policy in the mid-1970s. Sudan, it was said, could play a central role in the new Arab economic order. The Arab oil-producing states, especially after the 1973 war, were accumulating vast revenues which were in search of productive investment. Most important to the Arab oil-producing states was to invest in food production within the Arab world, as this would alleviate the Arab world's critical dependence on the outside world for food. Of Sudan's 80 million feddans of cultivated land, only 17 million feddans were actually under cultivation, and an additional 200 million feddans were available as grazing land.[110] The investment of Arab oil revenues in Sudan's land resources, making use of the substantial Sudanese labour force and the adequate supply of water from the Nile (in addition to rain-fed supplies), could therefore achieve a developmental breakthrough. Sudan would become the bread-basket of the world. The developmental effort would involve a three-concerned cooperation: Sudan's natural and manpower resources cooperating with Arab finance and with Western technology. The cooperation would bring benefit to all three partners: Arab revenues would be productively and usefully invested; the Western economies would earn recycled petrodollars through the sale of technology and know-how; and Sudan would undergo immense economic development.

Although the Five Year Plan remained formally in existence, and was indeed extended to cover two more years, actual economic policy proceeded differently. The 'Interim Programme (1973/4–76/77)' laid the basis for a more ambitious development effort, envisaging much higher expenditure than that proposed by the Five Year Plan.[111] The production of sugar, wheat and textiles was given particular encouragement: Sudan was to achieve short-term self-sufficiency in these products and would then develop a long-term export potential. In part this involved state-owned schemes which were supposed to lay a basis for further investment in allied fields; in part it involved cooperative ventures between the state and private investors; and in part it was a question of creating a framework within which private investment could be attracted. The major aspect in which the balance of investment would differ from that envisaged under the original plan, however, was in the emphasis given to public expenditure in the transport and communications sector – the road, rail and port facilities necessary to the expansion of production and trade. Table 7.2 gives details of the change which occurred in the pattern of sectoral investment, between the original version of the Five Year Plan and the Interim Programme (i.e. 'Amended Plan').

The first International Monetary Fund (IMF) 'stabilisation programme' (since 1969) was adopted in 1972, in return for a $24 million loan. This and subsequent stabilisation programmes had their impact on economic policy through the 1970s and into the 1980s. Initially at least, however, the IMF was probably pushing Sudan's technocratic

Table 7.2   Public Sector Investment Pattern, 1965–75

Sector	1965/70 (actual)	1970/75 (original plan)	1970/75 (amended plan)	1970/75 (actual)
Agriculture and irrigation	35	38	23	27
Industry and mining	6	17	18	21
Power	9	6	6	
Transport and communications	18	14	34	32
Services	19	19	14	16
Miscellaneous (including technical assistance)	13	6	6	4
Total	100	100	100	100

Source: Sayed Nimeiri, *The Five Year Plan (1970–75): Some Aspects of the Plan and its Performance* (DSRC, Khartoum, 1976), p. 18.

neutrals in a direction in which they wished to go. The principal elements of IMF programmes over this period were the following:

(i) Privatisation and reducing the role of the public sector:
—introducing a land-water charge system in the Gezira scheme to replace the old partnership between the scheme and the farmers;
—eliminating state monopolies in import and export trade;
—dissolving public industrial corporations and re-forming the units within them as private companies;
—introducing foreign management where necessary.

(ii) Liberalisation of trade and elimination of subsidies:
—abolishing the foreign exchange control system;
—removing subsidies from basic commodities (wheat, sugar and petroleum) and from services;

(iii) Anti-inflationary policies:
—reducing state expenditure, especially on social services.

(iv) Devaluation of the Sudanese currency so as to correct the balance of payments crisis.[112]

The Six Year Plan (1977–83) followed the pattern laid down by the Interim Programme and was geared to consistency with IMF doctrines. External resources were to account for some 52 per cent of total investment. As private investors had so far shown some reluctance to invest directly in the Sudanese economy, however, the public sector would account for 59 per cent of total investment. Much of the investment undertaken, therefore, would consist of the government spending funds borrowed from abroad.

Within the framework set by the Interim Programme, the Six Year Plan and IMF policies, considerable development activity was engendered in Sudan in the middle and late 1970s. Annual development expenditure rose from £S278 million in 1972/3 to £S432.9 million in 1973/4, and to £S666.2 million in 1974/5. In 1976/7 it exceeded £S1000 million.[113] In the agricultural sector, a number of large irrigated schemes were initiated, most notably at Rahad, Seleit, Damazine and Kenana. The emphasis in these schemes was on the production of sugar and wheat, but it was intended also to grow millet, cotton and vegetables. Mechanised dry farming was also greatly expanded.

Infrastructure also attracted significant expenditure. New rolling stock was brought in for the railway system, new port facilities were created in Port Sudan, a tarmac road was constructed between Khartoum and Port Sudan (completed in 1980), new electric power stations were constructed, and the digging of the Jonglei canal was initiated. The latter project was intended to divert some 20 million cubic metres of water a day away from the marshlands of the *sudd*, such that the water could be used to irrigate an extra 3–4 million feddans of land in the central Sudan – together with a similar area in Egypt.

One other field of development activity, which had not been envisaged in the Interim Programme, was the oil sector. The Chevron oil company began prospecting for oil in 1974, followed in the late 1970s by other oil companies. Figure 7.2 shows the distribution of oil concessions and 'areas of interest' among the different oil companies. By 1980 it was clear that oil was present in exploitable quantities along the northern fringe of Bahr el Ghazal province (under the Chevron concession). While the main burden of expenditure in this sector fell on the oil companies, the Sudanese government was responsible for some of the associated infrastructural expenses. The government also needed, once the decision to exploit the reserves was made, to raise finance for the projected pipeline which would carry the oil the 1000 miles to Port Sudan.

The flurry of development activity in the mid- and late 1970s, however, led the Sudan into a deepening economic crisis. By the end of the 1970s a clear pattern was emerging: few of the projects which were initiated were completed on time; once they had been completed, projects rarely fulfilled the production targets which had been set for them; and the output from previously existing agricultural schemes and industries gradually declined. Gross domestic output, far from increasing, actually decreased in the years which followed 1977 – falling by 4.3 per cent in 1978/9 and 1 per cent in 1979/80.[114] Having borrowed vast sums of money in the expectation that loans could be repaid out of increased production, therefore, the Sudanese government found itself burdened with an immense debt and no new revenue with which to make repayment. The external debt, standing at $3 billion in 1978, had risen to $5.2 billion at the beginning of 1982. By the time the Nimairi regime had fallen from power (April 1985) it was approaching $9 billion.

Sudan found itself in a cycle of increasing debt and declining production. With much of the foreign exchange which was raised through exports now being needed to meet interest payments, there was inevitably insufficient foreign exchange to satisfy the requirements of industry and agriculture for imports of fuel and spare parts. This naturally affected output in the agricultural and industrial sectors, which in turn reduced exports and thus the availability of foreign exchange. The balance of payments became critically unbalanced; inflation rose in the early 1980s to an effective rate of about 60 per cent per annum; the Sudanese pound steadily lost its value; and standards of living declined severely.

Two basic causes lay behind the Nimairi regime's failure to realise the ambitious development hopes of the early 1970s. First, the planning behind the development programme was deficient. Despite the existence of a Five Year Plan, an Interim Programme and a Six Year Plan, decisions on development expenditure were taken in an *ad hoc* fashion. Projects were often adopted simply because the necessary financing for them could be arranged, not because any of the plans had scheduled them for implementation. The costs and benefits of each project seem to have been assessed individually, with little attention given to the impact which all projects together would have on the economy (i.e. in terms of manpower resources, foreign exchange, use of infrastructure, etc.). Some ministries took the initiative of starting projects, financed by external loans which they negotiated themselves, without obtaining the prior approval of the central planning agency. The latter body, in any case, was headed by a minister of state who was in no position to impose his will on the more senior ministers. Inevitably critical bottlenecks and shortages

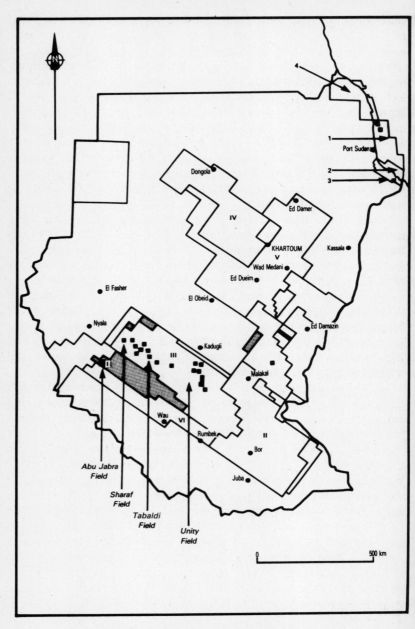

Figure 7.2   Oil Companies Holding Concessions in South-Central Region

soon emerged. These delayed the completion of projects, reduced the effectiveness of such projects as were completed, and undermined the viability of existing industrial and agricultural undertakings.

This 'deficient planning' was not simply a matter of incompetent management. Corruption played a major role. The motivation for many of the projects which materialised at this time could be found more in the financial gain which would accrue to individual ministers and officials than in an impartial assessment of their real value to the economy.

The second cause of economic failure was the combined effect of external factors over which the Sudanese government had no control. The multiple consequences of rising oil prices could not realistically have been predicted by the government when the Interim Programme was being framed in 1972. The most immediate impact was to increase substantially Sudan's fuel bill. Given the considerable energy requirements of the development programme, both for project construction and subsequent operation, the economic calculations on which projects were based were seriously skewed. Foreign exchange costs were thus much higher than had been predicted.

Of greater long-term importance were some of the indirect effects. Rising oil prices gave a new impetus to development programmes in the Gulf states, which in turn increased the demand there for externally recruited professionals, skilled workers and manual labourers. The Sudanese labour market was well placed to respond to this

---

I   Shaded areas: Areas relinquished by Chevron Oil Company in 1980. Taken by Total.
II   Total Exploration + International Energy Development (145 000 km^2). Concession agreed November 1980.
III Chevron Oil Company (204 200 km^2). Concession has been worked since 1974.
IV   Phillips Petroleum Company (120 000 km^2). Concession agreed October 1981.
V   US Sunmark (a division of Sun Oil of Dallas) area of interest (172 000 km^2).
VI   Transpacific (Canada) area of interest.

Red Sea Area
1 Texas Eastern (27 500 km^2). Concession agreed December 1979.
2 Total Exploration (6 400 km^2). Concession agreed November 1979.
3 Union Texas (4 249 km^2). Concession agreed May 1980.
4 Transpacific (Canada) area of interest (70 000 km^2).

demand. While jobs in the Gulf brought private gain to the many individuals who obtained such employment – and also brought some foreign exchange to Sudan through remittances, albeit in smaller amounts than first anticipated – the overall impact was to limit the Sudanese government's ability to control the economy. Shortages of skilled and technical labour suddenly arose as workers migrated to higher salaries in the Gulf. To deter skilled, technical and professional elements from leaving, the government found itself forced to raise salaries, thereby adding to inflationary pressures and widening social and economic disparities within the population. Exchange controls had to be loosened and import controls lifted to provide migrants with an incentive to bring their earnings home.

The migrant remittances themselves also increased the stress on the economic system. They were spent on the purchase of imported cars, consumer durables, houses and land. The increasing number of cars and consumer durables entering the country raised demand for fuel and electricity, thereby creating a further drain on foreign exchange. Expenditure on houses and land drove up real estate prices. The rising price of agricultural land forced up the cost of food products, giving yet another twist to the inflation spiral.

The indirect effects of labour migration on Sudan, therefore, were that labour could not be effectively regulated or planned; prices could not be effectively controlled; fuel and energy requirements grew more quickly than the government had envisaged, devouring huge quantities of foreign exchange; salaries and wages of scarcity-value personnel were forced upwards; and the government lost control over foreign exchange dealing (which itself was an IMF policy prescription).

While other labour-exporting countries have experienced some of the same negative effects of labour migration as Sudan, the Sudanese case was compounded by the faulty economic planning. The interaction of faulty economic planning and the systemic factors stemming from rising oil prices in the Gulf account for the extent of Sudan's economic failure. The Sudanese economy, in fact, could only have drawn real benefit from rising oil revenues in the Gulf if the government had retained a stronger control over the economy, had regulated more closely the flow of migrant labour, and had ensured that the pace and pattern of development were determined by a well-conceived set of priorities laid down by government planners. This was a period, however, in which government policy-making was moving in a different direction.

X THE DYNAMICS OF THE NIMAIRI REGIME'S DISINTEGRATION

The problems faced by the Sudanese economy in the early 1980s created the dynamics which ultimately led to the re-emergence of civil conflict in southern Sudan and to the fall of the Nimairi regime. The immense foreign debt and the severe imbalances in the economy left the government with little room for manoeuvre. Such funds as the government had at its disposal had to be spent on making operational and productive those projects already undertaken, and on eliminating the bottlenecks which inhibited their productivity. Most of the projects which had been undertaken, and on which the ultimate hopes of being able to pay back Sudan's debt rested, were located in central Sudan. Effectively, the outlying parts of the country were starved not only of development funding but even of funds for recurrent expenditure. They experienced, therefore, all of the negative effects of Sudan's economic position (high inflation, shortages of essential products, etc.) and none of the positive aspects (the influx of funds for selected development projects).

These immediate economic policy dilemmas were reinforced by external pressures. The IMF and the consortium of Sudan's creditors created a framework from which there was no escape, short of Sudan's reneging on its international debts. Both insisted that government expenditure be cut back sharply, that no new projects should be undertaken, and that expenditure be concentrated on existing agricultural and industrial schemes. Gulf investors, enjoying links with senior members of the Sudanese administration, intoned the same refrain.

The regime showed some awareness of the political dangers inherent in the situation. In 1979/80 it introduced new 'decentralisation' and 'regionalisation' policies, intended to shift administrative and development concentration away from the central Sudan and towards the provinces. There was much to be said in favour of these policies. The reality, however, was that the Sudanese government simply did not possess the resources to support them. The policies required increased expenditure, while the government was having to reduce expenditure. The policies became simply instruments for diverting popular attention from economic failure and for ensuring the continued allegiance of those locally influential individuals who could emerge as 'ministers' in the regional governments.

The economic problems had the greatest political significance in southern Sudan. Lacking a secure flow of funds for development, and confronted by conditions of considerable economic hardship, the regionally autonomous government in southern Sudan fell apart. A development programme that was effective as well as ambitious might well have been able to overcome the ethnic and personal antagonisms of southern Sudanese politics. Without such a focus for popular attention, however, the South's political arena became increasingly divisive. The credibility of the existing institutions was sapped by a prolonged dispute on whether the South should retain its unity or be divided into three regions. Creating three regions in the southern Sudan would, some claimed, lessen the tendency for southern Sudanese politics to be dominated by the Dinka tribe.

It was in this context that civil conflict re-emerged in southern Sudan. In January 1983 dissidents attacked the town of Aweil in Bahr el Ghazal province, killing twelve northern Sudanese merchants. In February of that year battalion 105 of the Sudanese army (based in the South and constituted mainly of southern Sudanese) mutinied. Some 1000 soldiers and officers fled to the bush, taking their weapons with them. Further incidents occurred during the summer. The formation of the Sudanese Popular Liberation Movement (SPLM) in August 1983 gave the resistance movement in the South a formal structure. By mid-1984 much of the land to the east of the White Nile appeared to be either under SPLM control or subject to SPLM incursions. The movement which had now developed, however, was different in character from earlier southern-based armed organisations: it was opposed to secession and called for the establishment of a unitary socialist Sudan.

Just as economic failure led to political disintegration, so also did political disintegration intensify the economic failure. Guerrilla attacks on personnel employed by the French company CCI, in December 1983, halted work on the Jonglei canal project. Similar attacks in February 1984 on oil workers employed by Chevron brought oil exploration to a stop. These developments extinguished any hope that the Sudanese economy could stage a short-term economic recovery.

The drought which afflicted Sudan in 1984–5 was, of course, a natural disaster which would have had a crushing effect on Sudan whatever economic policies had been pursued. The severity of the impact of the drought, however, was intensified by the experience which Sudan's 'outlying regions' had undergone since the late 1970s. Having suffered several years of declining living standards and economic disruption, the populations of eastern and western Sudan were in no position to face up to a major natural disaster.

The central rationale which had been put forward after 1971 to justify the regime – that it constituted an effective instrument to achieve development and national unity – was undermined by the evident failure of the development strategy and by the re-emergence of civil conflict in southern Sudan. The Nimairi regime gradually began to change its objectives and orientation. President Nimairi gave increasing emphasis to creating a basis of Islamic legitimacy for his regime, ultimately attempting to change fundamentally the permanent constitution which he himself had introduced. The political oppression and economic deprivation which Nimairi had imposed on the greater part of the Sudanese population, however, ultimately prevented the full fruition of this new mutation in the regime. In the meantime, several hundred people nonetheless suffered the butchery of limbs, under legal arrangements which could scarcely be dignified by reference to Islamic legitimacy.

Epilogue

On 26 March 1985 demonstrations broke out in the streets of Khartoum. The immediate cause of the demonstrations was the increase in the price of bread and sugar which had just been announced, and the earlier 75 per cent rise in the price of petrol. After President Nimairi left Sudan on the following day for a medical check-up in the United States, the demonstrations spread. Many different elements of the population were drawn, largely spontaneously, into the demonstrations, which were increasingly directed towards the overthrow of the regime itself. Political, professional and trade union groupings began to form (or re-form) so as to organise and promote the opposition movement. On 6 April, the Minister of Defence and commander-in-chief of the armed forces, General Siwar al-Dahab, spoke on Radio Omdurman:

> The Sudan armed forces have been observing the deteriorating security situation all over the country, and the extremely complex political crisis that has affected the country over the past few days. In order to reduce bloodshed and to ensure the country's independence and unity, the armed forces have decided unanimously to stand by the people and their choice and to respond to their demands by taking over power and transferring it to the people after a specified transitional period.

The removal from power of President Nimairi, together with his deputies, assistants, consultants and ministers, was announced. The constitution was suspended, a state of emergency declared, and the borders closed. Authority was placed in the hands of a Transitional Military Council (TMC).

The record of the Nimairi regime had been one of missed opportunities and political repression. The regime had initially appeared well placed to pursue a coherent development policy, creating a more egalitarian society and a more self-sufficient economy. The state enjoyed considerable freedom of action, or relative autonomy. It was not directly dependent on that bourgeoisie which, through the interlinked social and economic power of the old Sudanese establishment, had made it impossible for earlier regimes to envisage structural changes in economy and society. Yet such autonomy as the regime enjoyed, as against indigenous social groupings, was ultimately lost to international capital. The contours of economic policy were no longer determined by the political, social and economic interests of Sudan, but by the requirements of those individuals, banks, companies, corporations and governments who were prepared to invest in and lend money to Sudan, and who subsequently became Sudan's creditors. A combination of corruption and mismanagement, complemented by the failure to maintain a popular base, impelled the regime in this direction.

Having failed to base his regime on those elements in the population which favoured the radical changes initially espoused by the May 'revolution', Ja'afar Nimairi used national policies more as tactics to gain temporary semblances of popular support than as well-conceived strategies for furthering the country's welfare. The political arena, rather than constituting a forum within which national problems could be discussed and solutions proposed, became a theatre where the president could arrange spectacles. The spectacles were designed to distract the population from immediate economic problems and to weld together a shifting basis of proclaimed yet insubstantial support. Foreign and domestic issues were both used in this manner. The 1972 crisis in relations with Egypt, the anti-Libyan and anti-Ethiopian alarmism of the late 1970s and early 1980s, the short-lived 'national reconciliation' with Sadiq al-Mahdi and some elements of the opposition national front (1977–9), the decentralisation and regionalisation policies (1979–80), the change to a new system of local government (1980), and finally and most notably the adoption of the Islamic *shari'ah* as the basis of Sudan's laws – all these were important not so much for their policy content as for their utility as spectacles. The real issues were submerged by the spectacles, leaving a population which had possessed great political vitality without any effective input into the system. Meanwhile, the critical reality was covered up: the framework of economic decision-making was now set by external forces, whether in the capitalist world's financial institutions, in the oil-producing states, or in Washington.

Sudan's future seems beset by economic problems. Yet the great vitality of the Sudanese population, the immense natural resources which the country possesses, and a political tradition marked by considerable sophistication suggest a more hopeful vision of the future. The means need to be found whereby the recently regained democratic liberties, which in the past have created a high level of intellectual creativity among the Sudanese people, can be safeguarded within a political system responsive to the interests of the less privileged elements of society. The differences and diversities among the people of this vast and varied land – whether based on religion, culture or ethnic group – should, furthermore, be regarded as constituting a strength, where interactions between different cultural and religious groups add to the cultural vitality of the whole community, and not an inevitable source of disunity and weakness.

Notes

INTRODUCTION

1. The distinction between cultivators and nomads is not in fact clearcut. Many people straddle the dividing line between the two occupations. This obviously complicates a description of the socio-economic structure, in so far as the dividing line between social groups based on these different occupations itself becomes blurred.
2. The distinction between the modern and traditional sectors of the Sudanese economy is, with respect to agriculture, embodied in law. The use of tractors and other modern machines is forbidden outside of areas designated for the purpose by the government. The object of this much-broken regulation is to conserve the environment.
3. All land in Sudan which is not registered as private property legally belongs to the state. This has been true ever since the Land Ordinance of 1905. The state, however, recognises customary rights of use to the land, and the communities which enjoy these rights naturally consider themselves the real owners of the land. See Saeed Mohamed Ahmed El Mahdi, *A Guide to Land Settlement and Registration* (Khartoum University Press, 1971) Ch. 2.

CHAPTER 1

1. The account given here of economic developments in the Sudan between the 16th and 18th centuries relies heavily on the able historical work of R. S. O'Fahey and J. L. Spaulding. Their principal writings on this period are: R. S. O'Fahey and J. L. Spaulding, *Kingdoms of the Sudan* (Methuen, London, 1974); J. L. Spaulding, 'Kings of Sun and Shadow: A History of the 'Abdullab Provinces of the Northern Sinnar Sultanate, 1500–1800', unpublished PhD thesis, Columbia University, 1971; R. S. O'Fahey, 'The Growth and Development of the Keira Sultanate of Dar Fur', unpublished PhD thesis, University of London, 1972; R. S. O'Fahey, 'Slavery and the Slave Trade in Dar Fur', *Journal of African History*, vol. XIV/I, 1973.

    Another important historical work from which information is taken is: O. G. S. Crawford, *The Funj Kingdom of Sennar* (John Bellows, Gloucester, 1951).

    The accounts of European travellers who visited the area at this time are also instructive, as for example: J. Bruce, *Travels to Discover the Source of the Nile in the Years 1768–1773* (Edinburgh University Press, 1805); J. L. Burckhardt, *Travels in Nubia* (Murray, London, 1819); G. W. Browne, *Travels in Egypt, Syria and Africa* (Cadell and Davies, London, 1799).
2. For a discussion of what is meant by 'administered trade', see K. Polanyi,

Primitive, Archaic and Modern Economies (The Free Press, New York, 1968), pp. 280–3.

3. O'Fahey and Spaulding, *Kingdoms*, p. 56.

4. The information which follows in this paragraph is taken from O'Fahey and Spaulding, *Kingdoms*, pp. 55–6.

5. Information on the goods traded can be found in 'Awad al-Sid al-Karsani, 'Trade and Society in ad-Damer Town', unpublished typescript, p. 4; in El-Sayed el-Bushra, 'Towns in the Sudan in the Eighteenth and Early Nineteenth Centuries', *Sudan Notes and Records*, vol. LII, 1971, pp. 63–70; and M. A. Amin, *Historical Geography of Trade Routes and Trade Centres in the Northern Sudan: 1500–1939*, unpublished PhD thesis, University of California, 1968.

6. The main evidence for this is found in the developments which followed later. There must have been a sizeable number of traders in subsistence goods in existence by the end of the 17th century for, as explained later, such traders had become strong enough to take away some of the sultan's prerogatives in international trade at this time.

7. The main form of artificial irrigation before the 19th century was that based on the *shaduf*. The *shaduf* is a hand-operated lever in the form of a pole pivoted at the middle like a seesaw with a skin bucket at one end and a counterweight (usually a stone) at the other. By this means, water was raised from the river to feed shallow canals.

8. See G. Brausch, 'Problèmes du travail au Gezira', *Civilisations*, no. 3, 1965.

9. O'Fahey and Spaulding, *Kingdoms*, p. 55.

10. Ibid., pp. 158–61.

11. See the references given under note 5 above.

12. See Browne, *Travels*, p. 57.

13. The information contained in the four paragraphs which follow is taken from O'Fahey and Spaulding, *Kingdoms*, pp. 68–74, 78–82, and 85–8.

14. O'Fahey and Spaulding, *Kingdoms*, p. 80.

15. Ibid., p. 85.

16. See El-Sayed el-Bushra, 'Towns in the Sudan in the Eighteenth and Early Nineteenth Centuries', *Sudan Notes and Records*, vol. LII, 1971, p. 65.

17. O'Fahey and Spaulding, *Kingdoms*, p. 86.

18. See G. Brausch, 'Problèmes du travail'.

19. For some examples of such charters, see M. I. Abu Salim, 'Some Land Certificates of the Fung', Occasional Papers No. 2, Sudan Research Unit (Khartoum), 1967.

20. See O'Fahey and Spaulding, *Kingdoms*, p. 82.

21. See R. Hill, *Egypt in the Sudan 1820–1881* (Oxford University Press, 1959), pp. 7–8.

22. For the development of communications in Sudan at this time, see ibid., pp. 99–101, 129–33 and 156–60.

23. 'Basins' were areas adjacent to the Nile where the level of the land was lower than the river-level during the Nile flood. By cutting irrigation canals through the river banks, the areas concerned could be watered while the flood was at its height. The basin land could thus be brought

under cultivation. There had been a number of basins in use in Meroitic times, but these had fallen into disuse thereafter. The petty tribal chiefs along the river were not able to organise the labour needed to maintain the irrigation system.

24. For the development of the economy and of trade at this time, as outlined in the three paragraphs which follow, see Hill, *Egypt*, pp. 49–59, 62–4, 73–4, 97–9, 122–5, and 153–6.

25. For the activities of the traders at this time, as outlined in this paragraph and the three which follow, see R. O. Collins, *The Southern Sudan, 1883–1898: A Struggle for Control* (Yale University Press, New Haven, 1962). Also see Abbas Ibrahim Muhammad Ali, *The British, the Slave Trade and Slavery in the Sudan* (Khartoum University Press, 1972), pp. 3–21.

26. See Hill, *Egypt*, p. 98.

27. See O'Fahey and Spaulding, *Kingdoms*, pp. 179–80.

28. See P. M. Holt, *The Mahdist State in the Sudan 1881–1898* (Oxford University Press, 1970), pp. 255–7.

29. The map is reproduced in F. Rehfisch, 'A Sketch of the Early History of Omdurman', *Sudan Notes and Records*, vol. XLV, 1964, pp. 44–5. The book from which the map was taken is P. Rossignoli, *I Miei Dodici Anni di Prigonia* (Mondini, 1898). Other first-hand accounts of the economic conditions during the Mahdiyyah can be found in J. Ohrwalder, *Ten Years' Captivity in the Mahdi's Camp* (Macmillan, London, 1892); R. C. Slatin, *Fire and Sword in the Sudan* (Arnold, London, 1896); and F. R. Wingate, *Mahdism and the Egyptian Sudan* (Macmillan, London, 1891). See also S. M. Nur, 'The Memoirs of Yusuf Mikhail', unpublished PhD thesis, University of London, 1956.

30. For further discussion of the state of the economy under the Mahdiyyah see Abd al-Muhsin Mustafa, 'The Structural Malformation of the Sudanese Economy', Bulletin No. 24, Economic and Social Research Council (Khartoum), 1975, pp. 6–10.

31. Slatin, *Fire and Sword*, pp. 357–9.

32. The information given here on the needs of the Lancashire cotton industry is taken from A. Barnett, 'The Gezira Scheme: Production of Cotton and Reproduction of Underdevelopment', in I. Oxaal, A. Barnett and D. Booth (eds), *Beyond the Sociology of Development* (Routledge and Kegan Paul, London, 1975), pp. 187–9.

33. This point was stressed at the time by MPs from Lancashire constituencies in debates in the House of Commons. See *Hansard Parliamentary Debates*, fifth series, vol. 50, vol. 17, 1913. Mentioned in Barnett, 'Gezira Scheme', p. 188.

34. A number of the memoirs of British officials who served the Condominium in the early years refer to this point. See, for example, H. C. Jackson, *Sudan Days and Ways* (Macmillan, London, 1954), p. 130–2.

35. The pattern of financing gives credence to the contention of Mustafa Kamil and the Egyptian nationalists at the time that Sudan had become a British colony at the expense of Egypt's 'blood and money'. See Mekki Shibeika, *The Independent Sudan* (Robert Speller, New York, 1959), pp. 461–2.

36. For a discussion of this, see D. M. Benn, 'The Theory of Plantation Economy and Society: A Methodological Critique', *Journal of Commonwealth and Comparative Politics*, vol. XII, no. 3, November 1974.

37. For the early developments see W. F. Tewson, *Golden Jubilee, 1904–1954: The Sudan Plantation Company and the Kassala Co. Ltd. and Their Work in Sudan* (SPS, London, 1954).

38. One feddan is equal to 1.036 acres.

39. The basic information given here on the schemes which came under the SPS is taken from A. Gaitskell, *Gezira: A Story of Development in the Sudan* (Faber, London, 1959). See also W. A. Hance, 'The Gezira, an Example in Development', *The Geographical Review*, vol. 44, 1954, pp. 253–70; and Khattab Saggar al-Ani, 'The Gezira Scheme in Sudan, unpublished PhD thesis, Columbia University, 1959.

40. See E. Mackinnon, 'Blue Nile Province', in J. D. Tothill (ed.), *Agriculture in the Sudan* (Oxford University Press, 1948).

41. See Gaitskell, *Gezira*, pp. 83–6.

42. This was in accordance with a land settlement ordinance laid down in 1905. See Saeed Mohamed Ahmed El Mahdi, *A Guide to Land Settlement and Registration* (Khartoum University Press, 1971), Ch. 2.

43. 100 piastres = 1 Egyptian pound (the official currency within the Sudan at that time). The Egyptian pound at this time was worth marginally less than the pound sterling.

44. The 'landowning tenants' did not necessarily own the land on which their tenancies stood. It was quite normal for the tenancy not to be even in the vicinity of the land owned.

45. See Farah Hassan Adam, 'Agricultural Policy', unpublished mimeo, no date.

46. See pp. 87–8.

47. Information on the Kassala Cotton Company taken from K. M. Barbour, *The Republic of Sudan* (Athlone Press, London, 1961), p. 222.

48. The term 'Fellata', as used in Sudan in such a context, refers to those who have entered the country from beyond the western frontier. Most of them originally came from northern Nigeria, making their way as pilgrims to Mecca.

49. The KCC's scheme in the Gezira drew water from the main Gezira scheme. The feddans managed by the KCC are included in the total given earlier for the Gezira irrigated area.

50. See C. B. Tracey, 'Northern Province', in J. D. Tothill (ed.), *Agriculture in the Sudan* (Oxford University Press, 1948).

51. The writer has no information specifically on gains made by tenants in the early period. It seems probable, however, that these did not change substantially over the years. L. B. Tracey, in describing the gains made by an average tenant on an average scheme in 1944, calculates the economic dealings as follows:

Income	£
Sale of crops	30
Sale of other farm produce	10
Gross	40

Expenditure in the course of production

Water rate	20.4
Land tax	2.1
Payment for hired labour	3.0
Total gain	14.5

This, however, does not take into account the food crops which the tenant grew for his and his family's own consumption. Tracey, 'Northern Province'.

52. For information on the development of the railways see Barbour, *Republic of Sudan*, p. 267.
53. See D. Roden, 'The Twentieth Century Decline of Suakin', *Sudan Notes and Records*, vol. LI, 1970, pp. 1–22.
54. See R. L. Hill, *Sudan Transport* (Oxford University Press, 1965), pp. 57–67.
55. Such shows were held from 1904 onwards. See the annual *Reports of Governors of Provinces* (McCorquodale, London).
56. See D. F. M. Mcloughlin, 'Labour Market Conditions and Wages in the Three Towns, 1900–1950', *Sudan Notes and Records*, vol. LI, 1970, pp. 105–18.
57. Ibid.

CHAPTER 2

1. For the figure for 1901 see Mekki Shibeika, *The Independent Sudan* (Robert Speller, New York, 1959), p. 464. For the remaining figures see Republic of Sudan, *Internal Statistics 1960 and 1961* (Department of Statistics, Khartoum, 1961), p. 66.
2. H. A. L. Tunley, 'Revenue from Land and Crops', in J. D. Tothill (ed.), *Agriculture in the Sudan* (Oxford University Press, 1948), pp. 203–7.
3. See Sudan Government, *Sudan Almanac 1942* (Government Printing Press, Khartoum, 1942).
4. During the Second World War cotton prices on the London market were frozen and the price of 1 lb of Sudanese cotton always remained below 11 pence. After 1945 the restrictions were lifted, and the price rose to 19 pence in 1947 and 38.5 pence in 1948. See T. B. Founou, 'De Facto Wage-earners in the Gezira Scheme', unpublished mimeo, African Institute for Economic Development and Planning, November 1974.
5. See Table A.2 in the Appendix.
6. See Republic of Sudan, *Internal Statistics 1960 and 1961*, pp. 62–5.
7. Ibid.
8. See Table A.2 in the Appendix.
9. Republic of Sudan, *Internal Statistics 1960 and 1961*, pp. 62–5.
10. Ibid.
11. See Table A.2 in the Appendix.
12. See Sudan Government, *Sudan Almanac* (Government Printing Press, Khartoum) for the years in question.
13. See Table A.2 in the Appendix.

14. A Gaitskell, *Gezira: A Story of Development in the Sudan* (Faber, London, 1959), pp. 290–2.
15. K. M. Barbour, *The Republic of Sudan: A Regional Geography* (Athlone Press, London, 1961), p. 222.
16. E. Mackinnon, 'Blue Nile Province' in Tothill (ed.), *Agriculture in the Sudan*, pp. 798–803.
17. H. E. Hurst, *The Nile* (Constable, London, 1951), p. 104.
18. The largest of the schemes which came under the WNALB was in fact not a pump scheme and is not one of those referred to in this paragraph. The Abdel-Magid scheme (38 000 feddans in 1944) was an offshoot of the Gezira scheme, obtaining its water from the Gezira scheme's canal system. Its area, therefore, has been included in the figures given earlier for the expansion of the Gezira scheme.
19. See C. B. Tracey, 'Northern Province', in Tothill (ed.), *Agriculture in the Sudan* pp. 749–55.
20. It should be noted that Blue Nile province covered the pump-scheme areas of the White Nile as well as of the Blue Nile.
21. See W. N. Allan, 'Irrigation in the Sudan', in Tothill (ed.), *Agriculture in the Sudan*, p. 617.
22. Republic of Sudan, *A Report on the Census of Pump Schemes*, vol. 1 (Department of Statistics, Khartoum, 1967), p. 17a.
23. See Republic of Sudan, *A Report on the Census of Pump Schemes: vol. i A Co-ordinated Picture of Area Irrigated by Pump Schemes in the Republic of Sudan* (Department of Statistics, Khartoum, 1967), p. 27a.
24. *Salukah* land is the land which lies directly on the river bank or on islands in the river. This land is flooded when the river is at its highest and it thus receives sufficient water to produce a crop. It is also sometimes referred to as '*jarf*' (bank). The *salukah* is the wooden planting-stick which is usually employed to cultivate the *jarf*.

    Sagiah land lies at the highest levels which are not reached by the river's flood. Such land was traditionally watered by *sagiah* or by *shaduf* (see p. 8 above, and note 7 of Chapter 1).
25. All figures given in the text relating to tenants therefore include these landowning tenants.
26. See M. C. Jedrej and G. Stremmalaar, 'Guneid Sugar Scheme: A Sociological Consideration of Some Aspects of Conflict Between Management and Tenant', *Sudan Notes and Records*, vol. LII, 1971, p. 72.
27. See Republic of Sudan, *Report on the Census of Pump Schemes*, vol. 1, p. 39.
28. See Jedrej and Stremmalaar, 'Guneid Sugar Scheme', p. 72.
29. Most of the information given here on the Zande scheme is taken from H. Ferguson, *The Zande Scheme* (Agricultural Publications Committee, Khartoum, 1954). For the anthropological and sociological aspects see C. C. Reining, *The Zande Scheme: An Anthropological Case Study of Economic Development in Africa* (Northwestern University Press, Evanston, 1966).
30. This is based on impressions given to the writer by political personalities from the Zande area. It finds some support in Reining, *The Zande Scheme*.

31. See Barbour, *Republic of Sudan*, p. 258.
32. An event which had occurred on the Zande scheme, however, was itself one of the factors which triggered off the 1955 mutiny. Following a strike and demonstration by workers in the cotton mill, calling for higher pay, tough police action led to the death of a number of the strikers. The soldiers of the Southern Corps reacted sharply to this incident, seeing in it an example of how Southern Sudanese could expect to be treated by Northerners after independence. The strike move indicates the radicalisation brought about by transforming peasants into industrial workers, and the frustration felt towards the benevolently-intended scheme which had been imposed upon the Azande.
33. See M. Mekkawi, 'Textile Industry in the Sudan', in Faisal Beshir Imam (ed.), *Industry in the Sudan: Papers Presented to the First Erkowit Conference* (Government Printing Press, Khartoum, 1973), pp. 249–65.
34. There had in fact been a few other small experimental pump schemes started by foreign entrepreneurs in Northern province before the First World War. These, however, were of little economic significance. They were mostly sold to, and thereafter expanded by, local entrepreneurs in the 1930s and 1940s.
35. See Republic of Sudan, *Report on the Census of Pump Schemes*, vol. 1, pp. 17a, 17b, 22a and 22b. Not all of the c. 1000 schemes mentioned in the text enjoyed the same irrigation rights. There were distinctions between perennial, flood (extendable), flood (non-extendable) and restricted licences, according to whether the scheme was or was not able to draw water from the river at all times of the year – or if not, at which times. To simplify matters, however, these distinctions are not brought in here.
36. Ibid.
37. The term 'scheme operator' is used rather than 'scheme owner' because, as explained below, those who operated the schemes did not necessarily own the land. Government publications tend to refer to the operators as 'licencees' – i.e. those who hold a licence to use a pump.
38. The information given in the remainder of this paragraph and in the one that follows is taken from Farah Hassan Adam, 'Agricultural Policy', unpublished mimeo, Department of Rural Economy (University of Khartoum, undated).
    Other valuable accounts of the operation of private pump schemes in Sudan and the relationship between operators and tenants can be found in Abdel-Rahman el Hadari, 'The Economics of Agricultural Production in the Private Pump Schemes', unpublished mimeo, Department of Rural Economy (University of Khartoum), Research Bulletin No. 135, 1968; D. S. Thornton, 'A Comparative Study of Pump Schemes in the Northern Province', unpublished mimeo, Department of Rural Economy (University of Khartoum, 1965); R. F. Wynn, 'The Development, Present Economic Performance and Future Prospects of Nile Pump Irrigated Agriculture in Sudan', unpublished mimeo, Department of Rural Economy (University of Khartoum), Research Bulletin No. 9, 1967; R. F. Wynn, 'The Economics of Pump Irrigation from the Nile in the Sudan', *Sudan Notes and Records*, vol. XLIX, 1968, pp. 98–100; Farah

Hassan Adam, 'Economic Appraisal of Agrarian Reform in the Private Cotton Estates, Sudan', unpublished mimeo, Department of Rural Economy (University of Khartoum), Research Bulletin No. 20, 1971; Abdel-Rahman el Hadari, 'Cotton Production in the Private Pump Schemes: Kosti', *Sudan Agricultural Journal*, no. 1, 1969, pp. 51–65; Omer Mohamed Osman, 'Some Economic Aspects of Private Pump Schemes', *Sudan Notes and Records* vol. XXXIX, 1958, pp. 40–8; J. R. Thomson, 'Pump Scheme Management on the White Nile', unpublished mimeo, Ministry of Agriculture (Khartoum), Bulletin No. 7, 1951; and D. S. Thornton, 'Pump Schemes on the White and Blue Niles', unpublished mimeo, Department of Rural Economy (University of Khartoum, 1964).

39. See Farah Hassan Adam, 'Economic Appraisal'.
40. For the information in this paragraph see Republic of Sudan, *Report on the Census of Pump Schemes, vol. i*, pp. 22a and 22b. Also Republic of Sudan, *A Report on the Census of Pump Schemes: Blue Nile Province* (Department of Statistics, Khartoum, 1967), pp. 34 and 35; and Republic of Sudan, *A Report on the Census of Pump Schemes: Northern Province* (Department of Statistics, Khartoum, 1967), pp. 36 and 37.

Blue Nile province and Northern province are the only provinces for which individual information is provided here. As the remaining provinces only account for 15 per cent of the land under private irrigation schemes, it was not considered worth treating them individually.

The statistics on pump schemes which are given in the text are deficient in one respect. Only pumps with a diameter measuring more than 3 inches required a licence. Pump schemes based on pumps of 3 inches or less, therefore, are not included in the statistics given in the *Census of Pump Schemes* reports. A 3-inch pump, however, would only irrigate 20 feddans at maximum. While there were quite a large number of such pumps used on small farms beside the river, they would have accounted for only a very small percentage of irrigated land.

41. See Republic of Sudan, *Report on the Census of Pump Schemes, vol. i*, pp. 26–9. In Northern and Khartoum provinces the proportion of government land was generally lower than in Blue Nile, Upper Nile and Kassala provinces.
42. 100 piastres = £E1.
43. The licence fee varied according to the size of the pump and whether it was for perennial use or just for use during the flood season. On a perennial use licence for a 16 -inch (relatively large) pump, for example, the fee stood at £E10.37 in 1944, while for a flood-use licence for a 6-inch pump (relatively small) it was £E0.64.
44. The information given here was supplied by the Ministry of Irrigation, Khartoum. Their estimates for 1956 are an approximate calculation based partly on the trends which were known to exist in the mid-1950s and partly on the subsequent (1963) census of pump schemes.
45. The 30 000-feddan scheme on Aba Island, for example, was built up by Sayyid Abd al-Rahman al-Mahdi. It was registered, however, as belonging to the Mahdi Commercial Company.

46. Most of the information on the pump-scheme cooperatives given here is taken from Farah Hassan Adam, 'The Cooperative Sector in the Sudanese Economy', unpublished mimeo, Department of Rural Economy (University of Khartoum), Research Bulletin No. 22, 1973, pp. 23–30; and M. Bardeleben, *The Cooperative System in the Sudan* (Weltforum Verlag, Munchen, 1973) pp. 31–9.

Other important references on this subject are: W. K. H. Campbell, *Report on Cooperative Possibilities in Sudan* (Government Printing Press, Khartoum, 1946); Republic of Sudan, *Co-operation in the Sudan* (Department of Cooperation, Khartoum, 1966); Mahassin Khider El Sayed, 'The Development of Agricultural Co-operation in the Sudan', unpublished MA thesis, University of Khartoum, 1967; Mahassin Khider El Sayed and M. C. Simpson, 'Co-operatives and Agricultural Development in the Sudan', *The Journal of Modern African Studies*, vol. 6, no. 4, 1968, pp. 509–28; and D. J. Shaw, 'Agricultural Co-operation (with Reference to the Sudan)', *The Agricultural Magazine*, vol. 4, 1963, pp. 35–51.

47. The writer has no information about the infrastructural and other costs of initiating a scheme in the 1930s and 1940s. To give some idea of the scale of cost, however, estimates made in the mid-1960s can be quoted. At that time, to start an 85-feddan vegetable scheme on the Blue Nile was estimated to cost about £S1000, while to start a 500-feddan scheme near Meroe in Northern province would cost about £S17 000. (See R. F. Wynn, 'The Economics of Pump Irrigation', pp. 83–103). To raise such capital was obviously beyond the means of a group of farmers living close to subsistence level.

48. The commercial banks and some of the trading companies did provide finance for pump schemes, but the cooperative societies tended to be regarded as bad risks. Most of the finance from these sources, therefore, went into schemes under individual, partnership or company ownership.

49. Due to the pressures caused by a rising population confronting limited quantities of cultivable land, emigration had been a prominent characteristic of the areas adjacent to the main Nile since the 18th century.

50. Government of Sudan, *The Co-operative Societies Ordinance* (Government Printing Press, Khartoum, 1948), p. 16.

51. See Campbell, *Cooperative Possibilities*, paras 6545–55.

52. See Bardeleben, *The Coopertive System*, p. 33.

53. Theoretically it should not have been possible for a minority of wealthy members to manage things in this way. The 1948 Ordinance laid down that the executive committee of each cooperative should be elected at an annual general meeting at which each member had the same voting rights regardless of his share in the company. Moreover the executive committee was obliged to allow members to examine the company books at any time and to report on its annual account at the general meeting. The majority of members, whose interests probably lay in the cooperative paying a low dividend and using accumulated funds for improving the scheme's facilities, should therefore have been able to defeat the manoeuvres of the minority of members whose primary interest was to gain

a good profit. In practice, however, the cooperative's dependence on the wealthy elements for finance meant that the interests of the majority might not predominate.

54. The information which follows regarding the development of mechanised agriculture in the Sudan is taken from H. R. J. Davies, 'Agricultural Revolution in the African Tropics: The Development of Mechanised Agriculture on the Clay Plains of the Republic of Sudan', *Tijdshrift voor Economische en Sociale Geographie*, no. 4, April 1964, pp. 101–8.

Other important references on mechanised agriculture, concentrating more on current organisation, are: Abdel-Rahmann el Hadari, 'Dura Production and Marketing in the Mechanised Crop Production Schemes', unpublished mimeo, Department of Rural Economy (University of Khartoum), Research Bulletin No. 16, 1968; Farah Hassan Adam, 'Annual Leasehold in the Mechanised Crop Production Schemes', *Economic Journal* (Khartoum), vol. 1, no. 2, April 1967, pp. 27–36; Ahmed Abdalla Osman, 'Results of Four Case Studies at Singa-Dali Mechanised Crop Production Schemes', unpublished mimeo, Ministry of Agriculture (Khartoum), 1958; A. G. McCall, 'Working Party's Report on the Mechanised Crop Production Schemes', unpublished mimeo, Ministry of Agriculture (Khartoum), 1959; R. G. Laing, 'Mechanisation in Agriculture in the Rainlands of the Anglo–Egyptian Sudan, 1948–51', unpublished mimeo, Ministry of Agriculture (Khartoum), 1953; Mohamed Osman Shazali, 'The Possibilities and Problems of the Mechanisation of Agricultural Production in the Sudan', in D. J. Shaw (ed.), *Research in Agricultural Economics in the Sudan: proceedings of the 12th Annual Conference of the Philosophical Society* (University of Khartoum, 1964); and I. G. Simpson, 'The Developing Balance Between Manpower and Machinery, Land and Water in the Sudan', *Tropical Agriculture*, vol. 45, no. 2, 1968, pp. 79–89.

55. The 'under-utilised' land which came to be used for mechanised agriculture was not entirely vacant. Much of it formed part of the traditional grazing lands of the nomadic tribes. When mechanised agriculture became established here, the nomadic tribes sometimes posed a threat to it – partly as a result of their resentment at being deprived of their traditional grounds. They were not loath to drive their animal herds on to the schemes and to permit them to feed off the growing crops. On occasions armed force had to be used to protect the schemes.

56. The tradition of crop-sharing in the Nile valley arose, of course, from the existence of *sagiahs* and the fact that the owner of the *sagiah* was not necessarily the owner of the adjacent land. The traditional sharing system on land watered by *sagiah* was as follows: the owner of the land was entitled to 1/10 of the gains from the land, the owner of the *sagiah* to 1/10, the owner of the cattle used to drive the *sagiah* to 2/10, the owner of the agricultural implements used to 1/30, the supplier of labour to 4/10 and 2/30 would go to feed the cattle. See Tothill (ed.), *Agriculture in the Sudan*, p. 300.

57. See Farah Hassan Adam, 'Annual Leasehold', p. 27.

58. See Davies, 'Agricultural Revolution'.

59. The figure for gross domestic product is taken from C. H. Harvie and

J. G. Kleve, *The National Income of Sudan 1955/56* (Department of Statistics, Khartoum, 1959), p. 14. The figure for private capital formation is taken from Republic of Sudan, *Capital Formation and Increase in National Income in Sudan 1955–59* (Department of Statistics, Khartoum, 1961), p. 98.

60. Even those who built houses primarily for their own use, of course, stood to profit considerably by so doing. With the steady rise in house prices, they owned pieces of property whose value was constantly appreciating. This put them at a marked advantage over those who did not own a house. The latter had to face rising rents, and an increasingly large outlay if they wanted to buy property.

61. Republic of Sudan, *Population and Housing Survey 1964/65: Omdurman* (Department of Statistics, Khartoum, 1966), p. 39.

62. Civil servants were only supposed to obtain loans for the construction of houses which they themselves were going to live in. This was in practice not upheld, however. Many civil servants rented out the houses they had built, while living in government houses at concessionary rates.

63. Harvie and Kleve, *National Income of Sudan*, p. 14.

64. Republic of Sudan, *Capital Formation 1955–59*, p. 98.

65. Republic of Sudan, *First Population Census of Sudan 1955/56* (Department of Statistics, Khartoum, 1957), vol. II, p. 1.

66. For the 1939 and 1945 figures see Omer Mohamed Osman, 'The Development of Transport and Economic Growth in the Sudan, 1899–1957', unpublished PhD thesis, University of London, pp. 124 and 170. For the 1956 figure see Republic of Sudan, *National Income of Sudan 1960/61* (Department of Statistics, Khartoum, 1963), p. 35.

67. The limited development of the manufacturing sector meant that few lorries and trucks would have been used in that sector. Some were probably owned by construction companies. The vast majority, however, could only have been used for commercial purposes.

68. The writer does not know of any cases where merchants or trading organisations owned large fleets of taxis. There were cases, however, where merchants or commercial organisations did own a small number of taxis.

69. The companies are listed in Republic of Sudan, *Trade Directory of Sudan 1957/58* (Diplomatic Press and Publishing, London, 1958), pp. 130–1.

70. Small-scale manufacturing should not be confused with craft industry. The former involves units where modern machinery is used and where (according to the definition applied here) more than five people are employed. In craft industry only traditional tools or modernised simple hand tools are used.

71. Harvie and Kleve, *National Income of Sudan*, p. 14.

72. Republic of Sudan, *Capital Formation 1955–59*, p. 98.

73. Farid Atabani, 'Public Policy and Private Enterprise in Sudan', unpublished PhD thesis, Harvard University, 1965, p. 35.

74. Ibid., p. 72.

75. Ibid., p. 42.

76. Harvie and Kleve, *National Income of Sudan*, p. 30.

77. Ibid., p. 14.

78. Republic of Sudan, *Capital Formation 1955–59*, p. 98.
79. Harvie and Kleve remark that there were many small contractors whose names were not even known. Harvie and Kleve, *National Income of Sudan*, p. 35.
80. *Marisah* is a local beer.
81. Harvie and Kleve, *National Income of Sudan*, p. 14.
82. See Sudan Government, *Sudan Almanac 1950* (Government Printer Khartoum, 1950).
83. For a fuller definition of the two sectors see Mohamed Abdel-Rahman Ali, *Government Expenditure and Economic Development: The Case of Sudan* (Khartoum University Press, 1974), p. 8.
84. Republic of Sudan, *National Income of Sudan in 1960/61* (Department of Statistics, Khartoum, 1963), p. 49.
85. 'Irrigated agriculture', within the modern sector, covers pump irrigation gravity irrigation and flush irrigation on centralised schemes. It does not include irrigation by *sagiah* which is considered to fall within the traditional sector. The number of *sagiah*s in use in Sudan declined steadily from 1943 onwards. From a total of over 10 000 in 1943 the number had fallen to 6733 by 1956. See Harvie and Kleve, *National Income of Sudan* p. 108.
86. Information on remunerations for workers, tenants and others is given in Chapter 3.
87. For further information on Sudan's foreign trade see Ali Abdalla Ali 'The Sudan's Balance of Payments, 1956–66', unpublished BLitt thesis University of Oxford, 1970; Ali Mohamed el Hassan, 'The Sudan' Terms of Trade', *Economic Journal* (Khartoum), vol. 1, no. 1, 1966; R H. Condie, 'Cotton Export and Economic Development in the Sudan' *Sudan Notes and Records* vol. XXXVII, 1956, pp. 70–8; Girges Abd Marzouk Daoud, 'The Sudan's Balance of Payments, 1938–53', unpublished PhD thesis, University of London, 1955; R. A. Henin, 'Recent Developments in Sudan's Foreign Trade, 1949–61', *Sudan Notes and Records*, vol. XLV, 1964, pp. 113–32; and Khidir Mohamed Ahmed *Effects of the Terms of Trade on the Balance of Payments of the Sudan, 1945–70* (University of Khartoum Press, 1978).
88. See Republic of Sudan, *Economic Survey 1961* (Department of Statistics, Khartoum, 1962), p. 55; and Harvie and Kleve, *National Income of Sudan*, p. 14.
89. For a contrary view, however, see Condie, 'Cotton Export'.
90. Republic of Sudan, *The National Accounts and Supporting Tables* (Department of Statistics, Khartoum, 1968), p. 35.
91. Henin, 'Sudan's Foreign Trade', pp. 120–32.
92. See Sudan Gezira Board, *Annual Report* (SGB, Wad Medani), for each of the years in question.
93. For further information on taxation and revenue in Sudan see Sayed Mohamed Nimeiri, *Taxation and Economic Development: A Case Study of the Sudan* (Khartoum University Press, 1974); and Ali Ahmed Suleiman *Al-Dara'ib fi al-Sudan* (Khartoum University Press, 1970).
94. Harvie and Kleve, *National Income of Sudan*, p. 60.

CHAPTER 3

1. 'Economic elite' is not used here as a social category. The term denotes simply those individuals who benefited economically under the Condominium. The nature of the class groupings is made clear later in the chapter.

2. For further information on the Sufi orders, see the appendix to this chapter. The Mahdist movement, although it has come to share many of the Sufi orders' characteristics, should not be classified as such. Prior to proclaiming his Mahdiship, the Mahdi had been initiated into the Sammaniyyah and Idrisiyyah orders. Once he had proclaimed his Mahdiship, however, he sought the dissolution of all the Sufi orders. He saw himself as instituting a new world order – the rule of God on earth – not as propounding a means for individuals to gain direct experience of God, the Sufi objective.

3. 'Abd al-Rahman al-Mahdi (1885–1959) was a posthumous son of Muhammad Ahmad al-Mahdi. For information on his rise to political eminence see Chapter 5.

4. S. al-Mahdi, *Jihad fi Sabil al-Istiqlal* (Government Printing Press, Khartoum, 1965), p. 13.

5. M. O. Beshir, *Revolution and Nationalism in the Sudan* (Rex Collings, London, 1974), p. 141.

6. Al-Mahdi, *Jihad.*, p. 20.

7. E. A. Abdel-Salam, 'The Umma Party, 1945–1969', unpublished MSc thesis, University of Khartoum, 1979, p. 47.

8. Ali ibn Muhammad 'Uthman al-Mirghani (1878–1968) spent the period of the Mahdiyyah in Cairo, returning to Sudan after the Anglo–Egyptian reconquest. For information on the Khatmiyyah *tariqah*, whose political leadership he assumed, see pp. 104–5. For details of his own rise to national political eminence, see Chapter 5.

9. Yusuf ibn Muhammad al-Amin al-Hindi (c. 1865–1942) founded the Hindiyyah *tariqah*, an offshoot of the Sammaniyyah. From a family which was recognised as being *ashraf* (descendants of the prophet), Yusuf al-Hindi fought on the side of the Mahdist forces leading up to and during the Mahdiyyah. After 1898, however, he gave strong support to the Anglo–Egyptian regime.

10. J. O. Voll, 'A history of the Khatmiyyah *tariqah* in the Sudan', unpublished PhD thesis, Harvard University, 1969, p. 611.

11. Quoted from a letter from the Director, Intelligence Department, to the Director of Lands, dated 10.4.1923. Central Records Office (Khartoum) archives, Blue Nile Province/1/20.

12. Information on the means whereby tribal leaders controlled and managed the economic resources which fell within their tribes' domains can be found in the anthropological works on Sudan. Particularly recommended (for Northern Sudan) are: T. Asad, *The Kababish Arabs: Power, Authority and Consent in a Nomadic Tribe* (Hurst, London, 1970); I. Cunnison, *Baggara Arabs: Power and Lineage in a Sudanese Nomadic Tribe* (Clarendon Press, Oxford, 1966); L. Holy, *Neighbours and Kinsmen: A Study of the Berti People of Darfur* (Hurst, London,

1974); A. A. Mohamed, *White Nile Arabs: Political Leadership and Economic Change* (Athlone Press, London, 1980); A. M. Ahmed, *Shaykhs and Followers: Political Struggle in the Rufa'a al-Hoi Nazirate in the Sudan* (Khartoum University Press, 1974).

13. A clear account of Condominium government policy towards the role of tribal leaders in the early years after 1898 is to be found in G. Warburg, *The Sudan under Wingate: Administration in the Anglo–Egyptian Sudan, 1899–1916* (Frank Cass, London, 1971), pp. 142–7.

14. See ibid., p. 147.

15. See p. 15.

16. Warburg, *The Sudan*, p. 157.

17. Mohamed, *White Nile Arabs*, p. 166.

18. This process is described in the thesis by F. Mahmoud, 'Origin and Development of the Sudanese Private Capitalist Class', PhD thesis, University of Hull, 1978. Dr Mahmoud shows that incoming Muslim merchants integrated into the local merchant community rather more easily than did incoming Christian merchants – mainly because the family members of the former could intermarry with family members of the existing indigenous merchants (pp. 173–218).

19. Mahmoud, 'Origin and Development', p. 322.

20. A. A. Bishai, *Export Performance and Economic Development in Sudan 1900–1967* (Ithaca Press, London, 1976), p. 119.

21. Mahmoud, 'Origin and Development', p. 86.

22. Ibid., p. 89.

23. Ibid., pp. 89–90.

24. See Bishai, *Export Performance*, Chaps 6 to 8.

25. C. H. Harvie and J. G. Kleve, *The National Income of Sudan 1955/56* (Department of Statistics, Khartoum, 1959), p. 31.

26. Mahmoud, 'Origin and Development', p. 194–6.

27. M. Abd al-Rahim, *Imperialism and Nationalism in the Sudan* (Clarendon Press, Oxford, 1969), p. 158.

28. H. Macmichael, *The Sudan* (Ernest Benn, London, 1954), p. 226.

29. P. Woodward, *Condominium and Sudanese Nationalism* (Rex Collings, London, 1979), p. 145.

30. Macmichael, *The Sudan*, p. 227.

31. For an overall perspective of the occupational categories into which the Sudanese population was divided at the time of independence, see Table A.6 in the Appendix.

32. A major part of the land used for peasant production was under communal management, formally owned by the state. 'Communal management', however, refers to the process whereby individuals obtained permission to use the land, not to the means whereby the land was cultivated. In most cases the village or tribal leaders would grant permission to individual members of the community to cultivate particular stretches of land (without rent). The right to cultivate such land would usually remain with the individual to whom it had been granted for as long as he or she continued to cultivate the land. While communal labour was often used to complete the most rigorous parts of agricultural work, the usufruct of the land was appropriated by the individual. In the Fur

area of western Sudan, the labour of fellow-villagers was drawn in to help gather an individual farmer's harvest by the holding of beer parties for those who gave assistance; in the central Sudan, the practice of *nafir* (mutual assistance, or communal self-help) involved the members of a community working collectively to clear the fields or bring in the harvests of individual farmers, with the farmer subsequently obligated to make his own labour available to clear the fields or bring in the harvests of others. See F. Barth, *Economic Spheres in Darfur* (University of Bergen Press, 1967).

Land cultivated by peasants in the valley of the Nile north of Khartoum was mostly privately-owned and not under communal management.

33. See Republic of Sudan, *First Population Census of Sudan 1955/56* (Department of Statistics, Khartoum, 1962), vol. 2, p. 124. The table from which this figure is taken is reproduced as Table A.6 in the Appendix.

34. The concept of 'needing to work for others so as to supplement one's income' is, of course, in part subjective to the individual. The need depends in part on the standard of living which the individual wishes to maintain and the goods he wishes to buy. The 'need to work', therefore, can be encouraged by making available to an individual a wider range of goods which he would wish to buy, or else by depriving the individual of some of his existing purchasing power (such that he would need to work more to maintain his existing level of purchases). The Condominium government appears to have sought deliberately to encourage the 'need to work' in this manner (for reasons to be explained in the text): taxation of peasant agriculture, albeit raising very little revenue for the government, was a useful means whereby the government could restrict the purchasing power resulting from peasant agricultural production; facilitating the expansion of commercial networks in the peasant areas (at least in northern Sudan) meant that peasants were offered a wider and more attractive range of goods to buy than had been the case before. Both activities fostered the need of peasants to supplement their incomes.

It should be noted that the need to supplement income was not necessarily met. Poorer peasants in southern Sudan, for example, would have found it extremely difficult (for both geographic and administrative reasons) to travel to the Gezira for harvest work. In such cases basic subsistence needs were simply not met.

35. This classification of peasants is one used by A. El-Hardallo in 'Zur Entwicklung der sozialen Struktur der städtischen Bevölkerung im Sudan und ihre gesellschaftlich-politische Rolle nach dem 2. Welt-krieg', unpublished PhD thesis, Karl Marx University, Leipzig, 1975, pp. 51–5.

36. El-Hardallo, *Zur Entwicklung*, p. 54.

37. Republic of Sudan, *First Population Census of Sudan 1955/56* (Department of Statistics, Khartoum, 1962), vol. 3, p. 372.

38. See R. Henin, 'Economic development and internal migration in the Sudan', *Sudan Notes and Records*, vol. XLIV, 1963, pp. 100–19.

39. The use of the term 'shepherds' is inappropriate. Most of the 'shepherds' would have been herding cattle or camels.

40. See Republic of Sudan, *First Population Census*, vol. 2, p. 124.
41. It is true that settled cultivators kept significant numbers of animals and that some of the 'shepherds' enumerated in the census would have been looking after these animals. Settled cultivators, however, often entered arrangements with nomadic tribesmen whereby the latter looked after the animals belonging to cultivators. Even the 'shepherds' of animals belonging to settled cultivators, therefore, were often themselves nomads.
42. Calculated from the information presented in Table A.6 in the Appendix.
43. Republic of Sudan, *First Population Census*, vol. 2, pp. 414–15.
44. Harvie and Kleve, *The National Income*, pp. 14.
45. Ibid., p. 18.
46. The Taxation of Animals Act, 1925, laid down that province governors had the right to levy taxes on ownership of camels, cattle, donkeys, goats, horses, mules and sheep. The level of taxation on each animal was made subject to certain stipulated maxima; these maxima were changed from time to time. See Democratic Republic of Sudan, *Laws of the Sudan* (Khartoum University Press, 1975), pp. 398–402.
47. See Cunnison, *Baggara Arabs*, p. 68.
48. The only major exceptions to this were the cotton growing areas in the Nuba hills.
49. Harvie and Kleve, *The National Income*, pp. 14.
50. Bishai, *Export Performance*, p. 48.
51. In some cases the tenant would hand over the management to a *wakil* and reside elsewhere himself. The census, however, would not have counted such individuals as tenants.
52. Reference here is to the amount of land actually being farmed, not to the size of the tenancy. The same applies to the other figures given for areas of land farmed by tenants.
53. See M. W. Wilmington, 'Aspects of moneylending in northern Sudan', *Middle East Journal* vol. 9, 1955, p. 141.
54. Republic of Sudan, *The Sudan Gezira Board: What It Is and How It Works*, (Ministry of Information, Khartoum, 1967), p. 31.
55. Republic of Sudan, *A Report on the Census of Pump Schemes, June–August 1963: A Coordinated Picture of Area Irrigated by Pump Schemes in the Republic of Sudan* (Department of Statistics, Khartoum, 1967), p. 39.
56. Ibid.
57. Mahmoud, 'Origin and Development', p. 59.
58. The tenants themselves seemed to experience some psychological unease over their status and role. They generally insisted on being called 'farmers' rather than 'tenants'. See A. Barnet, *The Gezira Scheme: An Illusion of Development* (Frank Cass, London, 1977), p. 168.
59. Ibid., pp. 168–9.
60. Although no change occurred until 1956 in the 'main account' percentage of rewards going to tenants, changes occurred in the organisation of costs – i.e. some costs which were initially the responsibility of the tenants subsequently became the responsibility of the Board. See A. Gaitskell, *Gezira: A Story of Development in the Sudan* (Faber, London, 1959), Chap. 19.

61. This was after the SPS contract had expired and the government had taken over the share of the proceeds (20 per cent) formerly going to the SPS.

62. Y. Abd al-Majid, *'Ujara al-Rif* (Khartoum, 1954), p. 32.

63. Surprisingly, the population census of 1955/56 gives very inaccurate figures for seasonal rural labourers. 'Subsidiary occupation rural labourers' are estimated at 58 689. This is a severe underestimate, presumably caused by the difficulty of obtaining information. The figure given in the text is based on the information presented in El-Hardallo, *Zur Entwicklung*, p. 54. It is consistent with the usual land/labourer ratio on Sudanese irrigated land, where 1 000 000 feddans of land generally require 250 000–300 000 labourers.

64. Abd al-Majid, *'Ujara*, p. 25.

65. Republic of Sudan, *First Population Census*, vol. 2, p. 122.

66. Ibid., vol. 3, pp. 366 and 368.

67. Bank of Sudan, 'Report on Modern Manufacturing in the Sudan Since Independence 1955/6–1968', unpublished report, 1968, p. 4.

68. A good description of the role played by this social element is to be found in El-Hardallo, *Zur Entwicklung*, pp. 107–9.

69. Significant differences did exist between different groups of investors. These differences, however, were not simply between industrial, commercial and agricultural investors. Sid Ahmed Nugdallah, for example, has shown that there were important differences between those pump scheme owners who maintained a feudal relationship with their tenants and those who maintained a purely economic relationship. See S. A. M. Nugdalla, 'The Sudanese Political Leadership', unpublished PhD thesis, University of Manchester, 1973.

   The assertion that no significant differences existed between industrial, commercial and agricultural entrepreneurs in Sudan would seem to negate a key element in the Communist Party of Sudan's political programme: namely the belief that a 'national bourgeoisie unconnected with imperialism' could be drawn into alliance with less priveleged class groupings, as against a 'comprador bourgeoisie linked to imperialism'. If the strands of manufacturing, importing and exporting, local commerce, and agricultural investment were all intertwined, it would seem unlikely that any entrepreneurial elements would have economic interests clearly independent of the advanced capitalist world. There were, however, obviously different degrees to which Sudanese merchants were linked to the economic interests of the Western world; the Communist Party was perhaps right in perceiving that most of Sudan's merchants (the petty merchants in Table 3.11) could survive equally well – and perhaps better – under a socialist economy.

70. Seasonal labourers do not constitute free wage-labour. Their economic lives are not dependent on this labour alone. See Barnet, *Gezira Scheme*, p. 23.

71. In keeping with a term used elsewhere, the bourgeoisie could be described as being mainly 'absentee'.

72. One exception here is that of some middle-level salaried personnel, who could expect to move upwards on the administrative ladder. The

'transfer of gains to another field of economic activity' refers mainly to tenants moving into commercial activities.

73. The abundance of urban labour stemmed mainly from the pressures impelling people to leave the rural areas. These pressures were partly ecological (drought, etc.) and in part resulted from government action: the imposition of taxes on land and animals, which peasants and nomads had difficulty in meeting. Sudan's position on the pilgrimage route from West Africa to Mecca also increased the availability of urban labour: many pilgrims sought employment in Sudanese towns so as to finance their journeys.

74. See p. 88.

75. It is interesting to note the provenance of the orders which became established in Sudan. As they were brought to Sudan from (or through) the Hijaz, rather than from (or through) Egypt, the nature of Sufi orders in Sudan is quite different from those in Egypt.

76. All information given here on individual Sufi orders is in Sudan taken from J. S. Trimingham, *Islam in the Sudan* (Frank Cass, London, 1965), pp. 187–241.

77. This, however, was not the seal which gave its name to the *tariqah*. Al-Mirghani, before starting his own order, passed through many other orders: the Naqshabandiyyah, the Qadiriyyah, the Junaidiyyah, the Shadhiliyyah and the Idrisiyyah. He regarded his own order as setting the seal on all other orders.

78. British support for Sayyid 'Ali and for the Khatmiyyah was of importance in the early years of the Condominium – going up to 1924. By the time Sayyid 'Ali emerged as a patron of the pro-Egyptian grouping in the nationalist movement (from the late 1930s) he no longer stood in need of British support to strengthen his position.

CHAPTER 4

1. See A. Gaitskell, *Gezira: A Story of Development in the Sudan* (Faber, London, 1959), p. 307.

2. M. O. Beshir, *Revolution and Nationalism in the Sudan* (Rex Collings, London, 1974), pp. 191–3.

3. The exact relationship between the workers' society, its leader 'Ali Ahmad Salih, and the White Flag League is not clear. J. M. A. Bakheit, in his pamphlet *Communist Activities in the Middle East* (Institute of African and Asian Studies, Khartoum, 1968), contends that 'Ali Ahmad Salih was simply organising a workers' branch of the WFL. This impression also comes across from the report written by the Governor of Khartoum, mentioned in the text. Recent work by M. N. el-Amin, however, suggests that 'Ali Ahmad Salih was only peripherally involved with the White Flag League, see M. N. el-Amin, 'The Origins of Communism in the Sudan', unpublished DPhil thesis, University of Oxford, 1983, pp. 59–70. In view of the large number of strikes and demonstrations which occurred (as listed in Beshir, *Revolution and Nationalism*, pp. 91–101), it is evident that – whatever the truth

of the conflicting versions – urban workers were being organised as part of the nationalistic activity in 1924. Further information on the WFL and the events of 1924 is to be found in Chapter 5.

4. El-Amin, 'The Origins of Communism', p. 58.
5. Beshir, *Revolution and Nationalism*, pp. 91–100.
6. Ibid., p. 191.
7. Ibid., p. 191.
8. Bakhiet, *Communist Activities*, p. 12.
9. I. Davies, *African Trade Unions* (Penguin, Harmondsworth, 1966), p. 91.
10. S. E. Fawzi, *The Labour Movement in the Sudan, 1946–55* (Oxford University Press, 1957), p. 34.
11. Democratic Republic of Sudan, *Laws of the Sudan, 1901–25* (Attorney-General's Office, Khartoum, 1975), p. 238.
12. For an account of the effects of the deteriorating standard of living, see Abd al-Mun'im al-Ghazali, *Al-Shafi' Ahmad al-Shaikh wa al-Harakah al-Naqabiyyah wa al-Wataniyyah fi al-Sudan* (Dar al-Farabi, Beirut, 1972), p. 15.
13. Davies, *African Trade Unions*, p. 91.
14. Sudan Government, *Report of the Independent Committee of Inquiry* (Government Printer, Khartoum, 1948), pp. 14–15.
15. Fawzi, *The Labour Movement*, p. 22.
16. Beshir, *Revolution and Nationalism*, p. 192.
17. J. Robertson, *Transition in Africa: From Direct Rule to Independence* (Hurst, London, 1974), p. 125.
18. K. D. D. Henderson, *Survey of the Anglo–Egyptian Sudan, 1898–1944* (Longman, London, 1946), pp. 57–8.
19. Robertson, *Transition in Africa*, p. 124.
20. Sudan Workers' Trade Union Federation, *Min Tujarib al-Harakah al-'Umaliyyah* (SWTUF, Khartoum, 1965), p. 4.
21. Interview, Abd al-Majid Abu Hasabu, 1974.
22. Robertson, *Transition in Africa*, p. 125.
23. A. E. A. Taha, 'The Sudanese Labour Movement', unpublished PhD thesis, University of California Los Angeles, 1968, p. 59.
24. P. M. Holt, *A Modern History of the Sudan* (Weidenfeld and Nicolson, London, 1961), p. 158.
25. For information on the activities of the railway and engine schools see Henderson, *Anglo–Egyptian Sudan*, p. 37.
26. Robertson, *Transition in Africa*, p. 125.
27. Henderson, *Anglo–Egyptian Sudan*, p. 38.
28. Robertson, *Transition in Africa*, p. 124.
29. Henderson, *Anglo–Egyptian Sudan*, p. 52.
30. Fawzi, *The Labour Movement*, p. 25.
31. From the minutes of the board's 16th meeting. Quoted in ibid., p. 26.
32. The board, it appears, took the idea from the British Ministry of Labour's *Industrial Relations Handbook* (1944 edition).
33. Prior to the general meetings convened between 29 June and 16 July, small secret meetings among those who were to become the nucleus of

the WAA had been taking place since 1944. Shafi' Ahmad al-Shaikh was the principal instigator of these meetings. See al-Ghazali, *Al-Shafi'*, pp. 17–18.

34. Fawzi, *The Labour Movement*, pp. 38–9.
35. Ibid., p. 41.
36. Ibid., Chap. 5.
37. Ibid., pp. 52–3.
38. Beshir, *Revolution and Nationalism*, p. 195.
39. Further information on these ordinances, together with information on the Wages Tribunal Ordinance (1952) and the Employment Exchange Ordinance (1955), can be found in Fawzi, *The Labour Movement*, Chap. 7.
40. Robertson, *Transition in Africa*, p. 125.
41. Ibid., p. 126.
42. S. El-Agabani, 'Industrial Relations and Economic Development: The Case of Sudan', unpublished MA thesis, Institute of Social Studies (The Hague), 1977, p. 9.
43. Davies, *African Trade Unions*, p. 92.
44. The writer's own calculation, based on the cost of living indices.
45. For further information on developments at this stage see al-Ghazali, *Al-Shafi'*, p. 22–4.
46. See, for example, Henderson, *Anglo–Egyptian Sudan*, p. 99.
47. Government legislative activity provided some ground for these fears. In 1950 the government introduced some amendments to the Defence of the Sudan Ordinance, giving the Governor-General additional powers in the case of strikes. In 1952, the government drafted a series of measures which, trade unionists believed, could be used to restrict trade union activities. These measures were incorporated into a law on subversive activities.
48. Quoted in Fawzi, *The Labour Movement*, p. 72.
49. P. Woodward, *Condominium and Sudanese Nationalism* (Rex Collings, London, 1979), p. 195, n. 33.
50. Fawzi, *The Labour Movement*, p. 104–5.
51. Ibid.
52. El-Amin, 'The origins of communism', p. 249.
53. Fawzi, *The Labour Movement*, p. 116. See also the account of these events given in al-Ghazali, *Al-Shafi'*, pp. 20–5. The SWTUF attempted to organise a general strike in April 1952 to secure the immediate release of its imprisoned officers. Some of the principal trade unions, including the Sudan Railways Workers' Union, however, failed to give support to the idea and the strike was called off two days before it was due to begin. Eleven members of the SWTUF executive were sentenced to two years' imprisonment for their attempt to 'abet a strike of public employees without 15 days' notice'. Four of these sentences were reduced on appeal to six months. The SWTUF was weakened by the division in its own ranks as to the desirability of the strike.
54. Taha, 'The Sudanese Labour Movement', p. 85.
55. Ibid.

56. Some of the proclamations issued and petitions made in the later part of the campaign can be found in Muhammad Sulaiman, *Al-Yasar al-Sudani fi 'Asharah 'Awam, 1954–64* (Maktabah al-Fajr, Wad Medani, 1971), see, for example, p. 18.
57. SWTUF annual report, pp. 50–1. Quoted in Taha, 'The Sudanese Labour Movement', p. 86.
58. Al-Ghazali, *Al-Shafi'*, p. 23.
59. Quoted in A. Y. El-Khalifa, 'The Labour Movement and Politics in the Sudan', unpublished diploma dissertation, Institute of African and Asian Studies (Khartoum), 1974, p. 19.
60. Further information on the resolutions can be found in A. El-Hardallo, 'Zur Entwicklung der sozialen Struktur der städtischen Bevölkerung im Sudan und ihre gesellschaftlich-politische Rolle nach dem 2. Weltkrieg', unpublished PhD thesis, Karl Marx University, Leipzig, 1975, pp. 51–5.
61. Tables 7–9 in the Appendix give information on the economic returns drawn by the tenants, the government and the syndicate companies from the Gezira Scheme over the 1926–50 period.

    The account given in this paragraph of the origins and development of the 1946 strike is taken from Gaitskell, *Gezira*, pp. 226–8.
62. Ibid., pp. 258–9.
63. Ibid., p. 259.
64. One such 'richer tenant' who was active on the TRB and later emerged as chairman of the Gezira Tenants' Association was Shaikh Ahmad Babikir al-Izairiq. Shaikh Ahmad, in addition to managing a tenancy, was involved in commerce. He also owned a coffee-shop in Khartoum.
65. Information on the critical attitudes which some tenants held with regard to the TRB is taken from an interview with Shaikh al-Amin Muhammad al-Amin, conducted on behalf of the writer in March 1974. Shaikh al-Amin became president of the Gezira Tenants' Union in 1953.
66. Gaitskell, *Gezira*, p. 305–8.
67. It is significant that Shaikh al-Amin was a half-tenant (i.e. farming only half a normal tenancy), as also were many others in the 'radical tenant' grouping. Shaikh al-Amin was an active member of the SMNL.
68. The issues in dispute between the GTU and the Gezira Board at this stage are described in Gaitskell, *Gezira*, pp. 308–10.
69. Documents on the GTU's 'wider campaigns' may be found in Sulaiman, *Al-Yasar al-Sudani*, pp. 39–44, 47–51, and 56–9.
70. It seems that the SWTUF played a prominent role in the establishment of these associations. See Fawzi, *The Labour Movement*, p. 115.
71. K. D. D. Henderson, *Sudan Republic* (Benn, London, 1965), p. 76.
72. M. O. Beshir, *Educational Development in the Sudan, 1898–1956* (Oxford University Press, 1969), p. 159.
73. Details of total KSM student numbers after 1943 can be found in Table 4.6.
74. Article II(ii) of the treaty.
75. A full account of the commission's report is given in Beshir, *Educational Development*, p. 117.

76. For more information on the development of secondary education see ibid., chaps. ix–xi.
77. See Republic of Sudan, *Sudan Almanac* (Government Printer, Khartoum) for each of the years in question.
78. Beshir, *Educational Development*, p. 141.
79. For the information in this paragraph see ibid., pp. 141–4.
80. Ibid., p. 166.
81. Information from Dr Habib 'Abdallah, the writer's father-in-law. Dr Habib was a student at Gordon College at the time of the strike.
82. The 1931 strike will therefore be examined further in Chapter 6.
83. Quoted from an article by A. Misha'al in *Gordon College Magazine*, vol. 1, no. 1 (May 1946).
84. The information in this paragraph is taken from ibid.
85. S. E. E. El-Tayeb, *KUSU: The Students' Movement in the Sudan* (Khartoum University Press, 1971), p. 10.
86. Quoted in ibid., p. 10.
87. The information given in this paragraph and that which follows is taken from ibid., pp. 9–11.
88. For further information on the Ashiqqah grouping, see Chapter 6.
89. A detailed account of the formation and development of the Muslim Brothers and other Islamic political movements in Sudan can be found in H. M. Ahmad, *Harakah al-'Ikhwan al-Muslimun fi al-Sudan 1944–1969* (Dar al-Fikr, Khartoum, 1983). The origins of the ILM go back to a group formed at Hantoub secondary school in 1948, also under the leadership of Babikir Karar.
90. A similar conception lay behind the creation of the Sudan Workers' Trade Union Federation. The conception, in both cases, came from the Sudan Movement for National Liberation.
91. The information in this paragraph is taken from Beshir, *Educational Development* pp. 45, 50, 84 and 86.
92. Rufaa was chosen due to the presence there of Babikir Badri, who became the first headmaster of the new school. An active supporter of girls' education, Babikir Badri had been running a small private venture girls' school in Rufaa since 1907. His own account of these early developments can be found in Babikir Badri, *Memoirs* (Ithaca Press, London, 1980), vol. 2, pp. 109–70.
93. See M. Hall and B. A. Ismail, *Sisters under the Sun: The Story of Sudanese Women* (Longman, London, 1981), pp. 55–9.
94. See Table 4.5.
95. Ibid.
96. Information from University of Khartoum records.
97. See F. B. Mahmoud, 'The Role of the Sudanese Women's Union in Sudanese Politics', unpublished dissertation for BSc degree, University of Khartoum, p. 12.
98. This was, however, largely at the elementary level.
99. Conflicting material in some of the books relating to the Sudanese women's movement makes it difficult to present an accurate picture of the movement's development in the early years. The account given here relies primarily on Mahmoud, 'The Role of the Sudanese Women's

Union', which is in turn based on interviews with some of those who established and ran the early organisations (including Khaldah Zahir, Fatmah Ahmad Ibrahim and Hajah Kashif). There are some discrepancies between the information presented by Mahmoud and that found in Hall and Ismail, *Sisters under the Sun*. The latter appears to rely for source material on Z. E. El-Badawi, *The Development of the Sudanese Women's Movement* (Ministry of Information and Social Affairs, Khartoum, no date). As Mahmoud conducted extensive interviews her account appears authoritative.

100. At the time, Fatmah Talib Isma'il was a teacher. She later became an inspector in the Ministry of Education.
101. At the time, Khaldah Zahir was a medical student. She later became one of the first two Sudanese lady doctors.
102. See p. 200.
103. The information on the association in this paragraph is taken from Mahmoud, 'The Role of the Sudanese Women's Union', pp. 18–21.
104. See Fawzi, *The Labour Movement*, p. 125.
105. Established in 1947 to advise on local government.
106. The information in this paragraph is taken from Mahmoud, 'The Role of the Sudanese Women's Union', pp. 24–7.
107. The information in this paragraph is taken from ibid., pp. 28–30.
108. Ibid., pp. 30–31.
109. Traditional hair style, requiring considerable work.
110. Traditional mourning dress.
111. Mahmoud, 'The Role of the Sudanese Women's Union', p. 31.
112. For further information on the 1924 revolution see pp. 163–9.
113. See Table 4.3.
114. See H. MacMichael, *The Anglo–Egyptian Sudan* (Faber, London, 1934), pp. 120–1.
115. The concern here is only with Sudanese involvement in *modern* military organisation. It seems a reasonable assumption that a military force organised along modern lines is more likely to breed the attitudes necessary for nationalist organisation than would a tribally-based, religious-based or other form of traditional military force.

    Much has been written elsewhere about the traditional fighting qualities of different tribes and population groups in Sudan. For further information see H. C. Jackson, *The Fighting Sudanese* (Macmillan, London, 1954); Y. Abu Qurun, *Qaba'il al-Sudan al-Kubrah* (Dar al-Nashr al-Islami, Omdurman, 1969); and W. Nicholls, *The Shaikiya* (Dublin Press, London, 1913). Most accounts of the Battle of Omdurman give credit to the bravery of the 35–40 thousand Sudanese fighting on the Mahdist side.

116. The thesis by U. M. Salih, entitled 'The Military in Sudanese Politics' (unpublished MA thesis, University of Khartoum, 1974) gives a very useful account of the antecedents of the Sudanese army.

    The specific information given here on the projects of Napoleon and Muhammad 'Ali is taken from B. I. Bashir, 'The Early History of the Sudanese Army', unpublished paper presented at the Institute of African and Asian Studies, University of Khartoum, November 1972.

117. See R. Kirk, 'Sudanese in Mexico', *Sudan Notes and Records*, vol. 24, 1924, pp. 110–18.
118. This term, which occurs frequently in official reports written by British army officers about the development of the Sudanese military, refers to Sudanese whose family origin lay either in the southern provinces or else on the southern fringes of Kordofan and Darfur. Most 'blacks' would appear to have been of either Dinka or Nuba origin. Their families, however, may have been resident in the riverain northern Sudan for a substantial period.
119. The desire, on the part of the British officers responsible for training the Egyptian army, to keep Sudanese officer cadets outside Egypt stemmed from an event which occurred in January 1900. Some soldiers and officers of the 14th batallion of the Egyptian army, which was stationed at that time in Omdurman, mutinied, seized a quantity of ammunition, and arrested their British officers. The 14th battalion was one of the six Sudanese battalions which had entered Sudan under Kitchener's command in 1898. An investigatory report written by Colonel Jackson suggested that the unrest was in part a reaction to events occurring – or believed to be occurring – in Egypt. It followed that, in order to prevent further mutinies. Sudanese officers should be kept distant from the nationalistic consciousness which was becoming widespread in Egypt (see Beshir, *Revolution and Nationalism*, pp. 56–8).
120. See P. F. Martin, *The Sudan in Evolution* (Negro Universities Press, New York, 1970), p. 145. Originally published by Constable, London, 1921.
121. Ibid., p. 146.
122. Salih, 'The Military in Sudanese Politics', p. 55.
123. The potential for conflict between British officials and the Egyptian government is well reflected in the position of the Governor-General of Sudan at this time. Since the re-conquest of Sudan, every Governor-General had concurrently served as *sirdar* (Commander-in-Chief) of the Egyptian army. Contradictions between the two roles were not likely to arise for as long as Egypt remained securely under British control. When that control began to weaken, however, contradictions inevitably arose.
124. For an account of these developments, see MacMichael, *Anglo–Egyptian Sudan*, p. 161.
125. H. MacMichael, *The Sudan* (Ernest Benn, London, 1954), p. 184.
126. Ibid.
127. In a memorandum to the British prime minister, despatched on 19 August 1924, the Governor-General of Sudan wrote: ' . . . the only solution which will ensure for the Sudan an efficient and economical armed force for the preservation of internal police security is the formation of a purely Sudan force . . . It is proposed therefore . . . to arrange for the withdrawal to Egypt of all Egyptian units stationed in the Sudan.' [E/7134/735/16]
128. Salih, 'The Military in Sudanese Politics', p. 40.
129. Ibid., p. 40. The Egyptian contribution was arranged following a memorandum which the Egyptian government sent to the British

government on 13 March 1929. The memorandum expressed Egypt's desire to sustain its ties and interests in Sudan and conveyed the Egyptian Council of Ministers' decision to allot a sum of £E750 000 annually to the Sudan government for military expenditure. When the 1936 Anglo–Egyptian treaty was signed, the decision was taken to phase out the payments. The contribution for 1938 was set at £E562 500, that for 1939 at £E312 500, and that for 1940 at £E62 500. Thereafter no further payments were made.

130. A full account of the development of the SDF in the early days, with details regarding recruitment of officers and number of soldiers, can be found in 'Abd al-Rahman al-Faki, *Tarikh Quwwah Difa' al-Sudan* (Al-Dar al-Sudaniyah, Khartoum, no date).
131. The best account is that in Al-Tahir Mohi al-Din, *al-Lahzat al-Harijah fi al-Harb al-Alimiyah al-Thaniyah* (Khartoum University Press, 1974).
132. W. Gutteridge, *Military Institutions and Power in New States* (Pall Mall Press, London, 1964).
133. Republic of Sudan, *First Population Census of Sudan, 1955/6* (Department of Statistics, Khartoum, 1962), pp. 2–3.
134. A. Paul, *A History of the Beja Tribes of the Sudan* (Frank Cass, London, 1954), pp. 72–8.
135. Republic of Sudan, *First Population Census*, pp. 2 and 184.
136. Mukhtar Mohamed Ali, 'Communalism in Northern Sudan', unpublished dissertation, Institute of African and Asian Studies, University of Khartoum, 1974, p. 77.
137. Ibid., p. 77.
138. M. D. Isma'il, *Kifah al-Bija* (Khartoum, 1953).
139. Ibid., p. 34.
140. See Abdulrahman Abbaker Ibrahim 'Politics and Regionalism in Sudan', unpublished dissertation, Department of Political Science, University of Khartoum, 1975, pp. 172–3.
141. See, for example, C. Eprile, *War and Peace in the Sudan 1955–72* (David and Charles, Newton Abbot, 1974), pp. 15–17.
142. J. Howell, 'Political Leadership and Organisation in the Southern Sudan', unpublished PhD thesis, University of Reading, 1978, p. 43. Howell's criticism of misrepresentations of 19th century southern Sudanese history is particularly good.
143. Howell, 'Political Leadership in Southern Sudan', p. 43.
144. Abbas Ibrahim Muhammad Ali, *The British, the Slave Trade and Slavery in the Sudan, 1820–81* (Khartoum University Press, 1972), pp. 3–32.
145. Ibid., p. 130.
146. H. Velin, 'General Gordon and Education in the Sudan', *Missionary Review of the World*, vol. 31, 1908, pp. 360–4. Quoted in Mohamed Omer Beshir, *The Southern Sudan: Background to Conflict* (Hurst, London, 1968), p. 27.
147. R. O. Collins, 'The Sudan: Link to the North', in F. G. Burke and S. Diamond (eds), *The Transformation of East Africa* (New York, 1966), p. 373.
148. Howell, 'Political Leadership in Southern Sudan', p. 47.

149. Beshir, *The Southern Sudan*, p. 31.
150. Missionary activity in northern Sudan was restricted to certain specified roles, mainly concerned with servicing the existing Christian community.
151. See R. Hill, 'Government and Christian Missions in the Anglo–Egyptian Sudan', *Middle Eastern Studies*, vol. 1, no. 2. January 1965.
152. L. Sanderson, 'Educational Development in the Southern Sudan, 1900–1948', *Sudan Notes and Records*, vol. XLIII, 1962, p. 105.
153. From a Sudan Government memorandum to the Rejaf language conference, entitled 'Note on the Case for the Vernacular'. Quoted in Beshir, *The Southern Sudan*, p. 44.
154. R. K. Winter, 'Education in the Sudan', in J. A. de C. Hamilton, *The Anglo–Egyptian Sudan from Within* (Faber, London, 1935), p. 353.
155. R. O. Collins, 'British Policy in the Southern Sudan, 1898–1953', unpublished paper, African History Seminar, Boston University, 1962, p. 1.
156. Muddathir Abdel-Rahim, *The Development of British Policy in Southern Sudan, 1899–1947* (Khartoum University Press, 1968), p. 6.
157. Ibid., p. 7.
158. Sudan Government, *Laws of the Sudan* (Government Printer, Khartoum, 1941), pp. 137–43.
159. Ibid., p. 146.
160. Ibid., p. 151.
161. The memorandum, from which this quotation is taken, is reproduced in Muddathir Abdel-Rahim, *Imperialism and Nationalism in Sudan* (Oxford University Press, 1969), pp. 244–9.
162. Abdel-Rahim, *British Policy in Southern Sudan*, pp. 10–11.
163. J. W. Sommer, 'The Sudan: A Geographical Investigation of the Historical and Social Roots of Political Dissension', unpublished PhD thesis, Boston University, 1968, p.221.
164. Collins, 'British Policy', p. 38.
165. For further information on the Graduates' Congress memorandum, see p. 193.
166. The memorandum, from which the quotation is taken, is reproduced in Beshir, *The Southern Sudan*, pp. 119–21.
167. Howell, 'Political Leadership in Southern Sudan', p. 55.
168. P. Woodward, *Condominium and Sudanese Nationalism* (Rex Collings, London, 1979), pp. 145 and 148.
    It should be noted that the Sudanisation Committee, responsible for appointing Sudanese to the posts vacated by British and Egyptian officials, was acting in a professionally correct manner. Principles of competence and seniority were adhered to rigorously.
169. From the civil secretary's opening address to the Juba Conference. Sudan Government Archives, 'Proceedings of the Juba Conference on the Political Development of the Southern Sudan, June 1947'.
170. The crucial switch in the views of the southern participants took place on the evening of the first day, outside the conference itself. Southern and northern delegates had come together informally at the house of Dr Habib 'Abdallah, one of the northern participants who was resident in

Juba. Credit for persuading the southerners to accept the South's representation in the Legislative Assembly is usually given to Muhammad Salih Shinqiti who, closely linked to the political leaders emerging in northern Sudan, was well-placed to speak on behalf of the North. The role played by Dr Habib 'Abdalla, however, was probably more significant: he had served as a doctor in the South for 12 years and was known and trusted by most of the southern participants. Academic objectivity nevertheless obliges the writer to admit that his favourable assessment of Dr Habib 'Abdalla's role may stem from personal factors.

171. Howell, 'Political Leadership in Southern Sudan', p. 107.
172. In particular, see Muddathir Abd al-Rahim, *Imperialism and Nationalism in the Sudan* (Oxford University Press, 1969).
173. Ibid., p. 33.

CHAPTER 5

1. Of particular note are Afaf Abu Hasabu, 'Factional Conflict in the Sudanese Nationalist Movement, 1918–48', PhD thesis, University of Khartoum, 1978; Mohammed Nuri El-Amin, 'The Origins of Communism in the Sudan', unpublished DPhil thesis, University of Oxford, 1982; Ga'afar Mohamed Ali Bakhiet, 'British Administration and Sudanese Nationalism, 1919–39', unpublished PhD thesis, University of Cambridge, 1965; A. S. Cudsi, 'The Rise of Political Parties in the Sudan, 1936–46,' unpublished PhD thesis, University of London, 1978; Mohamed Omer Beshir, *Revolution and Nationalism in the Sudan* (Rex Collings, London, 1974); and P. Woodward, *Condominium and Sudanese Nationalism* (Rex Collings, London, 1979).
2. Taken from article 3 of the Constitution of the Graduates' General Congress.
3. Abd al-Qadir Wad Habbuba's rising would appear to have been rather different from the others listed here. Although the British official who first reported the rising referred to Wad Habuba's claim to be the *nabi 'Isa*, subsequent investigations did not bear this out. His objective may simply have been the re-establishment of the Madhist state. See A. S. Cudsi, 'Sudanese Resistance to Colonial Rule, 1900–1920', unpublished MA thesis, University of Khartoum, 1969, pp. 30–45.
4. For detailed information on the first three uprisings listed here see Cudsi, 'Sudanese Resistance', pp. 18–45. For information on the latter two see Beshir, *Revolution and Nationalism*, p. 55.
5. Cudsi, 'Sudanese Resistance', pp. 64–193.
6. The formation of the Sudanese Union Society is described well in Hassan Abdin Mohammed, 'The Growth of Nationalist Movements in the Sudan, 1919–25', unpublished PhD thesis, University of Wisconsin, 1973.

The intention to maintain secrecy by adopting the cell structure was in practice unrealistic. The Society's literary events at the Graduates' Club inevitably brought the membership together. Members were generally well aware of which other graduates were members of the society.

7. The Sudan Schools' Graduates' Club in Omdurman was established in Omdurman in 1918. It constituted the focal point of graduates' social activity at that time.

8. 'Ubaid Haj al-Amin and Muhi al-Din Jamal Abu Saif were clerks; Ibrahim Badri and Tawfiq Salih Jibrail were sub-*ma'murs*.

9. See Bakhiet, 'British Administration', p. 66.

10. Ibid., pp. 66–7. The spelling of the names in this extract has been adapted by the writer so as to conform to the transliteration system used elsewhere in the book.

11. A member of the Egyptian royal family, Prince 'Umar was known for his concern with, and interest in, Sudan.

12. The letter was signed 'Secretary of the Sudanese Union'. 'Ubaid, however, had a copy of the letter under his own name. See Bakhiet, 'British Administration', p. 68, note 2.

13. This distinction was first suggested to the writer by Dardiri Muhammad 'Uthman (interview, February 1973). Other sources describe the differences between 'Ubaid and his colleagues as only emerging in 1923, when 'Ubaid favoured an open political struggle and the others wished to restrict political activities to the secretive leafleting and article-writing campaign undertaken so far. As 'Ubaid seems to have been much more deeply involved in political activities than his colleagues prior to 1923, however, Dardiri's view seems nearer the truth.

14. See p. 316, n.118.

15. See the 'Report of the Ewart Commission' (1925), Sudan Government Archives (D.I. File), p. 30.

16. Ibid., p. 5.

17. See Sulaiman Kishah, *Al-Liwa' al-Abiad* (Khartoum, 1969), p. 7.

18. Quoted in Bakhiet, 'British Administration', p. 71.

19. Beshir, *Revolution and Nationalism*, p. 75.

20. The British authorities in Khartoum believed that the formation of the White Flag League was undertaken directly by Egyptian nationalists. There is, indeed, some evidence that the league was funded from Egyptian sources (see El-Amin, 'The Origins of Communism', p. 126). Whether or not this is true is irrelevant to the theme pursued here: the White Flag League involved, and articulated the objectives of, some authentically Sudanese social forces, whoever instituted its formation or funded it.

21. When 'Ubaid Haj al-Amin was arrested in July 1924 he was found to be carrying a list of the key members of the White Flag League. There were 150 names on the list.

22. Bakhiet, 'British Administration', p. 74.

23. Ibid., p. 75.

24. Ibid., p. 75.

25. The incidents are listed in Beshir, *Revolution and Nationalism*, pp. 91–101.

26. Bakhiet, 'British Administration', p. 87.

27. Of particular importance here was the 'Petition of the Sound Elements', despatched to the government on 10 June 1924. The petition

was signed by the main religious leaders, major merchants, tribal leaders and senior Sudanese officials in government service.

28. *Al-Hadarah*, 25 June 1924. Quoted in Bakhiet, 'British Administration', p. 88.

29. *Al-Hadarah*, 28 June 1924. Quoted in Bakhiet, 'British Administration', p. 88. It is interesting to note that the article in question was written by Sulaiman Kishah, a founding member of the Sudanese Union Society. This is indicative of the dilemma in which members of the Sudanese Union Society (virtually defunct by 1924) found themselves. Supposedly strong nationalists, they felt alienated from the White Flag League, sharing some common views with the 'collaborators' of the Sudanese establishment. Most of them seem eventually to have adopted the position which a majority of graduates probably espoused; favouring no immediate change in the political order, but calling for a time-limit to British rule.

30. 'Ubaid Haj al-Amin died while under detention; 'Ali 'Abd al-Latif chose self-exile in Egypt following his release from detention.

31. In the writer's view, this factor has been given undue emphasis in much of the literature. There were certainly some White Flag League activists, such as 'Arafat Muhammad 'Abdallah, whose disillusionment with Eygpt drew them into the moderate, 'gradualist', camp. It is equally clear, however, that for some gradualists of later years the 'disappointed hopes of 1924' constituted an excuse more than a cause. Many such had themselves been antipathetic to the White Flag League, and so had no cause for disappointment.

32. It is true that most (but not all) educated Sudanese in Sayyid 'Abd al-Rahman's coterie came from *ansar* families, and that most (but not all) educated Sudanese in Sayyid 'Ali's coterie came from *khatmi* families. It was, however, the family links which drew an educated Sudanese towards a particular coterie, not his personal religious beliefs.

33. Cromer to Mitchell-Innes, 22 December 1896, F.O. 633/VIII. Quoted in Bakhiet, 'British Administration', p. 16.

34. P.P. Cmd. 95 (1900). Quoted in ibid., p. 24.

35. Ibid., p. 23.

36. C. Harold to Intelligence Office, Khartoum, 1901. Quoted in J. O. Voll, 'A History of the Khatmiyyah Tariqah in the Sudan', unpublished PhD thesis, Harvard University, 1969, p. 391.

37. See p. 162.

38. Sayyid 'Ali, at the proposal of Lord Cromer, received a decoration in 1900. For details of the material assistance see p. 52.

39. In 1915 the leading members of the establishment placed their signatures on a document which pledged their loyalty to Britain in the First World War. The document, known as the Book of Loyalty, was signed by *'ulama, tariqah* leaders, tribal leaders and merchants. A copy is kept in the Sudan Government Archives.

40. Sudan Intelligence Report, no. 197, December 1910. Quoted in Voll, 'History of the Khatmiyyah', p. 410.

41. A good account of Sayyid 'Abd al-Rahman's activities at this stage is

given in El Fatih Abdullahi Abdel Salam, 'The Umma Party 1945–69', unpublished MA thesis, University of Khartoum, 1979, pp. 52–9.

42. See Beshir, *Revolution and Nationalism*, p. 68.

43. The most notable omissions were Sayyid 'Ali al-Mirghani and Sharif Yusuf al-Hindi. As is explained below, Sayyid 'Ali took offence at the manner in which Sayyid 'Abd al-Rahman seized the initiative in organising the petition. Sharif Yusuf gave his support to Sayyid 'Ali on this matter.

44. Although government policy in this sphere began to change after Sir Stewart Symes became Governor-General in 1933, and more distinctly after the Anglo-Egyptian Treaty of 1936, the main framework of this policy remained intact through to 1938.

45. See statement by J. C. Penny, controller of the public security branch, to the northern governors' meeting, 15 December 1934 (Sudan Government Archives CS/SCR/32/B/12). Quoted in Bakhiet, 'British Administration', p. 277.

46. Ibid., p. 279.

47. Ibid., pp. 282–5.

48. See p. 51.

49. Bakhiet, 'British Administration', p. 279.

50. Although the Condominium authorities did not permit the collection of *zakat* for Sayyid 'Abd al-Rahman, the practice still continued.

51. Beshir, *Revolution and Nationalism*, pp. 147–8.

52. Quoted in Abu Hasabu, 'Factional Conflict', p. 66.

53. Quoted in Abdel Salam, 'The Umma Party', p. 77.

54. Sayyid 'Ali had, for example, taken the initiative over the Book of Loyalty in 1915, had organised the collection of signatures for the 1919 petition, had led the Sudanese delegation which met King George V in 1919, and had headed the group of Sudanese notables who expressed their pro-British feelings to Lord Allenby during the latter's visit to Sudan in 1922.

55. These salaries remained at £E$4\frac{1}{2}$ monthly.

56. The members of the committee were Ahmad al-Sayyid al-Fil, Siddiq Farid, Muhammad 'Ali Shawqi, Muhammad al-Hasan Diab, 'Abd al-Majid Ahmad, 'Uthman Hasan 'Uthman, 'Umar Ishaq, Muhammad Nur Khojali, Mirghani Hamzah, and Ahmad 'Uthman al-Qadi.

57. The salary-cuts issue was eventually concluded on the basis of the 'compromise salary' proposed by Muhammad 'Ali Shawqi (and supported by Sayyid 'Abd al-Rahman). Family pressures ultimately forced the students to abandon their strike.

58. Some rivalry had occurred between Shawqi and al-Fil prior to 1931. This rivalry, however, had not been of such a kind as to divide the Graduates' Club into mutually antagonistic groupings.

59. A good account of developments in the Graduates' Club is given in Abu Hasabu, 'Factional Conflict', pp. 41–68.

60. Al-Fil had been an associate of Sayyid 'Ali's since the early 1920s. He was, however, a member of the Tijaniyyah religious order, not a *khatmi*.

It is interesting to note that neither of the graduate leaders shared the religious allegiance of their religious patrons. Shawqi, who was of part-Egyptian origin, came from a family which was inimical to Mahdism.

61. Abu Hasabu, 'Factional Conflict', pp. 93–4.
62. The best account of the activities of the Abu Ruf group is given in Khidir Hamad, *Muzakkirat Khidir Hamad* (Sharjah, 1980). The views and perspectives of the al-Fajr group come across clearly in the pages of the newspaper, *al-Fajr*, which members of the group published after 1934.
63. The ideological views of the two groups are presented well in the highly informative thesis by El-Amin, 'The Origins of Communism', pp. 164–202.
64. *Al-Fajr*, 1 May 1935. Quoted in El-Amin, 'Origins of Communism', p. 186.
65. This listing is given in Abu Hasabu, 'Factional Conflict', p. 95.
66. Unlike most members of the al-Fajr and Abu Ruf groups, 'Arafat Muhammad 'Abdallah had been active in the White Flag League in 1924. He spent the years which followed 1924 in Egypt, where he became disillusioned by the lack of practical support extended by the Egyptian authorities to Sudanese nationalists. After spending some time in the Hijaz, he returned to Sudan in 1929.
67. See Abu Hasabu, 'Factional Conflict', p. 98.
68. Condominium intelligence sources sometimes viewed the Abu Ruf group as a branch of the Egyptian Wafd party.
69. Edward 'Atiyah's position was unusual. An intellectual and an advocate of Arab cultural renaissance, he had a natural personal interest in the literary activities of Sudanese graduates. It is hardly surprising, however, that his role as an intelligence officer caused some graduates to view him askance.
70. Abu Hasabu, 'Factional Conflict', p. 102.
71. Among the government policies which indicated a more favourable governmental attitude towards educated Sudanese were the revision of salary scales for Sudanese government employees, the appointment of more Sudanese to responsible administrative positions, and the establishment of the 'higher schools' after 1935.
72. The possibility of creating a 'union' to represent graduates had been mentioned in *al-Fajr* magazine on 1 August 1935. It had also been raised in correspondence between one of the founders of the Abu Ruf group, Hasan Ahmad al-Kidd, and Dr 'Abd al-Halim Muhammad at about the same time. See Abu Hasabu, 'Factional Conflict', pp. 147–8.
73. *Al-Fajr*, 16 May 1937. Quoted in Abu Hasabu, 'Factional Conflict', pp. 150–1.
74. Some of the younger graduates, especially those in the Abu Ruf group, favoured the immediate establishment of an explicitly nationalist organisation modelled on the Egyptian Wafd. Such a project, however, would have drawn the graduates into an early and direct confrontation with the government, which most graduates sought to avoid; see Ahmad Khair, *Kifah Jil* (Al-Dar al-Sudaniyah, Khartoum, 1970), p. 95.
75. The Condominium authorities initially expressed reservations over the

Congress' concern with 'the general welfare of the country'. The Congress president, however, allayed government fears by explaining that questions of political welfare would not be covered.

76. For further information on these developments see Khair, *Kifah Jil*, Chap. 4.

77. The memorandum was presented to 'Ali Mahir during a party which the congress hosted in his honour. The contacts with 'Ali Mahir were to have a significant impact on Egyptian government attitudes towards the congress. Up to this time, the Egyptian government had viewed the congress simply as a British-inspired device to cultivate Sudanese identity and thwart Egyptian influence. The congress's nationalist potential was now appreciated.

78. Except where referred to otherwise, the material which is given in this and subsequent paragraphs on the political dynamics of the congress is taken from interviews conducted for the 'National Movement in Sudan' project, organised under the auspices of the Institute of African and Asian Studies, University of Khartoum. The writer participated in this project between 1972 and 1976.

79. As the committee was balanced in its composition, some of those who were seeking the committee's resignation were themselves members of the committee (e.g. al-Azhari).

80. Minutes of the Committee of 15, 2nd meeting, 5 January 1942. Quoted in Beshir, *Revolution and Nationalism*, p. 159.

81. The full memorandum is quoted in Muddathir 'Abd al-Rahim, *Imperialism and Nationalism in the Sudan* (Clarendon Press, Oxford, 1969), p. 127.

82. The best account of the events which followed the memorandum's rejection is given in Abu Hasabu, 'Factional Conflict', p. 228.

83. It should be noted here that the 'moderation' of some of the 1942 committee was quite different from the 'moderation' of the senior graduates who had previously dominated the congress. Unlike the latter, the 1942 moderates were committed to the congress playing a political role. Their diferences with the confrontationists were on strategy and tactics, not on the fundamental objectives of the congress.

84. Whereas the positions espoused by the al-Fajr and Abu Ruf groups were rooted in established attitudes (i.e. the al-Fajr group having rather more confidence in Condominium government goodwill than the Abu Ruf group), the line taken by al-Azhari and the Ashiqqah stemmed more from the requirements of political manoeuvring. Having lost control of the Committee of 15 in the December 1941 elections, they had now found an issue which could lead them back to the centre of the stage.

85. See A. S. Cudsi, 'The Rise of Political Parties in the Sudan, 1936–46', unpublished PhD thesis, University of London, pp. 238–49.

86. The issue of Sayyid 'Abd al-Rahman's break with the Ashiqqah became embroiled in an intra-Mahdi family dispute. Up to this time, 'Abdallahi al-Fadil had been regarded as Sayyid 'Abd al-Rahman's chief lieutenant. The *sayyid*'s own sons, Siddiq and al-Hadi, resented 'Abdallahi's favoured position and were eager to displace him. Those members of the Mahdi family who sought to persuade the *sayyid* to

break with the Ashiqqah were indirectly attacking 'Abdallahi. Once the break was made, 'Abdallahi lost his influence.

87. Whereas the Condominium government had sought between 1935 and 1938 to limit Sayyid 'Abd al-Rahman's economic power and social prestige, and had maintained a somewhat reserved attitude towards him between 1938 and 1940, in 1941 and thereafter he was restored to full governmental favour. The government now stood in need of his support. As a major government ally, he could exert a moderating influence on the Graduates' Congress, and could encourage cooperation with the proposed Advisory Council.

88. Cudsi, 'Rise of Political Parties', p. 241.

89. Sayyid 'Ali's support for the Ashiqqah was by no means popular among senior members of the Mirghani coterie. Although they never formally opposed the alliance, they sought on a number of occasions over the ensuing years to draw Sayyid 'Ali away from it. Mirghani Hamzah and Dardiri Muhammad 'Uthman, for example, consistently deemed the Ashiqqah untrustworthy.

90. The Ashiqqah's greater commitment to effective political manoeuvring than to consistent ideological positions is again evident here.

91. Some sources emphasise the experience of contact with Egypt as the key factor determining the adoption of the 'Unity of the Nile Valley' policy by the confrontationist groups. Whether the founding members of these groups really had more experience of Egypt than the founding members of the pro-independence groups is debatable. The popular followings which the confrontationist groups eventually developed certainly did have more contact with Egypt (through education, trade, etc.) than the popular followings of the pro-independence groups. The critical factor at the popular level, however, may have been the degree of political consciousness. It was the more politically aware townsmen, rather than the less politically aware rural peoples, who could best appreciate the advantages of a joint strategy with Egypt (at least until self-determination was achieved).

92. Whereas it is useful to describe the graduate political leaders initially as being influenced by elements in the establishment, it was of course not long before they became incorporated into, and themselves formed part of, the Sudanese establishment.

93. Confrontationists on the Council of 60 argued that the Advisory Council would undermine the credibility of the congress as a mouthpiece for Sudanese opinion, that Sudanese should be able to participate in decision-making rather than simply to offer advice, and that the system of nomination and election to the council ensured a pro-government consensus.

94. As political parties were not permitted in Sudan at this time, most of the parties which were formed in the mid-1940s were registered as clubs. In so far as the Ashiqqah operated through the Graduates' Congress, however, it was able to dispense with any form of official registration.

95. Taken from the formulation of congress policy whose adoption was secured by the Ashiqqah-led Committee of 15, April 1945.

96. Quoted in Abu Hasabu, 'Factional Conflict', p. 241.

97. The most significant such attempt was made in March 1946, when an all-party delegation was despatched to Cairo. A common statement of policy was agreed, on the basis of which the delegation was to negotiate with the Egyptian authorities. The deliberate ambiguity of the common statement, however, ensured that the delegation fell apart once it sought to negotiate.

98. As mentioned at the end of this section, some of the unionist parties had radical nationalist groups within them. Also worthy of note here are those groupings which called for the rejection of Western patterns of development and the re-organisation of the social and economic structure in a manner which reflected Islamic values. The principal grouping which propounded this view was the Muslim Brother movement, founded in 1944 among Gordon College students. In 1949 a new organisation, the Islamic Liberation Movement, was formed, representing the views of Islamic socialists. At this stage, however, these groups had little influence outside the educational institutions. See Hasan Makki Muhammad Ahmad, *Harakah al-Ikhwan al-Muslimin fi al-Sudan 1944–1969* (Dar al-Fikr lil-Tiba‘h wa al-Nashr wa al-Tawzi‘, Khartoum, 1983).

99. The single individual who appears to have had the most influence on this circle was Herbert Storey, a British soldier in his early twenties. What happened to Storey subsequent to his service in Sudan remains a mystery.

100. In what follows on the early development of the SMNL, I am relying strongly on El-Amin, 'Origins of Communism'.

101. ‘Abd al-Wahab was a medical doctor who had undergone part of his training in Egypt. Whatever one may say about his skill as a political leader, his medical skill was undoubted, as the writer can testify from personal experience.

102. See ‘Abd al-Khaliq Mahjub, *Lamahat min Tarikh al-Hizb al-Shuyu‘i al-Sudani* (Khartoum, 1965), pp. 26–7.

103. El-Amin, 'Origins of Communism', pp. 338–9.

104. The confrontation with the police which occurred during the demonstrations involved considerable violence. In a major demonstration in Atbara, five people were killed. In Wad Medani one was killed. Large numbers were injured in the demonstrations in Port Sudan and the Three Towns. These events are well portrayed in S. A. M. Nugdalla, 'The Sudanese Political Leaderhship: A Study of Elite Formation and Conflict in a Modernising Society', unpublished PhD thesis, University of Manchester, 1973.

105. El-Amin, 'Origins of Communism', p. 336.

106. Ibid., p. 343.

107. Ibid., p. 356

108. Ibid., pp. 352–3.

109. The seat was won by Hasan al-Tahir Zarruq, an SMNL member who had previously belonged to the Liberal Unionist Party.

110. P. Woodward, *Condominium and Sudanese Nationalism* (Rex Collings, London, 1979).

CHAPTER 6

1. Some writers characterise the differences between the major political factions at this time as conflicts between the commercial bourgeoisie, the agrarian bourgeoisie and the finance bourgeoisie. See, for example, Taysir Mohamed Ali, 'The Cultivation of Hunger: Towards the Political Economy of Agricultural Development in the Sudan', unpublished PhD thesis, University of Toronto, 1982. In this writer's view, however, such an approach exaggerates the state of development of class fractions at this time.
2. See Ibrahim Mohammed Rodwan, 'The NUP: A Rift Between the Secular and the Religious, 1952–8', unpublished BSc dissertation, Political Science Department, University of Khartoum, 1977, p. 23. Ibrahim Mohammed Rodwan was himself a member of the council and writes with a wealth of personal experience. The account given here of NUP–Khatmiyyah differences relies heavily on Rodwan's work.
3. Formally, differences between al-Azhari and the 'group of three' centred on the opposition of the latter ministers to union with Egypt. It is unlikely, however, that this constituted the real problem. The ministers would have been aware by December 1954 that al-Azhari was moving away from the unionist line. The group of three had acted together as advisers to Sayyid 'Ali for many years and appear to have continued to operate as an autonomous – and hence disruptive – element when they joined the cabinet.
4. Rodwan, 'The NUP', p. 46.
5. Ibid., p. 57.
6. It is interesting that the Mahdi–Mirghani meeting is often described as a great step towards national reconciliation. In fact its main significance was as a move towards removing from power a legitimately constituted government.
7. Rodwan, 'The NUP', pp. 60–1.
8. *Sudan Weekly News*, 16 November, 1955. Quoted in El Fatih Abdullahi Abdel Salam, 'The Umma Party 1945–69', unpublished MA thesis, University of Khartoum, 1975, p. 115.
9. The stand taken by Shaikh 'Ali 'Abd al-Rahman, who had formed part of the inner council of the Ashiqqah group, constituted a serious blow to al-Azhari. Shaikh 'Ali's own motives appear to have been personal. Following the defection from the NUP in mid-1955 of its then deputy-president, Muhammad Nur al-Din, Shaikh 'Ali had expected to become deputy-president of the party. When al-Azhari appointed Mubarak Zarruq to this position, a personal rift opened up between al-Azhari and Shaikh 'Ali.
10. Rodwan, 'The NUP', p. 76.
11. *Al-Ayam*, 30 October 1958.
12. Abdel Salam, 'The Umma Party', pp. 117–9.
13. P. Bechtold, 'Parliamentary Elections in the Sudan', unpublished PhD thesis, Princeton University, 1968, pp. 200–4.
14. J. Howell, 'Political Leadership and Organisation in the Southern

Sudan', unpublished PhD thesis, University of Reading, 1978, p. 122.

15. Quoted in ibid., p. 123.

16. For a full exposition of the factors behind the growing spirit of unrest see Government of Sudan, *Report of the Commission of Enquiry into the Southern Sudan Disturbances during August 1955* (Ministry of the Interior, Khartoum, 1956).

17. *Journal of the House of Representatives* (McCorquodale, Khartoum, 1957), p. 66. Motion moved by S. Mirghani Husain Zaki al-Din on 19 December 1955.

18. Committee of Enquiry into the Events Leading to the 17 November 1958 Coup, *Al-Tahqiq fi al-Asbab al-Lati 'Addat Ila Inqilab 17 November 1958* (Ministry of Justice, Khartoum, 1965), pp. 26–9.

19. Ibid., p. 18.

20. The text of the whole broadcast can be found in Umsalama Mohamed Salih, 'The Military in Sudanese Politics', unpublished MA thesis, University of Khartoum, 1974, pp. 293–5.

21. Given in full in Muhammad Sulaiman, *Al-Yasar al-Sudani fi 'Ashrah 'Awam 1954–64* (Maktabah al-Fajr, Wad Medani, 1967, pp. 358–9.

22. See Sadiq al-Mahdi (ed.), *Jihad fi Sabil al-Dimoqratiyah* (Al-Nil Publishing House, Khartoum, no date), p. 30. The idea of military involvement was on that occasion, however, 'discarded as impractical'.

23. General Ahmad 'Abd al-Wahab had enjoyed a close relationship with 'Abdallah Khalil ever since serving under him in the army.

24. As Sayyid 'Abd al-Rahman was not expected to live long (and in fact died the following year) the 'for life' did not carry long-term implications.

25. It is interesting and significant that General 'Abbud sought to solve the problem created by the two brigadiers by calling on the two *sayyid*s and 'Abdallah Khalil to mediate. 'Abbud evidently recognised his regime's dependence on the establishment.

26. The full memorandum can be found in Sulaiman, *Al-Yasar al-Sudani*, pp. 382–4.

27. See *Al-Rai al-'Am*, 28 November 1961.

28. The full text can be found in Sulaiman, *Al-Yasar al-Sudani*, p. 357.

29. These points are made in the 1965 programme of the PDP, in justification of the party's record during the 'Abbud regime.

30. See Sulaiman, *Al-Yasar al-Sudani*, pp. 387–90. It should be noted that Mirghani Hamzah did not follow his erstwhile PDP colleagues in giving support to the 'Abbud regime. He supported the national front.

31. See *Al-Rai al-'Am*, 18 November 1959.

32. As described in general 'Abbud's inaugural speech to the central council on 13 November 1959. See Sudan Central Council, *Weekly Digest*, November 1959, p. 9.

33. See Hassan Saad el-Din Hassan, 'The Central Council of the Abboud Regime', unpublished dissertation, Department of Political Science, University of Khartoum, 1976.

34. The references which are sometimes made to a '17-year civil war' in Sudan are incorrect. Although there had been occasional armed incidents in the southern Sudan ever since the mutiny of the Equatorial

Corps in 1955 (carried out by mutineers who had fled into the bush) these were isolated and of no great signficance. A generalised state of conflict did not come into being until 1963, lasting until 1972.

35. Apollo Loboka, 'The Policies of the Military Junta of General Abboud towards the Southern Sudan', unpublished dissertation, Department of Political Science, University of Khartoum, 1977, p. 10.
36. See J. Oduho and W. Deng, *The Problem of the Southern Sudan* (Oxford University Press, 1963), p. 35.
37. O. Albino, *The Sudan: A Southern Viewpoint* (IRR, London, 1970), p. 44.
38. See Howell, 'Political Leadership and Organisation', Chap. 7.
39. 'Anyanya' is usually described as the Madi word for snake poison. SANU sources, however, contend that it is a fusion of the Madi *inya nya* (snake poison) and the Moru *'manya nya* (soldier ant). See Howell, 'Political Leadership and Organisation', p. 194.
40. See Loboka, 'The Policies of the Military Junta', pp. 24–43.
41. Beshir, *The Southern Sudan*, p. 81.
42. Quoted in Howell, 'Political Leadership and Organisation', p. 183.
43. R. First, *The Barrel of a Gun* (Allen Lane, London, 1970), pp. 246–60.
44. Quoted in Asma Abdel Razig el Nagar, 'The October Revolution 1964', unpublished BSc dissertation, Department of Political Science, University of Khartoum, 1972, p. 66.
45. First, *Barrel of a Gun*, p. 256.
46. Ibrahim Muhammad Haj Musa, *Al-Tajrubah al-Dimoqratiyah wa Tatawwur Nuzum al-Hukm fi al-Sudan* (Matba'ah al-Ahram, Cairo, 1970), p. 291.
47. Quoted in Sadig El Rasheed, 'The Experience of Public Industrialisation in the Sudan', in Ali Mohammed El Hassan (ed.), *Essays on the Economy of Sudan*, vol. 1 (ESRC, Khartoum, 1977), p. 84.
48. Ibid.
49. Government of Sudan, *The Ten Year Plan of Economic and Social Development, 1961/2–1970/1* (Government Printer, Khartoum, 1962).
50. Abdalla Mohamed Elhassan, 'The State and the Development of Capitalism in Agriculture in Sudan: The Case of the Savannah Rainland', unpublished PhD thesis, University of East Anglia, 1985, p. 143.

CHAPTER 7

1. On occasions these officers also seem to have called themselves *al-Dhubat al-Shurafa'* (the Honourable Officers). The latter term may have been used so as to differentiate them, after 1956, from the Egyptian free officers.
2. Except where otherwise stated, the information given here on the free officers' movement of the 1950s is taken from an interview with 'Abd al-Rahman Kibaidah, November 1973.
3. This possibility seems to have been widely discussed in army circles. Information from Ma'mun 'Awad Abu Zaid, interview December 1973.
4. Among the civilians with whom the 1950s free officers would have been

prepared to cooperate were Ahmad Khair and Mirghani Hamzah. Their assessment of Ahmad Khair's trustworthiness, however, changed after 1958, when Ahmad Khair accepted a governmental position under General Ibrahim 'Abbud.

5. 'Abd al-Rahman Kibaidah and the other principal conspirators were tried and imprisoned. They were released six months after the 'Abbud regime came to power, in April 1959.

6. Neither of the two brigadiers were associated with the free officers. The two younger brothers of 'Abd al-Rahim Shannan, however, were members of the movement.

7. Whether the two brigadiers were really concerned with a 'more radical direction' could be questioned. Their main objective was to remove General Ahmad 'Abd al-Wahab – the son-in-law of 'Abdallah Khalil and a strong Umma party supporter – from the position of influence he had established within the regime. They were also personally affronted at not being offered governmental positions.

8. Despite the free officers' perception of themselves as capable and effective, their record in coup-management was scarcely creditable. On this occasion they were able to seize control of the White Nile bridge, the telephone exchange and a significant part of Khartoum, but failed to secure their control of the army headquarters. This enabled the regime to mobilise resistance to the coup.

9. Nimairi had been implicated in the 1957 coup attempt. Although the military authorities suspected his involvement, there was insufficient evidence for action to be taken against him.

10. 'Abd al-Khaliq Mahjub, secretary-general of the party, seems to have retained in his own hands responsibility for party contacts with army officers. Another member of the party's executive committee, 'Abd al-Qadir 'Abbas, was responsible for contacts with soldiers.

11. The account given here of the initiation of the post-1960 free officers' movement is based on information given to the writer by Ma'mun 'Awad Abu Zaid in a series of interviews between December 1973 and April 1974. Ma'mun had been a member of the movement.

12. *Sawt al-Quwwat al-Musallahah*, no. 1.

13. See Asma 'Abd al-Raziq al-Naqar, 'The October Revolution, 1964', unpublished dissertation, Department of Political Science, University of Khartoum, 1972.

14. Officers gathering in Juba for army examinations took the opportunity to discuss the deficiencies in living conditions and in equipment made available to soldiers and officers in the South. Telegrams were despatched to the minister of defence and the commander-in-chief of the army, instructing them to proceed immediately to Juba so as to discuss the grievances. After these discussions were held, the army command took punitive measures against the officers concerned. Major Faruq Hamadallah was among those dismissed from the army.

15. Whether this was a genuine coup remains a mystery. One officer, Lieutenant Khalid al-Kidd, and three NCOs were ultimately found guilty of attempting to carry out a coup. How so small a group could seriously have hoped to overthrow the government was never satisfactorily explained.

16. Information from interviews with Ma'mun 'Awad Abu Zaid, December 1973–April 1974.

17. Acting as unofficial secretary of this committee was Faruq Hamadallah. As Hamadallah was at this time a civilian (having been dismissed from the army in December 1965) he enjoyed greater freedom of action than serving officers.

18. Information given in this paragraph and subsequent paragraphs dealing with the planning of the 1969 coup is taken (except where otherwise noted) from interviews with Ma'mun 'Awad Abu Zaid, December 1973–April 1974. This information was corroborated in later conversations and interviews which the writer conducted with other members of the Revolutionary Command Council which gained power in 1969.

19. Three names were considered in this regard. One was that of General Sharif al-Habib, who had won a strong national reputation while in command of troops in the South. Another was that of Brigadier 'Uthman Husain, the Director of Ordnance, who was generally respected as a patriot. The third was that of Babikir 'Awadallah, a former chief justice who had played an eminent part in the overthrow of the 'Abbud regime.

20. The proposal for this came from Faruq Hamadallah, who had a strong personal relationship with Babikir 'Awadallah.

21. Major Khalid Hasan 'Abbas was of key importance here.

22. Major Abu al-Qasim Muhammad Ibrahim and Major Zain al-Abdin 'Abd al-Qadir were the principal free officers in the paratroops.

23. The effective leader of those officers associated with the Communist Party was Lieutenant-Colonel Babikir al-Nur. The principal non-communists in the majority grouping were Major Abu al-Qasim Hashim and Major Salah 'Abd al-'Aal.

24. From the army's intelligence section. Major Ma'mun's role in the army was, paradoxically, to monitor against attempted coups.

25. Faruq Hamadallah is referred to here as an officer even though he had in fact been dismissed from the army in 1965.

26. It is, however, difficult to believe that free officers in the majority block did not pick up some intimations as to what was afoot, especially in the few weeks which preceded 25 May.

27. Most of these colleagues only learnt of the widened membership of the Revolutionary Command Council when they attended a joint meeting between the Revolutionary Command Council and the Council of Ministers on the evening of 25 May.

28. The Arab Socialists were a small group with links to the Iraqi Ba'th Party. Within Sudan, they aligned themselves closely with the Communist Party. Lawyers were prominent in the group's leadership.

29. The Arab Nationalists were a diffuse grouping, possessing no organisational structure or central leadership. Their activities tended to centre around the Cairo University (Khartoum branch) campus. Some of the more radical members of the Democratic Unionist Party were associated with this grouping.

30. For the full text of this speech see Umsalama Mohamed Salih, 'The Military in Sudanese Politics', unpublished MA thesis, University of Khartoum, 1974.

31. *Khartoum News Service* (henceforth *KNS*) bulletin, 17 October 1969.
32. *Al-Ayyam*, 10 May 1970. Quoted in Salih, 'Military in Sudanese Politics', p. 217.
33. The 'Uthman Salih family was accused of having given support to the Imam al-Hadi al-Mahdi, whose armed uprising on Aba Island in March 1970 had posed a severe threat to the regime.
34. See Salih, 'Military in Sudanese Politics', p. 219.
35. The information in this paragraph is taken from ibid., pp. 220–1.
36. *The Times*, 28 May 1970. Quoted in ibid., p. 221.
37. Many of the central ideas which underpinned the plan emerged first in the proceedings of a conference entitled 'A Model Development Plan for the Sudan', held in August 1969 in Juba. See *Sudanese Economist*, no. 134, August 1969, p. 36.
38. 'Abdalla Mohamed El-Hassan, 'The State and the Development of Capitalism in Agriculture in Sudan: The Case of the Savannah Rainlands', unpublished PhD thesis, University of East Anglia, 1985, p. 148.
39. *KNS* bulletin, 29 June 1969.
40. *KNS* bulletin, 18 August 1969.
41. *KNS* bulletin, 12 July 1969.
42. *KNS* bulletin, 27 June 1969.
43. *KNS* bulletin, 25 November 1970.
44. *KNS* bulletin, 8 September 1969.
45. *KNS* bulletin, 15 June 1969.
46. *KNS* bulletin, 22 June 1969.
47. *KNS* bulletin, 5 June 1969.
48. *KNS* bulletin, 7 August 1969.
49. Information on these loans can be found in *KNS* bulletins dated the day after the announcements.
50. *KNS* bulletin, 30 September 1969.
51. *KNS* bulletin, 31 July 1969.
52. *KNS* bulletin, 3 September 1969.
53. *Al-Ayyam*, 29 December 1969.
54. *KNS*, 20 April 1970.
55. *KNS*, 17 November 1970.
56. Information from an interview with Mahdi Mustafa, who participated in the discussions. March 1972.
57. *Al-Jundi* (Tripoli), 5 December 1970.
58. There were serious differences within the Sudanese RCC and Council of Ministers on the issue of unity with Egypt and Libya. The leadership of the Communist Party favoured economic integration but opposed any institutionalised form of political unity. Arab nationalist elements were more favourable to institutionalised political unity. These differences, however, do not account for the Sudanese government's reluctance to envisage the early creation of federal institutions. Paradoxically, it was not until after the regime had broken with the Communist Party that the government withdrew from the federative scheme. The Sudanese government's primary concern was with the impact which the country's incorporation into a Federation of Arab Republics would have on opinion in southern Sudan – and hence on Sudan's national unity.

59. 'Declaration on the Southern Question', 9 June 1969. Quoted in full in D. M. Wai, *The Southern Sudan and the Question of National Integration* (Frank Cass, London, 1973), pp. 219–20.

60. Ibid.

61. *KNS* bulletin, 14 July 1969.

62. *KNS* bulletin, 16 June 1969.

63. All political parties were formally banned following the seizure of power on 25 May. In practice, however, the Communist Party was able to retain some freedom of action – at least through to November 1970.

64. Quoted from a speech by Abu al-Qasim Hashim, a member of the RCC. *Al-Ayyam*, 20 August 1969.

65. By 1966, the CPRL had divided into three groups, known as CPRL-A, CPRL-B, and CPRL-C. The few CPRL members (of any group) who were still active politically in the late 1960s were rounded up after the 25 May coup.

66. The only use of violent methods which the party leadership did permit was a limited campaign of bombings against American- or British-owned installations, instituted after the June 1967 Arab–Israeli war. The most significant action taken was a bomb attack on the United States Information Services building in 1968. It seems that the arms used in this campaign were brought from Egypt, with a senior figure associated with the People's Democratic Party acting as intermediary. A cache of these arms was unearthed on a farm in Gereif (south of Khartoum) following the 25 May coup.

67. *Al-Marxiyah wa Qadayah al-Thawrah* (Sudanese Communist Party, Khartoum, 1967), p. 209.

68. *Al-Ayyam*, 8 December 1968.

69. Information provided by Ahmad Sulaiman. Interview, June 1975.

70. The controversy over Ahmad Sulaiman's writings was not the only concern of the March 1969 meeting. Discontent over some aspects of 'Abd al-Khaliq's leadership had been rising, and some central committee members launched an attack on his style of leadership during the meeting.

71. Quotations taken from 'Abd al-Khaliq Mahjub's 'Report to the Consultative Conference of the Sudanese Communist Party', August 1970.

72. Information taken from the 'Twelve-Man Letter', circulated by Mu'awiyah Ibrahim and his supporters on the central committee to party members in mid-1970.

73. The Communist Party's objective in establishing revolutionary committees appears, in part, to have been to test RCC attitudes towards leftist political organisation.

74. *KNS* bulletin, 9 October 1969.

75. *KNS* bulletin, 10 October 1969.

76. *KNS* bulletin, 29 October 1969.

77. *Middle East News Agency*, 5 January 1970.

78. The RCC apparently intended 'Abd al-Khaliq's banishment to Egypt to last longer than three months. Nasser, however, was not prepared to keep 'Abd al-Khaliq under prolonged restriction in Egypt.

79. *Sudan News Agency* (SUNA) bulletin, 9 February 1971.

80. Garang had in fact sought to relinquish his ministerial position. As Ja'afar Nimairi respected his judgement on southern Sudanese affairs, however, he was not permitted to resign.

81. Hashim al-'Ata had masterminded 'Abd al-Khaliq's escape from detention at the Shajarah army camp on 29 June 1971. 'Abd al-Khaliq was subsequently secreted in the residence of one of the other officers who was to participate in the 19 July coup: the commander of the Republican Guard. Given Hashim al-'Ata's long association with the Communist Party, it is difficult to believe that he would have left 'Abd al-Khaliq ignorant of the intended coup, or that he would have deferred to 'Abd al-Khaliq's contrary instructions. Isolated from his senior party colleagues since November 1970, and now under the protection of leftist military officers, however, 'Abd al-Khaliq was scarcely well placed to tender judicious advice.

82. A secret meeting of the party's central committee on 30 May had passed a resolution calling for a concerted struggle to remove the Nimairi regime. The resolution did not, however, envisage the use of military means to achieve this objective. Shafi' Ahmad al-Shaikh and Joseph Garang had, it seems, argued strongly against military adventurism – a view which had carried majority support.

83. The spontaneous nature of Hashim al-'Ata's action in launching the coup is indicated by the fact that his two colleagues were in London when he seized power. The plane carrying Babikir al-Nur and Faruq Hamadallah back to Sudan on 21 July was forced down in Libya. The two men were detained in Tripoli until after the counter-coup had succeeded, and were then despatched to Sudan.

84. The abandonment of most of the socialist rhetoric does not indicate that the state was reverting to its pre-1969 dependence on the incipient Sudanese bourgeoisie. In the 1980s the regime was able to change tack again, alienating many of the elements which had welcomed its policies in the mid-1970s. The state retained, therefore, a considerable degree of relative autonomy from domestic social groupings.

85. The information on the political system given here is taken, except where otherwise stated, from T. Niblock, 'A New Political System in Sudan', *African Affairs*, vol. xv, no. 4, October 1974.

86. As stated in circular 653 of the Ministry of Local Government, Khartoum.

87. Information from an interview with Dr Ja'afar Bakhit, Minister of Local Government, in February 1974.

88. The architect of the November 1971 People's Local Government Act was Dr Ja'afar Bakhit, who had joined the government in February 1971.

89. President Nimairi frequently contended that the SSU was not a party at all, but a 'union of the Sudanese people'. To the (marginal) extent to which this distinction has any meaning, the 'union' concept became more significant in the mid-1970s than at the SSU's inception.

90. It is interesting to note, however, that a number of prominent technocratic neutrals had been together as students at the University of Khartoum, and in 1955–6 had belonged to the 'neutralist bloc' which

had sought to occupy the middle ground between right and left in students' union politics.

91. The best account of the regime's objectives in the mid-1970s is that given by Mansour Khalid in *Nimeiri and the Revolution of Dis-May* (KPI, London, 1985).

92. Sudan Socialist Union, *Basic Rules of the Sudan Socialist Union*, (SSU, Khartoum, 1972), pp. 4–6.

93. 'Regular meetings' are defined here as being at least one every two months. Meetings were supposed to be held at least once a month.

For more details on this project see T. Niblock, 'The Role of the Sudan Socialist Union in Sudan's System of Government', in Centre for African Studies, *Post-Independence Sudan* (University of Edinburgh, 1980), pp. 11–24.

94. 'Balgo Bindi' and 'Angudri' were both code-names rather than place names. They both related to places within the southern Sudan.

95. See Mom Kou Nhial Arou, 'Regional Devolution in the Southern Sudan', unpublished PhD thesis, University of Edinburgh, 1982, pp. 66–72.

96. *Observer*, 7 March 1971.

97. The information given in this paragraph is taken from an interview with Gordon Mortat Mayen, June 1974.

98. It is frequently contended that Joseph Garang was opposed to negotiations with the SSLM, and that such progress as occurred towards negotiations prior to Garang's dimissal and execution in July 1971 was attributable to President Nimairi placing increased responsibility for southern affairs in the hands of Abel Alier (Minister of Works) from March/April 1971. The writer, however, is not fully convinced by this contention. Garang met the AACC delegation during its May 1971 visit to Khartoum and appears to have reacted positively to its proposals. He had, moreover, sought to open up contacts with the SSLM through the Movement for Colonial Freedom (London) in the course of 1970. Garang did perhaps have a more extensive set of pre-conditions than did Abel Alier.

Details of the initiative towards negotiations taken by the Movement for Colonial Freedom (MCF) can be found in Mohamed Omer Beshir, *The Southern Sudan: From Conflict to Peace* (Hurst, London, 1974). As the MCF was regarded by the southern opposition as siding with the central government, the initiative did not progress far.

99. A four-man goodwill mission from the AACC visited Khartoum in December 1966, at the invitation of Sadiq al-Mahdi, the then prime minister.

100. Taken from the AACC account of developments, as given in K. Ankrah, 'In Pursuit of Peace in the Sudan', *Study Encounter*, vol. VIII, no. 2, 1972.

101. The most prominent non-Sudanese member of the Kampala Committee was Storrs McCall, a Canadian lecturer in the Philosophy Department at Makerere University. McCall appears to have had international links which drew in support for the SSLM.

102. Taken from Ankrah, 'In Pursuit of Peace'.

103. The writer has given a fuller account of these events in T. Niblock, 'Tajribah al-Hal al-Silmi li-Qadayah Janub al-Sudan', *Al-Siyasah al-Dawliyah*, no. 41, July 1975, pp. 114–29.

104. Information from an AACC official who participated in the negotiations.

105. Since the January 1971 coup in Uganda, when Iddi Amin had ousted Milton Obote, the Ugandan government (or at least the Ugandan armed forces) had been giving increased support to the Anyanya – by allowing the guerrillas greater access to facilities within Uganda, and by permitting arms to reach the Anyanya across Ugandan territory. Elements of the Anyanya appear to have been involved in Amin's seizure of power. In response to this development, the Sudanese government permitted Milton Obote to take up residence in Sudan and to build up an armed force (based at Owiny-Ki-Bul, a camp in the South which had been captured from the Anyanya) with which to invade Uganda. After the agreement between the Sudanese and Ugandan governments in March 1972, Obote and his armed force were despatched to Tanzania. See D. Martin, *General Amin* (Faber, London, 1974), pp. 170–7.

106. Information from Ja'afar Bakhit – Minister of Local Government, and a member of the government delegation in the Addis Ababa negotiations. Interview, April 1974.

107. Most Israeli military aid to the SSLM had been reaching the guerrillas by way of Uganda since Iddi Amin's January 1971 coup.

108. The full text of the Draft Organic Law is given in Beshir, *The Southern Sudan: From Conflict to Peace*, pp. 158–77.

109. Arou, 'Regional Devolution', p. 112.

110. Arab Fund for Economic and Social Development, *Basic Programme for Agricultural Development in the Democratic Republic of the Sudan 1976–85: Summary and Conclusions* (AFESD, Kuwait, 1976), p. 17.

111. The Interim Programme was also sometimes referred to as the Phased Action Programme.

112. This listing is taken from the excellent presentation of IMF policy in Sudan given in Abdalla Mohamed Elhassan, 'The State and the Development of Capitalism in Agriculture in Sudan', unpublished PhD thesis, University of East Anglia, 1985, pp. 153–7.

113. Figures from the National Planning Commission, Khartoum.

114. Elhassan, 'The State and the Development of Capitalism', p. 199.

Appendix: Economic and Social Statistics

Table A.1   Annual Government Revenue and Expenditure, 1899–1956

Year	Revenue (£E)	Expenditure (£E)
1899	126 596	230 238
1900	126 888	331 918
1901	242 300	407 335
1902	270 226	516 945
1903	462 605	616 361
1904	567 013	628 931
1905	665 411	681 881
1906	780 858	793 657
1907	923 630	960 918
1908	924 832	1 109 774
1909	982 302	1 100 620
1910	1 104 873	1 158 562
1911	1 236 446	1 286 120
1912	1 355 635	1 421 334
1913	1 568 352	1 533 063
1914	1 543 549	1 531 346
1915	1 495 227	1 462 934
1916	1 857 856	1 745 320
1917	2 195 355	1 901 941
1918	2 774 689	2 336 315
1919	2 992 792	2 720 513
1920	4 425 340	3 564 848
1921	4 069 235	3 900 242
1922	3 498 595	3 496 999
1923	3 766 133	3 392 470
1924	4 298 856	3 453 273
1925	4 866 883	4 375 670
1926	5 857 988	5 482 388
1927	5 929 944	5 504 890
1928	6 646 833	6 045 287
1929	6 981 590	6 610 274
1930	4 693 623	4 693 623
1931	4 396 180	4 396 180
1932	3 853 798	3 853 798
1933	3 639 570	3 521 957

Table A.1 continued

Year	Revenue (£E)	Expenditure (£E)
1934	3 774 911	3 794 488
1935	4 098 413	3 993 113
1936	4 402 309	4 204 917
1937	4 748 302	4 457 784
1938	5 131 635	4 857 784
1939	5 053 765	4 857 784
1940	4 632 351	4 543 790
1941	5 379 277	5 047 160
1942	5 814 165	5 337 991
1943	5 861 944	5 601 790
1944	6 578 769	6 529 662
1945	7 763 078	7 548 186
1946	8 288 985	8 207 802
1947	10 141 495	9 534 668
1948	12 697 809	11 318 589
1949	19 172 548	13 964 007
1950/1	41 867 359	23 596 510
1951/2	46 299 658	21 531 991
1952/3	30 295 657	25 658 747
1953/4	35 436 422	27 611 034
1954/5	38 110 530	30 588 642
1955/6	42 322 551	32 097 705
1956/7	45 869 401	32 698 857

Source: M. O. Beshir, *Educational Development in the Sudan, 1898–1956* (Oxford University Press, 1969), p. 196.

Table A.2 Summary of Central and Local Government Revenue and Expenditure, 1908-1955/56

Year	Central Government			Local Government (I)		
	Revenue (£E)	Expenditure (£E)	Surplus (+) Deficit (−) (2) (£E)	Revenue (£E)	Expenditure (£E)	Surplus (+) Deficit (−) (£E)
1908	518 696	703 638	− 184 942	54 510	53 882	+ 623
1918	1 814 098	1 375 724	+ 438 374	138 997	110 690	+ 28 307
1928	4 680 189	4 078 592	+ 601 597	133 577	116 743	+ 16 834
1938	5 131 635	4 857 784	+ 273 851	221 005	203 930	+ 17 075
1948	10 543 531	10 514 640	+ 28 891	302 408	289 348	+ 12 860
1952/53 (budget 12 months)	28 619 445	24 557 185	+4 062 260	2 587 967	2 491 266	+ 96 701
1953/54 (budget 12 months)	28 473 367	26 801 236	+1 672 131	2 992 121	2 758 567	+233 554
1954/55 (budget 12 months)	36 122 176	31 727 254	+4 399 922	3 573 598	3 345 972	+228 026
1955/56 (budget 12 months)	36 148 888	33 012 068	+3 136 820	4 025 868	3 707 228	+318 640

Source: *Internal Statistics 1960*, and *Internal Statistics 1961* (Department of Statistics, Khartoum).

Table A.3 Functional Classification of Central and Local Government Current and Capital Expenditure, 1955/56

Functional classification	Expenditure (thousand £E)			Percent of total expenditure	
	Central govt	Local govt	Combined total	Central govt	Local govt
1. General services:					
(a) General administration	5 399	1 823	7 222	13	41
(b) Police and justice	1 990	11	1 979	5	–
(c) Defence	3 633	–	3 633	9	–
2. Social services:					
(a) Education	3 868	521	4 389	9	11
(b) Social welfare	2 074	25	2 899	7	1
(c) Health	3 417	520	3 937	8	11
(d) Housing and community services	904	98	1 002	2	2
3. Economic services:					
(a) Agriculture	2 149	26	2 175	5	1
(b) Fuel and power	466	–	466	1	–
(c) Roads, highways and waterways	318	511	829	1	11
(d) Other transport and communications	4 292	54	4 346	10	1
(e) Other industry and commerce	1 028	1	1 029	3	–
4. Other and unallocable	10 869	933	10 170*	27	21
Total	41 207	4 501	44 076	100	100

* In the 'Combined total' the transfers between central and local government have been left out.

Source: C. H. Harvie and J. G. Kleve, *The National Income of Sudan* (Department of Statistics, Khartoum, 1959), p. 66.

Table A.4 Progress of Pump Irrigation, pre-1920–1963

Period	Number of schemes (No.)	(%)	Gross area (Feddans)	(%)	Cumulative number of schemes (No.)	(%)	Cumulative gross area (Feddans)	(%)
(1)	(2)	(3)	(4)	(5)	(6)	(7)	(8)	(9)
Up to 1920	15	0.7	31 200	2.4	15	0.7	31 200	2.4
1921–30	18	0.8	37 399	2.9	33	1.5	68 599	5.3
1931–40	56	2.4	55 847	4.3	89	3.9	124 446	9.6
1941–45	51	2.2	25 649	2.0	140	6.1	150 095	11.6
1946–50	269	11.8	115 361	8.9	409	17.9	265 456	20.5
1951–55	757	33.2	475 416	36.8	1 166	51.1	740 872	57.3
1956–60	785	34.4	417 778	32.4	1 951	85.5	1 158 650	89.7
1961–63	332	14.5	132 480	10.3	2 283	100.0	1 291 130	100.0
Total	2 283	100.0	1 291 130	100.0				

Source: Department of Statistics, *A Report on the Census of Pump Schemes, June–August 1963: A Coordinated Picture of Area Irrigated by Pump Schemes* (Department of Statistics, Khartoum, 1967), p. 17(c).

Table A.5 Progress of Pump Irrigation Schemes, pre-1920–1963, by Provinces

Period	Blue Nile				Northern				Khartoum			
	Number of schemes		Area		Number of schemes		Area		Number of schemes		Area	
	(No.)	(%)	(Feddans)	(%)	(No.)	(%)	(Feddans)	(%)	(No.)	(%)	(Feddans)	(%)
(1)	(2)	(3)	(4)	(5)	(6)	(7)	(8)	(9)	(10)	(11)	(12)	(13)
Up to 1920	—	—	—	—	12	1.2	26 888	11.7	2	0.9	4 307	11.7
1921–30	4	0.4	14 503	1.6	10	1.0	21 289	9.3	4	1.8	1 607	4.4
1931–40	17	1.7	47 666	5.4	26	2.6	7 034	3.1	13	5.9	1 147	3.1
1941–45	15	1.5	10 942	1.2	25	2.5	11 388	5.0	10	4.5	3 317	9.0
1946–50	114	11.6	68 640	7.7	113	11.1	33 374	14.6	34	15.5	6 653	18.1
1951–55	431	43.9	388 590	43.7	244	24.1	48 042	21.0	54	24.6	5 148	14.0
1956–60	360	36.7	323 096	36.4	340	33.5	55 865	24.4	66	30.0	2 439	6.6
1961–63	40	4.1	35 072	4.0	244	24.1	24 958	10.9	37	16.8	12 199	33.1
Total	981	100.0	888 509	100.0	1 014	100.0	228 838	100.0	220	100.0	36 817	100.0

Period	Upper Nile				Kassala				All provinces			
	Number of schemes		Area		Number of schemes		Area		Number of schemes		Area	
(1)	(No.) (14)	(%) (15)	(Feddans) (16)	(%) (17)	(No.) (18)	(%) (19)	(Feddans) (20)	(%) (21)	(No.) (22)	(%) (23)	(Feddans) (24)	(%) (25)
Up to 1920	1	1.9	5	0.0	—	—	—	—	15	0.7	31 200	2.4
1921–30	—	—	—	—	—	—	—	—	18	0.8	37 399	2.9
1931–40	—	—	—	—	—	—	—	—	56	2.5	55 847	4.3
1941–45	1	1.9	2	0.0	—	—	—	—	51	2.2	25 649	2.0
1946–50	8	15.4	6 694	5.0	—	—	—	—	269	11.8	115 361	8.9
1951–55	24	46.2	32 886	24.5	4	25.0	750	28.0	757	33.2	475 416	36.8
1956–60	12	23.1	34 904	26.0	7	44.0	1 474	54.0	785	34.4	417 778	32.4
1961–63	6	11.5	59 766	44.5	5	31.0	485	18.0	332	14.5	132 480	10.3
Total	52	100.0	134 257	100.0	16	100.0	2 709	100.0	2 283	100.0	1 291 130	100.0

Source: Department of Statistics, ibid., p. 17(b).

Table A.6   Classification of the Sudanese Population's Occupational Status 1955/56

Occupational group/ occupation	Males		Females	
	5 and over to under puberty	Over puberty	5 and over to under puberty	Over puberty
(1) (2)	(3)	(4)	(5)	(6)
Total	1 322 484	2 851 009	1 049 295	2 996 812
No. gainfully employed	692 125	2 751 506	72 635	283 037
Percentage gainfully employed	52.3	96.5	6.9	9.4
1. *Professional, non-technical*				
(i) Accountancy, economics, statistics	—	197	—	—
(ii) University and secondary school teachers	—	652	—	141
(iii) Ministers, senior civil and local government service	—	1 028	—	16
(iv) Senior religious occupations	—	152	—	10
(v) Miscellaneous professional, non-technical	—	451	—	4
(vi) Other professional, non-technical	—	141	—	65
2. *Professional, technical*				
(i) Professional, medicine	—	259	—	17
(ii) Professional, engineering, surveying, architecture	—	563	—	—
(iii) Professional, natural sciences	—	108	—	4
(iv) Other professional, technical	—	178	—	—
3. *Managerial, Commerce and Industry*				
(i) Owners of large commercial undertakings	—	378	—	4
(ii) Managers of and in large commercial undertakings	—	281	—	4
(iii) Owners of large industrial undertakings	—	785	—	5
(iv) Managers of and in large industrial undertakings	—	42	—	2

Table A.6   continued

Occupational group/ occupation	Males		Females	
	5 and over to under puberty	Over puberty	5 and over to under puberty	Over puberty
(1) (2)	(3)	(4)	(5)	(6)
4. *Farm owners and farm managers*				
(i) Other farming occupations	1	5	—	—
(ii) Farm owners, farm managers	—	191	—	39
5. *Semi-professional, non-technical*				
(i) Book-keepers, cashiers, etc.	9	3 774	—	20
(ii) Intermediate and primary school teachers	3	4 971	2	1 421
(iii) Junior administrative in civil and local government service	1	705	—	10
(iv) Junior religious occupations	—	902	7	130
(v) Other semi-professional, non-technical	103	27 711	—	73
(vi) Entertainment	6	85	—	4
6. *Semi-professional, technical*				
(i) Semi-professional, medicine	125	4 331	1 406	2 068
(ii) Semi-professional, engineering, surverying, architecture	—	905	—	4
(iii) Semi-professional, natural sciences	8	921	—	1
(iv) Other semi-professional, technical	29	608	—	8
7. *Shop and workshop owners, supervisors in commerce and industry*				
(i) Shop-keepers	1 855	63 913	3	861

Table A.6 continued

		Males		Females	
	Occupational group/ occupation	5 and over to under puberty	Over puberty	5 and over to under puberty	Over puberty
(1)	(2)	(3)	(4)	(5)	(6)
(ii)	Other semi-supervisory occupations	8	1 509	—	3
(iii)	Supervisors in shops	—	19	—	—
(iv)	Workshop owners	—	123	—	—
(v)	Foremen	—	201	—	—
8.	*Senior clerical and* *kindred*				
(i)	Senior clerical in civil and local government service	—	2 712	—	43
(ii)	Other senior clerical and kindred	—	17	—	—
(iii)	Senior clerical in commerce and industry	3	940	—	40
9.	*Craftsmen, mechanics*				
(i)	Other craftsmen	709	6 083	—	29
(ii)	Metal industries craftsmen	902	12 649	—	17
(iii)	Metal industries mechanics	73	975	—	—
(iv)	Wood-working craftsmen	977	12 178	—	17
(v)	Building and kindred craftsmen	382	12 764	6	167
(vi)	Textile craftsmen	1 758	14 877	1 131	6 332
(vii)	Light industries craftsmen	964	19 992	2 427	14 177
10.	*Skilled personal services*				
(i)	Other skilled personal services	—	216	—	15
(ii)	Shop assistants	3 743	15 399	544	6 576
(iii)	Domestic servants	4 506	22 793	3 114	8 755
(iv)	Servants (other than domestic)	345	4 643	12	352
11.	*Farmers, hunters,* *fishermen*				

Table A.6   *continued*

Occupational group/ occupation		Males		Females	
		5 and over to under puberty	Over puberty	5 and over to under puberty	Over puberty
(1)	(2)	(3)	(4)	(5)	(6)
(i)	Other occupations allied to farming. hunting, etc.	5	48	—	2
(ii)	Farmers	261 920	1 863 099	23 974	222 652
(iii)	Hunters and Fishermen	683	5 169	—	41
2.	*Animal owners*				
(i)	Other animal owners	5 597	59 251	166	585
(ii)	Nomadic animal owners	3 868	90 774	77	1 055
3.	*Junior clerical and kindred*				
(i)	Sub-grade school teachers and equivalent	87	4 796	2	149
(ii)	Junior clerical in civil and local government service	48	10 149	14	215
(iii)	Other junior clerical and kindred	6	661	—	1
(iv)	Junior clerical in commerce and industry	99	4 420	—	193
4.	*Machinery operatives*				
(i)	Other machinery operatives	65	2 001	—	6
(ii)	Operatives of stationary machinery in industry	164	3 766	10	258
(iii)	Operatives in transport	388	26 896	56	38
5.	*Semi-skilled and unskilled personal services*				
(i)	Other semi-skilled and unskilled personal services	2 052	25 956	2 154	2 734
(ii)	Sanitary services	69	4 025	19	160
6.	*Labourers, except farm labourers*				
(i)	Other labourers except farm labourers	4 312	65 352	216	1 601

Table A.6   continued

Occupational group/ occupation	Males		Females	
	5 and over to under puberty	*Over puberty*	*5 and over to under puberty*	*Over puberty*
(1) (2)	(3)	(4)	(5)	(6)
(ii) Building and construction labourers	286	4 839	15	245
(iii) Road and railroad labourers	5	4 184	—	3
17. *Farm labourers and forestry workers*				
(i) Farm labourers	8 479	36 413	483	3 907
(ii) Forestry workers	45	1 267	117	6
18. *Shepherds*				
(i) Shepherds	387 199	279 214	36 680	7 722
19. *Protective services*				
(i) Armed forces	238	7 380	—	4
(ii) Police and prison wardens	—	9 342	—	26
(iii) Fire brigade	—	177	—	—
20. *Unproductive occupations*				
(i) Students, schoolboys, household duties	27 994	5 163	642 733	2 554 565
(ii) Unemployed, beggars	717	12 978	191	27 100
(iii) Unknown and no occupation	601 648	81 362	333 736	132 110

Source: Republic of Sudan, *First Population Census of Sudan* (Department of Statistics, Khartoum, 1962), pp. 122–5.

Table A.7 The Economic Returns of the Gezira Scheme to the Sudan Government, 1926–50 (Direct revenue compared with direct expenditure)

Crop Year (1)	Government share of net divisible return (£E) (2)	Direct expenditure (£E) (3)	Surplus (£E) (4)	Deficiency (£E) (5)	Cumulative Surplus (£E) (6)	Cumulative Deficiency (£E) (7)
1925–6	713 347	718 925		5 578		5 578
1927	1 150 191	721 412	428 779		423 201	
1928	958 835	814 009	144 826		568 027	
1929	1 256 076	970 504	285 572		853 599	
1930	337 785	1 027 245		689 460	164 139	
1931	150 016	1 023 103		873 087		708 948
1932	863 066	992 539		129 473		838 421
1933	330 267	896 219		565 952		1 404 373
1934	385 850	892 907		507 057		1 911 430
1935	836 444	952 483		116 039		2 027 469
1936	790 104	930 526		140 422		2 167 891
1937	1 120 093	956 217	163 876			2 004 015

Year						
1938	800 350	1 027 844		227 494		2 231 509
1939	862 314	1 032 313		169 999		2 401 508
1940	1 045 236	714 654	330 582			2 070 926
1941	1 147 076	696 740	450 336			1 620 590
1942	1 133 933	698 365	435 568			1 185 022
1943	1 434 824	716 792	718 032			466 990
1944	965 002	737 323	227 679			239 311
1945	1 559 636	752 519	807 117		567 806	
1946	939 481	773 543	165 938		733 744	
Totals	18 779 926	18 046 182	4 158 305	3 424 561		
1947	2 696 510	855 843	1 840 667		2 574 411	
1948	4 703 604	918 832	3 784 772		6 359 183	
1949	5 523 844	966 628	4 557 216		10 916 399	
1950	6 455 609	1 134 693	5 320 916		16 237 315	
Totals	38 159 493	21 922 178	19 661 876	3 424 561		

Note: The direct expenditure includes the rent of the land, the interest and amortisation of loans for the Gezira, and the cost of maintenance of the dam and the canal system.

Source: A. Gaitskell, *Gezira: A Story of Development in the Sudan* (Faber, London, 1959), p. 268.

Table A.8 The Economic Returns of the Gezira Scheme to the Tenants, 1926–50

Crop year	Yield	Price	Tenants' collective share of net divisible return (£E)	Equivalent to average credit per tenancy of (£E)	Deduct average tenants' loans (£E)	Results per standard tenancy			
						Deduct transfers to tenants' reserve fund (£E)	Balance being average profits paid (£E)	Add transfers from tenants' reserve fund (£E)	Net average profits paid (£E)
(1)	(2)	(3)	(4)	(5)	(6)	(7)	(8)	(9)	(10)
1925–6	4.8	18.0	936 246	117	50		67		67
1927	4.7	18.0	1 342 652	134	50		84		84
1928	3.3	19.7	1 025 361	101	43		58		58
1929	3.6	18.4	1 307 665	100	45		55		55
1930	2.3	7.9	354 362	20	34		Nil		Nil
1931	1.4	6.4	157 575	8	27		Nil		Nil
1932	4.1	8.5	908 395	46	31		12		12
1933	1.9	8.1	350 139	18	22		Nil		Nil
1934	2.3	8.6	410 130	23	23		5		5
1935	4.5	8.2	875 167	50	28	5	17		17
1936	3.7	7.9	831 143	49	27	6	16		16
1937	4.5	8.6	1 163 364	58	28	6	24		24
1938	4.6	5.9	836 765	40	27	2	11		11
1939	4.5	6.2	901 178	44	27	6	11		11

1940	3.8	9.6	1 088 963	53	24	12	17		17
1941	4.0	8.9	1 180 897	57	25	11	21		21
1942	4.0	9.1	1 169 037	57	25	9	23		23
1943	4.8	9.3	1 478 992	71	32	6	33		33
1944	3.1	10.6	1 114 915	54	26	2	26	2	28
1945	4.9	10.6	1 876 536	90	34	2	54		54
1946	3.4	10.3	1 148 658	58	26	3	29	20	49
Total			20 458 140						
1947	4.0	19.2	2 715 870	132	35	1	96		96
1948	3.4	38.5	4 700 999	228	36	3	189	15	204
1949	4.3	38.5	5 527 933	267	45	1	221		221
1950	4.6	41.3	6 447 262	312	32		281		281
Total			39 850 204						

Source: Gaitskell, ibid., p. 270.

Table A.9 *The Economic Returns of the Gezira Scheme to the Syndicate Companies, 1926–50*

Crop year	Companies' share of net divisible return	Companies' share including interest charged to joint account and tenants	Companies' expenses	Balance
(1)	(£E) (2)	(£E) (3)	(£E) (4)	(£E) (5)
1925–6	582 281	622 008	215 763	406 245
1927	759 319	821 487	278 888	542 599
1928	573 954	632 979	223 557	409 422
1929	699 630	771 666	237 226	534 440
1930	192 702	293 779	188 060	105 719
1931	85 552	211 653	226 237	14 584 (Loss)
1932	495 807	647 178	190 348	456 830
1933	193 299	309 867	214 288	95 579
1934	226 841	329 317	220 407	108 910
1935	470 425	574 742	250 355	324 387
1936	451 386	556 506	280 524	275 982
1937	618 832	715 201	311 647	403 554
1938	451 104	527 148	290 667	236 481
1939	485 285	568 195	274 878	293 317

1940	581 958	659 806	240 528	419 278
1941	621 993	709 871	217 809	492 062
1942	616 261	693 687	214 870	478 817
1943	776 878	847 266	221 545	625 721
1944	533 584	608 303	237 131	371 172
1945	837 611	912 602	260 047	652 555
1946	516 938	584 692	270 189	314 503
Totals	10 771 640	12 597 953	5 064 964	7 532 989
1947	1 372 042	1 465 512	301 716	1 163 796
1948	2 339 120	2 447 716	336 423	2 111 293
1949	2 741 206	2 861 206	401 243	2 459 963
1950	3 189 374	3 319 374	541 108	2 778 266
Totals	20 413 382	22 691 761	6 645 454	16 046 307

Source: Gaitskell, ibid., p. 271.

Table A.10   Composition of GDP by Economic Sectors, 1955/56–1973/74
(percentages)

	1955/56	1960	1965	1971/72	1973/74
GDP, factor cost (£S million)	284.2	352.4	441.3	632.4	698.6
Agriculture, livestock, forestry and fishing	61.0	57.3	47.7	38.2	38.2
Mining, manufacturing and handicrafts	4.5	4.8	6.0	8.3	8.3
Electricity and water	4.5	4.3	3.7	2.7	2.7
Construction	5.7	6.3	5.1	4.2	4.1
Commerce and hotels	6.0	6.7	14.7	16.1	16.6
Transport and communications	7.5	7.6	7.0	8.1	8.1
Finance, insurance, real estate, etc.	3.7	3.6	3.8	6.4	6.4
Government services	6.7	8.6	10.4	14.5	14.5
Others	0.4	0.8	1.6	1.5	1.1
Total	100.0	100.0	100.0	100.0	100.0

Source: Economic Planning Secretariat (Khartoum), *Ten Year Plan of Economic and Social Development, 1961/62–1970/71*; National Planning Commission, *Economic Survey*, of 1972, 1973, and 1974.

Table A.11   Sudan's Exports, Imports and Balance of Trade, 1970–80

Year	Exports (£S million)	Imports (£S million)	Balance of trade (£S million)	Imports as % of exports
1970	101.6	108.3	−6.7	106.6
1971	114.4	123.6	−9.2	108.0
1972	124.5	123.1	+1.4	98.9
1973	143.5	166.9	−23.4	116.3
1974	152.8	246.2	−93.4	161.1
1975	147.6	348.3	−200.7	236.0
1976	199.5	355.9	−156.4	178.4
1977	223.3	378.8	−155.5	169.6
1978	183.1	374.8	−191.7	204.7
1979	252.8	458.5	−205.7	181.4
1980	292.1	856.3	−564.2	293.2

Source: Compiled by the writer from the *Statistical Abstracts* for the relevant years

Table A.12   Medium- and Long-term External Public Debt and Debt Service Payments, 1976–81

	1976	1977	1978	1979	1980	1981
			($US million)			
Total outstanding debt	1 722.4	1 949.0	2 250.2	2 856.9	3 487.0	3 694.2
Debt service payments	159.0	124.1	130.9	140.0	163.4	234.8
Principal	80.9	62.6	72.5	51.1	100.9	96.7
Interest	78.1	61.5	58.4	88.9	62.6	138.1
Debt service payments/ exports of goods and services (%)	23.5	15.1	15.2	13.4	20.6	27.5

Source: Abdalla Mohamed Elhassan, 'The State and the Development of Capitalism in Agriculture in Sudan: The Case of the Savannah Rainland', unpublished PhD thesis, University of East Anglia, 1985, p. 202.

Glossary of Arabic Terms

al-dajjal: the impostor
ansar: followers (of the Mahdi)
ashiqqah: blood brothers
ashraf: descendants of the prophet Muhammad
barakah: blessedness; supernatural power
dammur: cotton cloth
darb al arba'in: the 40-day camel route from Kordofan province to Assiut in Egypt
durah: millet (*Sorghum vulgare*)
hafir: water-hole
hidd: traditional mourning dress and customs
imam: religious leader, or official of mosque
jallabah: petty traders
jihad: holy war
khalifah (pl. *khulafa*): successor, local leader in a religious order
khatmi: of the Khatmiyyah *tariqah*
mahkamah: court of law
makk: chieftain
ma'mur: civilian administrative assistant to a district commissioner
maqdum: senior political representative of the Sultans of Darfur
marisah: beer made from various grains, but chiefly *durah*, in the central and southern Sudan
miralai: colonel
mufti: official head of Islamic religious notables
muqaddam: subordinate officer
mushat: traditional hair-style, requiring many hours to produce the many tiny plaits
nafir: a system of co-operative agriculture
nazir: head of a tribe
qadi: Islamic law judge
qurair: cracked soil near river; river soil
sagiah: water-wheel
saluqah: a digging-stick with foot-rest; also applied to land cultivated by the *saluqah*
samadiah: village agricultural unit
sayyid: religious title indicating sanctity
shaduf: a hand-operated water-lifting device
shaikh: tribal chief or religious notable
shail: bartered loan arrangement
shari'ah: Islamic law
shartai: hereditary sub-chiefs under whom are tribal elders among the Fur
silsilah: chain
sirdar: commander-in-chief of the Egyptian army during the Condominium
sultan: Muslim sovereign; tribal leader in Darfur

tariqah: (pl. *turuq*): *sufi* order
'ulama: orthodox Islamic religious leaders
'umda: head of an administrative unit, usually a collection of villages
wakil: deputy
wali: saint or religious notable
wazir: chief minister of a *sultan*
zakat: religious tax in Islam

Index